IFRS PRIMER
International GAAP Basics

Irene M. Wiecek, FCA
University of Toronto
Toronto, Ontario

Nicola M. Young, MBA, FCA
Saint Mary's University
Halifax, Nova Scotia

John Wiley & Sons

ACQUISITION EDITOR   Jeff Howard

EDITORIAL ASSISTANT   Kara Taylor

PUBLISHER   George Hoffman

MARKETING MANAGER   Julia Flohr

PRODUCTION MANAGER   Micheline Frederick

PRODUCTION EDITOR   Kerry Weinstein

PRODUCTION ASSISTANT   Mary Alma

DESIGNER   Natalia Burobina

COVER DESIGNER   Jeof Vita

MEDIA EDITOR   Greg Chaput

To order books or for customer service, please call 1-800-CALL WILEY (225-5945).

ISBN 978-0-470-48317-6

Printed in the United States of America

10 9 8 7 6 5 4 3 2 1

ABOUT THE AUTHORS

Irene M. Wiecek, FCA, and is a Senior Lecturer in Accounting at the Rotman School of Management, University of Toronto and the University of Toronto, Mississauga. Currently, she teaches financial reporting at the undergraduate level in the Accounting Specialist Program and financial reporting and accounting theory and research at the graduate level in the Master of Management & Professional Accounting Program (MMPA). She is the Associate Director of the MMPA Program and is Co-Director and founder of the ICAO/Rotman Centre for Innovation in Accounting Education. Since 2002, Irene has chaired the Canadian Academic Accounting Association's CICA Exposure Draft Response Committee. Irene is involved in professional accounting education and has taught at the ICAO School of Accountancy for many years. At the CICA, she is Director of the In-Depth GAAP Program, a member of the Financial Reporting and Governance Working group, and past Ontario representative of the CICA Qualifications Committee. Her interests lie in the area of international accounting and multiple intelligences as a framework for accounting education. She is the recipient of the MMPA Faculty of the Year award for 2004 and 2006 and is the Canadian co-author of the leading text Kieso, Weygandt, Warfield, Young, Wiecek: *Intermediate Accounting*, Eighth Canadian Edition.

Nicola (Nickie) M. Young, MBA, FCA, is a Professor of Accounting in the Sobey School of Business at Saint Mary's University in Halifax, Nova Scotia. Her teaching responsibilities have varied from the introductory offering to final year advanced financial courses to the survey course in the Executive MBA program. She is the recipient of teaching awards, and has contributed to the academic and administrative life of the university through chairing the Department of Accounting, membership on the Board of Governors, and the pension and other committees. Nickie was associated with the Atlantic School of Chartered Accountancy for over 25 years in a variety of roles, including program and course development, teaching, and program reform. In addition to contributions to the accounting profession at the provincial level, Nickie has served on national boards of the Canadian Institute of Chartered Accountants (CICA) dealing with licensure and education. For the over 15 years, she has worked with the CICA's Public Sector Accounting Board (PSAB) as an Associate, as a member and chair of the Board, and as chair and member of PSAB task forces. Nickie is the Canadian co-author of the leading text Kieso, Weygandt, Warfield, Young, Wiecek: *Intermediate Accounting*, Eighth Canadian Edition.

PREFACE

The increasing use of international financial reporting standards (IFRS) on a global basis provides some amazing research and teaching opportunities. A common language for reporting information about business and economic activities brings us one step closer to a global capital marketplace. Students who learn IFRS now will be that much more valuable in the workplace.

However, there are a number of challenges. How do we teach multiple GAAPs? Should we teach IFRS as a stand-alone course or integrate it into our existing curriculum? Should we even try to teach multiple GAAPs given the risk of overload? There are only so many courses in a degree and so many hours in a day. Instead, should we go back to teaching basics? These are all questions that every university and college are grappling with.

Since we have started to introduce IFRS into our own courses, we have found that students are developing a greater appreciation for the complex judgments and decisions that go into financial reporting. This, in turn, is encouraging greater student engagement with the material, better class discussion, and, correspondingly, more critical thinking. This is all very exciting!

This book—*IFRS Primer: International GAAP Basics*—introduces instructors and students to the basics of IFRSs. The following discusses what this book contains and how it can be used.

- The book was written primarily for college-level educators and students, although it is also useful for recent, and not-so-recent, graduates and those working for public accounting firms and reporting entities. Our goals are to provide a snapshot and understanding of each international accounting standard. It is not written for the accounting professional who needs to know all the detailed requirements and how to apply them to complex situations.

- The *IFRS Primer* is meant to be a supplement to, rather than a substitute for, existing introductory, intermediate, and advanced accounting texts. How it will be used in each of the three levels of an accounting program depends on the approach taken in the specific course, the capabilities and interests of the students, and how a particular program is designed.

- The *IFRS Primer* could also be used in a stand-alone IFRS course, for those students who have already taken accounting courses.

- This book is an excellent tool for the IFRS-GAAP transition period, bridging the gap until the next generation of textbooks incorporates IFRS in the same way that they explain, illustrate, and provide pedagogical aids for GAAP. The *IFRS Primer* is not meant to be the final solution to teaching IFRSs.

- Each chapter in the *IFRS Primer* describes and explains fundamental international reporting standards as of early 2009, following the same general organization that makes up each specific IFRS. Areas of significant high-level difference between IFRS requirements and U.S. standards are identified by chapter icons. The last question in every chapter's End-of-Chapter Practice section draws the students' attention to the icons, provides the relevant website that identifies what the differences are, and asks them to prepare a concise summary of the differences between the international standard and GAAP. The suggested solutions to these questions are on the Instructor Resource Site that accompanies the *IFRS Primer*.

- The End-of-Chapter Practice questions are a mix of short qualitative and quantitative exercises, most of which zero in on areas that are new to the students and instructors. The numbers used are small (e.g., equipment with a cost of $100) in order to focus attention on the underlying concepts rather than the numbers. The *IFRS Primer* is not meant to be an extensive source of end-of-chapter material.

Other Hallmark Features

We begin each chapter by identifying the **specific IFRS**, its **U.S. counterparts**, and a list of **other IFRSs related** to the chapter topic.

The content of each chapter generally follows the **same headings as used in the IFRS**: objective and scope, recognition, and measurement, ending with disclosure requirements.

Illustrations and tables are included to enhance students' understanding with walk-through **mini scenarios and exercises** interspersed throughout the chapter. Situations requiring numerical analysis are identified by a toolkit icon placed beside the applications box. Those where professional judgment is needed to interpret a standard or apply a principle are identified with a marginal conceptual framework or accounting principle icon.

Short excerpts and note disclosures from a variety of **actual financial statements** prepared under IFRSs are also provided to help illustrate how the disclosures are made.

We end every almost every chapter with a **Looking Ahead** feature. Accounting standards are not static—they are in a constant state of flux. All the standards described in each chapter are formally approved by the IASB as of the spring of 2009, but many of these are on the Board's active agenda. The Looking Ahead feature explains what the current issues are in relation to the chapter IFRS, what stage of development the project is in, and when new standards are expected to be developed and approved. A list of abbreviations printed on the inside back cover of the book offers a quick guide to the abbreviations used in the text. We use a variety of **icons** to indicate other features common to all chapters.

Measurement icon: A measurement chart appears on the inside front cover of the book. It captures the measurement models that IFRSs either require or permit for each major category of asset and liability reported on the statement of financial position. The chart also indicates the accounting treatment for the unrealized fair value gains and losses that result from using a fair value measure. This summary is useful for both instructors and students. An icon of the chart with the appropriate segment shaded appears at the beginning of each chapter that relates to one of the balance sheet elements.

Conceptual framework icon: International standards have often been described as principles-based standards. We insert a conceptual framework/accounting principle icon in the chapter margins whenever major accounting principles underlying the specific IFRS are stated and discussed. This icon is a reminder of the financial accounting framework explained in Chapter 1.

Definitions icon: This icon signals where a term is defined. A complete glossary of these terms is provided on the companion website. Because all IFRSs are dealt with in the *IFRS Primer*, this glossary is a useful supplement of major IASB terminology.

U.S. GAAP differences icons: Icons of the U.S. flag indicate that there is a significant difference between the IASB requirement being addressed at that point in the chapter and the corresponding U.S. GAAP standards. As indicated above, the last question in each chapter's End-of-Chapter Practice section addresses these differences. All significant differences are identified on the Instructors' Resource Site.

Research icon: Occasionally, we refer to related articles or studies that have been carried out about the chapter topic. We identify these and other interesting references with a research icon.

We have also provided an **Instructor Resource Site** to supplement the *IFRS Primer*. This site contains suggested solutions to the End-of-Chapter Practice questions and comprehensive Power Point presentations covering each chapter. Instructors can use all or some of these presentations, or use specific slides in their own presentations.

Acknowledgments

A book like this does not just happen, especially in such a short time frame. The team at John Wiley & Sons, both in New York and Canada, rose quickly to the challenge. For this and for believing in this project, we thank Jeff Howard in New York. In Canada, we thank Veronica Visentin, Publisher; Zoë Craig, Acquisitions Editor; Karen Staudinger, Editorial Manager; Karen Bryan, Publishing Services Director; Aida Krneta, Marketing Manager; Dela Hirjikaka, Developmental Editor; Alison Arnot, copyeditor; Laurel Hyatt, proofreader; Charlene McDonald and Andrew Golobic, solution manual authors; Shelley Coyle, solutions checker; and Sibongile Mukandi for her work on the glossary.

We want to acknowledge the continuing cooperation we receive from the principals and staff of the Accounting Standards Board of the CICA. We thank them for this. We are also grateful for the generosity of the major professional service firms and their international umbrella organizations in making so much information so freely available. Our thanks go particularly to Deloitte and to Ernst & Young, whose websites we used extensively for comparing international and U.S. GAAP standards.

Finally, we want to thank our families for their patience and support during the countless hours we devoted to this *IFRS Primer*.

We have made considerable efforts to produce an error-free book, but if anything has slipped through the variety of checks, please let us know so corrections can be made to subsequent printings. Your suggestions and comments on matters related to this material are always appreciated.

Happy transitioning.

Irene M. Wiecek   Nicola M. Young
Wiecek@rotman.utoronto.ca   nicola.young@smu.ca

August 2009

This book is dedicated to all the accounting professionals working to make one set of high-quality international standards a reality...
...to national and international standard setters, preparers of financial reports, professional advisers and assurance providers, and to the educators who facilitate the transition of the current and next generation of accountants to a new world of GAAP.

CONTENTS

Chapter 1

Introduction and the IAS Framework

A COMMON SET OF GLOBAL ACCOUNTING STANDARDS

Do we need a common set of global accounting standards?

Different generally accepted accounting principles (GAAP) have been developed in various countries over the past few decades. These differences have arisen largely due to unique legal, regulatory, litigious, social, economic, religious, and cultural environments. They result in financial statements that are not comparable and difficult for users to interpret. This in turn acts as a barrier for global capital movement, potentially resulting in less than optimal allocation of capital.

More recently, there has been a movement toward harmonization and convergence of GAAP. The most significant initiative has been led by the International Accounting Standards Board (IASB),[1] formerly known as the International Accounting Standards Committee.

---

[1] The oversight body is the International Accounting Standards Committee Foundation (IASCF), which appoints members (12 full-time and 2 part-time members) to and funds the IASB. The IASCF is governed by trustees that represent global standard setters. North America currently has 6 of the 22 trustees. In addition to the IASB, the International Financial Reporting Interpretations Committee (IFRIC) assists the IASB through timely identification, discussion, and resolution of issues. IFRIC is much like the Emerging Issues Task Force (EITF) in the United States.

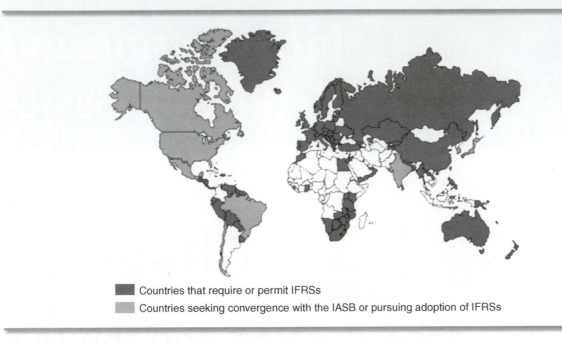

Countries that require or permit IFRSs

Countries seeking convergence with the IASB or pursuing adoption of IFRSs

Illustration 1-1 IFRS Convergence (source: www.iasb.org)

The IASB'S mandate is

. . . . . . developing, in the public interest, a single set of high quality, understandable and enforceable global accounting standards that require transparent and comparable information in general purpose financial statements.[2]

The IASB also works with national accounting standard setters to move toward global convergence. To date, nearly 100 countries have converged (require or allow IFRS) or are on the path to convergence. (See Illustration 1-1.)

The International Organization of Securities Commissions (IOSCO) is also working with the IASB in this regard. IOSCO's objective is to join together securities regulators, such as the Securities and Exchange Commission (SEC), to promote cooperation and high standards of regulation in order to maintain "just, efficient, and sound markets" on a global basis.

Political and Regulatory Issues

One of the issues with international convergence of GAAP is enforcement. Enforcement is generally carried out on a country-by-country basis. For instance, in the United States, the SEC is the main regulatory body. Once standard setting moves to a global setting, this fragmented, country-by-country regulatory environment will prove to be a challenge. With so many entities regulating the markets, is it possible to be consistent? IOSCO provides the various regulators with a forum to meet and work together. In October 2005, IOSCO announced that it would create an IFRS database for regulators to share decisions on the application of IFRS. The database allows global regulators to see what their counterparts are doing in terms of regulation so that each country is aware of various rulings that have been made regarding the application

---

[2] IASB website, <www.iasb.org>.

of IFRS. This is the first step toward ensuring that securities regulators do not inadvertently create GAAP differences.

Another question is whether there is or can ever be total acceptance of IFRS. While standard setters have come a long way, there is still a long way to go toward obtaining full acceptance of a global set of standards. Although the map at left looks like global convergence is at hand, a closer look reveals where IFRS is required versus where it is merely allowed as an option. Note further that even where it is required, it may be required only for consolidated financial statements and for public companies. National GAAPs are still in existence and are widely used.[3]

Can one set of standards meet the needs of all users?

Currently, there is a concern that private companies—specifically small and mid-sized ones—would not benefit from using IFRS. They operate in a local market and often (although not always) have more simplified business models. On the international front, there is a move to establishing more simplistic standards for these entities.

Principles or rules—which are better?

International financial reporting standards (IFRS) are sometimes referred to as being principles-based—that is, they are more loosely framed—allowing for professional judgment to be applied. This results in accounting that is more flexible to deal with unique economic and business circumstances. Some argue that allowing professional judgment introduces bias.

At the other end of the spectrum is a rules-based GAAP model that is more prescriptive—providing a rule for every situation. Many feel that this tightens up the accounting; however, a rules-based system soon becomes unwieldy in size because you need a rule for every situation. The complexity works against good financial reporting because fewer and fewer people can claim to have mastery of the body of knowledge. It is just too large and complicated. Although more guidance is a comfort to some, it becomes difficult to ensure that the standards are all consistent.

There is significant discussion as to which is better, and the trend seems to be moving away from a pure rules-based system. In January 2008, the CEOs of the Big 6 accounting firms met to discuss this issue and decided the following:[4]

> To begin with, however, we may be well served by acknowledging that neither a purely rules-based nor a purely principles-based system has ever existed or will ever exist. Every accounting standard will exist somewhere along a spectrum between rules and principles. The goal must be to seek the "sweet spot" on the spectrum.

In their deliberations, the CEOs concluded that the key elements of a principles-based accounting standard were as follows:

1. Faithfully representing economic reality
2. Responsive to users' needs for clarity and transparency
3. Consistent with a clear conceptual framework
4. Based on an appropriately defined scope that addresses a broad area of accounting
5. Written in clear, concise, and plain language
6. Allowing for the use of reasonable judgment

No matter how the standards model is labelled, what is needed is a robust, consistent model that is manageable.

---

[3] For instance, in the European Union, IFRS is required for public company consolidated statements only.
[4] Global Public Policy Symposium, *Principles-based Accounting Standards* (January 2008).

CONCEPTUAL FRAMEWORK FOR THE PREPARATION AND PRESENTATION OF FINANCIAL STATEMENTS

What is the role of a conceptual framework?

The conceptual framework (sometimes referred to as the framework) sets out the concepts that underlie the preparation of the financial statements.[5]

The purpose of the framework is to[6]:

(a) assist the IASC [Board] in the development of future International Accounting Standards and in its review of existing International Accounting Standards;

(b) assist the IASC Board in promoting harmonization of regulations, accounting standards, and procedures relating to the presentation of financial statements by providing a basis for reducing the number of alternative accounting treatments permitted by International Accounting Standards;

(c) assist national standard-setting bodies in developing national standards;

(d) assist preparers of financial statements in applying International Accounting Standards and in dealing with topics [that are not dealt with in International Accounting Standards];

(e) assist auditors in forming an opinion on whether financial statements conform with International Accounting Standards;

(f) assist users of financial statements in interpreting the information contained in financial statements prepared according to International Accounting Standards; and

(g) provide those who are interested in the work of IASC with information about its approach to the formulation of International Accounting Standards.

What is the formal status of the conceptual framework?

The framework is not an international accounting standard in and of itself and nothing in the framework overrides a specific accounting standard. The IASB notes that there may be a few rare cases where the framework is in conflict with a specific standard and, in these cases, the standard would override the framework. Where there is no specific standard, the framework should govern the accounting. It applies to the financial statements of all entities, whether in the public or private sector, where the users rely on the statements as a major source of information for decision-making.

 Illustration 1-2 is a pictorial representation of the framework.[7] We will refer to this throughout the book and will reference back to it using the icon shown in the margin at left. Note that the conceptual framework is currently the subject of a joint project between IASB and FASB. See the section "Looking Ahead" for a summary of the proposed changes.

A Quick Recap of the Conceptual Framework

The framework is similar to North American frameworks although some of the labels are different. Illustration 1-2 provides a quick recap of the framework.

Users and Objectives

According to the framework, users of financial statements include present and potential investors, employees, lenders, suppliers and other trade creditors, customers, governments and their agencies, and the public. This definition is fairly broad and encompasses anyone who uses general purpose financial statements to make decisions.

---

[5] International Accounting Standards Committee Foundation (IASCF), *International Financial Reporting Standards, Introduction*.

[6] International Accounting Standards Committee Foundation (IASCF), *International Financial Reporting Standards, Introduction*.

[7] Adapted from Kieso et al., *Intermediate Accounting*, 8e, John Wiley & Sons, Canada, Toronto, 2007.

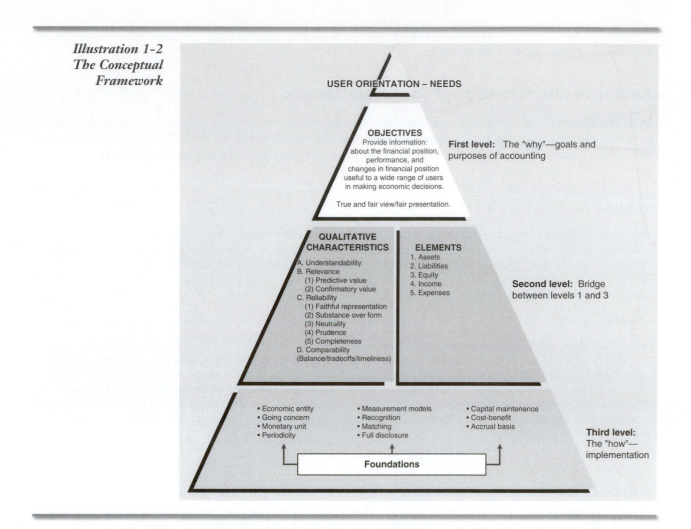

*Illustration 1-2
The Conceptual
Framework*

The overall objective of financial reporting is to produce financial statements that present fairly the results of operations and the financial position. This is sometimes referred to as a "true and fair view" of the company and its financial position.

The objective is articulated in the framework as follows:[8]

12   The objective of financial statements is to provide information about the financial position, performance and changes in financial position of an entity that is useful to a wide range of users in making economic decisions.

13   Financial statements prepared for this purpose meet the common needs of most users. However, financial statements do not provide all the information that users may need to make economic decisions since they largely portray the financial effects of past events and do not necessarily provide non-financial information.

14   Financial statements also show the results of the stewardship of management, or the accountability of management for the resources entrusted to it. Those users who wish to assess the stewardship or accountability of management do so in order that they may make economic decisions; these decisions may include, for example, whether to hold or sell their investment in the entity or whether to reappoint or replace the management.

---

[8] International Accounting Standards Committee Foundation (IASCF), *International Financial Reporting Standards*, Framework par .12-.14.

In short, the objective is to provide useful information to users when making economic decisions (including decisions about management stewardship).

Qualitative Characteristics of Useful Information

Understandability.   Financial statements that are not understandable are of no use. One of the benefits of a common set of high quality accounting standards is that they create less confusion and are more likely to be understood by users internationally. However, the IASB still recognizes that users will have differing knowledge levels.

Situation

Financial Analysts Incorporated (FAI) analyzes the financial statements of international companies for its clients and provides buy and sell recommendations with respect to the shares of these companies. These analysts follow all publicly available news relating to the companies. In contrast, Franco First is a second-year accounting student who has only some basic knowledge of accounting theory and bookkeeping. Which knowledge level should a company assume when preparing its financial statements?

Analysis

Both the analyst and the student are potential users of the financial statements and therefore the statements should provide information that is useful to both of them. The framework assumes that users have a reasonable knowledge of business and economic activities as well as accounting, and a willingness to study the information with reasonable diligence.[9] The student may not yet have the business background, nor have mastered the fundamentals of economics, and so would likely struggle with the statements. This is not ideal; however, the objective of the preparers of financial statements is not to educate users on the fundamentals of business and economics, but rather to communicate company-specific information.

Relevance.   Decision relevance is fundamental to financial reporting. In other words, the information must be useful to the user in making the decision at hand. This is not as simple as it sounds, especially given the number and diversity of users as well as their differing knowledge level. Relevant information must at least have the following characteristics:

1. *Predictive value*—many users use historic information to predict the company's future profits and cash flows. Although the past does not necessarily allow users to predict the future, it does provide information that can be used to assess the future potential of the entity.
2. *Confirmatory value*—many users use the information to confirm their prior expectations and to assess management performance (sometimes referred to as management stewardship).

There are a multitude of bits of information available about an entity and the transactions it enters into. How much information is needed in the statements? If there is not enough information, users will be left with unanswered questions. However, if there is too much, information overload results; that is, the user is inundated with so much information that he or she cannot sift through it to determine what is important and what is not. The concept of materiality is useful in that it defines the level of inclusion of information. As noted in the framework, information is *material* and useful if its omission or misstatement could influence the economic decisions of users.[10]

---

[9] International Accounting Standards Committee Foundation (IASCF), *International Financial Reporting Standards*, Framework par .25.

[10] International Accounting Standards Committee Foundation (IASCF), *International Financial Reporting Standards*, Framework par .30.

Once again, the focus is on the user and therefore it is not so straightforward, given the differing users and knowledge levels. Information might be material based solely on its nature (regardless of size or dollar value) or alternatively it might be material based solely on its size or dollar value.

Situation

Company A is in the mining industry and has operations all over the world. When the auditors were completing their annual audit, they found that the company had been making payments to government employees to facilitate the processing of applications to mine. These payments were going to the individual government employees (and not the government). The employees promised to ensure that the applications were expedited, which indeed they were. The amounts were not significant. Would this information be material?

Analysis

Some users of the financial statements might feel that the company was engaging in illegal or at least unethical activities and may choose not to invest in the company on that basis (regardless of the size of the payments). As you can see, what is material and what is not is also a matter of professional judgment.

Currently the standard does not have a quantitative definition for what is material and what is not. This is in line with the IASB view that "bright-line" tests are not desirable and are more often found in rules-based standards models. The term "bright-line" in the context of standard setting refers to the inclusion of a specific number or threshold in the standard. For instance, often in the past, materiality has been defined as an item that is larger than 5–10% of income. There is a concern that the inclusion of bright-lines draws the standard more toward a rules-based approach.

Reliability. Information is considered reliable if it has the following characteristics (included are brief definitions of each):

1. *Faithful representation*—the objective of financial reporting is to communicate information about the entity. In other words, it should faithfully represent the economic events and transactions in the statements since this is one of the main vehicles for sharing information about the company. In the proposed framework, this concept replaces reliability.
2. *Substance over form*—this is often referred to as economic substance over (legal) form. Accounting should reflect the substance of a transaction. It should look beyond the legal form. The following example illustrates this.

Situation

Airline Co Limited (ACL) leases planes under long-term leases. The company uses the lease contracts as a means of financing the acquisition of the planes. The intent is to keep the planes for the longer term. How should the leases be reflected in the statements?

Analysis

The planes should be shown as assets of the company with the related obligation to pay lease payments as a liability. The planes are essential assets to the company and the commitment (although legally structured as a lease as opposed to a loan and acquisition of the asset) is a liability. This reflects the reality or substance of the transaction.

---

3. Neutrality—unbiased information is better information. Biased information is of lesser quality since it is not objectively prepared.
4. Prudence—this concept is similar to conservatism. Many uncertainties are associated with capturing information in the financial statements. Prudence acts to ensure that the assets and income are not

overstated. Interestingly, this introduces its own bias to the statements and so is in conflict with (3) above. In the proposed framework, this concept disappears.

5. Completeness—complete information is critical for making decisions. Note that this is tempered by materiality and cost/benefit. Completeness refers only to material items and, in terms of the other criteria, the benefits must exceed the costs.

Comparability.   The main benefit of having one set of global standards is comparability. Use of the conceptual framework by all entities, whether they are publicly accountable or not, would enhance this. The IFRS body of knowledge still allows a fair bit of choice in the various standards—especially those standards that have been around for a while. IASB is trying to reduce choice by minimizing the number of incidences where choices are available.

Balance/trade-offs.   The qualitative characteristics noted above are not viewed in isolation. Sometimes there are trade-offs, i.e., preparers must choose which one to emphasize. This is another area where professional judgment must be applied. The proposed framework separates the qualitative characteristics into two categories— "fundamental" and "enhancing." The fundamental characteristics are dominant. It is proposed that fundamental characteristics will include relevance and representational faithfulness. In addition, enhancing characteristics will include comparable, verifiable, timely, and understandable. Materiality and cost will be seen to be pervasive constraints.

Elements of Financial Statements

When looking at financial statements, it is important that users know what to expect. Basic elements, including their defining characteristics, are noted below (as defined in the framework). Elements are recognized when probable and measurable with reliability.

Assets—a resource controlled by the entity as a result of past events and from which future economic benefits are expected to flow to the entity.

> The airplane in the applications box on page 7 is an example of an asset. In a lease situation, the entity does not have legal title to the plane; however, the terms of the lease entitle the entity to the future benefits through possession.

Liabilities—a present obligation of the entity arising from past events, the settlement of which is expected to result in an outflow from the entity of resources embodying economic benefits. Liabilities may be legally enforceable via a contract or law, but need not be, i.e., they can arise due to normal business practice or customs.

Equity—a residual interest in the assets of the entity after deducting all its liabilities.

Income—increases in economic benefits that result in increases in equity (other than those related to contributions from shareholders). Income includes both revenues (resulting from ordinary activities) and gains. Gains are not treated as a separate element since they may also arise due to ordinary activities. Income may be realized or unrealized.

Expenses—decreases in economic benefits that result in decreases in equity (other than those related to distributions to shareholders). Expenses result from ordinary activities. Similar to gains, losses may also result from ordinary activities so are not treated as separate elements. Expenses may be realized or not realized.

Foundations

IFRSs are supported by certain generally accepted foundational concepts and conventions, as noted in Illustration 1-2. Most of these are not discussed separately here since they are covered in introductory and intermediate accounting textbooks.

GAAP HIERARCHY

IAS 8 identifies the GAAP hierarchy; i.e., where we should look to determine what particular GAAP should be applied, as follows:[11]

1. IFRS (including IFRS, IAS, IFRIC, and SIC) and implementation guidance;
2. If no standards exist, financial statement preparers may look to similar situations and related issues that are covered by IFRS and the conceptual framework; and, finally,
3. If there is no guidance, we may look to other standard-setting bodies as long as they do not conflict with the above.

THE U.S. EXPERIENCE TO DATE

As previously noted, U.S. GAAP has essentially evolved as a rules-based GAAP. This is due to many reasons but is partially due to the more litigious legal environment. Rules-based standards are considered to provide more support for preparers and auditors. Although IASB and FASB are working together to harmonize/converge standards, it is not clear whether this means full convergence (one standard for both) or whether this is more like a harmonization mandate (separate but similar standards).

The rise of principles-based standards?

Historically, U.S. GAAP developed without much outside influence and has been viewed as being a very robust model and gold star standard. The pressures to converge are mounting, however. Due to the recent and not-so-recent abuses of the rules-based GAAP (Enron, WorldCom, and others), the caché associated with rules-based accounting is declining. Standard setters, regulators, and financial statement users are asking whether a more principles-based approach would be better. Indeed the *Sarbanes-Oxley Act of 2002* (which was a reaction to the turmoil and fraud in the capital markets) called for a study of principles-based accounting standards. In 2003, the SEC issued a Staff Report dealing with the issue of principles-based standards and their desirability. The report introduced the term "objectives-oriented standards" as explained below:

> [T]he optimal principles-based accounting standard involves a concise statement of substantiate accounting principle where the accounting *objective* has been incorporated as an integral part of the standard and where few, if any, exceptions or internal inconsistencies are included in the standard. Further, such a standard should provide an appropriate amount of implementation guidance given the nature of the class of transactions or events and should be devoid of bright-line tests. Finally, such a standard should be consistent with, and derive from, a coherent conceptual framework of financial reporting.[12]

---

[11] IASCF, IAS 8. IFRS and IFRIC are pronouncements produced by the current standard-setting bodies (IASB and IFRIC), and IAS and SIC were originally produced by the predecessor standard-setting bodies (IASC and SIC). IAS and SIC were inherited by IASB and IFRIC and are part of the IFRS body of knowledge.

[12] SEC Staff Report, *Adoption by the United States Financial Reporting System of a Principles-Based Accounting System* (July 2003).

IFRS for Foreign Filers

Since the SEC has now allowed foreign filers to use IFRS without a reconciliation, the question arises as to why U.S. companies are not able to follow IFRS.[13] In August 2007, the SEC issued a Concept Release asking this question.

Convergence with IASB

In terms of the convergence/harmonization mandate, the following steps have been taken:

- *The Norwalk Agreement*—In 2002, FASB signed an agreement with the IASB to work toward convergence. Under this agreement, both parties agreed to working toward making their respective standards compatible with each other.
- Roadmap for convergence—In 2006, both parties reaffirmed the goal of compatibility and issued a roadmap for convergence, which involves short-term and longer-term projects.

Will the current partnership between FASB and IASB result in actual convergence, or will the two sets of standards continue to exist side by side but separately? Will the SEC, by allowing IFRS for U.S. companies, drive the change? Although the answers to these questions remain to be seen, the SEC recently issued a statement that would support a mandatory transition to IFRS for the year beginning on or after December 15, 2014, given certain milestones. These include continued/ongoing improvement of IFRS, new funding and accountability models for the IASCF, more use of interactive databases, increased education and training in IFRS in the U.S., and limited early use by eligible companies.

Roadblocks in the Roadmap

Some of the issues being raised in the U.S. are as follows:

1. What will happen with the Codification project? The Codification project seeks to reorganize the "thousands of pronouncements" currently known collectively as U.S. GAAP into roughly 90 topics in an on-line database. Once complete, it will be the single source of authoritative U.S. GAAP and supersede all prior pronouncements (except for SEC pronouncements). The database will include standards from FASB, the Emerging Issues Task Force, the AICPA, and SEC. The database is now in its verification phase, meaning that it is substantially complete and is open for review and comment. FASB has invested a substantial amount of resources in this project. Should they/can they abandon it now for IFRS?
2. Additional disclosures and safe harbor rules: Safe harbor is a legal concept that reduces or eliminates a party's liability under law. In the case of financial reporting, it would potentially provide protection for a reporting company and its auditors as long as they have performed their duties diligently and in good faith. There is a concern that with the additional disclosures required under IFRS, the incidence of lawsuits will increase. Should safe harbor rules be applied to financial statement disclosures?
3. Decreasing influence: U.S. stakeholders will have a decrease in influence on international standard setting, which by definition, must also take into consideration the needs of global users. Will the resulting financial reporting still meet the needs of U.S. users?
4. Funding model for IASB: Optimally, the funding model should ensure that international standards are free from bias. IASB has already proposed a model where a levy is charged on capital market transactions. There has been some concerns that the current model of funding, which relies on corporate donations, may result in the IASB being unduly influenced.

---

[13] According to Deloitte and Touche's *IFRS in your pocket*, of the 15,000 companies whose securities are registered with the SEC, 1,100 are non-U.S. companies or foreign filers.

LOOKING AHEAD

In a very significant and time-consuming project, the IASB is currently overhauling the framework with FASB. The first four phases are in progress and include the following: (1) objectives/qualitative characteristics, (2) elements/recognition, (3) measurement, and (4) reporting entity. An Exposure Draft has been issued on objectives/qualitative characteristics as well as a Preliminary Views discussion paper on the reporting entity. Once this is done, the next step will be to go through each of the IFRS standards to ensure that the framework is consistently applied. It will therefore be an ongoing project. In the meantime, the existing conceptual framework will be in place.

According to the proposed framework:

The objective of general purpose financial reporting, as clarified, is to provide financial information about the reporting entity that is useful to present and potential investors and creditors in making decisions in their capacity as capital providers. The objective should pertain to financial reporting as a whole, not just financial statements.

The emphasis is on resource allocation (lending and investing). It also incorporates the notion of assessment of management stewardship since capital providers assess not only an entity's potential future cash flows, but also management's ability to deliver those cash flows. It emphasizes those who have a claim (or potentially have a claim) on the entity's resources (including equity investors, lenders, and other creditors).

Below is an excerpt from the IASB/FASB project regarding qualitative characteristics:

Qualitative Characteristics of Financial Reporting

The Boards made the following decisions related to the proposed material on the qualitative characteristics of decision-useful financial reporting information:

1. Relevance and faithful representation are fundamental qualitative characteristics that must be present for information to be useful.
2. Information is relevant if it is capable of making a difference in decisions. Information is capable of making a difference when it has predictive value, confirmatory value, or both.
3. Faithful representation is attained when the substance of an economic phenomenon is depicted completely, accurately, and neutrally.
4. Comparability, verifiability, timeliness, and understandability are enhancing qualitative characteristics that complement the fundamental qualitative characteristics. Enhancing qualitative characteristics distinguish more useful information from less useful information and enhance the decision usefulness of information.
5. Conservatism/prudence should remain excluded from the qualitative characteristics of accounting information.

The new framework provides additional guidance and refinements to the model. Note that reliability is now gone from the framework.

The IASB and FASB have agreed on the following changes in definitions.[14] Note that these views have not yet been exposed in an Exposure Draft and so could change.

In terms of the definition of **assets/liabilities,** the Boards decided the following:

- Some users interpret the words "expected/probable" to mean that there must be a *high likelihood* of future economic benefits or outflows of cash. This results in some assets/liabilities not being recognized.
- There is too much emphasis on the **potential** for future economic benefits/outflows instead of focusing on the **present** resources/obligations.

---

[14] www.iasb.org under "conceptual framework project."

- Some users interpret the word "control" (in the definition of an asset) to mean the same as for consolidation of subsidiaries. This may be too strict a test.
- Users focus on *past* transactions or events as opposed to deciding whether the entity has *present* access to the benefits or has *present* obligations at the balance sheet date. This may result in more or fewer assets/liabilities being recognized.
- It is unclear how the definition applies to contractual obligations.

Therefore, the following definitions have been proposed:

Asset

An *asset* of an entity is a **present economic resource** to which, through an **enforceable right** or other means, the **entity has access** or can limit the access of others.

The text of the standard will describe economic resources as follows:

An *economic resource* is something scarce that has positive economic value. It is capable of being used to carry out economic activities, such as production and exchange. It can contribute to producing cash inflows or reducing cash outflows, directly or indirectly, alone or together with other economic resources. Economic resources include non-conditional contractual promises that others make to the entity, such as promises to pay cash, deliver goods, or render services. Rendering services includes standing ready to perform or refraining from engaging in activities that the entity could otherwise undertake.

Liability

A *liability* of an entity is a present economic obligation that is enforceable against the entity.

The framework will have a differing perspective, defining a liability as an economic obligation rather than a probable future sacrifice. The emphasis will be on present (i.e., when an entity is committed to a particular action that is capable of resulting in cash outflows) as opposed to past or future. There must also be a mechanism to enforce the obligation (such as a law or regulation).

The Boards distinguished a present obligation from a business risk. Note that any time that an entity does anything, it could result in an obligation but does not necessarily do so. Actions of a company that expose it to risk are normal business risks but do not necessarily result in present obligations. There must also be a mechanism to enforce the obligation.

In terms of contractual obligation, the Boards proposed that entities analyze contracts to see if they contain unconditional obligations (sometimes referred to as stand ready obligations) and/or conditional ones (those relating to uncertain future events). Stand ready obligations describe situations where the entity has some sort of duty that it may or may not have to fulfill but stands ready to do so. The concept of stand ready obligation assists with establishing whether a present obligation exists.

The Boards are now discussing measurement models. Under discussion are level of confidence that can be placed on various measurements and separation of current values from information about future cash flows that may be generated by the asset. The IASB has also issued a Discussion Paper on fair value measurements. The paper reviews the concepts established in FAS 157.

MEASUREMENT MODEL

The rest of the book will look at recognition, measurement, presentation, and disclosure issues under IFRS. Illustration 1-3 summarizes measurement models used under IFRS. We will refer back to this illustration throughout the book. Note how pervasive the use of fair value is. Note further that in many cases fair value is an option and not mandatory.

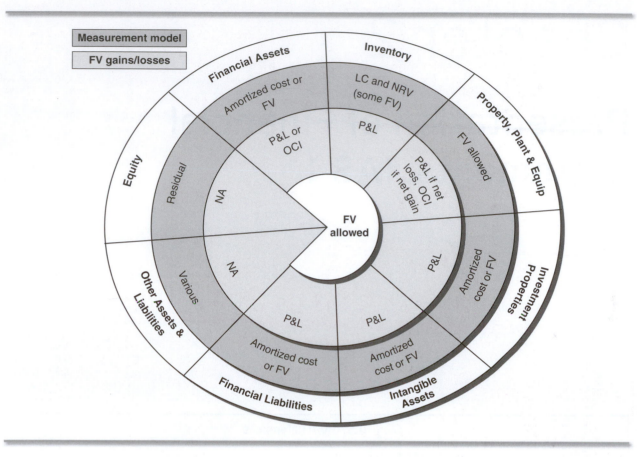

Illustration 1-3 Measurement Models under IFRS

END-OF-CHAPTER PRACTICE

1-1 Define and discuss the merits of a principles-based and rules-based approach to standard setting. How do they differ? Are there any similarities? What is an objectives-based standard-setting model? How does it compare with the other two?

1-2 Go to the IASB and FASB websites and look up the project summary relating to the conceptual framework project. Identify some of the main differences between the old frameworks and the proposed framework.

1-3 Discuss the relative merits of a single set of global accounting standards. What are some of the impediments or barriers?

1-4 Standard setters often refer to bright-line tests. What are these and do you believe they are useful in standard setting? What are some of the drawbacks to the use of bright-lines?

1-5 Identify what is meant by the IASB/FASB Roadmap to IFRS. Research this on the IASB and FASB websites. What are the various components of the roadmap? What is the objective? What are some of the short-term and longer-term projects being worked on?

Chapter 2

Presentation of Financial Statements: IAS 1

U.S. GAAP References
FAS 129 Disclosures of Information About Capital Structure
FAS 130 Reporting Comprehensive Income
CON 5 Recognition and Measurement in Financial Statements of Business Enterprises
In addition to the above, U.S. GAAP for financial statement presentation is spread across numerous specific standards.
In addition, public companies must follow the requirements of the SEC.

Related IFRSs
IFRS 5 Non-current Assets Held for Sale and Discontinued Operations
IFRS 7 Financial Instruments: Disclosures
IAS 8 Accounting Policies, Changes in Accounting Estimates and Errors

OBJECTIVE AND SCOPE

Comparable financial statements are more useful to users in making decisions. IAS 1 provides guidance regarding financial statement presentation in order to enhance comparability. It applies to all general purpose financial statements.

PURPOSE AND COMPONENTS OF FINANCIAL STATEMENTS

"Financial statements are a structured representation of the financial position and financial performance of the entity."[1] They exist to provide useful information to a wide range of users in making decisions. A common structure helps ensure that information about economic events and transactions is **consistently** represented from one company to another and from year to year. The standard therefore defines what is included in a complete set of financial statements.

The main statements are as follows (although an entity may use different titles for these statements):

1. Statement of financial position
2. Statement of comprehensive income (which may be augmented by a separate income statement)
3. Statement of changes in equity
4. Statement of cash flows
5. Notes including significant accounting policies and explanatory information
6. Statement of financial position at the beginning of the earliest comparative period when an entity applies an accounting policy retrospectively or makes a retrospective restatement

OVERALL CONSIDERATIONS

Fair Presentation and Compliance with IFRSs

According to IAS 1, the financial statements should fairly present the underlying position and financial performance of the entity. In order to do this, they must **faithfully represent** the underlying economic reality. It is presumed that application of IFRSs, with additional disclosures if deemed necessary, will result in fair presentation. Implicit in this is that the entity will do the following:

- select and apply appropriate accounting policies keeping in mind the GAAP hierarchy;
- present the information so that it provides relevant, comparable, and understandable information; and
- provide additional disclosures where necessary.

Note disclosures are not a substitute for proper accounting. There may be situations where application of IFRSs does not result in fair presentation. In this case, the entity departs from IFRSs and augments the statements with additional disclosures. This would be appropriate only in rare situations.

Going Concern and Accrual-Based Accounting

Financial statements should be prepared on an **accrual basis** assuming that the company will continue to operate as a **going concern**. Going concern would be assumed unless management intends to liquidate or to cease trading or has no realistic alternative but to do so.[2] If there is a doubt as to the ability of the company to continue to operate as a going concern, this must be disclosed in the financial statements. If the entity decides not to assume going concern, this must also be disclosed along with the reasons and the basis of accounting used.

Materiality, Aggregation, and Offsetting

Materiality is defined as follows:

. . . .Omissions or misstatements of items are material if they could, individually or collectively, influence the economic decisions of users taken on the basis of the financial statements. Materiality depends on the size and nature of the

---

[1] IASCF, IAS 1.9.
[2] IASCF, IAS 1.25. An entity would take into account information about the future looking forward at least one year.

omission or misstatement judged in the surrounding circumstances. The size or nature of the item, or a combination of both, could be the determining factor.[3]

Financial statement elements such as assets, liabilities, and revenues are aggregations of many smaller amounts representing numerous transactions or balances. When should these items be grouped together and when should they be shown separately? This depends on how material the items are. If they are material, they should be presented separately. Materiality is assessed in the context of users so it is important to understand what decisions are being made.

Care should be taken when grouping items together to ensure that items are not inappropriately offset. Offsetting is the process of netting unlike elements together (e.g., an asset offset against a liability or an income item offset against an expense). It is one thing to group like items such as receivables together, but it is entirely a different thing to group things like receivables and payables (debits and credits). As a general rule, things should not be offset unless an IFRS requires or permits this treatment and/or it reflects the economic substance of the transaction or balance.

Situation

Berringer Corp. sells concrete statues that are used to adorn buildings. The statues are made from cement using large cement mixers. During the year, the entity sold one of its cement mixers at a loss that is material. The entity purchases the raw material for the statues from abroad and therefore has foreign exchange gains and losses. In terms of absolute dollars, the gains and losses are both material; however, when netted, they are insignificant.

Analysis

The sale of concrete statues should be recognized gross as sales or revenues with the cost of sales presented separately. However, the sale of the cement mixer should be reflected on a net basis as a loss on sale (equal to revenue from sale less the carrying cost of the asset). This is because the sale of the cement mixer and the resulting loss are incidental or peripheral to the main revenue-generating activities. The gains and losses relating to foreign exchange may normally be offset since they represent a group of similar transactions. However, in this case, because they are material, they should be shown separately. IAS 1.34 and 35 support this.

Frequency of Reporting

According to IAS 1.36, the entity should produce, at a minimum, annual statements.

Comparative Information and Consistency of Presentation

Comparative information enhances comparability and therefore is required unless IFRS permits or requires otherwise. Entities should present at least two statements and a third (opening statement of financial position) where there has been a retrospective application or restatement.

Presentation and classification should stay the same unless it is determined that another alternative presentation/classification is more appropriate or an IFRS requires a change.

STRUCTURE AND CONTENT

Identification of Financial Statements

It is important to identify what is included as part of the statements since IFRSs apply to the financial statements only and not other information that may be reported. According to IAS 1, the following information must be displayed prominently:

---

[3] IASCF, IAS 1.7.

1. the name of the entity,
2. whether the financial statements are consolidated or not,
3. the date of the balance sheet or period covered,
4. the reporting currency, and
5. the level of rounding (e.g., $000s).

Statement of Financial Position

Information to Be Presented in the Statement of Financial Position

Items that are sufficiently different and material should be presented separately on the face of the balance sheet. This decision is based on the size, function, nature, and liquidity of the assets and the nature and timing of liabilities. Where different measurement bases are used, this would normally require separate presentation. The standard requires the following items to be presented separately:[4]

(a) property, plant, and equipment;
(b) investment property;
(c) intangible assets;
(d) financial assets (excluding amounts shown under (e), (h), and (i));
(e) investments accounted for using the equity method;
(f) biological assets;
(g) inventories;
(h) trade and other receivables;
(i) cash and cash equivalents;
(j) total of assets classified as held for sale and assets included in disposal groups classified as held for sale;
(k) trade and other payables;
(l) provisions (liabilities of uncertain timing or amount);
(m) financial liabilities (excluding amounts shown under (k) and (l));
(n) liabilities and assets for current tax;
(o) deferred tax liabilities and deferred tax assets;
(p) liabilities included in disposal groups classified as held for sale;
(q) non-controlling interests, presented within equity; and
(r) issued capital and reserves attributable to owners of the parent.

Entities may present or disclose relevant subcategories on the face of the balance sheet or in the notes. In addition, details about the nature of share capital should be presented either in the notes or on the balance sheet.

Current Assets and Liabilities

In most instances, the balance sheet is segregated between current and non-current assets and liabilities as this gives relevant information about the available working capital of the entity. However, there may be situations where it is more relevant to present the balance sheet in terms of liquidity, in which case the elements should be grouped and presented in order of liquidity. An entity may present some of its assets/liabilities using the current/non-current classification and some using the liquidity classification. The entity should also disclose amounts to be recovered/settled beyond 12 months. If using the current/non-current classification, the following applies.

---

[4] IASCF, IAS 1.54.

An entity classifies assets as *current assets* when[5]

    (a)   it expects to realize the asset, or intends to sell or consume it, in its normal operating cycle;

    (b)   it holds the asset primarily for the purpose of trading;

    (c)   it expects to realize the asset within 12 months after the reporting period; or

    (d)   the asset is cash or a cash equivalent (as defined in IAS 7) unless the asset is restricted from being exchanged or used to settle a liability for at least 12 months after the reporting period.

An entity classifies liabilities as *current liabilities* when[6]

    (a)   it expects to settle the liability in its normal operating cycle;

    (b)   it holds the liability primarily for the purpose of trading;

    (c)   the liability is due to be settled within 12 months after the reporting period; or

    (d)   the entity does not have an unconditional right to defer settlement of the liability for at least 12 months after the reporting period.

Professional judgment is used in determining whether something should be presented as current or non-current.

Situation

Jab Inc. has some long-term debt that is currently due this year. It has negotiated with Jonathan Bank (a large reputable bank) to refinance the debt with a five-year loan. A written agreement is in place; however, the actual refinancing will not take place until after year end.

Analysis

The debt would be classified as long term even though it is technically due in the upcoming year and thus meets the definition of a current liability. In this case, the existence of a written agreement with a solvent reputable bank for new long-term financing provides evidence that the debt should not be presented as current. The refinancing will not use up any of the company's cash flows since the debt does not need to be repaid. If the agreement was reached after year end, the debt would be classified as current.

Deferred tax assets/liabilities may not be classified as current.

Statement of Comprehensive Income

Information to Be Presented in the Statement of Comprehensive Income

The following items are included in the Statement of Comprehensive Income:[7]

    (a)   revenue;

    (b)   finance costs;

    (c)   share of the profit or loss of associates and joint ventures accounted for using the equity method;

    (d)   tax expense;

    (e)   a single amount comprising the total of

        (i)   the post-tax profit or loss of discontinued operations, and

        (ii) the post-tax gain or loss recognized on the measurement to fair value less costs to sell or on the disposal of the assets or disposal group(s) constituting the discontinued operation;

---

[5] IASCF, IAS 1.66.

[6] IASCF, IAS 1.69.

[7] IASCF, IAS 1.82.

(f)   profit or loss;

(g)   each component of other comprehensive income classified by nature (excluding amounts in (h);

(h)   share of the other comprehensive income of associates and joint ventures accounted for using the equity method; and

(i)   total comprehensive income.

Total comprehensive income is defined as follows:[8]

". . . the change in equity during a period resulting from transactions and other events, other than those changes resulting from transactions with owners in their capacity as owners."

Total comprehensive income includes all components of profit or loss and of **other comprehensive income** as noted above.

Items that are required to be included in other comprehensive income are the following:

1.   changes in the revaluation surplus for property, plant, and equipment and intangible assets;
2.   certain actuarial gains/losses on defined benefit plans;
3.   gains/losses arising on translation of financial statements of foreign operations;
4.   gains/losses arising from remeasuring securities available for sale; and
5.   gains/losses on cash flow hedges.[9]

Subsequent chapters will examine how these items arise. These items may be reclassified to profit or loss when certain events occur. For instance, when an available-for-sale investment is sold, any unrealized gain/loss previously booked to other comprehensive income would be reclassified to profit or loss. These reclassifications are referred to as *reclassification adjustments*.

When items are material, the nature and amount should be presented separately either on the face of the statements or in the notes. Expenses are presented in a way that highlights their nature or function within the entity. Consideration should be given to frequency, potential for gain or loss, and predictability. The two presentation methods are the nature of expense method and the function of expense method. The nature of expense method focuses on the type of expense itself, i.e., payroll or depreciation, whereas the function of expense method focuses on the nature of the activity that the expense relates to, i.e., production, distribution and selling, or administrative.[10]

Illustration 2-1 is an example of the nature of expense method.

Illustration 2-1 Nature of Expense Presentation			
Revenue			X
Other income			X
Changes in inventories of finished goods and work in progress		X	
Raw materials and consumables used		X	
Employee benefits expense		X	
Depreciation and amortization expense		X	
Other expenses		X	
Total expenses			(X)
Profit before tax			X

---

[8] IASCF, IAS 1.7.

[9] IASCF, IAS 1.7.

[10] IASCF, IAS 1.102-.103.

Illustration 2-2 is an example of the function of expense method.

Illustration 2-2 ***Function*** ***of Expense*** ***Presentation***		
Revenue	X
Cost of sales	(X)
Gross profit	X
Other income	X
Distribution costs	(X)
Administrative expenses	(X)
Other expenses	(X)
Profit before tax	X

Either method may be used depending on historical and industry factors and the nature of the industry. An entity may not present items as arising from the activities that are outside the entity's normal activities (i.e., extraordinary items are not allowed).

A survey carried out by KPMG IFRG Limited in 2005 after the European Community adopted IFRS found that 55% of the reporting entities surveyed presented the statement by function of expense and 45% by nature of expense.

Statement of Changes in Equity

The statement of changes in equity presents the following:

1. total comprehensive income;
2. for each component of equity, the effects of retrospective application/restatement; and
3. reconciliation between the carrying amount of each component of equity at the beginning and end of the period.

Statement of Cash Flows

IAS 7 sets out the specific requirements for the statement of cash flows. See Chapter 3.

Notes

The notes augment the basic statements and include information about the way they have been prepared (accounting policies) and provide additional descriptive and supportive information that is not presented elsewhere. The notes should be cross-referenced to the statements and include a statement of compliance with IFRSs.

Disclosure of Accounting Policies

Since many choices are allowed in terms of accounting policies, it is important to disclose which policies have been applied. In addition, the measurement bases should be identified, along with any significant judgments made in applying accounting policies.

Key Sources of Estimation Uncertainty

Many numbers on the balance sheet and statement of profit and loss contain significant measurement uncertainty. Because the financial statements are presented using point estimates, it is important to convey this "softness," i.e., that they represent a point estimate within a range. The nature of the measurement uncertainty should be disclosed (e.g., the obsolescence provision for inventories), as well as the carrying amount of the element at the end of the reporting period. The IFRSs give as an example of these disclosures a sensitivity analysis of carrying amounts to the methods, assumptions, and estimates, including reasons for the sensitivity and the expected resolution of an uncertainty, as well as the range of reasonably possible outcomes.[11]

If it is impracticable to disclose the possible effects of the above, then the fact that it is reasonably possible that the carrying value might have to be materially restated should be disclosed.

Capital

The nature and structure of an entity's capital and how it is managed help provide information useful to users in assessing risk. The following disclosures are therefore required regarding capital:[12]

(a) qualitative information about its objectives, policies, and processes for managing capital, including

    (i) a description of what it manages as capital;

    (ii) when an entity is subject to externally imposed capital requirements, the nature of those requirements, and how those requirements are incorporated into the management of capital; and

    (iii) how it is meeting its objectives for managing capital.

(b) summary quantitative data about what it manages as capital. Some entities regard some financial liabilities (e.g., some forms of subordinated debt) as part of capital. Other entities regard capital as excluding some components of equity (e.g., components arising from cash flow hedges).

(c) any changes in (a) and (b) from the previous period.

(d) whether, during the period, it complied with any externally imposed capital requirements to which it is subject.

(e) when the entity has not complied with such externally imposed capital requirements, the consequences of such non-compliance.

(f) the amount of dividends proposed or declared before the financial statements were authorized for issue but not recognized as a distribution to owners during the period, and the related amount per share.

(g) the amount of any cumulative preference dividends not recognized.

(h) the domicile and legal form of the entity, its country of incorporation, and the address of its registered office (or principal place of business, if different from the registered office).

(i) a description of the nature of the entity's operations and its principal activities.

(j) the name of the parent and the ultimate parent of the group.

Samples of and Excerpts from Selected Statements

The following illustrations were taken from IAS 1 as examples of financial statement presentations. The standard notes that this is not the only way to present the financial statements; an entity may change the order of elements, the title of the statements, and level of detail in order to provide the most useful information.

---

[11] IASCF, IAS 1.129.
[12] IASCF, IAS 1.135-.138.

Illustration 2-3
Statement of
Financial Position

XYZ Group – Statement of financial position as at 31 December 20×7
(in thousands of currency units)

	31 Dec 20×7	31 Dec 20×6
ASSETS		
Non-current assets		
Property, plant and equipment	350,700	360,020
Goodwill	80,800	91,200
Other intangible assets	227,470	227,470
Investments in associates	100,150	110,770
Available-for-sale financial assets	142,500	156,000
	901,620	945,460
Current assets		
Inventories	135,230	132,500
Trade receivables	91,600	110,800
Other current assets	25,650	12,540
Cash and cash equivalents	312,400	322,900
	564,880	578,740
Total assets	1,466,500	1,524,200
EQUITY AND LIABILITIES		
Equity attributable to owners of the parent		
Share capital	650,000	600,000
Retained earnings	243,500	161,700
Other components of equity	10,200	21,200
	903,700	782,900
Non-controlling interests	70,050	48,600
Total equity	973,750	831,500
Non-current liabilities		
Long-term borrowings	120,000	160,000
Deferred tax	28,800	26,040
Long-term provisions	28,850	52,240
Total non-current liabilities	177,650	238,280
Current liabilities		
Trade and other payables	115,100	187,620
Short-term borrowings	150,000	200,000
Current portion of long-term borrowings	10,000	20,000

Current tax payable	35,000	42,000
Short-term provisions	5,000	4,800
Total current liabilities	315,100	454,420
Total liabilities	492,750	692,700
Total equity and liabilities	1,466,500	1,524,200

Illustration 2-4
Statement of
Comprehensive
Income

XYZ Group – Statement of comprehensive income for the year ended 31 December 20×7

(illustrating the presentation of comprehensive income in one statement and the classification of expenses within profit by function)

(in thousands of currency units)

	20×7	20×6
Revenue	390,000	355,000
Cost of sales	(245,000)	(230,000)
Gross profit	145,000	125,000
Other income	20,667	11,300
Distribution costs	(9,000)	(8,700)
Administrative expenses	(20,000)	(21,000)
Other expenses	(2,100)	(1,200)
Finance costs	(8,000)	(7,500)
Share of profit of associates	35,100	30,100
Profit before tax	161,667	128,000
Income tax expense	(40,417)	(32,000)
Profit for the year from continuing operations	121,250	96,000
Loss for the year from discontinued operation	–	(30,500)
PROFIT FOR THE YEAR	121,250	65,500
Other comprehensive income:		
Exchange differences on translating foreign operations	5,334	10,667
Available-for-sale financial assets	(24,000)	26,667
Cash flow hedges	667	4,000
Gains on property revaluation	933	3,367
Actuarial gains (losses) on defined benefit pension plans	(667)	1,333
Share of other comprehensive income of associates	400	(700)
Income tax relating to components of other comprehensive income	4,667	(9,334)
Other comprehensive income for the year, net of tax	(14,000)	28,000
TOTAL COMPREHENSIVE INCOME FOR THE YEAR	107,250	93,500

Illustration 2-5
Statement of
Changes in
Equity

XYZ Group – Statement of changes in equity for the year ended
31 December 20×7
(in thousands of currency units)

	Share capital	Retained earnings	Translation of foreign operations	Available-for-sale financial assets	Cash flow hedges	Revaluation surplus	Total	Non-controlling interests	Total equity
Balance at 1 January 20×6	600,000	118,100	(4,000)	1,600	2,000	–	717,700	29,800	747,500
Changes in accounting policy	–	400	–	–	–	–	400	100	500
Restated balance	600,000	118,500	(4,000)	1,600	2,000	–	718,100	29,900	748,000
Changes in equity for 20×6									
Dividends	–	(10,000)	–	–	–	–	(10,000)	–	(10,000)
Total comprehensive income for the year	–	53,200	6,400	16,000	(2,400)	1,600	74,800	18,700	93,500
Balance at 31 December 20×6	600,000	161,700	2,400	17,600	(400)	1,600	782,900	48,600	831,500
Changes in equity for 20×7									
Issue of share capital	50,000	–	–	–	–	–	50,000	–	50,000
Dividends	–	(15,000)	–	–	–	–	(15,000)	–	(15,000)
Total comprehensive income for the year	–	96,600	3,200	(14,400)	(400)	800	85,800	21,450	107,250
Transfer to retained earnings	–	200	–	–	–	200	–	–	–
Balance at 31 December 20×7	650,000	243,500	5,600	3,200	(800)	2,200	903,700	70,050	973,750

LOOKING AHEAD

The financial statement presentation project is part of the Memorandum of Understanding between the IASB and FASB. It is divided up into several parts as follows:

- *Phase A: bring the accounting in line with U.S. standards for comprehensive income.* A revised IAS1 standard has already been released and incorporated into the material in this chapter.
- *Phase B: address more fundamental issues, such as how the entity can present an integrated financial picture of its financial portion and performance.* Concerns have been raised regarding how financial statements are presented, as there is no common approach, information is not linked between statements, and dissimilar items are sometimes aggregated. A discussion paper entitled *Preliminary Views on Financial Statement Presentation* has been issued for comment by April 2009. The following model has been proposed:

Statement of Financial Position	Statement of Comprehensive Income	Statement of Cash Flows
Business • Operating assets and liabilities • Investing assets and liabilities	*Business* • Operating income and expenses • Investment income and expenses	*Business* • Operating cash flows • Investing cash flows
Financing • Financing assets • Financing liabilities	*Financing* • Financing asset income • Financing liability expenses	*Financing* • Financing asset cash flows • Financing liability cash flows
Income taxes	*Income taxes* on continuing operations (business and financing)	*Income taxes*
Discontinued operations	*Discontinued operations,* net of tax	*Discontinued operations*
	Other comprehensive income, net of tax	
Equity		*Equity*

- *Phase C: address interim financial reporting.* This process has not yet begun.

END-OF-CHAPTER PRACTICE

2-1 Entities may present their statement of profit and loss using the nature of expense method or the function of expense method. Discuss the value of each method.

2-2 The accrual method requires that companies estimate the impact of transactions on the financial statements before the cash flows occur. This requires significant amounts of estimation. Review the assets of Rentokil Initial PLC (2007 Annual Report) and identify any assets that require estimation. Identify which estimates need to be made.

2-3 Review the balance sheet for L'Oreal (2007 Annual Report). How does it present its balance sheet? Discuss, comparing with how balance sheets are currently presented in North America.

2-4 Review the accounting policy note for GlaxoSmithKline (2007 Annual Report). Identify any areas where the accounting policy choices require significant judgment or measurement uncertainty. See also the key accounting judgments and estimates note. Relate these to the underlying business.

2-5 IAS 1 defines materiality. Compare the definition to the North American definition. Why is it important to relate the concept of materiality to the users?

2-6 Access IAS 1 (through the school's library) and identify the level of knowledge expected of a typical user of the financial statements. Does this differ at all from knowledge required by U.S. GAAP?

2-7 In this chapter, the flag icons identify areas where there are GAAP differences between IFRS requirements and national standards.

Instructions

Access the website(s) identified on the inside back cover of this book, and prepare a concise summary of the differences that are flagged throughout the chapter material.

Chapter 3

Statement of Cash Flows: IAS 7

U.S. GAAP References
FAS 95 Statement of Cash Flows
FAS 102 Statement of Cash Flows—Exemption of Certain Enterprises and Classification of Cash Flows from Certain Securities Acquired for Resale
FAS 104 Statement of Cash Flows—Net Reporting of Certain Cash Receipts and Cash Payments and Classification of Cash Flows from Hedging Transactions

Related IFRS
IAS 1 Presentation of Financial Statements

OBJECTIVE AND SCOPE

The cash flow statement provides key information to users to help in their assessment of an entity's prospects for future cash flows and to confirm or change their past expectations. Cash, critical to the survival and success of every organization, is needed to carry out day-to-day operations, invest in new long-term resources, meet debt obligations, and provide a return to investors. The cash flow statement, required of all entities, provides historical information on these operating, investing, and financing cash flows and how cash balances have changed as a result of these flows.

Investors, creditors, and others use cash flow information to assess an entity's solvency and liquidity and to understand the relationship between profit or loss and cash generated by operations. The statement also provides a link between the statement of financial position at the beginning and end of the accounting period.

CASH FLOWS

The statement of cash flows reports the change in cash during the accounting period and summarizes the cash flows according to whether they were a result of operating, investing, or financing activities. **Cash flows** refer to more than cash on hand and demand deposits. They are inflows and outflows of cash **and cash equivalents**. *Cash equivalents* are defined in IAS 7.6 as "short-term, highly liquid investments that are readily convertible to known amounts of cash and which are subject to an insignificant risk of changes in value."

Cash equivalents are included in cash flows because they are used in an entity's cash management activities. For example, excess funds are often placed in near-cash investments until needed in the short term. Cash equivalents do not include instruments held for investment purposes, debt instruments with a maturity date more than three months from the date acquired, or equity instruments in general.[1] Bank overdrafts that are payable on demand and fluctuate between positive and negative amounts are deducted when determining the amount of cash and cash equivalents because these overdrafts also result from an entity's cash management activities. Other bank borrowings are usually treated as financing cash flows. Throughout this chapter, the term cash is used to refer to both cash and cash equivalents.

REPORTING OPERATING CASH FLOWS

Operating Activities

Operating activities are the principal revenue-producing activities of the entity and those activities that are not classified as investing or financing activities.[2] Because operations vary from one industry to another, what an operating activity is will differ as well. Most operating cash flows result from transactions and events that are recognized in profit or loss, such as

(a) cash received from customers for the sale of goods and provision of services, or on account of royalties, fees, or commissions;

(b) cash payments to suppliers for goods and services provided, and to and on behalf of employees for their services; and

(c) cash received from or paid for financial instruments held specifically for dealing or trading purposes.

Companies in specialized industries, such as financial institutions, insurance companies, and mutual funds, have different types of operating cash flows than manufacturers, for example. The key to deciding whether a transaction is an operating activity is to zero in on what the entity's primary revenue-producing activities are.

Operating Cash Flows Are Important

Entities need surplus cash flows from their operating activities to maintain their existing operating capability, invest in increased capacity, meet their debt obligations, and provide a return to their shareholders. The greater the potential for generating these operating flows without incurring additional debt, the higher the value of the entity to an investor and the lower its cost of capital. Details about a company's past operating cash flows are useful in projecting future operating cash flows.

Reporting Standards

Two methods of reporting cash flows from operating activities are permitted: the direct method and the indirect method. Regardless of which method is used, and whether the information is taken directly from the cash accounts or by adjusting items reported on the income statement for differences between the revenue or expense

---

[1] Holdings of preferred shares acquired shortly before their fixed maturity date qualify as a cash equivalent.
[2] IASCF, IAS 7.6.

reported and their cash effect, the net cash flow from operations has the same meaning. Each method, however, provides different detailed information about what makes up the net result.

Common adjustments needed to convert profit or loss to cash from operating activities include

- changes in the balances of operating working capital accounts, such as inventory and operating receivables and payables;
- elimination of non-cash items related to depreciation, provisions, deferred taxes, and a variety of other accrual and deferral adjustments;
- other items where the related cash flows are financing or investing in nature, such as gains and losses on the disposal of long-lived assets or the elimination of debt.

The **direct method,** in which the major sources of operating cash receipts and cash payments are separately reported, is preferred but not required. Illustration 3-1 indicates how the operating cash flow section of the statement appears under this method.

Illustration 3-1 *Cash from Operations Direct Method*		
	Cash received from customers	$95
	Cash paid to suppliers of goods and services	(50)
	Cash paid to employees	(28)
	Income taxes paid	(5)
	Net cash from operating activities	**$12**

The **indirect method** presented in Illustration 3-2 reconciles the profit or loss reported to the net cash from operating activities. The example provided could be for the same company and the same period.

Illustration 3-2 *Cash from Operations Indirect Method*		
	Profit reported	$9
	Adjustments:	
	Depreciation	20
	Increase in trade accounts receivable	(6)
	Increase in trade accounts payable	5
	Decrease in deferred income tax liability	(3)
	Non-operating gain on sale of land	(13)
	Net cash from operating activities	**$12**

An alternative presentation is sometimes used, in which operating revenues and expenses are reported on the statement and presented as a subtotal, followed by changes in working capital.

Both the direct and indirect methods provide useful, but different, information. A survey carried out by KPMG IFRG Limited (a U.K. company) after the European Community adopted IFRS in 2005 found that 8% of the 199 companies in its sample that moved to IFRS used the direct method and 92% used the indirect.[3]

---

[3] KPMG and Prof. Dr. Isabel von Keitz, *The Application of IFRS: Choices in Practice*, KPMG IFRG Limited, December 2006, p. 5.

REPORTING INVESTING CASH FLOWS

Investing activities are the "acquisition and disposal of long-term assets and other investments not included in cash equivalents."[4] The objective of this classification is to identify those cash flows related to the pool of long-term assets that make up the operating capability of the entity, and only expenditures that result in a recognized asset are included. Examples of investing cash flows from IAS 7 include the following:

(a) Cash payments to acquire property, plant, and equipment; intangibles; and other long-term assets, including capitalized development costs
(b) Cash receipts from the disposal of items in (a)
(c) Cash payments to acquire debt and equity instruments of other entities or interests in joint ventures, excluding investments held for trading or in cash equivalents
(d) Cash receipts from the disposal of items in (c)
(e) Cash advances and loans to other parties and their cash repayments
(f) Cash payments for and receipts from futures, forwards, options, and swaps unless they are held for trading or are classified as financing flows. However, a contract accounted for as a hedge of an identifiable position is classified in the same way as the position hedged.

Wienerberger AG, an international building materials group headquartered in Vienna, Austria (reporting in thousands of euros), included the investing cash flow section in Illustration 3-3 on its statement of cash flows for the year ended December 31, 2007.[5]

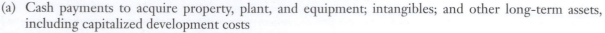

Illustration 3-3 Wienerberger AG—Investing Cash Flow Section	2007	2006
Proceeds from the sale of assets (including financial assets)	24,884	29,206
Purchase of property, plant and equipment and intangible assets	−319,604	−360,659
Payments made for investments in financial assets	−10,539	−3,946
Increase/decrease in securities	38,099	−5,118
Net payments made for the acquisition of companies	−326,015	−169,743
Net proceeds from the sale of companies	0	574
Cash flow from investing activities	**−593,175**	**−509,686**

Why are investing cash flows relevant to investors and other financial statement readers? Long-term assets provide an entity's operating capacity and the potential for generating operating profits and cash flows in the future. This section of the statement of cash flows allows readers to assess whether the entity is only maintaining or whether it is increasing its pool of long-term operational investments, whether capacity is being depleted, and whether it is investing in passive debt and equity instruments.

REPORTING FINANCING CASH FLOWS

Financing activities are those "that result in changes in the size and composition of the contributed equity and borrowings of the entity."[6] Examples of financing cash flows include the following:

(a) Cash receipts from the issue of the entity's shares or other equity instruments, and cash payments to reacquire these instruments

---

[4] IASCF, IAS 7.6
[5] From http://www.wienerberger.com/servlet/
[6] IASCF, IAS 7.6

(b) Cash receipts as a result of bank loans, the issue of bonds, notes or other short- or long-term borrowing, and cash payments to repay principal amounts borrowed, including payments by a lessee to reduce the principal on finance leases

Continuing with Wienerberger AG's 2007 statement of cash flows, Illustration 3-4 shows how this company reported its financing cash flows for 2007 and 2006.

Illustration 3-4 Wienerberger AG—Financing Cash Flow Section		**2007**	**2006**
	Increase/decrease in long-term financial liabilities	−2,602	−293,242
	Increase/decrease in short-term financial liabilities	−479,049	510,536
	Dividends paid by Wienerberger AG	−94,923	−86,415
	Dividends paid to minority shareholders and other changes in minority capital	−7,596	840
	Dividend payments from associates	4,087	3,676
	Capital increase Wienerberger AG	424,136	0
	Capital increase Wienerberger AG (hybrid bond)	492,896	0
	Cash inflows from exercise of stock options	7,672	5,268
	Purchase of treasury stock	−13,392	−8,892
	Cash flow from financing activities	**331,229**	**131,771**

Users of financial statements are interested in financing cash flows because they provide important information about changes in the capital structure of the entity. This affects the relative interests of the groups with claims to the entity's future cash flows.

SPECIFIC ITEMS

Netting

Investing and financing cash flows are generally reported at their gross amounts. For example, if an entity acquires land and building for $100, borrowing $75 from the bank to help finance the purchase, this is reported as an investing outflow of $100 and a financing inflow of $75. If an entity borrows $100 early in the year and repays $90 of it by year end, a financing cash inflow of $100 and a cash outflow of $90 are reported separately.

Operating, investing, and financing cash flows may be reported on a net basis only in two limited circumstances:

- when the cash flows received and paid on behalf of customers reflect the activities of the customer rather than the reporting entity; and
- when the cash receipts and related cash payments happen close together, are large in amount, and have short maturities.

An example of the first condition is the collection of rents by an entity that then turns the proceeds over to the owner of the property. Credit card companies are a good example of the second condition. The principal amounts they collect from customers and transfer to a retail entity, for example, may be netted in the statement of cash flows of the credit card company. A series of short-term borrowings each with a maturity of three months or less may also be reported as a net amount. Due to the type of transactions they enter into, further guidance is provided in the standard for financial institutions.

Interest and Dividends

Entities are required to provide separate disclosure of their cash flows from interest and dividends received and interest and dividends paid, **but have a choice** as to whether each is classified as an operating, investing, or financing flow. Once a choice is made, it is applied consistently.

Research conducted by KPMG IFRG Limited indicates that a significant majority of companies in its sample of 199 companies classify interest and dividends received and interest paid as operating flows, and dividends paid as a financing outflow. The next most common choice is to report interest and dividends received as investing inflows, interest paid as a financing outflow, and dividends paid as an operating outflow.[7]

Taxes on Income

Cash flows from taxes on income, including total taxes paid, require separate disclosure. Because tax cash flows are difficult to trace to specific transactions, cash flows resulting from taxes on income are classified as operating cash flows unless they are specifically identifiable with investing or financing activities.

Non-cash Transactions

Investing and financing transactions that have no cash flow effect are not included on the statement of cash flows. Examples include entering into a finance lease, acquiring property and assuming an existing mortgage, and converting debt into equity. Because such transactions often affect the capital or asset structure of an entity, information about them is required to be disclosed outside the statement of cash flows.

Cash Flows Related to Investments in Subsidiaries, Associates, and Joint Ventures

Only cash flows between an entity and a subsidiary, associate, or joint venture accounted for using the cost or equity method—such as dividends or advances—are captured on the statement of cash flows. If a joint venture is proportionately consolidated, the entity's share of the joint venture's cash flows is incorporated into its statement of cash flows.

Changes in Ownership of Subsidiaries and Other Businesses

Cash payments made to acquire (or cash received from losing) control of a subsidiary or business are presented separately as investing cash outflows (or inflows), with specific note disclosures required. Illustration 3-3 indicates that the payments made by Wienerberger for the acquisition of control over other companies was the single largest use of cash for investment in 2007. Cash effects of changes in ownership of a subsidiary without a change in control are reported as financing flows similar to other transactions with owners.

Foreign Currency Cash Flows

An entity records cash transactions denominated in a foreign currency using the exchange rate at the date of the cash flow, and translates the cash flows reported by a foreign subsidiary using the rates when the cash flows occurred. An adjustment is needed in preparing the statement of cash flows for the cash and cash equivalents held in a foreign currency during the period as the exchange rates change. The item is reported separately as a reconciling item at the bottom of the statement. Illustration 3-5 shows how Wienerberger reports the reconciling item on its 2007 statement of cash flows.

---

[7] KPMG and Prof. Dr. Isabel von Keitz, *The Application of IFRS: Choices in Practice*, KPMG IFRG Limited, December 2006, pp. 6–10.

Illustration 3-5 Wienerberger AG—Foreign Currency Item		2007	2006
	Change in cash and cash at bank	99,578	−26,316
	Effects of exchange rate fluctuations on cash held	264	−29
	Cash and cash at bank at the beginning of the year	193,531	219,876
	Cash and cash at bank at the end of the year	293,373	193,531

DISCLOSURES

In addition to the reporting standards explained in this chapter, the following disclosures are required:

- The components of cash and cash equivalents, and a reconciliation of the amount reported on the statement of cash flows with the amount reported on the statement of financial position
- An explanation of any significant cash balances not available for use

A variety of additional disclosures are suggested, but not mandatory. These include identifying separately cash flows that increase operating capacity from those that merely maintain capacity, and reporting cash flows by operating segment.

LOOKING AHEAD

Significant changes are anticipated in the future when the joint FASB-IASB *Financial Statement Presentation* project is completed. Both Boards issued a Discussion Paper (identical except in terms of style and format) in October 2008 that sets out their preliminary views on financial statement presentation. If accepted, the statement of cash flows would see the following changes:

- The change in cash, not cash and equivalents, is explained.
- The direct method of presenting operating cash flows is required, with a new schedule included in the notes to the financial statements that reconciles cash flows to comprehensive income.
- Cash flows are classified into business (with separate reporting of operating and investing flows), financing (with separate reporting of financial asset cash flows and financial liability cash flows), income taxes, discontinued operations, and equity flows.

In 2009, the IASB is field-testing the proposed presentation model; the Board expects to issue an Exposure Draft in 2010 and a final standard in 2011.

END-OF-CHAPTER PRACTICE

3-1 Ace Manufacturing Ltd. reports the following items on its June 30, 2008 statement of financial position:

	June 30, 2008	June 30, 2007
Available-for-sale investment in ABC Co. bonds	$28	$30
Bank overdraft	(8)	0
Cash on hand and in bank	15*	20
Trading investment in FPA Inc. common shares	12	0
Temporary investment in 60-day T Bill	0	5

*Includes $3 in an account of a foreign subsidiary in a country with restrictions on the repatriation of funds.

Instructions

Prepare the bottom portion of Ace Manufacturing's statement of cash flows, along with any related disclosures required, beginning with the line "Change in cash and cash equivalents for the year."

3-2 A list of assets from a variety of companies is provided below.
1. Heavy equipment owned by a construction company
2. Income taxes receivable on overpayment by an advertising agency
3. Development costs on product X34 of a manufacturing company
4. Golf course acquired under a finance lease by a hospitality company
5. Bulldozers acquired by a heavy equipment dealer
6. Long-term portion of installment account receivable of a furniture retailer
7. Held-for-trading investment in bonds in a portfolio of a technology solutions company
8. Temporary investment in 30-day commercial paper of a major company by a department store retailer

Instructions
(a) For each asset listed above, indicate whether its acquisition is an operating, investing, or a financing activity. If a choice is allowed, indicate what the choices are and explain which you would choose and why you would choose it.
(b) For each asset listed above, indicate whether cash flows from its use and/or disposal are operating, investing, or financing cash flows. If a choice is available, explain your answer.

3-3 Companies are affected by a number of events and transactions, some of which have an effect on their cash and cash equivalents, and some which do not. Following are some examples of such events and transactions:
1. Annual payment of $100 on a finance lease obligation, $2 of which is interest
2. Acquisition of a $100, 3%, 90-day government treasury bill
3. Payment of $25 to a pension fund trustee
4. Cash received on the maturity of the treasury bill in item 2. above
5. Annual payment of $100 on an operating lease for sales office space
6. Receipt of $10 on the sublease of excess sales office space
7. Acquisition of the company's treasury shares at a cost of $75
8. Conversion of convertible debt into common shares
9. Payment of $30 of a portion of long-term debt reported in current liabilities along with $3 of interest
10. Costs incurred to repair a customer's product under warranty—inventory supplies used $1; labor paid $4

Instructions
For each item listed above
(a) identify the effect on the company's cash and cash equivalents; and
(b) indicate how the transaction or event will be reported on the company's statement of cash flows, if at all, and if any special disclosures are required.

3-4 IAS 7 *Statement of Cash Flows* permits a choice in how interest and dividends received and paid are classified on the statement of cash flows.

Instructions
For interest received, dividends received, interest paid, and dividends paid, identify two likely ways in which each might be reported. Provide a reasonable explanation for each choice.

3-5 In this chapter, flag icons identify areas where there are GAAP differences between IFRS requirements and national standards.

Instructions
Access the website(s) identified on the inside back cover of this book, and prepare a concise summary of the differences that are flagged throughout the chapter.

Chapter 4

Non-current Assets Held for Sale and Discontinued Operations: IFRS 5

U.S. GAAP References
FAS 144 Accounting for the Impairment or Disposal of Long-lived Assets
FAS 131 Disclosures about Segments of an Enterprise and Related Information

Related IFRSs
IFRS 8 Operating Segments
IAS 36 Impairment of Assets
IAS 1   Presentation of Financial Statements

OBJECTIVE AND SCOPE

IFRS 5 addresses two key topics:

1. the classification, measurement, and presentation of assets held for sale; and
2. the presentation and disclosure of discontinued operations.

The objective of this IFRS is to provide information that is useful to users in assessing the amount, timing, and risk associated with an entity's future cash flows, particularly those related to non-current assets and disposal groups with carrying values that will be recovered through sale rather than through use.

The term **assets held for sale** refers to all such recognized non-current assets, as well as **disposal groups**. When a number of assets making up a cash-generating unit are disposed of together, the disposal group may include current assets and directly related current and non-current liabilities. IFRS 5 applies to all items in a disposal group; however, other IFRSs cover the **measurement** of the following specific assets and liabilities: deferred tax assets (IAS 12 *Income Taxes*), employee benefit assets (IAS 19 *Employee Benefits*), financial assets within IAS 39 (IAS 39 *Financial Instruments: Recognition and Measurement*), non-current investment property applying the fair value model (IAS 40 *Investment Property*), non-current agricultural assets measured at fair value less estimated point-of-sale costs (IAS 41 *Agriculture*), and contractual rights under insurance contracts (IFRS 4 *Insurance Contracts*).

A **discontinued operation** is a defined subset of assets that are either held for sale or disposed of during the period.

CLASSIFICATION AS HELD FOR SALE

An entity classifies non-current assets or disposal groups (referred to generally as assets in this section) as **held for sale** only when their carrying amount is expected to be converted to cash primarily through sale rather than through use. The assets cannot be reclassified as current assets until they meet the reclassification criteria of IFRS 5. To qualify for held-for-sale classification at the balance-sheet date, the assets must meet stringent conditions:

(a) They must be available for immediate sale in their existing condition, and the sale must be **highly probable**. Highly probable means that management has put in place an active plan to sell them, including marketing them at a reasonable price.

(b) It is likely that significant changes will not be made to the plan and that the sale will qualify for accounting recognition within one year from the date the assets are classified as available for sale. Exceptions to completion of the sale within one year are permitted, but only when caused by circumstances outside management's control and management is still committed to its plan.

The additional guidance provided in the standard is based on ensuring that only assets that recover their carrying value through their sale are included in the classification:

- **Asset exchanges** that have commercial substance (see IAS 16.25 *Property, Plant and Equipment*) are included as sales transactions.
- **Assets acquired solely for disposal** in the near future are classified as held for sale when acquired only if the one-year requirement is met and the criteria in (a) above will be met soon after acquisition, usually within three months.
- Assets are not permitted to be classified as held for sale if the criteria in (a) above will not be met until **after the date of the financial statements**. However, if the conditions are met before the financial statements are authorized for release, information about the assets or group, the sale or likely disposal, and the business segment affected is disclosed.
- **Assets to be abandoned** rather than sold are **not** classified as held for sale. If an asset is temporarily taken out of service, this is not an abandonment.

MEASUREMENT

Measurement of the Non-current Asset or Disposal Group

Prior to classification and measurement as held for sale, the carrying amounts of the assets or assets and liabilities in the disposal group are determined according to the IFRS related to each specific asset or liability. When reclassified as held for sale, they are measured at **the lower of their carrying amount and fair value less costs to sell**. If any of the selling costs are not expected to be incurred for more than one year, they are discounted to their present value and then are adjusted as time passes. The associated interest cost and other expenses related to the liabilities of a disposal group are recognized in profit or loss.

Accounting for Impairment Losses and Reversal of Losses

Write-downs to adjust the carrying amounts of such assets to a lower fair-value-less-selling-costs measure are recognized in profit or loss as **impairment losses**. At each balance sheet date, the non-current assets and disposal groups held for sale are remeasured. **Any increase in fair value less costs to sell**—to a maximum of the cumulative impairment losses previously recognized in IFRS 5 or IAS 36 *Impairment of Assets*—is recognized as a **gain and included in profit or loss**.[1] Further gains or losses are recognized when the assets or disposal groups are sold.

No depreciation is taken on non-current assets or disposal groups while they are classified as held for sale, even if they are still used in operations. The goal of accounting for this classification of assets is one of valuation, not cost allocation. As indicated in the Basis for Conclusions on IFRS 5, "the remaining use in operations of an asset that is to be sold is incidental to the recovery of the carrying amount through sale."[2]

Changes to a Plan of Sale

If the criteria required for classification as held for sale are no longer met for a non-current asset alone or as part of a disposal group, the item is reclassified and remeasured to the lower of

(a) its carrying amount before it was classified as held for sale, net of any depreciation, amortization, or valuation adjustments that would have been made if it had not been classified as held for sale; and

(b) its recoverable amount when the held-for-sale criteria were no longer met. *Recoverable amount* refers to the higher of its fair value less costs to sell and the present value of the expected future cash flows from continuing use and disposal by the entity (also known as *value in use*).

Any adjustment to the assets' carrying amount is recognized in profit or loss from continuing operations. Illustration 4-1 sets out the accounting requirement.

PRESENTATION AND DISCLOSURE

The goal of the presentation and disclosure requirements for non-current assets and disposal groups classified as held for sale is to allow financial statement readers to assess the effects of these items whose cash flows will come from their sale rather than from their use. In addition, providing information separately about continuing and discontinued operations is useful in assessing the potential for future returns and operating cash flows.

Income Statement

A discontinued operation needs to be carefully defined because it is reported on the income statement separately from other operating and ancillary results. Appendix A of IFRS 5 defines a *discontinued operation* as "a **component of an entity** that either has been disposed of or is classified as held for sale and

(a) represents a separate major line of business or geographical area of operations,

(b) is part of a single co-ordinated plan to dispose of a separate major line of business or geographical area of operations, or

(c) is a subsidiary acquired exclusively with a view to resale."

---

[1] Special standards apply to any assets or liabilities in a disposal group that are excluded from the measurement provisions of IFRS 5.

[2] IASB, Basis for Conclusions on IFRS 5 *Non-current Assets Held for Sale and Discontinued Operations*, paragraph BC29.

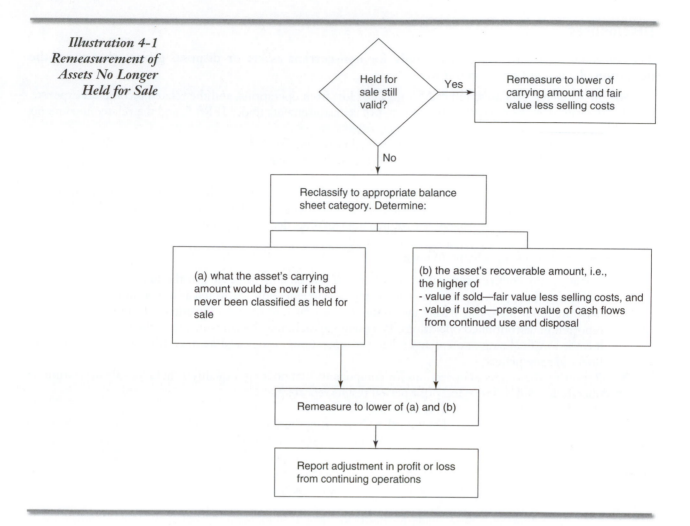

***Illustration 4-1
Remeasurement of
Assets No Longer
Held for Sale***

In addition, a ***component of an entity*** must have "[o]perations and cash flows that can be clearly distinguished, operationally and for financial reporting purposes, from the rest of the entity." [3]

The following business components are included in Daleara Corp. Determine whether the disposal of each is likely to meet the definition of a discontinued operation:

- A start-up operation that has incurred expenses but no revenues yet
- Division A that manufactures a primary component part that is sold only to Division B
- An information technology (IT) department that services the rest of the organization, internally billing other departments to recover its costs

Discussion: The **start-up operation** does not qualify as a discontinued operation because it has not begun operations, even though expenses have been recognized. It is not considered a separate major line of business. **Division A's** classification as a discontinued operation depends on whether the intermediate product is considered a separate and major line of business. It is likely that Division A's operations and cash flows are distinct from the rest of the entity. The **IT department** does not meet the definition of a discontinued operation. Its activities do not qualify as a major line of business.

---

[3] IASCF, IFRS 5, Appendix A.

Disclosures

The following disclosures are required **only for non-current assets or disposal groups that meet the definition of a discontinued operation:**

    (a) the revenues, expenses, and pre-tax profit or loss from operations, and the related income tax expense;

    (b) the gain or loss on disposal or as a result of remeasurements under IFRS 5, and the related income tax expense;

    (c) the total of the after-tax amounts determined in (a) and (b); and

    (d) the net cash flows from operations, investing, and financing.

The total of (c) is required to be reported separately on the face of the income statement, identified specifically as relating to discontinued operations. The other details may be reported on the face of the financial statements or in the notes. Only the information in item (c) is needed for disposal groups that are newly acquired subsidiaries that qualify as held for sale when acquired.

Other requirements include the following:

- Restating any comparative prior period's income statements presented in the financial statements, by reclassifying the past operating results of any components now identified as discontinued.
- Separate reporting of the nature and amount of any current period adjustments to amounts previously reported in discontinued operations. For example, there may be adjustments to the sales price or costs incurred in finalizing agreements related to operations recognized as discontinued on a prior year's financial statements.
- Reporting the results of operations for components that no longer qualify as held for sale in continuing operations, and reclassifying prior period results reported.

Marks and Spencer Group plc, based in the United Kingdom, operates in 34 countries and has 240 retail stores worldwide. In its financial statements for the 52 weeks ended March 31, 2007, the company reports the sale of its Kings Super Markets Inc. business. The excerpts reproduced in Illustration 4-2 show how this discontinued operation is reported on the face of the income statement and the statement of cash flows, and the additional details that are provided in the notes.[4] Marks and Spencer Group uses British pounds as its reporting currency.

Tentative decisions have been made by the IASB that, if implemented, will change the definition of a discontinued operation and the disclosures that are required. Additional information is provided in the **Looking Ahead** section at the end of the chapter.

Statement of Financial Position

Non-current assets classified as held for sale and those included in any disposal groups are reported separately from other assets on the statement of financial position. Liabilities included in disposal groups are reported as liabilities, separate from other liabilities. Unless the disposal group is a newly acquired subsidiary acquired specifically for resale, information about the major categories of assets and liabilities is disclosed either in a note or on the face of the statement. Any related amounts reported in equity, such as unrealized gains or losses on available-for-sale financial instruments or foreign currency adjustments, are also presented separately.

---

[4] http://www.marksandspencer.com/gp/node/n/56268031

*Illustration 4-2
Marks and
Spencer Group
plc—Income
Statement and
Statement of
Cash Flows
Disclosures*

Consolidated income statement

	Notes	52 weeks ended 31 March 2007 £m	52 weeks ended 1 April 2006 £m
Profit on ordinary activities after taxation – continuing operations		**659.2**	520.6
Profit from discontinued operation	7A	**0.7**	2.5
Profit for the year attributable to shareholders		**659.9**	523.1

Consolidated cash flow information

CASH FLOW STATEMENT

	Notes	52 weeks ended 31 March 2007 £m	52 weeks ended 1 April 2006 £m
Cash flows from operating activities			
Cash generated from operations – continuing	29A	**1, 442.6**	1,183.6
Cash generated from operations – discontinued	29B	**0.7**	13.9
Tax paid		**(150.8)**	(101.5)
Net cash inflow from operating activities		**1, 292.5**	1,096.0
Cash flows from investing activities			
Disposal of subsidiary, net of cash disposed		**48.8**	–
Capital expenditure and financial investment	29C	**(712.8)**	(266.3)
Interest received		**13.2**	12.9
Net cash outflow from investing activities		**(650.8)**	(253.4)

7 DISCONTINUED OPERATION

On 31 March 2006, the Group announced the sale of Kings Super Markets Inc to a US investor group for $61.5m excluding cash in the business at the date of disposal. The disposal of the business was completed on 28 April 2006.

A. Profit from discontinued operation	2007 £m	2006 £m
Revenue	**13.0**	228.2
Cost of sales	**(8.2)**	(144.7)
Gross profit	**4.8**	83.5
Net operating expenses	**(4.5)**	(80.5)
Net interest receivable	**–**	0.2
Profit before taxation	**0.3**	3.2
Taxation on results	**–**	(0.7)
Profit after taxation	**0.3**	2.5
Gain on disposal of subsidiary net assets	**0.4**	–
Taxation	**–**	–
Net gain on disposal	**0.4**	–
Profit from discontinued operation	**0.7**	2.5

Unlike reporting discontinued operations on a comparative basis on the income statement, no reclassifications are permitted on the comparative balance sheets of prior periods for the assets and liabilities now classified as held for sale.

As shown in Illustration 4-3, Switzerland-based Nestlé Group reports this information about its non-current assets and disposal groups held for sale on its December 31, 2007 financial statements.[5] Nestlé Group uses Swiss francs as its reporting currency.

Illustration 4-3
Nestlé Group—
Statement
of Financial
Position
Disclosures

Consolidated balance sheet as at 31 December 2007
before appropriations

In millions of CHF	Notes	2007	2006
Assets			
Current assets			
Assets held for sale	25	22	74
Liabilities and equity			
Current liabilities			
Liabilities directly associated with assets held for sale	25	7	-

25. Discontinued operations and Assets held for sale and Liabilities directly associated with assets held for sale
Assets held for sale and Liabilities directly associated with assets held for sale

In millions of CHF	2007	2006
Property, plant and equipment	10	57
Financial assets	2	–
Net working capital	5	17
Employee benefits, deferred taxes and provisions	(2)	–
Net assets held for sale	**15**	**74**
Reflected in the balance sheet as follows:		
Assets held for sale	22	74
Liabilities directly associated with assets held for sale	(7)	–
Net assets held for sale	**15**	**74**

[5] http://www.nestle.com/Resource.axd?Id=24E5A5E2-93F8-43A3-956E-0F259448CB90

Other Disclosures

Notes to the financial statements also provide the following information:

(a) A description of the non-current assets or disposal groups, including information about their sale or how and when they are expected to be disposed of, and, if applicable, which reportable segment they are (were) a part of.

(b) The amount of any losses on initial or later write-downs to fair value less disposal costs, any subsequent gains or recoveries, and where these are reported on the income statement.

(c) The facts and circumstances around any decision to remove assets or all or a part of a disposal group out of the held-for-sale classification, along with the effects on the current and prior years' results of operations presented.[6]

LOOKING AHEAD

What qualifies as a "component" for the purposes of defining a discontinued operation has been a continuing source of difference between IFRS and U.S. GAAP. Both groups of standard setters have now proposed a common definition of what should be included as a discontinued operation, in effect limiting this category to disposal activities that represent a strategic shift in operations.

As a result, in late 2008 the Board of the IASB issued an Exposure Draft and the FASB issued a proposed FASB Staff Position (FSP FAS 144-d) to establish a common definition of a component of an entity that would be reported in the discontinued operations section of the income statement. They also set out common disclosures for components of an entity that have been disposed of or are classified as held for sale.

The IASB's Exposure Draft indicates that "a discontinued operation is a component of an entity that:

(a) is an *operating segment* (as that term is defined in IFRS 8) and either has been disposed of or is classified as held for sale or

(b) is a *business* (as that term is defined in IFRS 3 *Business Combinations* (as revised in 2008)) that meets the criteria to be classified as held for sale on acquisition."

Similar to FAS 131, IFRS 8.5 defines an operating segment as a "component of an entity

(a) that engages in business activities from which it may earn revenues and incur expenses (including revenues and expenses relating to transactions with other components of the same entity),

(b) whose operating results are regularly reviewed by the entity's chief operating decision maker to make decisions about resources to be allocated to the segment and assess its performance, and

(c) for which discrete financial information is available."

Using the IFRS 8 definition of operating segment simplifies the question about what to include as a discontinued operation as this decision is already made for other financial reporting purposes. Because the definition is based on how the chief operating decision maker allocates resources, treatment as a discontinued operation should also be limited to strategic shifts within the entity.

The IASB Exposure Draft also proposes that reconciliations be provided. The first reconciles the amounts disclosed in the notes for major categories of assets and liabilities held for sale to the amounts reported as held for sale on the statement of financial position. The second proposes that the following information be reported for all components that have been or will be disposed of, separately indicating whether the item is presented as a discontinued operation or outside this category:

---

[6] IASCF, IFRS 5.41 and 42.

(a) the profit or loss, together with major income and expense items making up that profit or loss, including impairments, interest, depreciation, and amortization;

(b) where a non-controlling interest, the profit or loss in (a) attributable to the owners of the parent company; and

(c) the operating, investing, and financing cash flows.

The Exposure Draft proposes various exemptions from disclosure for businesses that qualify as held for sale on acquisition.

A revised IFRS is expected to be finalized in late 2009, although this date could be pushed later if the Board opens up the possibility of eliminating the requirement to present discontinued operations in the income statement (with limited exceptions), a position taken by some respondents to the Exposure Draft.

END-OF-CHAPTER PRACTICE

4-1 Subs and Grub (SG) is a franchisor that operates several corporate-owned restaurants, as well as many franchised restaurants. SG provides its franchisees with advertising support, general management advice, and SG-labelled supplies. SG recovers from the franchisees the cost and a small mark-up on the supplies and an annual fee for other services. The annual fee is 2% of each franchisee's total sales. In February 2008, SG sold its corporate-owned restaurants to a franchisee, but continues to oversee all franchisee operations.

Instructions

Will SG report a discontinued operation on its financial statements for its year ended March 31, 2008? Explain how you determined your answer.

4-2 Glassio Corp. has an April 30 fiscal year end. Glassio's board of directors approved a formal and detailed plan on October 31, 2007 to sell its head office tower. The building has a carrying amount of $100 and an expected selling price of $95. The company will continue to use the tower, pending completion of its new head office building that is slated to begin construction in January 2008.

Instructions

(a) Discuss the financial reporting issues as April 30, 2008 approaches.

(b) Would any of the issues change if Glassio Corp. were a heavy equipment manufacturer and the building was the company's only rental property? Explain.

4-3 The controller of Shikkiah Corp. (SC) is on sick leave and you are asked to draft the financial statements for the company's year ended May 31, 2008. You determine that the company has total revenues of $962 and expenses of $762 in the current fiscal year (revenues of $950 and expenses of $753 one year earlier) before recognizing income taxes. Additional information is provided below:

1. SC pays taxes at a rate of 25% on all items of income and loss.

2. Included in the current year results are revenues of $43 and operating expenses of $41 related to a division of SC that was sold in February 2008, as well as a loss of $6 on the division's net assets that were sold. This division had performed better in the preceding year, reporting revenues of $62 and expenses of $49.

3. In April 2008, the local government began the process of expropriating some of the company's land that was being held for future expansion; however, this was not finalized by year end. The government has agreed to cover the $1 land transfer costs and to pay SC $10 for the land. The land is on SC's books at a carrying amount of $13. No accounting entries have yet been made in relation to this event.

Instructions

(a) Prepare a summary income statement for Shikkiah Corp. for its year ended May 31, 2008 and a comparative income statement for the previous year.

(b) Identify how the land that is in process of being expropriated will be measured and reported on the May 31, 2008 financial statements.

(c) Identify all the note disclosures that are required as a result of the events described above.

4-4 Acme Manufacturing Inc. (AMI) decided to outsource the supply of several minor components of its manufacturing process instead of making them in its subcomponents division, Division X. AMI entered into a contract with a supplier and put Division X on the market for sale. Division X comprises the following assets and liabilities:

	Carrying Amount	Fair Value
Building	$100	$110
Equipment	50	45
Land	40	40
Miscellaneous supplies	4	2
Mortgage note payable	65	65
Accounts payable, trade	3	3

The commercial property market is strong in the division's location and it is expected to sell quickly. The only cost that AMI expects to incur on the disposal of the division is a 5% transfer tax payable on the sales value of the land and building sold.

Instructions
    (a) Prepare any accounting entries AMI makes as Division X is reclassified as held for sale.
    (b) Indicate how this disposal group will be reported on AMI's statement of financial position.
    (c) Indicate how any adjustments on reclassification will be reported on the financial statements.

4-5 JayCee Corp. acquired equipment on June 29, 2005 to produce a specialized version of its basic and best-selling product. The equipment cost $100, had an estimated production capacity of 45 units, and a residual value of $10. JayCee uses the units of production method of depreciation for all its equipment. On June 1, 2008, after JayCee produced and sold 28 units, management decided that the company would discontinue production of this product. A plan was immediately put in place to sell the equipment and it was appropriately reclassified as held for sale. Management expected that the equipment could be sold for $45, but a 10% commission would be payable to the sales agent.

During June 2008, the equipment was used to produce two final units. Due to depressed market conditions, the equipment continued to be held and available for sale. When it was still not sold on December 31, 2008, management reduced its posted selling price to $42. In the second quarter of 2009, conditions improved and the fair value of similar equipment rose to $50. Management finally sold the equipment on August 12, 2009 for $49.

Instructions
    (a) Assuming JayCee Corp. prepares financial statements each June 30 and December 31, prepare all entries required to account for the equipment on June 1, 2008; June 30, 2008; December 31, 2008; June 30, 2009; and August 12, 2009.
    (b) Explain how these events will be reported on the income statements for each six-month period ended June 30 and December 31, 2008, and June 30 and December 31, 2009.

4-6 In this chapter, flag icons identify areas where there are GAAP differences between IFRS requirements and national standards.

Instructions
Access the website(s) identified on the inside back cover of this book, and prepare a concise summary of the differences that are flagged throughout the chapter.

Chapter 5

Provisions, Contingent Liabilities and Contingent Assets: IAS 37

U.S. GAAP References
FAS 5 Accounting for Contingencies
FAS 143 Accounting for Asset Retirement Obligations
FAS 146 Accounting for Costs Associated with Exit or Disposal Activities
CON 5 Recognition and Measurement in Financial Statements of Business Enterprises
CON 6 Elements of Financial Statements
CON 7 Using Cash Flow Information and Present Value in Accounting Measurements

Related IFRSs
Framework for the Preparation and Presentation of Financial Statements
IFRS 4 Insurance Contracts
IAS 1 Presentation of Financial Statements
IAS 11 Construction Contracts
IAS 12 Income Taxes
IAS 17 Leases
IAS 19 Employee Benefits

OBJECTIVE AND SCOPE

This standard seeks to ensure that provisions and contingencies are appropriately dealt with in terms of recognition, measurement, and disclosure. It does not cover executory contracts unless they are onerous (this term will be defined later). Nor does it cover provisions or contingencies that are covered by other standards, including financial instruments, revenues, construction contracts, income taxes, leases, employee benefits, and insurance contracts. Finally, it does not deal with depreciation and impairments.

IAS 37.10 defines provisions, contingent liabilities, and contingent assets respectively as follows:

A ***provision*** is a liability of uncertain timing or amount.

A ***contingent liability*** is

    (a) a possible obligation that arises from past events and whose existence will be confirmed only by the occurrence or non-occurrence of one or more uncertain future events not wholly within the control of the entity; or

    (b) a present obligation that arises from past events but is not recognized because

        (i) it is not probable that an outflow of resources embodying economic benefits will be required to settle the obligation, or

        (ii) the amount of the obligation cannot be measured with sufficient reliability.

A ***contingent asset*** is a possible asset that arises from past events and whose existence will be confirmed only by the occurrence or non-occurrence of one or more uncertain future events not wholly within the control of the entity.

The key thing that separates a provision from other liabilities is the uncertainty associated with it, including

- uncertainty of the timing of a future expenditure, or
- uncertainty of measurement.

Note that accrued expenses for items such as unpaid bills or vacation pay are not referred to as provisions because there is much less uncertainty associated with these types of items.

How are provisions differentiated from contingencies? Both have significant uncertainty associated with them, although contingencies have considerably more—relating either to the outcome of a future event or the measurement of the element. The terms contingent assets/liabilities are used to refer to assets/liabilities that *are not recognized* in the financial statements because of the significant uncertainty. Provisions, by contrast, are recognized. They reflect an existing obligation that is measurable and probable.

The following diagram illustrates the interrelationship among accruals, provisions, and contingencies.

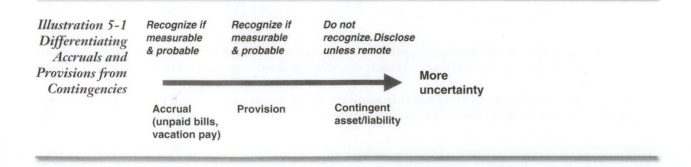

Illustration 5-1 Differentiating Accruals and Provisions from Contingencies

RECOGNITION

Provisions

Provisions are recognized only when all of the following criteria are met:[1]

(a) an entity has a present obligation (legal or constructive) as a result of a past event;
(b) it is probable that an outflow of resources embodying economic benefits will be required to settle the obligation; and
(c) a reliable estimate can be made of the amount of the obligation.

The above definition is essentially the definition of a liability, including recognition criteria. The paragraphs that follow examine this definition more closely.

Present Obligation Resulting from a Past Event, Which Is Independent of an Entity's Future Actions

The determination of whether we should recognize a liability or not depends on whether an obligation exists at the *present time*. This is differentiated from a *future commitment*, although the latter may create a present obligation if there are significant negative consequences (e.g., if the agreement is irrevocable or there is a substantial penalty).

The obligation must also result from a past event (sometimes referred to as an *obligating event*). According to IAS 37.17, with an obligating event, there is no realistic alternative to settling the obligation (in other words, there is little or no discretion to avoid settlement). The standard notes that this would be the case, for instance, where the obligation is

- enforceable by law (known as a *legal obligation*), or
- where a valid expectation has been created that the entity will discharge the obligation (known as a *constructive obligation*).

Constructive and legal obligations are specifically defined as follows:[2]

A *constructive obligation* is an obligation that derives from an entity's actions where

(a) by an established pattern of past practice, published policies, or a sufficiently specific current statement, the entity has indicated to other parties that it will accept certain responsibilities; and
(b) as a result, the entity has created a valid expectation on the part of those other parties that it will discharge those responsibilities.

A *legal obligation* is an obligation that derives from

(a) a contract (through its explicit or implicit terms),
(b) legislation, or
(c) other operation of law.

An entity may have a constructive obligation to make refunds to customers if it has established a past practice of doing so. Customers may come to expect that they will be able to get a refund even though it is not explicitly stated.

An entity should take care to avoid accruing provisions for things that it can avoid through future actions. For instance, if a new law is approved that requires a company to install certain noise restriction barriers around

---

[1] IASCF, IAS 37.14.
[2] IASCF, IAS 37.10.

its factory, a liability does not necessarily exist at the present time since the company can change the way it operates in order to reduce the noise, making the barriers unnecessary. An obligation may exist for a penalty for not being in compliance in the meantime, however.

The following scenario illustrates some of these points.

Situation

Fruition Inc. is interested in installing solar panels on its roof under a new program to reduce its carbon footprint. It has signed a contract to take delivery of the panels early in the new year (after year end). It has not put any advance deposit down and the contract is cancellable. In addition, the company is considering installing "carbon scrubbers" on its coal-burning facility smokestacks. It has publicly announced the program since it has been receiving significant pressure to reduce pollution. In response to the announcement, its stock price increased. Currently, it is within the government guidelines for pollution control; however, the government has drafted a new law, currently being debated, which will introduce significantly more stringent requirements for pollution control.

Analysis

The purchase contract does not in itself create a present obligation since it is cancellable. It therefore results in a future obligation. The company can get out of the contract with no economic hardship.

The decision to install the coal scrubbers does not create a present obligation either; however, the decision plus the announcement may do so. The question is whether the announcement is sufficiently specific to create a valid expectation that an obligation exists and that the entity will fulfill it. Even though there is no legal obligation, there may be a constructive obligation and the company would have to record the provision as long as a reasonable estimate could be made of the amount. The existence of the new draft legislation is not relevant since the legislation is still being debated and is not yet finalized.

If the law is finalized before year end, does an obligation exist? Not necessarily. By definition, the obligation arises from a past event that is independent of the entity's future actions. In this case, the entity may decide to adjust its operations to avoid polluting altogether (i.e., outsource the process). In other words, the entity has some choices and can avoid having to incur the cost. Therefore, no liability would be recognized (except as noted above for any penalties for non-compliance of the law).

Probable Outflow of Resources Embodying Economic Benefits

For recognition, there is a probability threshold that must be met. In this case, the potential outflow of resources must be probable (*more likely than not*).[3] If it is not probable, then note disclosure is required, unless the probability is remote.

Reliable Estimates of an Obligation

Provisions, by definition, are very uncertain and therefore may be difficult to measure. In general, the standard presumes that the entity should be able to determine a reliable range of outcomes; however, if the provision is not estimable (in rare situations), then note disclosure is required.

Contingent Liabilities and Assets

Contingent assets and liabilities are note disclosed only, unless the probability of occurrence is remote, in which case note disclosure is not required.

---

[3] *More likely than not* is generally seen to mean >50%.

MEASUREMENT

Best Estimate and Risks/Uncertainties

According to IAS 37, an entity must accrue the best estimate of the amount for the provision. **_Best estimate_** is defined as follows:

> The best estimate of the expenditure required to settle the present obligation is the amount that an entity would rationally pay to settle the obligation at the end of the reporting period or to transfer it to a third party at that time.[4]

Entities must gather evidence to support the assessment of best estimate. This may involve historical or market data and may require the use of independent experts. Management must apply professional judgment and consider the nature of the provision. There are differing methodologies for measuring the provision, and the technique chosen depends upon the nature of the item that the provision relates to. The following illustrates this.

Provision relating to	Methodology
Large number of items	Expected value method—assess all outcomes and assign probabilities to each outcome.
Large number of items with a continuous range of possible outcomes, each as likely as the other	Use the midpoint of the range.
Single item	Use the most likely outcome but take into account the probability of possible outcomes to refine if the information is available.[5]

Situation

Garaway Limited produces machines that are used in large institutions to make soft ice cream. It sells its products globally. All sales are accompanied by a one-year warranty, under which the company will fix the machine (on-site) or replace it. At year end, the accounting staff is looking to estimate the warranty provision and have the following historical data:

- 1,000 units were sold during the year.
- Over the past five years, 3% of the machines were defective in some way and had to be fixed.
- Of the above-noted 3%, half required a full replacement of the equipment at a cost of $5,000 per unit and half were fixable at an average cost of $500.

Garaway feels that the data are indicative of the current situation.

In addition, the company is concerned about a potential liability relating to a recent lawsuit. The company's lawyers estimate that it is likely that it will lose the lawsuit and have to pay $100,000.

---

[4] IASCF, IAS 37.36.

[5] This could end up being equal to the expected value method. In the opinion of the authors, the difference in approach likely has to do with the fact that the probabilities may be more difficult to assess for specific unique items (rather than multiple items where a history of experience might be used to project forward). In addition, for a single item, where the most likely outcome is close to the expected value, it may make the most sense to accrue the most likely outcome since this is the most relevant estimate of likely cash outflows.

Analysis

For the warranty costs (since there are multiple items and the likelihood of outcomes are different):

$(1{,}000 \times 3\% \times 50\% \times \$5{,}000) + (1{,}000 \times 3\% \times 50\% \times \$500) = \$82{,}500$

For the lawsuit (since this is a single item and this is the most likely outcome): $100,000

The standard goes one step further and notes that the probability of other outcomes must be taken into account for single items. In this case, we do not have the information to refine the estimate; however, if we did have the additional probabilities, then the provision might be adjusted. This is a matter of judgment since any other amount would be different from the amount most likely to be paid out, i.e., the $100,000.

Present Value

Where the time value is material, the present value of the cash flows must be used in estimating the amount. The discount rate shall

". . . . be a pre-tax rate (or rates) that reflect(s) current market assessments of the time value of money and the risks specific to the liability. The discount rate(s) shall not reflect risks for which future cash flow estimates have been adjusted."[6]

Although the standard gives little guidance as to how to discount, the following approaches would be acceptable:[7]

1. Adjust the discount rate to reflect the riskiness of the cash flows (useful where cash flows are defined and articulated, e.g., a bond). This is sometimes referred to as the ***traditional present value technique*** or a ***discount rate adjusted approach***. The discount rate is referred to as a risk adjusted rate and is adjusted for risks in amount, nature, and timing of the cash flows associated with the item. If the amount, nature, and timing of the cash flows are articulated as part of the contract, this simplifies the calculation. The rate would be adjusted for the risk that the cash flows will not be paid (credit risk).

2. Use a risk-free rate as the discount rate but consider multiple cash flow scenarios that reflect differing outcomes and their probability of occurrence. This technique would be useful where the cash flows are not clearly defined and may be based on uncertain outcomes (like warranty costs). This method is sometimes referred to as the ***expected present value technique***. A risk-free rate might be seen as being equal to the rate of return on a government bond.[8]

Either the discount rate or the cash flows are adjusted for risk but not both. The following scenarios illustrate two possible approaches to measuring the provisions. Recall that the standard gives little guidance and thus leaves it to professional judgment.

---

[6] IASCF, IAS 37.47.

[7] Care must be taken during this move to IFRS, that country-specific "legacy accounting practices" are not inadvertently brought forward since they may work against the goal of a single set of high quality, comparable standards. In this case, however, the methods suggested are commonly used in the area of finance as measurement tools and are not accounting specific, even though they are found in U.S. accounting literature at present. These methods are grounded in economic and finance research and so transcend accounting.

[8] In the study of finance, portfolio theory identifies two types of risk. The first is unsystematic or diversifiable risk; that is, the risk identifiable with a particular asset or liability. The other risk is systematic risk or non-diversifiable risk; that is, the risk that is inherent in the general marketplace that cannot be diversified away. Under the expected present value technique, cash flows should be adjusted for systematic risk (general market risk in any portfolio of assets/liabilities that is not diversifiable). In practice, instead of adjusting the cash flows for this systematic risk, the discount rate is often adjusted (only for this one particular risk). Either technique is okay as long as both the cash flows or discount rate are not adjusted for the same risk at the same time (e.g., adjust either the cash flows or the discount rate). Note that if the discount rate is adjusted, then it must be adjusted only for the systematic risk. Either version should result in the same estimate. It is just a different way of arriving at the answer. FAS 157, Appendix B (paragraphs .18 and .19) gives a good example of this.

Situation 1

Lease contracts

   A company leases head office space under a five-year contract, which has been accounted for as an operating lease. Due to downsizing, it has relocated its head office. Despite numerous attempts to sublet the space, it has had little success due to a recession that has hit the area pretty hard. It is not anticipated that the recession will abate in the near future. Unfortunately, the landlord will not allow the lease to be cancelled and, therefore, the payments must still be made. Payments are $5,000 per year and there are three years left on the lease. The company's interest rate on financing that was recently obtained from the bank is 8%. The risk-free rate on government bonds is 5%. Although the company is in a cost-cutting mode, it is still very much a going concern. Calculate the provision for the lease.

Analysis

Since the cash flows are well defined, the company would likely use the traditional approach and discount the cash flows using a risk-adjusted rate of 8%. This is the rate that external parties (the bank) have recently charged the company. When the bank determined what interest rate to charge, it would have assessed the riskiness of the cash flows and added on a risk premium to the risk-free rate. This rate may be seen to be acceptable for the payment of the lease amounts as well, although in practice, the rates might differ slightly due to different riskiness of the payouts under the loan versus the lease (e.g., contractual, legal, or other).

   PV $5,000 (3 years, 8%) = $12,885

Situation 2

Cleanup costs

   Vertigon Inc. is a petrochemical plant owned and run by the government for profit. Despite continued and mostly successful efforts to filter contaminated air and water that results from the production process, the company is still polluting the surrounding property. The property is leased and the landlord and Vertigon have agreed that when the lease expires in 10 years, Vertigon will ensure that this excess pollution is cleaned up before the land is transferred back. The lease has a renewal option for another 10 years. If this option is exercised, then the cleanup would be done at the end of the renewal period. There is a 60% chance that the lease will not be renewed and the cleanup will cost $100,000. There is a 40% chance that the lease will be renewed and the cleanup costs at the end of 20 years will be $200,000. Calculate the provision for cleanup. These estimates have been derived from past experience and incorporate management's best estimates of likely outcomes. In addition, the company has obtained cleanup cost estimates from engineering firms. The risk-free rate is 5%.

Analysis

Since there are multiple possible scenarios here and the various amounts and probabilities are estimable (based on historical data and external independently derived information), the expected present value technique might be used as follows (using present value factors from present value tables):

   ($100,000 × 60% × .61391) + ($200,000 × 40% × .37689) = $66,986

   It is very difficult to assign probabilities in actuality—especially if there are no historical data or the likelihood of the outcomes depend on factors beyond the company's control. Even where there are historical data, it cannot necessarily be assumed that the past will reflect the future. In the end, significant judgment is used in measuring provisions. Note that it may not be appropriate to use the same risk-free rate for multiple years. The annual risk-free rate will change from year to year depending on the interest yield curve.

   In addition, the cash flows should reflect all uncertainties, including the risk of the entity's inability to pay. In this case, since it is the government, this risk is assumed to be zero and no adjustment to the cash flows has been made. For corporations, however, this additional risk would always exist and have to be taken into consideration. Where does a company get this information from? In practice, this information has already been incorporated by the marketplace and is reflected in the company's borrowing rates (which reflect a credit adjusted risk-free rate specific to the company). Therefore, companies sometimes modify the present value calculation by adjusting the discount rate so that it reflects the risk-free rate adjusted for the company's credit risk only (not the riskiness of the cash flows as they relate to uncertain timing or amounts). This is acceptable as long as the cash flows are not adjusted for this specific risk at the same time.

Future Events

In estimating the provision, entities may consider future events if there is sufficient evidence regarding the occurrence of the events. In the scenario above, the engineering estimates should not take into account proposed new technology that is yet to be developed or if it is developed but not yet proven.

Expected Disposal of Assets

No gains are taken into income for assets that are expected to be sold. This is because they are not realized.

REIMBURSEMENTS

In some cases, some of the cash outflows will be reimbursed. This should be assessed separately and recognized when the receipt of cash inflows is virtually certain. In terms of presentation, the cost and the reimbursement may be offset in the statement of profit and loss.

CHANGES IN AND USE OF PROVISIONS

The provisions should be continually assessed, at a minimum, at the end of each reporting period. If the amount of the provision is discounted, then borrowing costs are recognized.[9]

APPLICATION OF THE RECOGNITION AND MEASUREMENT RULES

Future Operating Losses

Future operating losses are not accrued since they represent future events that an entity may be able to get out of. However, future losses may be indicative of asset impairment.

Onerous Contracts

According to IAS 37.10, an ***onerous contract*** is

"... a contract in which the unavoidable costs of meeting the obligations under the contract exceed the economic benefits expected to be received under it."

Present obligations under onerous contracts are recognized as provisions in the financial statements. Onerous contracts are often purchase commitments, where the entity is locked in and must settle the contract according to terms that are unfavorable to it.

Situation

Heinrich Limited purchases raw materials that are used to manufacture its products. Normally, the purchasing manager enters into purchase commitments to purchase a fixed amount of products over a fixed term at a fixed price. The contracts are non-cancellable. Currently, at year end, the company is locked in to buying 1,000 kilograms of raw materials at a cost that exceeds current market prices.

---

[9] IFRIC 1 concluded that although the discount would be recognized as a financing cost, it would not be eligible for capitalization under IAS 23, *Borrowing Costs*.

> **Analysis**
>
> This represents an onerous contract since the costs of settling the contract (the price the company is locked in at) exceed the benefits (receiving the raw materials that are worth less than what the company has agreed to pay). The contract is non-cancellable and so the obligation is unavoidable. The expected loss and obligation should be accrued in the financial statements at year end.

Restructuring

Restructuring includes termination of a line of business, closure or relocation of business, changes in management structure, and fundamental reorganizations. As a general rule, a restructuring provision should be recognized when the criteria for recognizing a provision is met, as discussed earlier, i.e.,

- the entity has a present obligation (legal or constructive) as a result of a past event (in the case of a restructuring, there may be an obligation to pay employees certain amounts);
- it is probable that an outflow of resources will be necessary to settle the obligation; and
- the restructuring is measurable (a reliable estimate can be made).

In addition, the following criteria must also be met, according to IAS 37.72, in order to argue that a constructive obligation exists:

(a) [the entity] has a detailed formal plan for the restructuring, identifying at least

    (i)   the business or part of a business concerned;
    (ii) the principal locations affected;
    (iii) the location, function, and approximate number of employees who will be compensated for terminating their services;
    (iv) the expenditures that will be undertaken; and
    (v) when the plan will be implemented; and

(b) [the entity] has raised a valid expectation in those affected that it will carry out the restructuring by starting to implement that plan or announcing its main features to those affected by it.

 In other words, the additional criteria include a detailed formal plan that has been communicated or implementation of the plan (at least in part). Communication must be in sufficient detail. The time frame involved should be short enough to signal that changes to the plan will be unlikely. The longer the time frame, the more likely changes may be made. A constructive obligation does not arise for a sale of an operation until the purchaser is identified and there is a binding agreement.[10] The entity may set up a provision for other parts of the restructuring and the assets would be assessed for impairment under IAS 36.

The provision under the standard includes only direct costs that meet both of the following criteria:

- the costs are necessarily entailed by the restructuring, and
- they are not associated with the ongoing activities of the entity.

IAS 37.81 excludes retraining/relocating continuing staff, marketing, and investments in new systems or distribution networks. These costs are accounted for when incurred and receive no special treatment. As previously mentioned, estimated future losses are not accrued unless they relate to onerous contracts.

---

[10] IASCF, IAS 37.78 and .79.

Situation

Restructuring Company Limited is currently undergoing a significant cost-cutting initiative in response to an economic slowdown. A detailed plan has been put in place and this has been approved by the board of directors. A press release has been prepared but not yet released. Below are some excerpts from the detailed plan:

The Retro Division will be sold. The company estimates it will be sold at a profit.

Remaining employees will have to be retrained early next year.

It is now year end and the company is drafting its financial statements.

Analysis

The company has a detailed approved plan; however, it has not begun to implement it and has not communicated the plan. Therefore, no provision will be booked. Even if it had communicated the plan in sufficient detail, the gain on the sale of the division would not be recognized since it is not realized. The training costs would not be accrued because they are future costs that are related to the ongoing operations.

DISCLOSURES

Appropriate detail regarding the nature of the provisions and uncertainties should be disclosed. In rare cases where the information to be disclosed may prejudice the outcome of a dispute with other parties, there is not a requirement to disclose, other than the general nature of the dispute and the reason why full disclosure is not being made.

LOOKING AHEAD

The IASB originally decided to review IAS 37 as part of its short-term convergence project with FASB. However, it became apparent that the issues being discussed were quite foundational and pervasive in terms of the entire body of knowledge. The IASB issued an Exposure Draft in 2005 and plans to issue a new standard in 2009. The standard proposes that all liabilities be recognized unless they cannot be reliably measured, and that uncertainty relating to the amount and timing of cash flows be reflected in the measurement of the liability.

Some of the items being proposed/clarified are as follows:

1. Scope: Performance obligations will not be covered by the standard (they are covered by IAS 18, *Revenue*).
2. Definitions: Provision will not be a defined term due to its ambiguity. The terms contingent liability and assets will be deleted. Differentiation of a business risk from a present obligation will be more explicit (an action does not give rise to a present obligation itself; there must be a mechanism to enforce). Expanded discussion on stand-ready obligations will be included (identifying whether there is a stand-ready obligation will help establish existence of a present obligation).
3. Recognition: Probability recognition criteria will be deleted.
4. Measurement: More guidance on measuring expected values and reimbursement rights will be included.

END-OF-CHAPTER PRACTICE

5-1 The concept of contingency is different under IFRS.

Instructions

Contrast and compare the definitions of contingencies and contingent liabilities under both IFRS and U.S. GAAP. How does the accounting differ? Start by looking up the respective definitions under the respective standards.

5-2 In accounting, many specific terms are used to deal with uncertainty.

Instructions
Write a short essay on the use of the terms "possible" and "probable" as they relate to recognition of provisions. Do these represent "bright line" tests? Discuss.

5-3 The following scenarios relate to expected cash outflows relating to several lawsuits. The company is in the process of trying to measure the provision:
- Lawsuit A - $1,000 to be paid out in one year with certainty.
- Lawsuit B - $1,000—uncertain but will be somewhere between $0 and $1000. The lawyers estimate an 80% probability regarding payout.
- Lawsuit C - $1,000 to be paid out in one year—possible that it may be as high as $1,500 and as low as $500.

Instructions
Assume that each of the lawsuits is unique. Prepare the journal entries to accrue the provision. Now, assume that the three lawsuits are part of a pool of similar lawsuits. Prepare the journal entry to accrue the provision. How do the entries differ and why? Discuss.

5-4 Assume the same information as 5-3 for lawsuit A, including the fact that the lawsuits are part of a pool of similar lawsuits. Assume further that the lawsuits will be paid out in five years. The risk-free rate is 5% and the company's credit adjusted borrowing rate is 8%.

Instructions
Prepare the journal entry to accrue the provision.

5-5 A vendor sells frozen hamburgers in a jurisdiction where the law stipulates that vendors must pay compensation to each customer who receives a contaminated hamburger. On December 31, 200X, the last day of the reporting period, the vendor sold one hamburger. The customer has not yet taken the hamburger out of the freezer.

Past experience indicates that one in every million hamburgers sold by the vendor is contaminated. No other information is available.

Instructions
Does the vendor have a liability at December 31, 200X?
(This case is taken from discussion material from the IASB website.)

5-6 In this chapter, the flag icons identify areas where there are GAAP differences between IFRS requirements and national standards.

Instructions
Access the website(s) identified on the inside back cover of this book, and prepare a concise summary of the differences that are flagged throughout the chapter material.

Chapter 6

Revenue: IAS 18

U.S. GAAP References
SAB 104 Revenue Recognition
SOP 81-1 Accounting for Performance of Construction-Type and Certain Production-Type Contracts
SOP 97-2 Software Revenue Recognition
SOP 98-9 Software Revenue Recognition, with Respect to Certain Transactions
FAS 45 Accounting for Franchise Fee Revenue
FAS 48 Revenue Recognition When Right of Return Exists
FAS 49 Accounting for Product Financing Arrangements
FAS 66 Accounting for Sales of Real Estate
EITF 99-19 Reporting Revenue Gross as a Principal Versus Net as an Agent
EITF 00-21 Revenue Arrangements with Multiple Deliverables
EITF 00-22 Accounting for 'Points' and Certain Other Time-Based or Volume-Based Sales Incentive Offers, and Offers for Free Products or Services to be Delivered in the Future
EITF 01-9 Accounting for Consideration Given by a Vendor to a Customer
CON 5 Recognition and Measurement in Financial Statements of Business Enterprises
CON 6 Elements of Financial Statements

Related IFRSs
IFRS 4 Insurance Contracts
IAS 11 Construction Contracts
IAS 17 Leases
IAS 28 Investments in Associates
IAS 39 Financial Instruments: Recognition and Measurement
IAS 41 Agriculture
IFRIC 13 Customer Loyalty Programs
SIC 31 Revenue—Barter Transactions Involving Advertising Services

OBJECTIVE AND SCOPE

The accounting body of knowledge for revenues is quite substantial in the United States, although it is spread across numerous sources. Because some of these other sources are very foundational, they have been included in the chart above. IAS 18 is much more compact and caution must be taken not to fall back on the very explicit and specific guidance provided by U.S. GAAP. Although the IFRS GAAP hierarchy allows for review of other sources of GAAP by other standard setters, the temptation to look for explicit guidance will risk eroding the principles-based nature of the IFRS and will eventually contribute to a lack of global comparability.

IAS 18 deals with general standards for recognition and measurement of revenues. Revenues are generated by ordinary business activities and, therefore, it is important to understand just how an entity makes money. Revenues may be generated by

- the sale of goods,
- the sale of services,
- fees,
- interest,
- royalties,
- dividends, and other sources.

IAS 18 is supplemented by an Appendix (which accompanies the standard but is not part of it). The Appendix provides expanded discussion but is not meant to provide a comprehensive discussion of all the issues.

According to IAS 18.6, the following are excluded from the standard:

(a) lease agreements (see IAS 17 *Leases*);
(b) dividends arising from investments, which are accounted for under the equity method (see IAS 28 *Investments in Associates*);
(c) insurance contracts within the scope of IFRS 4 *Insurance Contracts*;
(d) changes in the fair value of financial assets and financial liabilities or their disposal (see IAS 39 *Financial Instruments: Recognition and Measurement*);
(e) changes in the value of other current assets;
(f) initial recognition and from changes in the fair value of biological assets related to agricultural activity (see IAS 41 *Agriculture*);
(g) initial recognition of agricultural produce (see IAS 41); and
(h) the extraction of mineral ores.

The IAS framework defines income to include both revenues and gains. IAS 18.7 provides the following definition of revenue:

"Revenue is the gross inflow of economic benefits during the period arising in the course of the ordinary activities of an entity when those inflows result in increases in equity, other than increases relating to contributions from equity participants."

It is important to separate income from ordinary activities and income from atypical/infrequent activities since many users use the financial statements to assess the nature, timing, and amount of future earnings and cash flows. Income from ordinary activities is more likely to recur than income from atypical/infrequent activities.

MEASUREMENT OF REVENUE

Revenue is measured at the fair value of the consideration received or receivable, with fair value being defined in IAS 18.7 as follows:

"Fair value is the amount for which an asset could be exchanged, or a liability settled, between knowledgeable, willing parties in an arm's length transaction."

Amounts Paid Over Time

In general, the fair value is the amount of cash or cash equivalents received; however, when the amount due is paid over time, the cash flows are discounted using one of the following rates (whichever is more clearly determinable):

- a discount rate that reflects either the prevailing rate for a similar instrument (for a company with a similar credit rating), or
- an imputed rate of interest that equates the receivables to the current cash sales price.[1]

The choice of interest rate should reflect the riskiness of the cash flows. Generally, with sales, the amount and timing of the receivables is fixed, although there will often be credit risk (the risk that the customer might not be able to pay) attached to the cash flow stream. The discount rate might therefore reflect the customer's incremental borrowing rate. The incremental borrowing rate of the customer may not always be available to the supplier, although in theory the supplier should be able to approximate this rate after doing a credit check.

An alternate view is to impute an interest rate. If we know the cash selling price and the total cash flows to be paid under the arrangement, the difference should theoretically be interest. This approach is also problematic since the cash selling price may vary from customer to customer. Significant judgment is required. Where the imputed interest rate is unrealistic in relation to current economic conditions and the risk-free rate, the calculation should be revisited. The cash selling price may be unreasonable.

Barter Transactions

Barter transactions that deal with items that are similar in nature and value are not accounted for as revenues. What do we mean by "similar"? The standard contemplates situations (for instance) where commodities like oil or milk might be exchanged by suppliers to facilitate customer sales (where the supplier is in one geographic location but the customer is in another location close to the second supplier). The substance of this type of transaction is that it is more like a loan of the commodity by one supplier to the other. The loan will be repaid when the supplier who borrowed the commodity returns it.

If the goods are dissimilar, it is considered to be a sale and recorded as revenues. This is because the entity has transferred the risks and rewards of the one asset (a sale) and taken on new and different risks and rewards for the other asset (a purchase). The transaction is measured at the fair value of the asset received unless it cannot

---

[1] IASCF, IAS 18.11.

be reliably measured, in which case the fair value of the asset given up is used. This would be adjusted for any cash consideration.[2]

Barter transactions involving an exchange of advertising services are dealt with separately.[3] Barter transactions involving advertising may result in revenue recognition as long as the advertising services provided and received are different. This would normally be the case. The problem arises with measurement. Although it may be difficult to measure the services received, the entity may be able to measure the services rendered by looking at similar advertising contracts that occur frequently and represent a predominant number of transactions involving cash or cash-like consideration with other parties. Thus, these transactions may be measured based on the fair value of the services provided.

Situation

During the year, Jinx Inc. sold athletic footwear to several of its retail customers. The last four shipments were shipped just before year end under the following terms:

Transaction A – 100 units at $1,000 cash
Transaction B – 100 units to be paid at the end of next year at $1,100 (1 year hence)
Transaction C – 100 units shipped to a customer of another supplier. The supplier will replace the 100 units.
Transaction D – 100 units exchanged for $1,050 worth of computer equipment
Assume that all of the customers involved have incremental borrowing rates of 8%, which reflects the riskiness of the cash flows.

How should each of these be accounted for and why?

Analysis

Transaction A is a straight sale and should be measured at $1,000, which is the value of the consideration received. The cost of sales and inventory should also be adjusted for this (and all of the following transactions).

Dr. Cash	$1,000	
Cr. Revenues		$1,000
Dr. COS	XXX	
Cr. Inventory		XXX

Transaction B includes a financing aspect because the money is not due until the end of the year. This should be reflected in the journal entries. There is a choice of how to measure the transaction. One option is to use the customer's borrowing rate, which is 8%, and discount the cash flows using a present value factor (1 year, 8%) as follows:

$1,100 × .92593 = $1018.

Dr. Accounts receivable	$1,100	
Cr. Revenues		1,018
Cr. Unearned interest		82

The interest would be recognized as earned (as time passes).

The other option is to equate the present value of the cash flows to the cash selling price and calculate the imputed interest rate. In this case, the cash selling price is $1,000. The interest rate that equates the cash flows of $1,100 to the cash selling price is 10%.

---

[2] The similar/dissimilar approach to barter transactions is different from the model in IAS 16 and 38, where the transaction is recorded at fair value unless it lacks commercial substance or both the fair value of the asset given up and received is not reliably determinable.
[3] IASCF, SIC 31.

> Dr. Accounts receivable $1,100
>   Cr. Revenues   1,000
>   Cr. Unearned interest   100
>
>   Transaction C would not be recorded as a sale since it is an exchange of similar items to facilitate a sale. The inventory will be replaced with the same inventory. As previously noted, it is almost like a very short-term loan of the footwear to the other supplier.
>   Transaction D is a barter transaction. Because the items are dissimilar (footwear versus computer equipment), it may be recorded as a sale and would be measured at the fair value of the computer equipment (the consideration received).[4] This is treated as both a purchase (of the equipment) and a sale of the footwear.
>
> Dr. Computer equipment $1,050
>   Cr. Revenues $1,050
>
>   In all cases where a sale is recorded, the cost of sales and inventory accounts would be adjusted as done in transaction A.

IDENTIFICATION OF THE TRANSACTION

As noted earlier, in order to understand how to account for a transaction, we must understand what the substance of the business transaction is. In many cases, the transaction involves a collection of items or a bundle. For instance, a piece of equipment may be sold along with a service to install or maintain it. Because the revenue recognition points may be different depending on the asset sold or service rendered, we must break the transaction down into separately identifiable components. Each component is then accounted for separately. The standard does not give concrete guidance as to how to divide the transaction into separate units so judgment must be used. The standard walks though several examples of bundled sales in the Appendix. These are summarized in Illustrations 6-1 and 6-2.

SALE OF GOODS

Criteria for recognition of revenue for the sale of goods are as follows (all criteria must be met):[5]

(a) significant risks and rewards of ownership are transferred;
(b) neither continuing managerial involvement nor effective control over the goods sold is retained;
(c) the amount of revenue is reliably measurable;
(d) the economic benefits are probable; and
(e) the costs are reliably measurable.

For most sale of goods transactions, there is a critical event where the risks and rewards pass from the seller to the buyer. This is normally the point at which the legal title and possession pass. In certain cases, one or the other (but not both) will pass. This does not preclude revenue recognition. Judgment must be used in determining what the substance of the transaction is and whether significant risks and rewards have been transferred. Care should be taken to identify the shipping terms since they often define when the transfer occurs. In addition, there may be differing laws in different countries that dictate when legal title transfers.

---

[4] It is not so much that the items are dissimilar than it is the fact that the transaction is not a "loan" of goods to facilitate a sale to another customer, although the standard uses the words similar and dissimilar to articulate the point. In practice, judgment would be used to determine whether the risks and rewards related to the assets being exchanged (and their respective cash flows) are different. Companies would rarely exchange assets that have the exact same risks and rewards unless there was a valid business reason. This is because there are exchange costs to each transaction.
[5] IASCF, IAS 18.14.

If significant risks and rewards are retained or there is continuing managerial involvement, revenue is not recognized. This may be the case for instance[6]

(a) if an obligation for unsatisfactory performance is retained (other than that covered by a normal warranty provision);

(b) if the receipt of revenue is contingent upon resale of the goods by the buyer;

(c) if the goods must be installed and the installation is a significant part of the contract; and

(d) if the buyer can rescind the contract or back out of it and there is uncertainty relating to the probability of this.

Where there are insignificant risks and rewards or continuing managerial involvement, it may be okay to recognize revenues. Judgment is used to determine significant versus insignificant.

The appendix to the standard walks through several examples relating to the sale of goods that are worth looking at. Selected scenarios and comments are noted below in Illustration 6-1.

Illustration 6-1
Examples
of Specific
Transactions
Relating to the
Sale of Goods
Revenues[7]

Type of transaction	Relevant IFRS criteria for recognition of revenues (in addition to general revenue recognition criteria)
Bill and hold	When buyer takes title and (a) delivery is probable; (b) item is on hand, identified and ready for delivery; (c) buyer acknowledges the deferred delivery; and (d) payment terms are normal.
Goods shipped subject to conditions such as installation and inspection	Installation, acceptance, and completion, unless the installation process is simple or inspection is only for final determination of the price.[8]
Goods shipped subject to approval where the buyer has negotiated a limited right of return	Where there is uncertainty—upon formal acceptance, or when goods delivered and the acceptance time period has lapsed.[9] General rights of return do not preclude revenue recognition as long as returns are measurable.
Sale and repurchase agreements other than financial assets	May be a financing arrangement (not a sale) if criteria are not met.[10]
Sales to intermediaries (distributors, dealers, or others for resale)	General revenue recognition criteria for the sale of goods. May be a consignment arrangement in which case the criteria are not met. Under consignment accounting, revenue would be recognized at a later date, when the consignee sells the goods to the customer.

---

[6] IASCF, IAS 18.16.

[7] IASCF, IAS 18 Appendix.

[8] An example of a simple installation process is where the customer need only unpack the item and plug it in.

[9] Formal acceptance might for instance be evidenced by a customer signature.

[10] In a financing arrangement, the entity would retain the risks and rewards of ownership of the asset.

Subscriptions and similar items	Recognize over the life of subscription using the straight-line method if delivered items are of similar value. Recognize based on the relative sales value (individual item value as a percentage of the total value of the sales contract) if individual delivered items vary in value.[11]
Installment sales	Selling prices are measured as the present value of the consideration determined by discounting installments at the imputed rate of interest.[12]
Real estate sales	In some jurisdictions, legal title transfer may occur at a later point, but the purchaser may have the risks and rewards of ownership because he/she is able to access/utilize the property. When legal title passes or equitable interest is acquired by the purchaser, revenue may be recognized as long as there are no further substantial acts to complete. If there are substantial acts yet to perform, revenue would be recognized as significant acts are performed. Refer to IAS 11 and Chapter 8. Examples of continuing managerial involvement include sale and repurchase agreements and contracts where the vendor has made guarantees of occupancy rates or cash flows. Professional judgment must be applied in determining whether to account for the transaction as a sale, lease, financing, or profit sharing arrangement.
Customer loyalty programs[13]	If the entity supplies the award credits, separate the fair value of the award credits and recognize revenue for them when the obligation is fulfilled. If a third party supplies the award, use judgment to determine whether the entity collecting consideration is a principal or an agent. If an agent, recognize the difference between the amount allocated and the amount paid to the third party. If a principal, recognize the gross amount as revenue. The fair value may be determined using the amount for which the credits could be sold separately or by reference to the awards for which the credits could be redeemed (adjusted for the amounts not expected to be redeemed).

---

[11] This latter method of measuring revenues is sometimes referred to as the relative sales method.

[12] Since the Appendix is technically not part of the standard per se, another option exists under the standard for measurement. The entity may choose to discount using a rate that reflects the riskiness of the cash flows.

[13] IASCF, IFRIC 13.

The discussion on customer loyalty programs above brings up another issue. Should revenues be booked on a gross basis or net basis? The nature of the business transaction must be reviewed. Is the entity acting as a principal or an agent? According to the standard,

> Revenue includes only the gross inflows of economic benefits received and receivable by the entity on its own account. Amounts collected on behalf of third parties such as sales taxes, goods and services taxes and value added taxes are not economic benefits which flow to the entity and do not result in increases in equity. Therefore, they are excluded from revenue. Similarly, in an agency relationship, the gross inflows of economic benefits include amounts collected on behalf of the principal and which do not result in increases in equity for the entity. The amounts collected on behalf of the principal are not revenue.

Instead, revenue is the amount of commission.[14]

Situation

Realco Limited is in the business of developing parcels of land, building houses, and selling the houses to individuals. During the year, it sold homes worth $10 million. In addition to this line of business, Realco also has several real estate agents on staff. The real estate agents help potential customers who want to purchase a Realco home sell their existing homes. The company receives 1% of the value of the sale on these older homes. During the year, older homes worth $5 million were sold, netting the company a commission of $50,000.

Analysis

The income of $10 million from the sale of the Realco homes is revenue to the company. The company acts as a principal in the transaction since it builds the houses and has the risks and rewards of ownership prior to sale. The commission on the sale of the older "customer" homes is reported net as commission ($50,000). The company would never report the full amount that the older home is sold for as revenue since it is only acting as an agent in the sale. The company does not own the house that is being sold.

RENDERING OF SERVICES

The criteria for recognition of service revenues is as follows:[15]

    (a) revenue is reliably measurable;
    (b) economic benefits are probable;
    (c) stage of completion reliably measurable; and
    (d) costs reliably measurable.

Percentage of Completion Method Versus Other Methods

Part (c) above makes reference to the stage of completion. This refers to the method known as the percentage of completion method. In general, under this method, revenues are recognized over the life of the contract as services are provided. The percentage of completion method is discussed in more detail in Chapter 8 and IAS 11. Note that the method and standard also apply to rendering of services that are not related to construction contracts.

    When using the method, an estimate of the stage of completion must be made so that revenues can be estimated. According to IAS 18.24, the stage of completion may be determined using

    1. surveys of work performed,
    2. comparisons of work performed to total services to be performed, or
    3. comparisons of costs incurred to date versus total estimated costs.

---

[14] IASCF, IAS 18.8.
[15] IASCF, IAS 18.20.

The first two points above relate to outputs, i.e., what the entity is making/producing, and the last looks at input, i.e., how much the company has spent to date in terms of resources to produce the outputs. According to the standard, the straight-line method is used where there are an indeterminate numbers of acts over the life of the contract, unless there is evidence of a better method. Note that if there is an act that is more significant than the other acts, revenue recognition would be deferred until the significant act is executed.

The standard notes that an entity should be able to measure the transaction reliably when the following terms of the arrangement have been agreed upon:[16]

(a) enforceable rights;
(b) consideration; and
(c) manner and terms of settlement.

In cases where the transaction cannot be reliably measured, revenue is recognized only to the extent of costs incurred and then only to the extent that the amounts are recoverable. If the transaction is not measurable and collection is not probable, the costs would be expensed and no revenues recognized.

The appendix to the standard walks through several examples relating to service transactions that are worth looking at. Selected scenarios and comments are noted in Illustration 6-2.

Illustration 6-2 Examples of Specific Transactions Relating to Service Revenues[17]	Type of transaction	Relevant IFRS criteria for recognition of revenues (in addition to general revenue recognition criteria)
	Installation fees	If installation is incidental to the sale of the product, recognize as goods sold.[18]
	Servicing fees included in the price of the product (sales support and product enhancement for software)	Divide the services and account for them separately. The amount treated as service revenues should cover costs plus a reasonable expectation of profits.
	Insurance agent commissions	If there is no further obligation to provide services, recognize up front.
	Financial services fees	If they are an integral part of the effective interest rate, adjust the interest rate, unless the asset is recognized at fair value through profit/loss, in which case expense.[19] If they are not an integral part of the effective interest rate, recognize them as service is provided.[20]
	Franchise fees	General revenue recognition criteria for rendering of services. The initial fee is recognized when performance of initial services has been substantially accomplished. If there is significant uncertainty regarding collection, recognize them as cash installments received.

---

[16] IASCF, IAS 18.23.
[17] IASCF, IAS 18 Appendix.
[18] For instance, a supplier of large equipment might agree to deliver the equipment and ensure that it is in good working order before they leave.
[19] Examples are loan origination and commitment fees where it is probable that the entity will enter into a specific lending arrangement. Note that some of these will be covered under IAS 39.
[20] Examples are loan servicing fees, investment management fees, placement fees, and loan syndication fees. Note that some of these may be covered under IAS 39.

INTEREST, ROYALTIES, AND DIVIDENDS

For interest, royalties, and dividends, revenue shall be recognised on the following bases:[21]

- (a) interest shall be recognized using the effective interest method as set out in IAS 39, paragraphs 9 and AG5–AG8;
- (b) royalties shall be recognized on an accrual basis in accordance with the substance of the relevant agreement; and
- (c) dividends shall be recognized when the shareholder's right to receive payment is established.

DISCLOSURE

The following disclosures are required:[22]

- (a) the accounting policies adopted for the recognition of revenue, including the methods adopted to determine the stage of completion of transactions involving the rendering of services;
- (b) the amount of each significant category of revenue recognized during the period, including revenue arising from
    - (i) the sale of goods,
    - (ii) the rendering of services,
    - (iii) interest,
    - (iv) royalties, and
    - (v) dividends; and
- (c) the amount of revenue arising from exchanges of goods or services included in each significant category of revenue.

The following is an excerpt from the financial statements of Alfa Laval, a company that sells, installs, and services technology.[23]

Illustration 6-3
Excerpt from the
2007 Financial
Statements of
Alfa Laval

Revenue Recognition

Revenue recognition is made according to IAS 18 Revenue. Revenue from sale of goods is recognized when all of the following conditions have been fulfilled:

- the seller has transferred the significant risks and rewards of ownership of the goods to the buyer;
- the seller retains neither continuing managerial involvement to the degree usually associated with ownership nor effective control over the goods sold;
- the amount of revenue can be measured reliably;
- it is probable that the seller will get paid; and
- the costs incurred or to be incurred related to the transaction can be measured reliably.

The revenue recognition is usually governed by the delivery terms used in the sale. Net sales are referring to sales value less sales taxes, cancellations and discounts. Long-term construction projects are accounted for through the percentage of completion method.

To the extent that Alfa Laval also delivers services the three last conditions apply together with:

- the stage of completion at the balance sheet date can be measured reliably.

---

[21] IASCF, IAS 18.30.
[22] IASCF, IAS 18.35.
[23] http://alfalaval.halvarsson.se/2007en/#

LOOKING AHEAD

Revenue is currently the topic of a substantial joint project between IASB and FASB. The Boards hope to eliminate weaknesses in the current approach and to converge the standards, while at the same time clarifying the revenue recognition principles.

Current weaknesses are the following:

- The current focus on the critical event and/or earnings process. This is often difficult to identify and leads to lack of comparability in practice.
- Lack of guidance in IFRSs regarding multiple-element arrangements.
- The fact that approximately 200 sources of GAAP exist relating to revenue recognition under U.S. GAAP.

In December 2008, the IASB and FASB issued a Discussion Paper entitled *Preliminary Views on Revenue Recognition*. The paper proposes a single contract-based revenue recognition model which would be applied consistently across a range of industries. Revenue would be recognized when an entity has satisfied a performance obligation by transferring goods or services. To date, the Boards have agreed on the following preliminary views:

- The standard will apply to contracts with customers (there is some discussion as to whether to scope out financial instruments) and some non-financial instruments contracts covered by IAS 39, insurance contracts, and leasing contracts. Note that the Boards have yet to decide whether the standard will apply to revenues/gains in the absence of a contract (e.g., increases in the value of inventory).
- When an entity agrees to sell something or provide a service under contract, this gives rise to a net contract position (perhaps a receivable and a liability to perform). Revenue is recognized when the entity satisfies the obligation by transferring the goods or services to the customer.

The proposed standard may result in the following differences per IASB/FASB:

- revenue would only be recognized during construction contracts when the customer controls the asset under construction;
- items such as warranties would be accounted for as deliverables as opposed to cost accruals; and
- measurement criteria for multiple deliverables would be standardized.

The next step is to produce an Exposure Draft.

END-OF-CHAPTER PRACTICE

6-1 Foogle Inc. is in the Internet business. The company provides a search engine for free and advertises products. Every time a user of the services clicks on an advertisement, Foogle earns advertising revenues. In addition to these revenues, Foogle also has an arrangement with Gunigal Inc., another Internet company, in which they will each advertise on each other's sites. The company's auditor was looking for some evidence of the value of this transaction. Foogle and Gunigal decided on an amount for the year and swapped checks.

Instructions
Discuss the issues.

6-2 Inca Incorporated sells furniture wholesale. In an effort to get some new large customers, they are offering very lenient repayment terms. Customers do not have to pay for the goods purchased until one year after the shipment date. This recognizes the fact that sometimes the larger furniture pieces are used for showroom display purposes. On December 31 (the last day of the year), the company made a $100,000 sale to a new customer. The customer is a new company that just started up last year. No money was put down up front and payment is due December 31 the following year.

Instructions

Discuss the issues.

6-3 Assume the same facts as 6-2. Assume further that the cash price of the shipment is approximately $95,000. This information was obtained from several similar transactions with other customers.

Instructions

Prepare the journal entries to record the sale. The company uses a 50% markup policy.

6-4 Over the past six years, FASB and IASB have been meeting to discuss a new revenue recognition model. There have been two approaches to revenue recognition: (1) The Measurement Model and (2) the Allocation Model.

Instructions

Go to the FASB and IASB websites and access the minutes of the meetings where these models have been discussed. Write a short essay that explains the theoretical basis for both methods. Discuss.

6-5 The following is an excerpt from the minutes of the April 22, 2008 meeting of FASB, where the proposed joint IASB/FASB Discussion Paper was being deliberated:

> Mr. Batavick also noted that he disagrees with paragraph 40. He believes that revenue cannot arise at contract inception because the entity has not yet performed and a performance obligation has not been satisfied. Mr. Smith agreed and requested that this alternative view be included in the Discussion Paper. Mr. Wilks confirmed that the staff would make this addition.
>
> Mr. Linsmeier questioned whether recognizing revenue at contract inception was a measurement issue or a conceptual issue. Messrs. Batavick and Smith and Ms. Seidman responded that, for them, it is a conceptual issue. Mr. Linsmeier stated that he disagrees with their concept and that it is a measurement issue. Revenue-generating activities such as developing a business model and advertising start well before a contract has been arranged or signed. Often, getting the customer is the key event, so there should be at least a possibility of revenue at contract inception.

Instructions

Obtain and read the minutes. Discuss.

6-6 In this chapter, flag icons identify areas where there are GAAP differences between IFRS requirements and national standards.

Instructions

Access the website(s) identified on the inside back cover of this book, and prepare a concise summary of the differences that are flagged throughout the chapter material.

Chapter 7

Inventories: IAS 2

U.S. GAAP References
FAS 151 Inventory Costs—An Amendment of ARB 43
ARB 43 Inventories

Related IFRSs
IAS 11 Construction Contracts
IAS 32 Financial Instruments: Presentation
IAS 39 Financial Instruments: Recognition and Measurement
IAS 41 Agriculture

OBJECTIVE AND SCOPE

IAS 2 *Inventories* identifies what and how inventory-related costs are recognized as assets, and provides guidance on when these costs are transferred to the income statement as an expense. In addition, it sets out the minimum disclosures necessary for readers of the financial statements to understand the significance of inventories to the entity.

Inventories are defined as assets

(a) held for sale in the ordinary course of business,
(b) in the process of production for such sale, or
(c) in the form of materials or supplies to be consumed in the production process or in the rendering of services.[1]

Inventories can take a variety of forms, such as physical goods acquired for resale or manufacture, the cost of employee time in the case of a service provider, or livestock raised by an agricultural concern.

IAS 2 covers the entire range of inventories, **excluding** construction contract work in progress (see IAS 11 *Construction Contracts*), inventories of financial instruments (see IAS 32 *Financial Instruments: Presentation* and IAS 39 *Financial Instruments: Recognition and Measurement*), and biological inventory assets related to agricultural activity and agricultural produce at the point of harvest (see IAS 41 *Agriculture*).[2]

In addition, inventories held by the following businesses are excluded from the **measurement requirements** of IAS 2, provided the changes in the fair value measures they use are recognized directly in profit or loss:

1. producers of agricultural and forest products, agricultural produce after harvest, and minerals and mineral products, as long as these products are measured at net realizable value, consistent with long-accepted practice in these industries; and
2. commodity broker–traders with inventories that are carried at fair value less costs to sell.[3]

MEASUREMENT

Inventories are measured at the **lower of cost and net realizable value (LC and NRV)**. In order to apply this measurement principle, more information is needed about the costs that are included, the cost formulas that are appropriate to use, and how net realizable value is determined.

Costs Included

Inventory costs can be classified as

1. purchase costs,
2. conversion costs, or
3. other costs that can be inventoried.

All **purchase costs** are included in inventory cost. Similar to other non-financial assets that apply a cost-based measurement at acquisition—such as property, plant, and equipment—these include the purchase price, non-recoverable duties and taxes, and other costs directly associated with acquiring materials or services, including expenditures for their transportation and handling. Trade, volume, and similar discounts and rebates are deducted from the purchase cost.

Conversion costs include **direct labor** and indirect variable and fixed production overhead costs.

Variable production overhead costs are indirect plant costs that fluctuate directly with the volume of activity. Examples include indirect materials, indirect labor, and other variable costs such as electricity and unit-of-production-based depreciation. These costs are allocated to inventory based on actual usage.

Fixed production overhead—indirect plant costs that don't change significantly with the level of production—are allocated on a systematic basis to the inventory produced. Examples of fixed overhead costs charged to inventory include taxes on the plant property, and the salary and benefit costs associated with the factory manager.

---

[1] IASCF, IAS 2.6.
[2] IASCF, IAS 2.2.
[3] IASCF, IAS 2.3.

Fixed overhead costs are allocated to production based on the facility's **normal operating capacity**. Normal operating capacity is the average production volume expected over a number of periods under normal circumstances, taking down time for planned maintenance into account. This denominator is used so that the costs of inefficiency and idle capacity are not included in inventory, which happens if a lower volume is used. Inefficiency and idle capacity are period costs that should be recognized as an expense in the period incurred. Actual production volumes may be used if they are not significantly different from normal capacity. In periods of abnormally high production volumes, the actual volume is used as the denominator so that "cost" is not higher than actual cost.

Sometimes, the conversion process results in two or more **joint products** being produced so that the conversion costs incurred cannot be directly associated with any one product. In this case, the conversion costs are allocated between the joint products on a rational basis, often on the relative sales values of the products when they become separable or saleable. If a joint product that emerges is minor in value, as is the case with many by-products, the joint costs are not allocated. Instead the by-product is measured at its net realizable value and this amount is deducted from the main product costs. This is a reasonable and practical solution.

Other inventoriable costs are limited to costs incurred to bring the inventories to their present location and condition. For example, royalty fees payable to manufacture a licensed product or the amortization of capitalized development costs related to a product are properly chargeable to inventory.

Borrowing costs that are directly related to the acquisition, construction, or production of a qualifying inventory item are also capitalized as inventory. ***Borrowing costs*** are the interest and other costs associated with the borrowing of funds; in this case, for inventory items that take a substantial period of time to get ready for sale.[4] When these costs relate to inventory measured at fair value and items manufactured or produced in large quantities on a repetitive basis that take a substantial period of time to prepare for sale, the entity may, but is not required to capitalize them. IAS 23 *Borrowing Costs* addresses the specific scope, recognition, and disclosure requirements for including these costs in the acquisition costs of a variety of qualifying assets.

IAS 2 identifies specific costs that are **not capitalized** as part of inventory:

- Costs associated with abnormal amounts of wasted materials, labor, or overhead
- Storage or warehousing costs, unless the product is required to be held before another production stage
- Administrative overheads that are not necessary to bring inventory to its present location and condition
- Selling costs
- Interest or financing costs incurred above the purchase price for normal credit terms

Inventories of a Service Provider

The cost of inventories of a service provider is determined in much the same way as that of a manufacturer. It includes the cost of direct labor, indirect labor (supervisory personnel, for example), and allocated overheads. As with a manufacturing concern, the costs of selling and general administrative overhead are not considered inventoriable costs, and no profit margin is recognized in inventory cost.

Agricultural Produce Harvested from Biological Assets

Agricultural produce after harvest, according to IAS 41 *Agriculture*, is measured on initial recognition at fair value less costs to sell at the point it is harvested. This value then becomes its "cost" under IAS 2.

Measurement Techniques

Specialized techniques to measure inventory have been developed in specific industries. One technique is to apply **standard costs** to inventory units manufactured and sold rather than actual costs. The normalized costs, reviewed and updated on a regular basis, may be used for financial reporting purposes if they are close to actual cost.

---

[4] IASCF, IAS 23. *Borrowing Costs*, par. 23.5.

The retail industry often measures its inventory by using the **retail inventory method**. This method works by determining the retail value or selling price of the inventory on hand and then deducting from this an estimate of the gross profit. The result is an estimate of the inventory's cost. Ideally, separate calculations are performed for inventories with different markups, but average percentages by department are often used. In estimating the inventory's cost, the gross profit percentage used in the calculations includes both markups above and markdowns below original selling price.

Cost Formulas

Whenever acquisition and production costs change during a period, a method is needed to determine which costs should be identified with inventory left on hand and which with inventory that has been sold. Two general principles underlie the IAS 2 guidance on this issue:

1. costs assigned to ending inventories should be representative of recent costs, and
2. costs assigned should correspond closely with the actual physical flow of the goods and services.

Three different methods or formulas are used to attribute specific costs to inventory items: specific identification, first-in, first-out (FIFO), and weighted average cost.

Inventory costs are assigned using the **specific identification method** for inventory items that are not ordinarily interchangeable and for goods and services produced and segregated for specific projects.[5] This means that the **specific cost** of the items sold are assigned to the cost of goods sold, and the **specific cost** of those on hand at the end of the period make up the ending inventory cost. Where there are a large number of interchangeable goods, however, this method is not appropriate, and one of the other two methods is applied.

The first-in, first-out (FIFO) and the weighted average cost formulas are used to determine inventory cost for all other inventory. The **first-in, first-out** method, as its name suggests, assumes that the first inventory acquired is the first inventory sold. Therefore, the oldest costs are assigned to those units. Ending inventory, assumed to come from the latest purchases or production, is assigned the most recent costs. The **weighted average cost formula** applies the same weighted average cost of all units available for sale in the period to both the cost of goods sold and the ending inventory. This may be applied on either a perpetual or a periodic basis.

Aside from the two general principles referred to above, no guidance is provided on choosing between the FIFO and weighted average cost methods. It is clear, however, that an entity may choose one method for some inventories, such as those identified with a particular operating segment, and the other method for inventory with different characteristics. However, the **same cost formula** is used for all inventories with a **similar nature and use**.

A recent KPMG survey of 123 companies that apply IFRS found that 28 companies used both FIFO and weighted average cost formulas for different categories of inventory. In total, including entities that use both, there was a relatively even split—60% used weighted average and 40% used FIFO.[6]

Net Realizable Value

Similar to other assets, inventories cannot be reported on the statement of financial position at more than the net cash expected to be recovered from their sale or use. This means that the carrying amount of inventory has to be assessed at each balance sheet date for any effects of damage, obsolescence, reduction in selling price, or increase in completion and selling costs. If necessary, the inventory's carrying amount is written down so that it

---

[5] IASCF, IAS 2.23.
[6] KPMG and Prof. Dr. Isabel von Keitz, *The Application of IFRS: Choices in Practice*, KPMG IFRG Limited (December 2006), p. 15.

is reported on the balance sheet at the lower of cost and net realizable value (LC and NRV). ***Net realizable value*** is defined in IAS 2.6 as "the estimated selling price in the ordinary course of business less the estimated costs of completion and the estimated costs necessary to make the sale."

The adjustment to net realizable value is usually applied on **an item-by-item basis**; however, inventory items may be grouped in limited circumstances. IAS 2 suggests that to be grouped, the inventory items must have similar characteristics, such as being associated with the same product line with a similar purpose or end use, or produced and marketed in the same geographic area, and the items cannot be practicably evaluated separately from other items in that product line.[7]

Situation:

The December 31, 2008 inventory of Gwnyer Company consists of two products: 5 units of A105 and 7 units of BB32. Before adjustment, the cost and carrying amount of the total inventory is $100.

Product	Original Cost	Cost to Replace	Estimated Cost to Sell	Expected Selling Price	Normal Profit Margin
A105	$6	$6	$1	$8	20%
BB32	$10	$9	$4	$12	25%

Determine the amount of inventory to report on the December 31, 2008 statement of financial position and prepare any necessary adjusting entry.

Analysis:

Product	Cost (a)	Net Realizable Value (b)	Lower of (a) and (b)		Quantity		Inventory at LC and NRV
A105	$6	$8 − $1 = $7	$6	×	5	=	$30
BB32	$10	$12 − $4 = $8	$8	×	7	=	$56
							$86

Adjusting entry:

Inventory Loss − LC and NRV (P or L)	14	
Inventory (or Allowance account)		14

To write inventory down to the lower of cost and net realizable value: $100 − $86.

The net realizable value of inventory is reassessed at each financial reporting date and further reductions may be necessary or previous writedowns may be reversed. Reversals, also recognized in profit or loss, are allowed in the following circumstances:

1. the situation that caused the previous writedown no longer exists, or
2. there is clear evidence due to changed economic circumstances that an item's net realizable value has increased.

Valuation above the lower of cost and net realizable value is not allowed.

---

[7] IASCF, IAS 2.29.

Situation:

Assume that three units of inventory item BB32 from the example above remain in inventory at March 31, 2009. The cost to sell each unit is still $4, but the market has recovered for these items and their expected selling price is now $16. What adjusting entry, if any, is needed at March 31, 2009?

Analysis:

Product	Cost	Net Realizable Value	Lower of (a) and (b)		Quantity		Inventory at LC and NRV
	(a)	(b)					
BB32	$10	$16 − $4 = $12	$10	×	3	=	$30
	Carrying amount before adjustment:		$ 8	×	3	=	24
	Writedown reversal needed						$6

Adjusting entry:

      Inventory (or Allowance account)   6

          Inventory Loss Recovered − LC and NRV (P or L)   6

      To adjust inventory for recovery in NRV: ($10 − $8) × 3 units

EXPENSE RECOGNITION

The carrying amount of inventories sold is recognized as an expense in the same period that the related revenue is recognized. Other inventory losses, writedowns to the lower of cost and net realizable value, and reversals of such writedowns are recognized in the period they occur as an adjustment to the expense recognized in the period.

DISCLOSURE

Disclosures are required for the inventory accounting policies applied, for inventory remaining at the balance sheet date, and for inventory costs recognized in profit or loss.

The **accounting policies** used in measuring inventories are reported in the accounting policy note to the financial statements.

Balance sheet-related disclosures include

(a) the carrying amount of inventories in total, and the amount in each inventory category used by the entity;

(b) the carrying amount of inventory measured at fair value less the cost to sell, if any; and

(c) the carrying amount of inventories pledged as collateral for liabilities.

The most common inventory classifications are materials, work in progress (including inventories of service providers), finished goods, production supplies, and merchandise.

Disclosures related to **amounts recognized on the income statement** in the period include

(a) the amount of inventories recognized as an expense;

(b) the amount of any writedowns to NRV, or other inventory losses recognized as an expense;

(c) the amount of the reversal of any writedowns that reduced the amount recognized in (a); and

(d) a description of the circumstances that resulted in any reversals of writedowns.[8]

---

[8] IASCF, IAS 2.36.

The amount of inventories recognized as an expense is generally referred to as the cost of sales. This amount includes unallocated production overheads and abnormal production costs.

Siemens AG, headquartered in Munich, Germany, prepares its financial statements in accordance with international financial accounting standards. Siemens is a global operating giant in the fields of energy, healthcare, consumer products, financial services, information technology, communications, and other industries. The company's 400,000 employees work in about 190 countries around the world. Illustration 7-1 shows excerpts from Siemens' financial statements for its year ended September 30, 2007 that relate to its inventory disclosures.[9] Siemens uses euros (€) as its reporting currency.

Illustration 7-1
Siemens AG,
Inventory
Disclosures

Consolidated Statements of Income

For the fiscal years ended September 30, 2007 and 2006 (in millions of €, per share amounts in €)

	Note	Siemens 2007	2006
Revenue		72,448	66,487
Cost of goods sold and services rendered		(51,572)	(49,108)
Gross profit		20,876	17,379

Consolidated Balance Sheets

As of September 30, 2007 and 2006 (in millions of €)

	Note	Siemens 9/30/07	9/30/06
Assets			
Current assets			
Inventories	13	12,930	12,790

2 Summary of significant accounting policies

Inventories – Inventory is valued at the lower of acquisition or production cost or net realizable value, cost being generally determined on the basis of an average or first-in, first-out method. Production costs comprise direct material and labor and applicable manufacturing overheads, including depreciation charges. Net realizable value is the estimated selling price in the ordinary course of business, less the estimated costs of completion and selling expenses.

---

[9] http://w1.siemens.com/annual/07/pool/download/pdf/e07_00_gb2007.pdf.

13 Inventories

	September 30,	
	2007	2006
Raw materials and supplies	**2,201**	2,609
Work in process	**3,196**	2,975
Costs and earnings in excess of billings on uncompleted contracts	**7,099**	7,085
Finished goods and products held for resale	**2,558**	2,544
Advances to suppliers	**751**	667
	15,805	15,880
Advance payments received	**(2,875)**	(3,090)
	12,930	12,790

LOOKING AHEAD

There is nothing on the IASB's agenda that directly involves potential changes to IAS 2 *Inventories*.

END-OF-CHAPTER PRACTICE

7-1 The following costs have been incurred by a manufacturer of small leather goods:
1.   hides of various leather
2.   dyes to color the leather
3.   warehouse costs to store the dyed leather while drying
4.   patterns and dies used to guide the cutting of the pieces into the desired shape
5.   the salary of the plant manager's administrative assistant
6.   costs of the warehouse to store finished goods
7.   under-applied factory overhead

Instructions
Determine whether the cost of each of the above items is included in the cost of inventory. Provide a brief explanation of your answer for each.

7-2 Search Corp. (SC) provides executive search services to a variety of clients on a fee-for-service basis. A team of two human resource professionals is assigned to each client for each position SC is hired to fill. The professionals meet with the clients to establish what particular skills, abilities, and characteristics the ideal candidate should have; supervise meetings of the client's internal search team; advertise broadly; identify a list of potential candidates; contact a variety of associates across the country to expand this list; receive applications and dossiers; help the client develop a short list; and oversee the interview and selection process.

The human resource professionals are backed up by administrative assistants who work on 10 to 15 different client files at the same time, and by an executive team who provide strategic direction, and marketing, information systems, finance, and accounting capability to SC's operations. SC rents five floors of a major commercial building in a prime downtown location.

Instructions
Identify and briefly discuss the costs that are likely to be included in SC's inventory on its year-end balance sheet.

7-3 Kiji Appliances Ltd. (KAL) sells major household appliances through a chain of company-owned stores. In addition, the company stocks a wide variety of smaller appliances, such as electric can openers, irons, electric tea-kettles, and pots and pans. KAL pays its sales staff a base salary and a commission on the major appliances they sell.

Instructions
Identify inventory policies that would be appropriate for Kiji Appliances Ltd. to use for financial reporting purposes.

7-4 Khan Enterprises Inc. (KEI) reports the following information for the first three quarters of its 2008 fiscal year:

	Jan. 1, 2008	Mar. 31, 2008	June 30, 2008	Sept. 30, 2008
Inventory, at cost	$150	$251	$270	$230
Inventory, at LC and NRV	145	144	266	230
Purchases for the quarter		265	240	235
Sales for the quarter		475	210	500

Instructions
(a) Prepare quarterly income statements for the first three quarters of KEI's 2008 fiscal year. Report the inventory in the statements at cost, separately indicating the loss or loss recovery from adjusting inventory to the lower of cost and net realizable value.
(b) Assuming KEI records its LC and NRV adjustments in an allowance account, prepare the adjusting journal entries needed at March 31, June 30, and September 30, 2008.

7-5 In this chapter, flag icons identify areas where there are GAAP differences between IFRS requirements and national standards.

Instructions
Access the website(s) identified on the inside back cover of this book, and prepare a concise summary of the differences that are flagged throughout the chapter material.

Chapter 8

Construction Contracts: IAS 11

U.S. GAAP References
SAB 104 Revenue Recognition
SOP 81-1 Accounting for Performance of Construction-Type and Certain Production-Type Contracts
CON 6 Elements of Financial Statements

Related IFRSs
IAS 18 Revenue

OBJECTIVE AND SCOPE

This standard deals with revenue recognition for construction contracts. These contracts present special problems due to the nature of the arrangement with the customer. Specifically, these types of contracts often have the following unique features:

- The contract is signed up front before work is performed.
- Customer billings are stipulated in the contract (they are often used to finance the project).
- The contract is long term in nature, spanning several reporting periods.
- The earnings process is made up of many (often significant) events.

IAS 11 builds upon the revenue recognition criteria laid down in the framework and also upon IAS 18 *Revenue*. The standard provides the following term definitions:[1]

---

[1] IASCF, IAS 11.3.

A *construction contract* is a contract specifically negotiated for the construction of an asset or a combination of assets that are closely interrelated or interdependent in terms of their design, technology and function or their ultimate purpose or use.

A *fixed price contract* is a construction contract in which the contractor agrees to a fixed contract price, or a fixed rate per unit of output, which in some cases is subject to cost escalation clauses.

A *cost plus contract* is a construction contract in which the contractor is reimbursed for allowable or otherwise defined costs, plus a percentage of these costs or a fixed fee.

The standard differentiates between contracts where the overall price is fixed (and where the contractor has the risk of cost overruns) and cost plus contracts where the price is variable (depending on the costs). The latter type of contract allows for full cost recovery and therefore the risk of overruns rests with the customer. Contracts may have attributes of both of these. Because the risks are different, the accounting is different.

COMBINING AND SEGMENTING CONSTRUCTION CONTRACTS

There may be a need to group or subdivide contracts for accounting purposes.[2] This would depend on how the contract was negotiated. Contracts for construction of several assets would be grouped for accounting purposes if the contracts were:

- negotiated together,
- are closely interrelated, and
- are performed concurrently or in continuous sequence.

Contracts covering the construction of several assets would be treated as separate contracts for accounting purposes if

- separate proposals were submitted for each individual asset,
- each part of the contract was negotiated as a separate part, and
- the revenues and related costs are separable.

If the contract includes an option to build an additional asset, the arrangement would be accounted for as a separate contract if the additional asset differs from the rest of the assets or the price is negotiated separately.

The above flexibility allows the accounting to follow the economic substance of the contract negotiations. Grouping or segregating contracts also allows the appropriate treatments of costs and ensures that any losses are appropriately recognized.

CONTRACT REVENUE

Contract revenues include the amounts originally agreed to in the contract plus variations, claims, and incentive payments that are measurable and probable.[3] Variations, claims, and incentive payments are separately defined in the standard and reflect the differing nature of the revenues. Each has a different point for recognition of revenue. Illustration 8-1 provides a summary.

---

[2] IASCF, IAS 11.7-.10.
[3] IASCF, IAS 11.11-.15.

*Illustration 8-1
Variations,
Claims, and
Incentive
Payments*

Type of revenues	Description	Recognition criteria
Variations	• results from a change in the scope of the work as initiated by the customer (e.g., a customer may want additional work performed that was not originally intended and is willing to pay)	• probable that the customer will approve the variation and amount • reliably measurable
Claims	• represents an additional amount that the contractor seeks to collect due to incurrence of additional costs (e.g., the customer has ordered additional work done but is now of the opinion that it should have been included in the original price of the contract). These are more contentious and must be negotiated with the customer.	• probable that customer will accept (negotiations at advanced stage) • reliably measurable
Incentive payments	• additional amounts if certain targets are met or exceeded (e.g., performance standards, timing). For instance, the customer might agree to pay an additional 5% of the revenues if the contract is completed on time.	• probable that the target will be met or exceeded (contract must be sufficiently advanced) • reliably measurable

Although revenues are measured at the fair value of the consideration received or receivable, they may change from period to period. This would be treated as a change in estimate.

CONTRACT COSTS

It is important to identify all costs that are related to the contract in order to measure profit. In addition, sometimes the method used to estimate revenues is based on the costs incurred to date. Therefore, if the costs are incorrectly measured, the amount of revenue recognized will be incorrect as well. The standard provides the following guidance relating to which costs to include. Contract costs should include costs that are

- **directly related** to the contract (including materials and labor costs, depreciation, and other costs);
- **attributable to the contract activity in general** (such as insurance, design costs, construction overhead, payroll processing costs, and borrowing costs); and
- **specifically chargeable under the terms of the contract** (such as general and administrative costs, development costs).[4]

Contract costs may be shown net of incidental income such as income from resale of excess material that may have been ordered. Costs that are attributable to the contract activity may be allocated using systematic

---

[4] IASCF, IAS 11.16.-.21.

and rational allocation methods and must be allocated consistently to all costs that have similar characteristics. Allocations would be based on a normal level of activity.[5]

Selling costs and depreciation of idle plant and equipment should not be included. However, costs incurred in securing the contract may be included as long as they can be separately identified and reliably measured and as long as it is probable that the contract will be obtained.

RECOGNITION OF CONTRACT REVENUE AND EXPENSES

Revenue and costs are recognized **when the outcome of the contract can be estimated reliably**. Reference is made to the stage of completion of the contract and the calculations are done cumulatively each reporting period.

Determining whether the outcome of the contract can be estimated reliably depends on the type of construction contract as shown below in Illustration 8-2.[6]

Illustration 8-2 Recognition Criteria for Different Contract Types	Contract type	Criteria for determining whether the outcome of the contract can be estimated reliably
	• Fixed price contract	• contract revenue reliably measurable • economic benefits probable • contract costs and stage of completion reliably measurable • attributable contract costs clearly identified
	• Cost plus contracts	• economic benefits probable • attributable costs clearly identified and measured reliably

In general, the key terms of the contract (including enforceable rights under the contract, consideration and manner, and terms of settlement) must be established before an entity can make reliable estimates. Estimates by definition may require adjustment in subsequent periods. The percentage of completion method is used to determine how much revenue should be recognized for fixed price contracts. For cost plus contracts, the percentage of completion method is not necessary since the amount of revenue recognized each period is equal to the costs expensed plus an agreed upon profit margin or markup. As mentioned previously, different accounting is afforded each one since the risks are greater for fixed price contracts and therefore there is greater measurement uncertainty.

According to IAS 11.30, methods for estimating the stage of completion include the following:

- estimating the costs incurred to date as a percentage of total estimated costs (based on inputs to the process),
  - exclude costs relating to future activity on the contract from the numerator (e.g., supplies yet to be used and advance payments made to subcontractors),
- surveys of work performed (based on outputs—how much has been done), or
- estimating the proportion physically complete, e.g., the number of miles of highway completed (outputs).

As a default, when the outcome of the contract cannot be estimated reliably, costs incurred to date are expensed and equal revenue may be recognized as long as collection is probable. This may be the case for instance in the early stages of a contract. If total costs are likely to exceed total revenues, this excess loss must be recognized. Finally, any costs incurred that are not recoverable must be expensed even if no revenue is recognized.

Illustration 8-3 shows how revenue and cost recognition changes depending on the likelihood of the outcome.

Illustration 8-3
Recognition of Revenues and Costs under Fixed Price Construction Contracts

Profitable contract			Unprofitable contract
Recognize revenue equal to percentage complete (where outcome reliably estimable)	**Recognize revenue equal to costs incurred and expensed (where outcome not reliably measurable)**	**Recognize revenue less than costs incurred (where probable that contract costs will exceed revenues)**	**Recognize costs only (where recovery not probable)**

Situation

Contractor Limited has signed a contract to construct a building for $100 million. Costs are estimated to be $90 million. At the end of year one of the contract, costs of $40 million were incurred (and paid for in cash). Contractor uses the percentage of completion method for recognizing revenues where possible. Discuss how the contract should be accounted for under the following scenarios.

Analysis

1. Assume that the outcome is reliably measurable and that other revenue recognition criteria are met.
    At the end of year one, the journal entry to record the revenues would be as follows:

Dr. Construction expense	$40	
Dr. Construction in process	44	
Cr. Cash		40
Cr. Revenues		44

    (Revenues are equal to the percentage complete using costs incurred as an estimate = Costs incurred/ estimated total costs × revenues under contract = 40/90 × 100)

2. Assume that the outcome is not reliably measurable because, for instance, there is a concern about future significant cost overruns due to an impending strike in the construction industry.

Dr. Construction expense	$40	
Dr. Construction in process	40	
Cr. Cash		40
Cr. Revenues		40

    (Revenues are equal to the expenses recognized. Construction in process is equal to the costs incurred less the expected provision for loss)

3. Assume that losses of $10 million are probable on the contract.

Dr. Construction expense	$46	
Dr. Construction in process	30	
Cr. Cash		40
Cr. Revenues		36

(Revenues are equal to the percentage complete using costs incurred as an estimate = Costs incurred/estimated total costs × revenues under contract = 40/110 × 100). The entity must recognize the loss since it is probable and measurable. Construction in process is equal to the costs incurred less expected provision for the loss.

4. Assume that the outcome is not reliably measurable, and it is not clear that the costs are recoverable.

Dr. Construction expense	$40	
Cr. Cash		40

No revenues are recognized (nor assets)

5. Assume instead that the contract is a cost plus contract and that instead of including a fixed price in the contract, the entity may recover costs plus a 20% profit margin. All revenue recognition criteria are met.

Dr. Construction expense	$40	
Dr. Construction in process	48	
Cr. Cash		40
Cr. Revenues		48

DISCLOSURE AND PRESENTATION

Various disclosures are required including the following:[7]

- The amount of revenue recognized in the period.
- The method used to determine the above, as well as the stage of completion.
- For contracts in process, the amount of costs incurred and profit recognized to date, advance received, and amount of retentions (unpaid billings).
- Any contingent assets/liabilities.

On the balance sheet, the gross amount due from customers is presented as an asset if it is a debit (costs plus recognized profits less recognized losses and progress billings), or the gross amount due to customers is presented as a liability if it is a credit. Illustration 8-4 provides an excerpt from the annual financial statements of Siemens AG.[8]

Illustration 8-4 Excerpt from Siemens AG 2007 Annual Report

Revenue recognition on construction contracts – The Company's Groups, particularly PG, TS, I&S, PTD and SBT, conduct a significant portion of their business under construction contracts with customers. The Company generally accounts for construction projects using the percentage-of-completion method, recognizing revenue as performance on a contract progresses. This method places considerable importance on accurate estimates of the extent of progress towards completion. Depending on the methodology to determine contract progress, the significant estimates include total contract costs, remaining costs to completion, total contract revenues, contract risks and other judgments. Management of the operating Groups continually reviews all estimates involved in such construction contracts and adjusts them as necessary. The Company also uses the percentage-of-completion method for projects financed directly or indirectly by Siemens. In order to qualify for such accounting, the credit quality of the customer must meet certain minimum parameters as evidenced by the customer's credit rating or by a credit analysis performed by Siemens Financial Services (SFS), which performs such reviews in support of the Company's Corporate Executive Committee. At a minimum, a customer's credit rating must

---

[7] IASCF, IAS 11.39-.41.
[8] http://w1.siemens.com/annual/07/pool/download/pdf/e07_00_gb2007.pdf.

be single B from external rating agencies, or an equivalent SFS-determined rating. In cases where the credit quality does not meet such standards, the Company recognizes revenue for construction contracts and financed projects based on the lower of cash if irrevocably received, or contract completion. The Company believes the credit factors used provide a reasonable basis for assessing credit quality.

LOOKING AHEAD

The IASB is not currently looking at accounting for construction contracts specifically, although the accounting may be affected by the revenues project. Under the revenues project, it has been proposed that contract revenues only be recognized during the contract where the item being constructed is under the control of the customer.

END-OF-CHAPTER PRACTICE

8-1 Saturday Night Limited has signed a contract to construct a building for $1.5 million. Costs are estimated to be $1.2 million. At the end of year one of the contract, costs of $500,000 were incurred (and paid for in cash). Of this, half of the money was spent on construction materials, which are still in storage. The company uses the percentage of completion method for recognizing revenues where possible.

Instructions
Discuss how the contract should be accounted for under the following scenarios. Prepare journal entries.

1. Assume that the outcome is reliably measurable and that other revenue recognition criteria are met.
2. Assume that the outcome is not reliably measurable.
3. Assume that losses of $300,000 are probable on the contract.
4. Assume that the outcome is not reliably measurable and it is not clear that the costs are recoverable.

8-2 Sunday Night Limited signed a contract to build a building under a cost plus contract. Costs are estimated to be $5 million and, under the terms of the contract, Sunday Night Limited can recover all reasonable costs plus a 10% margin for profit. The costs incurred at the end of the first year are $2 million. It is probable that the costs plus profit will be recoverable. Costs are clearly identifiable.

Instructions
Prepare the journal entries to record the revenues in the first year.

8-3 Monday Morning Limited is a construction company. During the year, they had one very large, ongoing construction project. The five-year fixed price contract was signed at the beginning of the year, and the project is on schedule and is 20% complete to date. The following costs were incurred during the year:

*   materials costs (some of which are still on hand)
*   labor costs for builders
*   salary of site supervisor
*   salary of head office project manager
*   depreciation on construction machinery
*   insurance
*   head office secretarial (for typing up the contracts and doing the accounting for the contract)

Instructions
Discuss whether the costs are contract costs.

8-4 In this chapter, flag icons identify areas where there are GAAP differences between IFRS requirements and national standards.

Instructions
Access the website(s) identified on the inside back cover of this book, and prepare a concise summary of the differences that are flagged throughout the chapter material.

Chapter 9
Agriculture: IAS 41

U.S. GAAP References
FAS 144 Accounting for the Impairment or Disposal of Long-lived Assets
FAS 157 Fair Value Measurements
SOP 85-3 Accounting by Agricultural Producers and Agricultural Cooperatives

Related IFRSs
IAS 1 Presentation of Financial Statements
IAS 2 Inventories
IAS 18 Revenues
IAS 37 Provisions, Contingent Liabilities and Contingent Assets
IFRS 5 Non-current Assets Held for Sale and Discontinued Operations

OBJECTIVE AND SCOPE

This standard deals with accounting for agricultural activity. It specifically covers biological assets, agricultural produce at the point of harvest, and related government grants, but excludes land and intangible assets. Agricultural activities are excluded from Section 3031. IAS 41 is considered a significant addition to GAAP since the economies of many global countries rely on agriculture. Depending on the nature of the assets, they may meet the definition of assets held for sale and be covered by IFRS 5 (for example, a forest where the whole plot of living trees will be sold). Once an item has been harvested, it becomes inventory and is covered by IAS 2.

Illustration 9-1 highlights transitions in the development of a biological asset and identifies the standard that covers it.

Illustration 9-1
LifeCycle of a
Biological Asset
and Related
IFRSs

Seedling planted	Tree growing	Mature tree harvested	Logs processed into lumber	Lumber sold
IAS 41	IAS 41	IAS 2 Inventory (Fair value less costs to sell becomes new cost)	IAS 2 Inventory	IAS 18 Revenue (Cost of sales)

Biological assets ⟶ Agricultural produce ⟶

IAS 41 defines the following terms:[1]

Agricultural activity is the management by an entity of the biological transformation and harvest of biological assets for sale, or for conversion into agricultural produce, or into additional biological assets.

Agricultural produce is the harvested product of the entity's biological assets.

A *biological asset* is a living animal or plant.

Biological transformation comprises the processes of growth, degeneration, production, and procreation that cause qualitative or quantitative changes in a biological asset.

A *group of biological assets* is an aggregation of similar living animals or plants.

Harvest is the detachment of produce from a biological asset or the cessation of a biological asset's life processes.

The standard gives some examples of biological assets that it covers (sheep, trees, plants), agricultural produce that it covers only to the point of harvest (wool, felled trees, cotton), and products that are sold right after harvesting or are the result of processing after harvest, which are covered by IAS 2 and eventually IAS 18 when sold (yarn, lumber, clothing).

In general, agricultural activities have the following common characteristics: they are capable of biological transformation and this transformation is managed, facilitated, measured, and monitored by the entity.

RECOGNITION AND MEASUREMENT

Recall the general definition of an asset from Chapter 1 (taken from the IASB framework):

- *Future economic benefits* resulting from *past events*
- Resource *controlled by the entity*

Recall further that assets are recognized only when the economic benefits are

- probable and
- reliably measurable.

---

[1] IASCF, IAS 41.5.

The recognition criteria for biological assets are based on this foundation. Biological assets are recognized when

- the entity *controls* the asset as a result of *past events,*
- *future economic benefits* are *probable,* and
- the fair value or cost is *reliably measurable.*[2]

As biological assets grow and mature through biological transformation, they increase in value. Biological assets are measured at fair value less estimated costs to sell on initial recognition, unless fair value cannot be reliably measured. Costs to sell include commissions, taxes, and duties. Agricultural produce is measured at fair value less estimated costs to sell at the point of harvest. Situations where fair value is not reliably measured are discussed later in the chapter. Where fair value is used, assets are remeasured at each reporting date. Assets may be grouped for measurement purposes (e.g., assets of similar age or quality). Fair value represents the value in the present condition and location and thus equals market value less transport and other costs to get the asset to market.

Fair value is felt to be the most relevant measure since many of these assets trade in active markets and therefore objective information on their current value is available. Market values are more reliable and relevant than cost figures, which may be inconsistently accumulated from entity to entity due to differing choices regarding allocations. In addition, the life cycle and increase in value of many biological assets occur over numerous reporting periods; thus, it is misleading to reflect the gains only in the period sold.

In general, fair value is determined by reference to a market price if an active market exists for the asset in its present location and condition. An active market is a market where the items traded are homogeneous and there are buyers and sellers and publicly available prices.[3] Where an *active* market does not exist or where markets do not exist at all (for instance, for partially grown crops), the entity would do the following in attempting to estimate fair value:

1. First, try to estimate current market prices by looking at the prices of recent market transactions, market prices for similar assets (adjusting for differences), or sector benchmarks such as the price of cattle expressed by weight.
2. Second, if market-determined prices are not available for assets in their present condition (for instance partially grown crops), use a discounted cash flow approach to measuring the value.[4] This need not be carried out by an independent valuator.

Cost may be close to fair value if there has been little or immaterial biological transformation.

Where there is a range of estimates, the objective is to identify the most reliable estimate within a relatively narrow range.[5]

When using a discounted cash flow approach, the entity would

- use a market-determined discount rate;
- exclude cash flows for financing, taxation, or replacing the asset after harvest;
- incorporate risk by either using probability weighted cash flows or adjusting the discount rate or some combination of the two; and
- ensure assumptions for calculating the discount rate are consistent with calculating the cash flows to avoid double counting.

Where the biological assets are attached to land, the fair value of the land and assets would be measured and then the value of the land would be deducted since land is not covered by this standard.

---

[2] IASCF, IAS 41.10.
[3] IASCF, IAS 41.8.
[4] IASCF, IAS 41.18-20. All available market and market available information should be looked to first. Where more than one market is present, the entity should use the most relevant market information.
[5] IASCF, IAS 41.19.

Situation

Farm Co. grows strawberries and blueberries and sells them, as do other local farmers, to the local berry marketing board. Discuss whether an active market exists for the purposes of asset measurement.

Analysis

The standard calls for active markets to have buyers and sellers, homogeneous products traded, and publicly available prices. In this case, the prices would likely be made public, and there would be numerous sellers selling a homogeneous product (berries). The question arises as to whether the existence of only one buyer precludes this from being defined as an active market. On the one hand, an objective, relevant price would be produced in this marketplace and would thus be good for measuring the asset. On the other hand, a market with only one buyer (who might buy produce only at certain limited times) might be seen to be a market that is fairly illiquid and therefore inactive. Factors such as how often the assets are purchased/sold and how prices are determined would help the decision. In the end, the accounting is a matter of professional judgment.

If the entity has entered into a contract to sell the assets at a future date, the price fixed in the contract does not necessarily dictate the fair value since the contract price reflects an estimate of the future fair value and therefore includes a time value factor. In addition, the locked in contract price (which may be referred to as a forward price depending on the nature of the contract) may be higher or lower than the fair value at any point in time (spot price), including at the date of delivery. This is due to changing market conditions and expectations. Where an entity has locked into a price to sell the assets at a price less than the current fair value, this would be reflected in the statements as an onerous contract and IAS 37 would apply.[6]

Many costs go into the biological transformation process (planting, weeding, fertilizing, and others). The standard does not prescribe how to treat these. Some feel that it is inconsistent to capitalize these costs in a fair value model and that they should be expensed. Others feel that they should be capitalized and only the net amount should be recognized as gain or loss in the statement of profit and loss.

Situation

Cattle Co. Limited produces milk. The cattle live for several years and require housing and care. Typical costs incurred in looking after the cattle include medical bills, feed, and shelter. Assume that these costs are as follows for the current year:

Medical	$100
Food	$200
Shelter (cost of a new barn)	$1,000

---

[6] These contracts may take the form of a derivative contract. If the contract meets the definition of a derivative, it is covered by IAS 39 and would be recognized at fair value on the balance sheet with gains and losses through income. Contracts that are entered into for the purpose of taking receipt of the goods (in accordance with the entity's expected purchase, sale, or usage requirements) are excluded from IAS 39 and would not be recognized on the balance sheet unless they were deemed to be onerous. Accounting for derivative contracts is covered in Chapter 18.

Milk produced during the year was sold for $2,000 (net of point of sale costs). The value of the herd of dairy cows was estimated to have increased by $10,000 during the year. The entity uses fair value less point of sale costs to value its biological and agricultural assets. If there are differing treatments, discuss the options. Assuming that the entity chooses to expense the medical and food costs, prepare the journal entries to record.

Analysis

The standard does not mandate how the costs should be accounted for. On the one hand, they could be capitalized as part of the biological assets—the cows (medical and foods costs). On the other hand, the costs could be expensed directly. As long as the expenditures do not create assets that still exist at year end (i.e., barn), the net impact on the income statement should be the same. The barn qualifies for capitalization as property, plant and equipment; however, the other costs may be capitalized as part of the cost of the biological asset or expensed. Since the assets are carried at fair value, it might not make sense to capitalize the medical expenses and food.

The following journal entry assumes that the entity chooses to expense the food and medical costs.

Dr. PP&E	$1,000	
Dr. Biological assets	10,000	
Dr. Cash (2,000 − 1,000 − 200 − 100)	700	
Cr. Gain on biological assets		9,700
Cr. Milk revenues		2,000

(According to IAS 41.B61 and B62, the standard does not mandate whether to show the gains/revenues gross or net, nor the level of detail, although in general, the statements should be transparent.)

Gains and Losses

Gains or losses are recognized in income when they arise. This may result in a gain or loss arising upon initial recognition such as the birth of a calf.[7]

Inability to Measure Fair Value Reliably

In general, the standard assumes that fair value is measurable. This rebuttable presumption may be overcome for biological assets only if the market-determined prices are not available or fair value estimates are unreliable at the time of initial recognition. As a default measurement method, the asset would be measured at cost (amortized if relevant). The asset would also be tested for impairment. Once an asset is measured at fair value less point of sale costs (either as a biological asset or an asset held for sale), it is assumed that fair value is reliably measurable thereafter (no "going back"). Agricultural produce is always presumed to have a reliably measurable fair value.

GOVERNMENT GRANTS

Unconditional government grants are recognized as income when receivable. For conditional grants, conditions must be met before recognition of the grant. If the biological asset is measured at cost or amortized cost, the government grant is accounted for in accordance with IAS 20.[8]

---

[7] IASCF, IAS 41.27.
[8] IASCF, IAS 41.34 and .35.

DISCLOSURE

IAS 1 requires biological assets to be presented separately on the balance sheet.
The standard requires the following disclosures:[9]

- recognized gains/losses (on initial recognitions and on revaluation)
- description of each type of biological asset
- nature of activities relating to the assets
- non-financial measures or estimates of the physical qualities of the assets
- methods and significant assumptions to determine fair value
- fair value of harvested assets at point of harvest
- any restrictions on title
- commitments for the development or acquisition of biological assets
- financial risk management strategies
- a reconciliation of changes in the carrying amounts of biological assets between the beginning and end of the period
- additional disclosure if measured at cost
- additional disclosures related to government grants

An entity is also encouraged but not required to disclose the change in fair value due to physical changes (assets getting older) and price changes (e.g., the price of beef increases). Biological assets are categorized as being consumable (beef cattle) and bearer (dairy cows). Bearer biological assets are long-term assets that produce each year. Other examples are orchard trees and grapevines. Entities are encouraged to provide a description of different types of assets differentiating between consumable and bearer biological assets.

Illustration 9-2 shows an excerpt from the financial statements of Del Monte Pacific Limited.[10] The entity decided to measure growing crops (bearer biological assets) at cost less accumulated impairment losses—presumably because of the difficulty in arriving at fair value. The cost includes what the company refers to as nurturing costs (costs to look after the plants). It has also chosen to show the change in value due to physical changes versus price changes.

Illustration 9-2
Excerpt from the
Annual Report
of Del Monte
Pacific Limited

2.10 Biological Assets

Biological assets comprise growing crops and livestock.

Biological assets (growing crops), for which fair values cannot be measured reliably, are measured at cost less accumulated impairment losses. Expenditure on growing crops includes land preparation expenses and other direct expenses incurred during the cultivation period of the primary and ratoon crops. These expenditures on growing crops are deferred and taken into inventories based on the estimated total yield during the estimated growth cycle of three years.

Biological assets (livestock) are measured at fair value less estimated point-of-sale costs, with any changes therein recognised in income statement. Point-of-sale costs include all costs that would be necessary to sell the assets. Gains and losses arising from such measurement are included in the income statement in the period in which they arise.

---

[9] IASCF, IAS 41.40 - .57.
[10] http://www.delmontepacific.com/ir/media/ar_ipo/AR2007.pdf

9   Biological Assets

	Group	
	2007 **US$'000**	**2006** **US$'000**
Growing Crops (at cost)		
At 1 January	42,475	38,068
Additions	39,413	32,663
Harvested	(37,272)	(31,366)
Currency realignment	7,833	3,110
At 31 December	52,449	42,475
Livestock (at fair value)		
At 1 January	1,976	1,999
Purchases of livestock	4,462	5,138
Changes in fair value attributable to price changes	225	83
Sales of livestock	(2,116)	(5,407)
Currency realignment	365	163
At 31 December	4,912	1,976
Total biological assets	57,361	44,451

Growing Crops

Estimated hectares planted with growing crops are as follows:

	Group	
	2007	**2006**
Pineapples	11,262	10,776
Papaya	330	245
Passion fruit	62	48

Estimated fruits harvested, in metric tons, from the growing crops are as follows:

	Group	
	2007	**2006**
Pineapples	644,496	637,116
Papaya	5,869	7,721
Passion fruit	318	361

Source of estimation uncertainty

Growing crops is stated at cost which comprises actual costs incurred in nurturing the crops reduced by the estimated cost of fruits harvested. The cost of fruits harvested from the Group's plant crops and subsequently used in production is the estimated cost of the actual volume of fruits harvested in a given period. An estimated cost is necessary since the growth cycle of the plant crops is beyond twelve months, hence actual growing costs are not yet known as of reporting date. The estimated cost is developed by allocating estimated growing costs for the estimated growth cycle of two to three years over the estimated harvests to be made during the life cycle of the plant crops. Estimated growing costs are affected by inflation and foreign exchange rates, volume and labour requirements. Estimated harvest is affected by natural phenomenon such as weather patterns and volume of rainfall. Field performance and market demand also affect the level of estimated harvests. The Group reviews and monitors the estimated cost of harvested fruits regularly. Increases in cost of harvested fruits increases inventory cost and reduces the carrying amount of growing costs reflected as biological assets.

Livestock

Livestock comprises growing herd and cattle for slaughter and is stated at fair value. The fair value is determined based on the actual selling prices approximating those at year end less estimated point-of-sale costs.

Source of estimation uncertainty

The fair value of cattle for slaughter is based on the market prices from the various relevant markets. Fair value of the cattle for slaughter is measured on initial recognition and at each balance sheet date with changes in fair value recognised in income statement. The fair value is based on market prices of mature cattle ready for slaughter. Since market prices used as the basis for fair value refer to mature cattle, the market price for immature cattle already identified for slaughter is adjusted to account for the growing cost to be incurred for the immature cattle for slaughter to mature.

LOOKING AHEAD

The use of fair value in this standard means that the standard is intertwined with the larger fair value measurement project. The IASB has established an expert advisory panel to deal with the issue of fair value measurement in general. The panel met for the first time in June 2008. The panel's discussions will provide input for the IASB's work on financial instruments and fair value measurement in general. To date, the IASB has completed a standard-by-standard review of existing measurements in IFRSs that are identified as "fair value." As noted in Chapter 1, the IASB has also issued a Discussion Paper on the use of fair value.

    The IASB has decided to delete the requirement to use a pre-tax discount rate. Other than noted in footnote 6 and above, there are no other specific plans to make any changes in the standard in the near future.

END-OF-CHAPTER PRACTICE

9-1 IAS 41 requires that biological assets be valued at fair value less point of sale costs, as long as fair value is reliably measurable.

Instructions

Discuss why the measurement model is acceptable for this type of asset but not for inventories or property, plant and equipment. Identify other areas where fair value is used. What measurement models are supported by the framework? Discuss the issues. Hint: In researching this issue, refer to the basis for conclusions for IAS 41.

9-2 The standard has an informal fair value hierarchy embedded in it; that is, in determining the fair value of a biological asset, certain evidence is better than others.

Instructions

What is the fair value hierarchy for valuing biological assets? Discuss the pros and cons of having a prescribed hierarchy.

9-3 Farming Company Limited enters into forward selling contracts to sell its produce. One such contract has locked in the price of the most current crop at $100 per bushel. The harvest will take place after year end. As at year end, the crop is worth only $90.

Instructions

Discuss whether the entity should value the crop at $100 per bushel or $90.

9-4 Sheep Inc. raises sheep for wool. During the year, the sheep must be cared for, including feeding and veterinary bills.

Instructions

Discuss how these costs should be accounted for. Hint: review the basis for conclusion document for IAS 41.

9-5 In this chapter, flag icons identify areas where there are GAAP differences between IFRS requirements and national standards.

Instructions

Access the website(s) identified on the inside back cover of this book, and prepare a concise summary of the differences that are flagged throughout the chapter material.

Chapter 10

Property, Plant and Equipment: IAS 16

U.S. GAAP References
FAS 153 Exchanges of Non-monetary Assets
APB 29 Accounting for Non-monetary Transactions
FAS 146 Accounting for Costs Associated with Exit or Disposal Activities
FAS 144 Accounting for the Impairment or Disposal of Long-lived Assets
FAS 143 Accounting for Asset Retirement Obligations
FAS 34 Capitalization of Interest Cost

Related IFRSs
IAS 17 Leases
IAS 20 Accounting for Government Grants and Disclosure of Government Assistance
IAS 23 Borrowing Costs
IAS 36 Impairment of Assets
IAS 40 Investment Property
IFRS 2 Share-based Payment
IFRS 5 Non-current Assets Held for Sale and Discontinued Operations

OBJECTIVE AND SCOPE

To properly assess an entity's potential for future cash flows, users must have a solid understanding of its investment in long-term productive assets, the extent to which this investment has changed in the period, and the accounting policies applied. To this end, IAS 16 sets out requirements for the recognition and derecognition of property, plant and equipment assets; their measurement at and after recognition; and for financial statement disclosures.

    Property, plant and equipment are defined in IAS 16.6 as "tangible items that:

(a) are held for use in the production or supply of goods or services, for rental to others, or for administrative purposes; and

(b) are expected to be used during more than one period."

The standard does not apply to assets classified as held for sale, agricultural biological assets, or non-renewable natural resource rights and reserves. While IAS 40 is the specific accounting standard for investment property, it requires the IAS 16 cost model to be applied to investment property accounted for at cost.

RECOGNITION

A cost is recognized as an item of property, plant and equipment only if

1. it is **probable** that future economic benefits associated with the item will flow to the entity, and
2. the cost of the item can be measured **reliably** [IAS 16-7].

This general principle applies to costs as they are incurred, whether when acquiring or constructing the assets initially, or later when incurring costs to upgrade, replace, add to, or service items of property, plant and equipment. Although some costs, such as those for government-imposed pollution reduction equipment, may not appear to generate future economic benefits, these costs **are** recognized as items of plant and equipment. This is because they are needed in order to obtain economic benefits, or to increase the economic benefits from other assets.

    Costs incurred for ordinary servicing of property, plant and equipment are charged directly to profit or loss because these "repair and maintenance" type costs do not meet the definition of the asset, or the "future economic benefit" requirement of the recognition principle.

    An issue arises, however, when major repairs are carried out and parts of assets are replaced. The accounting principle in this situation is the same as for an original cost incurred: capitalize the replacement part if the definition and the two recognition criteria are met. If so, derecognize (i.e., remove from the asset account) the part that is replaced. The standards require that each part of an item of property, plant and equipment that is significant relative to the total cost of the item be depreciated separately. If the original part was not recognized as a separate asset when it was acquired, the estimated carrying amount left on the books representing the replaced part, adjusted for time and/or cost increases, must still be removed from the accounts. The cost of the replacement part may be used as a good indication of the original cost of the replaced part if it is not practicable to determine its carrying amount by other means.

Situation

Major inspections of each aircraft in Ajax Airlines' fleet are carried out every 12 to 18 months. This involves taking the plane out of service for a period and using a specialized maintenance crew to perform the inspection. Airplane X5 requires an inspection every 18 months, for a total cost of $100. How should the cost of the inspection be accounted for?

    Does the cost of the inspection meet the definition of property, plant and equipment? Is it probable that future economic benefits associated with the inspection will flow to the entity? Can the cost of the inspection be reliably measured?

Analysis

In this case, the inspection is an item related to the production or supply of goods or services, and it is expected to be used for more than one period. It is a cost that is required so economic benefits can be obtained from other assets, thereby meeting the first recognition criterion. The cost of the inspection can be reliably measured.

Therefore, the inspection cost of $100 is recognized as a **replacement** of an item of property, plant and equipment. The remaining actual or estimated carrying amount of the previous inspection is removed from the same asset category with a loss recognized to the extent of any undepreciated cost of the prior inspection that remains. Assuming the $80 cost of the previous inspection has been fully amortized, the entries are as follows:

Property, Plant and Equipment—Inspection Cost (new)	100	
Cash/Wages Payable		100
To recognize the new inspection asset.		
Accumulated Depreciation—Inspection Costs (old)	80	
Property, Plant and Equipment—Inspection Cost (old)		80
To derecognize the asset replaced.		

MEASUREMENT AT RECOGNITION

When an item meets the definition of a property, plant and equipment asset and qualifies for recognition, it is recognized at its cost. This requires

1. identifying what elements of cost are included, and
2. determining how cost is measured.

Cost Elements

The elements that are **included** in the cost of an item of property, plant and equipment include the following:

(a) The item's purchase price net of trade discounts and rebates, plus any non-refundable purchase taxes and duties.

(b) The expenditures directly attributable to bringing the asset to its required location and condition to operate as management intended. Directly attributable costs include employee costs needed to acquire or construct the asset; delivery and handling costs; site preparation, installation, and assembly costs; net material and labor costs incurred to ensure it is working properly; and professional fees.

(c) The estimate of the costs of the obligation associated with the asset's eventual disposition that arose from its acquisition. This includes, for example, costs of the asset's decommissioning and site restoration.

Once the asset is in place and ready to be used as intended, no further costs incurred to use the item or reorganize operations, or any initial operating losses, are included in its carrying amount. In addition, costs to open a new facility, introduce a new product or service, or operate in a new location, and administrative and general overhead type costs are specifically **excluded** as costs of property, plant and equipment assets.

The costs of self-constructed assets are determined by applying the same principles. Costs of abnormal amounts of material, labor, and other inputs are excluded from the assets' carrying amounts and are charged instead to profit or loss. IAS 23 sets out the accounting standards for recognizing interest costs as part of the cost of a self-constructed item of property, plant and equipment. In general, this standard indicates that borrowing costs that are directly attributed to the acquisition, construction, or production of an asset that requires a substantial time period to get ready for its intended use is part of the cost of that asset. Avoidable costs are permitted to be recognized, but only if they meet the specific recognition criteria identified above.

The costs of asset retirement obligations that arise from producing inventories during the period, rather than from the acquisition of the asset, are accounted for by applying IAS 2 *Inventories*.

IAS 20 *Accounting for Government Grants and Disclosure of Government Assistance* may also be relevant in determining an asset's cost. This standard indicates that the carrying amount of a property, plant and equipment item may be reduced by government grants.

Situation

Lili Corp. acquires new equipment at a cost of $100 plus 7% sales tax and 5% GST. (GST is a recoverable Canadian tax.) The company paid $10 to transport the equipment to its plant. The site where the equipment was to be placed was not yet ready and Lili Corp. spent another $5 for one month's storage costs. When installed, $3 of labor and $2 of materials were used to adjust and calibrate the machine to the company's exact specifications. The units produced in the trial runs were subsequently sold to employees for $4. During the first two months of production, the equipment was used only at 50% of its capacity. Labor costs of $30 and material costs of $20 were incurred in this production, while the units sold generated $55 of sales. Lili paid an engineering consulting firm $11 for its services in recommending the specific equipment to purchase and for help during the calibration phase. Borrowing costs of $1 were incurred because of the one month delay in installation. What is the cost of the equipment?

Analysis

The cost of the equipment includes the invoice cost ($100), sales tax ($7), transportation cost ($10), net direct costs of adjusting the equipment so it will work as intended ($3 + $2 − $4), and professional fees associated with the acquisition and installation ($11), for a total of $129.

The GST is excluded because it is recoverable. The $5 storage cost is not included in the cost of the equipment since it was not a required cost to bring the equipment to the location and to make it operational. The additional $30 labor and $20 material costs before the machine operated at full capacity are inventory production costs incurred after the equipment was in condition to operate as management intended and they, along with the sales of $55, are excluded. Lastly, the borrowing costs of $1 were not incurred to finance the acquisition or construction of a qualifying asset—one that requires a substantial period of time to get ready for its intended use.

Measurement of Cost

The second step in recognizing an asset's cost is to determine how cost is measured.

Cost is defined in IAS 16.6 as "the amount of cash or cash equivalents paid or the fair value of the other consideration given to acquire an asset at the time of its acquisition or construction or, where applicable, the amount attributed to that asset when initially recognized in accordance with the specific requirements of other IFRSs, e.g, IFRS 2 Share-based Payment."

Cost, therefore, is the cash cost that would have been exchanged when the asset is recognized. Any amount paid that represents interest after this date is expensed, unless it meets the criteria for capitalization as borrowing costs under IAS 23. What if the asset was acquired by giving up non-monetary assets instead of or in combination with monetary assets? When some portion of the consideration given is non-monetary, the cost of the property, plant and equipment asset acquired is measured as the fair value of the consideration given. This is consistent with the definition of "cost" provided above.

There is, however, an **exception** to using fair value as the cost of an asset in a non-monetary exchange. If the transaction lacks commercial substance, or if the fair value of neither the asset acquired nor of that given up can be reliably measured, the cost of the asset acquired is the **carrying amount** or book value of the asset(s) given in exchange. While the second reason for this exception is easily understood, what does it mean for a transaction to have, or to lack, commercial substance?

In general, an exchange transaction has *commercial substance* if it has an economic effect on the entity, i.e., if the future cash flows of the entity are changed in some way. Commercial substance exists if

(a) the amount, timing, and risk of the future cash flows of the asset received differ from those of the asset(s) transferred out; or

(b) the after-tax cash flows of the part of the business affected by the transaction (**entity specific value**) have changed as a result of the exchange; and

(c) the difference in (a) or (b) is significant relative to the fair values of the assets exchanged. [IAS 16.25]

MEASUREMENT AFTER RECOGNITION

After initial recognition, entities have a choice of models they can apply to account for their property, plant and equipment assets: the cost model or the revaluation model. A separate decision is made for each class of long-lived asset, so that an entity can use a different approach for different types of assets, but only one model within a specific class.

The following are examples of classes of property, plant and equipment assets:

- land   - land and buildings
- machinery   - ships
- office equipment   - aircraft
- motor vehicles   - furniture and fixtures

Cost Model

The cost model is by far the more commonly used method. This model states that property, plant and equipment assets are carried after acquisition at their cost less any accumulated depreciation and less any accumulated impairment losses.

Depreciation

Because many property, plant and equipment assets are made up of a variety of parts, the total cost recognized is allocated to the major component parts making up the whole. Consider a property made up of land and building, for example. The land is separable from the building and is usually not subject to depreciation. The building is made up of heating, cooling, electrical, and plumbing systems, as well as the basic structure, a roof, windows, and external siding, among other structural elements. The objective is to separate the larger asset into components so that each significant part can be depreciated separately using a depreciation method and useful life that is appropriate for that part.

Depreciation is usually recognized as an expense in profit or loss. However, the depreciation related to some assets may be charged to another asset as part of its cost. Consider the depreciation of factory equipment. It is an element of factory overhead that is added to work-in-process and finished goods inventory on the balance sheet. Similarly, the depreciation on heavy moveable equipment at a mine site may be capitalized as part of the development cost of the natural resource.

Depreciable Amount and Depreciation Period

IAS 16 reinforces the concept of depreciation being a method of cost allocation by requiring that the asset's depreciable amount be allocated over its useful life. Therefore, guidance is needed—and provided—on how to estimate the residual value needed to determine the depreciable amount, and what factors should be considered in determining useful life.

If the residual value of an asset is insignificant relative to its carrying amount, it is immaterial whether it is deducted or not in calculating the **depreciable amount** of the asset. However, many assets have residual values that are significant. *Residual value* is defined as "the estimated amount that an entity would currently obtain from disposal of the asset, after deducting the estimated costs of disposal, if the asset were already of the age and in the condition expected at the end of its useful life." [IAS 16.6]

The definition is very clear that it is **not** an asset's fair value in its **current** condition that is used. The standard also supports the concept that if the residual value, as defined, is greater than an asset's carrying amount, then no depreciation is warranted.

The **depreciation period** begins when the property, plant and equipment asset is in place and ready for use as intended by management; and depreciation continues as long as the asset is available for use. It ends when the asset is derecognized (removed from the accounts) or classified as held for sale (IFRS 5 *Non-current Assets Held for Sale and Discontinued Operations*), if earlier. Depreciation continues even if the asset is not used or is retired from active service.[1] This is justified on the basis that an asset's service potential is reduced by being held over time. Of course, no further charges are made once the asset is fully depreciated.

To calculate periodic depreciation, the estimated useful life of the asset needs to be determined. *Useful life* is defined as

(a) the period over which an asset is expected to be available for use by an entity, or

(b) the number of production or similar units expected to be obtained from the asset by an entity. [IAS 16.6]

Notice that the definition refers to the useful life **to the entity**, not to the asset's full economic life. A company may have a policy of turning over its fleet of sales vehicles every three years even though the automobiles have a longer economic life. Company policy limits the useful life of these assets to three years. Not all entities or all assets are governed by such policies, so other factors that zero in on the period of expected use will likely need to be considered. These include

- the capacity or physical output expected from the asset;
- physical wear and tear, including the effects of actual usage and maintenance policies on the asset's condition;
- obsolescence of the asset itself or changes in demand for the output of the asset; and
- contractual or other legal limits on the asset's use.

Depreciation Method

Because different types of property, plant and equipment deliver their benefits to an organization in different ways, IAS 16 requires that the depreciation method used reflect the pattern in which the economic benefits are expected to be consumed. Specific machinery may provide benefits based on use and physical wear and tear, while furniture and fixtures may deliver their benefits primarily as a function of time. Other assets such as automobiles may provide more benefits when new, with decreasing usefulness over time. Because of this, a variety of depreciation methods are permitted, but the choice is restricted to the method that best matches the estimated pattern in which the benefits are expected to be consumed.

The **straight-line** method, resulting in equal depreciation charges each period, is appropriate for the furniture and fixtures described above. The **declining balance** method, with high depreciation charges in the early years and reducing charges each period, is appropriate for the automobile that delivers benefits to the entity in the same pattern. The **units of production** approach results in depreciation amounts that correspond to benefits consumed as a function of use, such as the machinery example above.

The depreciation method chosen and applied to an item of property, plant and equipment must be reviewed at each fiscal year end at a minimum. If the pattern in which the future benefits will be consumed is expected to change, the depreciation method must be changed as well. This is considered a change in estimate and is accounted for on a **prospective basis**. This means that the remaining depreciable amount is allocated over the remaining depreciation period under the new appropriate method.

Revaluation Model

The other approach to accounting for property, plant and equipment assets is the **revaluation model**. Under this approach, the carrying amount of the property, plant and equipment asset is its **fair value at the date of the revaluation less any subsequent accumulated depreciation and subsequent accumulated impairment losses**.

---

[1] If an entity applies a usage method of depreciation and the asset has not been used in production in the period, IAS 16.55 indicates that it is acceptable to have $0 depreciation expense.

This model can be applied only to assets whose fair value can be reliably measured and revaluations must be carried out often enough that the carrying amount is not materially different from the assets' fair value at the balance sheet date. The frequency of revaluation depends on the specific assets. If values change rapidly, an annual revaluation may be appropriate. Other classes of asset may need to be remeasured only every three to five years. Fair values are usually market-based and often determined by appraisal.

The revaluation model is used by relatively few companies for their property, plant and equipment assets. It is included as an IFRS-allowed method mainly because it is particularly relevant in countries that experience **high rates of inflation**.

Accounting under the Revaluation Model

When an item of property, plant and equipment is revalued, its carrying amount will either increase or decrease. How is the change accounted for?

Asset carrying amount is <u>increased</u>	Asset carrying amount is <u>decreased</u>
Credit Revaluation Surplus, an equity account, unless the increase reverses a revaluation decrease previously recognized in profit or loss. If so, recognize the increase in profit or loss to the extent of the prior decrease.	Debit Revaluation Surplus, an equity account, to the extent of any credit balance associated with that asset. Any remaining amount is recognized in profit or loss.

The amounts debited or credited to the Revaluation Surplus account are reported in the statement of other comprehensive income. Note that over the life of the asset, this treatment does not permit any net revaluation increase to be recognized in profit or loss.

In adjusting the related asset accounts, there is a choice of how to account for the accumulated depreciation— either it is adjusted proportionately, or its balance is eliminated. The proportionate approach adjusts both the gross carrying amount of the asset and the accumulated amortization so that the net carrying amount is equal to the new valuation. The second approach eliminates the balance in the accumulated depreciation account against the asset's gross carrying amount. The asset itself is then adjusted to its new revalued amount. Let's look at an example.

Situation

On January 1, Year 1, ABC Co. acquires a building at a cost of $1,000. The building is expected to have a 25-year life and no residual value. The asset is accounted for under the revaluation model and revaluations are carried out every three years. On December 31, Year 3, the fair value of the building is appraised at $900, and on December 31, Year 6, its fair value is $750. Prepare the entries required on December 31, Year 3 and Year 6. (See pages 99–100 for the Analysis section for this Situation.)

Why would a company use the proportional method when the alternative method seems more straightforward? Two reasons have been suggested. First, many items of property, plant and equipment are revalued based on an index of specific prices. That is, the index is applied to both the asset and its accumulated amortization accounts, so the values for both are readily available. Second, the use of the proportional method provides additional information to the financial statement reader. Information about the relative age of the asset and assessments of when replacements are needed can be determined if both asset and accumulated depreciation amounts are maintained and reported. This is the reason why depreciation amounts are not credited directly to the asset account even under the cost method.

Analysis

Suggested approach:

December 31, Year 3

	Before Revaluation			Proportional after Revaluation
Building	$1,000	x	900/880	$1,023
Accumulated depreciation				
$1,000 /25 = $40/year for 3 years	(120)	x	900/880	(123)
Carrying amount	$ 880	x	900/880	$ 900

Revaluation amount is $900.
After-revaluation amounts = 900/880 of before-revaluation amounts

Entries, December 31, Year 3	
Proportional Method	**Gross Carrying Amount Method**

Building   23
   Accumulated Depreciation   3
   Revaluation Surplus (OCI)
     (900 − 880)   20
	Eliminate the accumulated depreciation:
	Accumulated Depreciation 120
	  Building 120
	[Building is now 1,000 − 120 = 880]
	
	Adjust building to revalued amount:
	Building (900 − 880) 20
	  Revaluation Surplus (OCI) 20

Balance Sheet Presentation, December 31, Year 3	

Building (1,000 + 23) $1,023
Accumulated depreciation
  (120 + 3)   (123)
         $ 900
	Building (1,000 − 120 + 20) $900
	Accumulated depreciation
	  (120 − 120) -0-
	         $900

Effective January 1, Year 4, the depreciation rate is adjusted to reflect the change in the depreciable amount. The $900 January 1, Year 4 carrying amount is now allocated over the remaining 25 − 3 = 22 years. The new rate, therefore, is $900/22 = $41 per year. Let's move ahead now to December 31, Year 6.

December 31, Year 6
(using the proportional method)

	Proportional before Revaluation			Proportional after Revaluation
Building	$1,023	x	750/777	$ 988
Accumulated depreciation				
$123 + ($41 x 3 = $123)	(246)	x	750/777	(238)
Carrying amount	$ 777	x	750/777	$ 750

Revaluation amount on December 31, Year 6 is $750.
After-revaluation amounts = 750/777 of before-revaluation amounts.

Under the alternative method, remember that the Accumulated Depreciation account was reduced to $0 at the end of Year 3. Its balance three years later on December 31, Year 6 therefore is 3 x $41 = $123, and the Building account under this method is still at the December 31, Year 3 revaluation amount of $900.

Entries, December 31, Year 6			
Proportional Method		**Gross Carrying Amount Method**	
Accumulated Depreciation		Eliminate the accumulated depreciation:	
(246 – 238)	8	Accumulated Depreciation	123
Revaluation Surplus (OCI)	20	Building	123
Profit or Loss Account		[Building is now 900 – 123 = 777]	
(777 – 750 – 20)	7		
Building (1,023 – 988)	35	Adjust building to revalued amount:	
		Revaluation Surplus (OCI)	20
		Profit or Loss Account	7
		Building (777 – 750)	27

Balance Sheet Presentation, December 31, Year 6			
Building (1,023 – 35)	$988	Building (900 – 123 – 27)	$750
Accumulated depreciation		Accumulated depreciation	
(246 – 8)	(238)	(3 x 41 = 123 – 123)	-0-
	$ 750		$750

Again, ABC Co. has to revise the depreciation rate going forward. The depreciable amount at the end of Year 6 is $750 and the depreciation period remaining is now 25 – 6 years = 19 years, resulting in a new annual rate of $39.

Disposition of the Revaluation Surplus Account

An entity may transfer amounts from the Revaluation Surplus directly to Retained Earnings as the asset is used. If this option is applied, the surplus transferred each period is the difference between the depreciation amount based on the revalued carrying amount and the depreciation based on the original cost.

Alternatively, the Revaluation Surplus could remain in equity until the asset is retired or disposed of. In this situation, it is transferred directly to Retained Earnings on derecognition, again without going through profit or loss.

To illustrate, assume on January 2, Year 4, ABC Co. sells the building referred to in the example above for $905.

Entries, January 2, Year 4			
Proportional Method		**Gross Carrying Amount Method**	
Cash	905	Cash	905
Accumulated Depreciation	123	Building	900
Building	1,023	Gain on Sale (P or L)	5
Gain on Sale (P or L)	5		
Revaluation Surplus (OCI)	20	Revaluation Surplus (OCI)	20
Retained Earnings	20	Retained Earnings	20

Impairment

IAS 36 *Impairment of Assets* sets out the accounting standards for the impairment of property, plant and equipment assets to ensure that such assets are not carried at more than their recoverable amount. Further discussion of impairment under both the cost and revaluation models is left to Chapter 16.

DERECOGNITION

When an item of property, plant and equipment is disposed of, or when no further economic benefits are expected to be received from its use or disposal, the carrying amount of the item is removed from the balance sheet: it is derecognized. At this time, a gain or loss is recognized and reported on the income statement. The gain or loss is the difference between the carrying amount of the asset—or part of an asset, if it is a replacement—and the net proceeds on disposal.

Any balance remaining in a Revaluation Surplus account related to a derecognized item under the revaluation model is transferred directly to Retained Earnings, not to profit or loss.

DISCLOSURE

A significant amount of disclosure is required about each class of property, plant and equipment assets:

(a) whether the cost or revaluation model is applied
(b) the depreciation methods used
(c) the depreciation rates or the assets' useful lives
(d) the opening and closing balances of the gross carrying amount and the total of the accumulated depreciation and accumulated impairment losses
(e) a complete reconciliation of the opening and ending carrying amount, including additions, disposals by type, changes due to revaluations, changes associated with impairment losses with details on how they were accounted for, depreciation, and foreign currency adjustments

For items carried at revalued amounts, entities are required to report the date of the revaluation, whether an independent valuation was performed, and the methods and valuation techniques used and assumptions made in estimating fair value. In addition, it is necessary to disclose the amount that would have been reported under the cost model, and details about the revaluation surplus and changes to it.

As shown in Illustration 10-1 the Switzerland-based Nestlé Group provides basic property, plant and equipment information on its December 31, 2007 balance sheet, accounting policy disclosures in an annex to its financial statements, and detailed supplementary disclosures in Note 11.[2] The Group's presentation currency is Swiss francs. It is interesting to note that Nestlé has not yet changed its policy to capitalize financing costs on self-constructed assets. This new standard was approved by the IASB in 2007 with prospective application required.

---

[2] http://www.nestle.com/Resource.axd?Id=24E5A5E2-93F8-43A3-956E-0F259448CB90.

Illustration 10-1
Nestlé Group
Property, Plant
and Equipment
Disclosures

Consolidated balance sheet as at 31 December 2007

before appropriations

In millions of CHF	Notes	2007	2006
Non-current assets			
Property, plant and equipment	11		
Gross value		49 474	47 077
Accumulated depreciation and impairment		(27 409)	(26 847)
		22 065	20 230

Annex

Accounting policies

Valuation methods and definitions

Property, plant and equipment

Property, plant and equipment are shown in the balance sheet at their historical cost. Depreciation is provided on components that have homogenous useful lives by using the straight-line method so as to depreciate the initial cost down to the residual value over the estimated useful lives. The residual values are 30% on head offices, 20% on distribution centres for products stored at ambient temperature and nil for all other asset types.

The useful lives are as follows:

Buildings	20–35 years
Machinery and equipment	10–20 years
Tools, furniture, information technology and sundry equipment	3–8 years
Vehicles	3–8 years

Land is not depreciated.

Useful lives, components and residual amounts are reviewed annually. Such a review takes into consideration the nature of the assets, their intended use and the evolution of the technology.

Depreciation of property, plant and equipment is allocated to the appropriate headings of expenses by function in the income statement.

Financing costs incurred during the course of construction are expensed. Premiums capitalized for leasehold land or buildings are amortised over the length of the lease.

11. Property, plant and equipment

In millions of CHF	Land and buildings	Machinery and equipment	Tools, furniture and other equipment	Vehicles	2007 Total
Gross value					
At 1 January	**13 245**	**25 455**	**7 446**	**931**	**47 077**
Currency retranslations	(156)	(478)	(171)	(86)	(891)
Capital expenditure	860	2 695	1 209	207	4 971
Disposals	(258)	(884)	(492)	(78)	(1 712)
Reclassified as held for sale	(30)	(38)	(3)	–	(71)
Modification of the scope of consolidation	90	51	3	(44)	100
At 31 December	**13 751**	**26 801**	**7 992**	**930**	**49 474**
Accumulated depreciation and impairments					
At 1 January	**(5 251)**	**(15 732)**	**(5 363)**	**(501)**	**(26 847)**
Currency retranslations	60	284	60	14	418
Depreciation	(398)	(1 307)	(800)	(115)	(2 620)
Impairments	(26)	(148)	(50)	(1)	(225)
Disposals	165	758	468	67	1 458
Reclassified as held for sale	22	30	3	–	55
Modification of the scope of consolidation	80	228	12	32	352
At 31 December	**(5 348)**	**(15 887)**	**(5 670)**	**(504)**	**(27 409)**
Net at 31 December	**8 403**	**10 914**	**2 322**	**426**	**22 065**

At 31 December 2007, property, plant and equipment include CHF 1178 million of assets under construction. Net property, plant and equipment held under finance leases amount to CHF 354 million. Net property, plant and equipment of CHF 117 million are pledged as security for financial liabilities. Fire risks, reasonably estimated, are insured in accordance with domestic requirements.

LOOKING AHEAD

While several of the IFRSs related to IAS 16 *Property, Plant and Equipment* are currently on the IASB's active agenda, the main requirements of IAS 16 are not expected to change in the foreseeable future. The IASB's fair value measurement project, expected to result in the convergence of international and U.S. GAAP, may affect the measurement guidance in this standard. An Exposure Draft (ED/2009/5) was issued in May 2009, with the publication of final guidance expected in 2010.

END-OF-CHAPTER PRACTICE

10-1 The following assets have been recognized as items of property, plant and equipment.
1. Head office boardroom table and executive chairs
2. A landfill site
3. Wooden pallets in a warehouse
4. Forklift vehicles in a manufacturing plant
5. Stand-alone training facility for pilot training, including a flight simulator and classrooms equipped with desks, whiteboards, and electronic instructional aids

Instructions

For each of the items listed
(a) Identify what specific costs are likely to be included in the acquisition cost.
(b) Explain whether any components of this asset should be given separate recognition, and why.
(c) Suggest what should be taken into consideration in determining each component's depreciable amount and depreciation period.
(d) Suggest and explain what depreciation method might be most appropriate for each component separately identified.
(e) Identify whether the periodic depreciation is recognized as an expense on the income statement, or whether another accounting treatment is more appropriate. Explain.

10-2 Vedat Corporation acquires new equipment with a list price of $100 to expand its product line. Vedat pays $50 of this cost on delivery and agrees to pay $25 of the remainder in one year's time and the final $25 in two years' time. The company extends a portion of its factory wall in order to fit the new machine in place and then rearranges existing equipment into a more efficient layout. The new equipment is dropped during installation, requiring repairs before it can be used. At the end of the equipment's useful life, Vedat Corporation is required to dismantle and dispose of it, paying a special environmental levy due to hazardous materials in its construction. Vedat is licensed to manufacture products with this equipment, and is required to pay a royalty for each unit produced.

Instructions

Discuss how the cost of the new equipment should be determined.

10-3 Teyal Limited has just finished the construction of its new head office building. At about the same time, one of Teyal's major suppliers, Layet Corporation, also moved into its new head office building. Layet Corporation did not construct its own building, but contracted it out in a fixed fee contract, and the total expenditures were approximately the same for both buildings.

Instructions

(a) Assume you are a co-op student in the accounting department of Teyal Limited. You are asked to write a short report on what the chief accountant needs to consider in accounting for the cost of the new building and its subsequent depreciation policy. Write the report.
(b) Assume you are a co-op student in the accounting department of Layet Corporation. If you were asked to write a report similar to the one required in part (a) above, identify in what respect it might differ, and why.

10-4 Resorts Ltd. has occupied its plant facility for 15 years, about one-third of its expected useful life. Although still very functional, numerous repairs have been required in recent months. The accounts indicate the original cost of the plant building was $500. The entire inside of the plant was painted at a cost of $2; the old wooden roof was replaced with a new one at a cost of $45; and part of the plumbing system was upgraded at a cost of $25 due to a change in the manufacturing process used. The plant was closed down while the roof was replaced, but overhead and administrative costs of $10 continued to be incurred even though production was at a standstill. The original roof had been identified as a separate component of the building when it was constructed with a cost of $30 and a useful life of 20 years. No separate records were kept of the original cost of the plumbing or painting.

Instructions

Prepare entries to record the recent repairs.

10-5 In this chapter, flag icons identify areas where there are GAAP differences between IFRS requirements and national standards.

Instructions

Access the website(s) identified on the inside back cover of this book, and prepare a concise summary of the differences that are flagged throughout the chapter material.

Chapter 11
Investment Property: IAS 40

U.S. GAAP References
FAS 153 Exchanges of Nonmonetary Assets
APB 29 Accounting for Nonmonetary Transactions
FAS 144 Accounting for the Impairment on Disposal of Long-lived Assets

Related IFRSs
IAS 2 Inventories
IAS 16 Property, Plant and Equipment
IAS 17 Leases
IAS 23 Borrowing Costs
IAS 36 Impairment of Assets
IFRS 5 Non-current Assets Held for Sale and Discontinued Operations

OBJECTIVE AND SCOPE

The objective of IAS 40 *Investment Property* is to set out the recognition, measurement, and disclosure requirements for this type of asset held by a reporting entity. The standard differentiates between **investment** property and items of property, plant, and equipment (**owner-occupied** property) addressed by IAS 16, and inventories of real estate properties under IAS 2, by defining *investment property* as:

"property (land or a building—or part of a building—or both) held (by the owner, or by a lessee under a finance lease) to earn rentals or for capital appreciation or both, rather than for:

(a) use in the production or supply of goods or services or for administrative purposes; or

(b) sale in the ordinary course of business."[1]

A distinguishing feature of investment property is that it **generates cash flows that are largely independent of the other assets** held by the entity. It is property that is under construction or being developed for future use as an investment property.

To qualify and be accounted for separately as an investment property when only **a portion of a property meets the above definition** and another part is owner-occupied, the investment portion must be able to be sold separately or leased out separately under a finance lease. If this is not possible, the entity classifies the investment property portion as an investment property only if the owner-occupied part is an insignificant portion of the total property.

When an entity **provides additional services** to the occupants of the property, it may be difficult to determine whether the property is an investment property under IAS 40 or an item of property, plant, and equipment under IAS 16. On one hand, a lessor may provide trash collection and general property maintenance services to lessees. These services are relatively minor in the total arrangement between the lessor and lessee, supporting the classification as an investment property. On the other hand, if an entity owns and manages a hotel providing innkeeper-type services to its clients, the services provided are so significant and fundamental to the arrangement that the property is, in reality, an owner-occupied property. Judgment is needed in many situations to determine the appropriate category of property, and entities are required to establish criteria so that judgment is exercised consistently.[2]

Although IAS 40 covers the measurement of a lessee's investment property interests classified as a finance lease and of a lessor's investment property under an operating lease, it leaves most other lease-related issues to IAS 17 *Leases*. Biological assets related to agricultural activity and mineral rights and reserves that are non-regenerative in nature are also **excluded** from the scope of IAS 40.

RECOGNITION

Investment property is **recognized** as an asset "when and only when

(a) it is **probable** that the future economic benefits that are associated with the investment property will flow to the entity, and

(b) the cost of the investment property can be **measured reliably**."[3]

Investment property costs—both those incurred initially and those incurred subsequently—are evaluated against this principle. Similar to the standards for property, plant, and equipment, the cost of a replacement component is recognized as an investment property asset and the carrying amount of the part replaced is removed.

A lessee that has a **property interest in an operating lease** that would otherwise meet the definition of an investment property may choose to recognize the lease as an investment property, and therefore, account for it like a finance lease. This can only be done, however, if the entity uses the fair value model (explained later in the chapter) to account for this and all other investment property. That is, "a lessee that uses the cost model for a property would not be permitted to recognize operating leases as assets."[4] The entity recognizes its **interest in the property** as the investment property, not the property itself.

---

[1] IASCF, IAS 40.5.

[2] IASCF, IAS 40.11-14.

[3] IASCF, IAS 40.16.

[4] IASCF, IAS 40 *Basis for Conclusions*, para. BC6. The classification choice is available on a property-by-property basis. That is, a lessee would have the choice of classifying some of its operating leases that would otherwise qualify as investment property as finance leases and others as operating leases.

MEASUREMENT AT RECOGNITION

An investment property is **measured initially at cost**, and the cost model in IAS 16 *Property, Plant and Equipment* is applied. This means that cost includes items directly attributable to the acquisition such as its purchase price, professional fees, transfer taxes, and other transaction costs. IAS 16 requirements are followed for an investment property acquired in a non-monetary exchange transaction, and interest charges resulting from delayed payment terms are expensed.

Leased investment property is measured according to IAS 17 *Leases* for a finance lease, with the cost of the property interest recognized at the lower of the fair value of the property and the present value of the minimum lease payments. The amount capitalized as the asset may differ from the amount recognized as the lease obligation. This happens when premiums paid for a lease, treated as a part of the minimum lease payments, are included in the asset cost but not in the obligation amount.

Situation

Nevine Corp. (NC) acquired a small 10-store shopping center outside a major city for $100 on June 2, 2008. On this date, nine of the stores were leased with remaining lease terms of two to four years. Costs and other information associated with this acquisition were the following:

Purchase price	$100
Costs to transfer property	5
Mortgage note payable assumed	73
Tenant deposits obligation assumed	14
Cost to paint empty store space	2
Legal fees for acquisition of property	3

Nevine Corp. classifies the acquired shopping center as an investment property. Determine the acquisition cost of the shopping center and prepare the journal entry to record the costs incurred.

Analysis

The investment property is measured at its cost—those costs directly attributable to its acquisition. This includes the $100 purchase price, the $5 transfer costs, and the $3 legal fees, for a total cost of $108. The cost to paint the empty store is a maintenance cost. The mortgage and the obligation for tenant deposits are both recognized as liabilities. Assuming the land acquired is approximately 25% of the value of the shopping center property, the entry to record these transactions is as follows:

Investment Property—Land ($108 × .25)	27	
Investment Property—Building ($108 × .75)	81	
Maintenance Expense	2	
Mortgage Note Payable		73
Tenant Deposits		14
Cash		23

To record acquisition of investment property.

MEASUREMENT AFTER RECOGNITION

After initial recognition and measurement, an entity is required to **measure all of its investment property under the fair value model (FVM) or all under the cost model (CM)**, with two exceptions:

1. As indicated in the Recognition section above, if a property interest under an operating lease is classified as an investment property (and therefore treated like a finance lease), it and all other investment property must be accounted for using the **fair value model**.

2. If an entity has investment property backing liabilities that pay a return linked directly to the fair value of or returns from specific assets including that investment property, this pool of properties is treated separately

from other investment properties. A decision about whether to use the cost model or fair value model is made **for the investment property in this pool and a separate decision is made for all other properties**.

An entity applies IAS 8 *Accounting Policies, Changes in Accounting Estimates and Errors* if it makes **a voluntary change** from one method to another. It is unlikely that a case can be made for a change from the fair value method to the cost method because it would be difficult to justify that the resulting information is more relevant.

We next look at how each of these models works.

Fair Value Model

Under **the fair value model**, the investment property assets are measured at fair value on the statement of financial position with changes in fair value recognized in profit or loss in the period of change. No depreciation is recorded.

Once a property has been measured at fair value, it continues to be measured at fair value until it is disposed of, becomes owner-occupied, or is developed for sale in the ordinary course of business. Fair values continue to be used while it is an investment property even if they become difficult to measure reliably.

Situation

Assume that Nevine Corp. (NC) introduced in the example above decides to apply the fair value model to all its investment property. NC has a May 31 year end and initially recognizes the property at its cost of $108 on June 2, 2008. The following fair values are determined:

Date	Fair Value
May 31, 2009	$ 105
May 31, 2010	$ 104
May 31, 2011	$ 110

You are asked to prepare the entries, if any, required at each year end. In addition, explain how the property would be reported if NC prepared a balance sheet shortly after acquisition in 2008.

Analysis

Because cost allocation and depreciation are not issues under the fair value model, it is likely that NC would not separate out the cost of the land from that of the building as indicated in the acquisition date journal entry above. Therefore, assume that the investment property is in an account entitled Investment Property—Shopping Center that is carried at $108 as of June 2, 2008.

On May 31, 2009 the property is written down to its fair value at that date of $105. On May 31, 2010 and 2011, the asset account is adjusted to $104 and $110 respectively. Changes in the fair values are recognized in profit or loss and the property is reported on the statement of financial position at its fair value at each balance sheet date. The following entries are made:

May 31, 2009	Loss in Value of Investment Property	3	
	Investment Property—Shopping Center		3
	To record loss in value of $108 − $105 = $3		
May 31, 2010	Loss in Value of Investment Property	1	
	Investment Property—Shopping Center		1
	To record loss in value of $105 − $104 = $1		
May 31, 2011	Investment Property—Shopping Center	6	
	Gain in Value of Investment Property		6
	To record appreciation in value of $110 − $104 = $6		

The cost of the investment property on June 2, 2008, as determined above, is $108. If a balance sheet were prepared shortly after that date, for example on June 5, 2008, what amount would be reported under the fair value model? Because fair value does not include transaction costs, the fair value would exclude the legal ($3) and transfer ($5) fees added into the cost of the asset. Its fair value at that time is $100 and a loss of $108 − $100 = $8 is recognized. At May 31, 2009 a gain of $105 − $100 = $5 is reported instead of a $3 loss.

Fair Value?

IAS 40 contains substantial guidance on what fair value means:

- **Fair value** is the price at which the property could be exchanged between knowledgeable, willing parties in an arm's-length transaction. It excludes any adjustments made to compensate for unusual arrangements, considerations, or concessions, and no deduction is made for transaction costs that may be incurred on disposal.[5]
- Fair value is a time-specific concept that reflects market conditions at the balance sheet date.
- The best evidence of fair value is provided by current prices in an **active market** for **similar property** in the **same location and condition** and subject to similar lease and other contracts.[6]
- If the best evidence is not available, fair value is based on adjustments made to other evidence such as different properties in an active market, or similar properties in less active markets, or on discounted cash flows using reliable estimates of future cash flows and other market-related external evidence.
- Fair value excludes synergies between the property and other investment properties or other company-specific rights or restrictions.

Inability to Determine Fair Value Reliably

IAS 40 requires entities to disclose fair values whether the FVM or CM is chosen. This presumes that the fair value of all investment properties can be reliably determined on a continuing basis. When an investment property is first acquired, there may be **exceptional** circumstances that indicate that the property's fair value will not be able to be measured reliably on a continuing basis. In this situation, the entity applies the cost model in IAS 16 to that specific property until its disposal. A residual value of zero is assumed for depreciation purposes.

If an entity cannot reliably determine the fair value of an investment property under construction, it may use cost as a proxy for fair value until construction is completed, at the latest.

Cost Model

After initial recognition and measurement, an entity that chooses **the cost model** applies the cost model set out in IAS 16 *Property, Plant and Equipment* and described in Chapter 10 of this text. That is, the investment property is reported on the statement of financial position at its cost less any accumulated depreciation and less any accumulated impairment losses. If the property meets the criteria to be classified as held for sale, the property is measured according to the requirements of IFRS 5 *Non-current Assets Held for Sale and Discontinued Operations*.

Situation

The Nevine Corp. (NC) shopping center acquisition set out in the Measurement at Recognition section above is used again, but now with the assumption that at acquisition, NC decides to apply the cost model to all its investment properties. NC expects the shopping center to have a 35-year useful life and a residual value of $11.

The fair values of the shopping center at the end of the next three years are the same as above: $105 at May 31, 2009; $104 at May 31, 2010; and $110 at May 31, 2011.

[5] IASCF, IAS 40.36-37.
[6] IASCF, IAS 40.45.

What entries, if any, are required each year, and how will the investment property be reported on each year-end statement of financial position?

Analysis

The cost model in IAS 16 requires the asset to be depreciated over its useful life using a method that corresponds to how NC receives the economic benefits the asset offers. For simplicity in this example, assume the straight-line method. The annual depreciation is calculated as follows:

Asset	Cost	Residual Value	Depreciable Amount	Useful Life	Annual Depreciation
Shopping center	$81	$11	$70	35 years	$2

Each May 31 the following entry is made to recognize depreciation:

Depreciation Expense	2	
Accumulated Depreciation—Shopping Center		2

Statement of Financial Position	May 31, 2009	May 31, 2010	May 31, 2011
Assets			
Investment Property:			
Shopping Center			
Land, at cost	$ 27	$ 27	$ 27
Building, at cost less			
accumulated depreciation	<u>79</u>	<u>77</u>	<u>75</u>
	$106	$104	$102

As can be seen from a comparison of the Nevine Corp. example under the FVM and the CM, there can be significant differences on the statement of financial position and in the amount of profit or loss reported. Anyone using financial ratios that involve total assets and/or the profit or loss has to be aware of the accounting policy choice and how this might affect the ratios.

The findings of a recent study carried out by KPMG IFRG Limited and Prof. Dr. Isabel von Keitz found that 42% of the companies applied the FVM and 58% used the cost model for investment properties. All of the Hong Kong companies in the sample used the FVM (about one-third of all the companies using the fair value model), perhaps because prior to applying IFRSs in 2005, Hong Kong GAAP required fair values to be used unless an underlying lease had 20 years or less to run.[7]

TRANSFERS

A change in use of an investment property results in a change in classification and in the IFRS that governs the accounting. IAS 40 sets out the specific requirements for changes in use of non-investment property to the investment property classification and for the reverse situations. The following table summarizes the effects of these changes.

---

[7] Prof. Dr. Isabel von Keitz and KPMG IFRG Limited, *The Application of IFRS: Choices in Practice* (December 2006), pp. 13–14.

Change in Use	Situation	Accounting
From investment property (FVM) to owner-occupied property or to inventory	Owner occupies the property or begins to develop it for sale	Deemed cost in IAS 16 or IAS 2 is FV at the date of change in use
From owner-occupied property in IAS 16 to investment property (FVM) in IAS 40	End of owner-occupation	Depreciate to the date of change; the difference between carrying amount and FV is accounted for according to the revaluation model in IAS 16
From inventory in IAS 2 to investment property (FVM) in IAS 40	Owner enters into an operating lease with a third party	Difference between IAS 2 carrying amount and IAS 40 FV is recognized in profit or loss
In progress investment property (CM) in IAS 40 to investment property (FVM) in IAS 40	Owners finish construction or development	Difference between carrying amount and FV is recognized in profit or loss

The accounting requirements are rational solutions that are internally consistent with the IFRSs involved.

DERECOGNITION

Investment property is **derecognized**, i.e., removed from the statement of financial position,

- on disposal—when sold or transferred under a finance lease, or
- on retirement—when permanently removed from use and no benefits are expected from its disposal.

When the CM is applied, the cost of a replacement is governed by IAS 16, which is discussed in Chapter 10. In summary, the carrying amount of the replaced part is removed from the accounts and the replacement part is added to the investment property's carrying amount.

If the FVM has been used and a part is replaced, the fair value of the replaced part, if known, is removed from the property's fair value. Alternatively, the cost of the replacement is added to the carrying amount of the property and then the fair value of the investment property as a whole is reassessed and adjusted.

Gains and losses on the disposal or retirement of investment properties are generally recognized in profit or loss. The gain or loss is the difference between the property's carrying amount and the net proceeds on disposal. IAS 17 *Leases* governs the recognition of gains and losses in sale and leaseback situations.

DISCLOSURES

IAS 40 requires a significant amount of general information to be disclosed for investment properties, with additional specific requirements for both the fair value and cost model properties. The IFRSs related to IAS 40 that are identified at the beginning of this chapter may also require additional disclosures. The list below is a summary of the major information required.

General Disclosures

- whether the FVM or the CM is applied
- if the FVM is applied, whether and when any operating leases are classified as investment property

- the criteria used to distinguish between owner-occupied property, investment property, and property held for sale where judgment is needed
- the methods and assumptions underlying fair value measurements, including the extent to which market-related evidence is used
- the extent to which the fair values were determined by an experienced, professional, and independent valuer
- the existence of restrictions and contractual obligations related to the properties
- amounts and specific types of income and expense recognized in profit or loss

Specific Disclosures

The following additional disclosures are specific to the type of measurement model chosen.

Fair Value Model	Cost Model
• A reconciliation between the carrying amounts at the beginning of the period and the end of the period, separately indicating the following:	
(a) additions from acquisitions and from subsequent expenditures and from business acquisitions	(a) additions from acquisitions and from subsequent expenditures and from business acquisitions
(b) assets classified as held for sale (see IFRS 5) and other disposals	(b) assets classified as held for sale (see IFRS 5) and other disposals
(c) foreign exchange effects on translation	(c) foreign exchange effects on translation
(d) transfers to and from inventories and owner-occupied property	(d) transfers to and from inventories and owner-occupied property
(e) net gains/losses from FV adjustments	(e) depreciation, and information about impairment losses
(f) other changes	(f) other changes
• A reconciliation between the valuation received and the adjusted valuation used on the financial statements, with details	• The depreciation methods used, and the useful lives or depreciation rates used
• If property is measured using the cost model because of an inability to reliably measure FV, additional descriptions and explanations	• The gross carrying amount and the accumulated depreciation at the beginning and end of the period
	• The fair value of investment property, or if unable to determine reliably, additional descriptions and explanations

Illustration 11-1 from Sponda Plc's financial statements for its year ended December 31, 2007 illustrates some of these requirements. Sponda Plc, headquartered in Helsinki, Finland, is a leading real estate investment company that owns, leases, and develops office, retail, and logistics properties in major cities in Finland and Russia.[8] The company's reporting currency is euros and amounts are reported on the financial statements in millions of euros. It is particularly interesting reading about how its fair values are determined.

---

[8] http://www.sponda.fi/www/In_english/Investors/Annual_reports.iw3

Illustration 11-1
Sponda Plc
Investment
Property Excerpts

Consolidated balance sheet (IFRS)

M€	Note	31 Dec. 2007	31 Dec. 2006
ASSETS			
Non-current assets			
Investment properties	14, 35	2,534.9	2,455.1

Consolidated income statement (IFRS)

M€	Note	1 Jan – 31 Dec. 2007	1 Jan – 31 Dec. 2006
Total revenue	1, 2, 3		
Rental income and service charges	4	193.4	115.4
Profit/loss on sale of investment properties	6	1.2	-
Valuation gains and losses		92.9	26.2

Accounting policies for the consolidated financial statements

Investment Properties

Investment properties are properties held by the company for the purpose of earning rental income or for capital appreciation, or both. Sponda measures its investment properties using the fair value method, as stated in IAS 40, *Investment Property*, under which the profit or loss from changes in fair values is recognized through profit and loss in the period in which it is incurred.

Investment properties are valued initially at acquisition cost, including transaction costs. The acquisition cost for investment properties that Sponda has completed comprises the construction and other costs incurred by the date of completion. In measurements after the initial recognition, the fair value is used. The fair value is the sum of money for which the property could change hands between parties who know the business, wish to carry out the transaction and are independent of each other. If a reliable market price is not available, the value can be determined using discounted cash flows.

The fair value of completed business properties is calculated by Sponda itself using the discounted cash flows method (DCF). Cash flows are calculated over a period of at least 10 years. Net cash flows in the period and the terminal value are discounted from the end of each accounting year to the assessment date. The terminal value is calculated by capitalizing the net cash flow of the year following the most recent accounting year with the required yield (Gordon growth model). The discount rate is determined by adding the expected long-term rate of inflation to the required yield. The yield is based on Sponda's own assessment of the market situation and on information from published sources including KTI Finland (Institute for Real Estate Economics).

Potential gross income is based on current lease contracts and, in the case of vacant premises, on estimated market rent levels. Potential gross income per property is adjusted annually by the estimated long-term vacancy rate taking into account any special aspects related to the property itself and the status of the lease contract. The estimated impact of inflation is calculated on maintenance expenses and on market and contract leases. Most of Sponda's lease contracts are linked to the cost-of-living index.

The value of non-developed sites and unused but usable building rights is determined using the sales price method.

Sponda's internal property assessment process, calculation methods and reporting are audited by an external valuer and are considered to fulfil the valuation criteria of the IFRSs and IVS (International Valuation Standards) as well as the AKA (Finnish authorized real estate auditors) criteria for good property valuation practice. In addition to auditing, Sponda also commissions at least once a year an external valuer to examine the material used in calculating the market value of the property portfolio, in order to confirm that the parameters and values used are based on market indications.

An investment property is derecognized from the balance sheet when it is divested or taken permanently out of use. Gains and losses on sales of investment properties are presented as a separate item in the income statement.

Notes to the consolidated financial statements

14. Investment properties

M€	2007	2006
Fair value of investment properties 1 Jan.	2,455.1	1,259.7
Kapiteeli acquisition	–	1,070.0
Acquisition of investment properties	115.1	94.3
Other capital expenditure on investment properties	138.9	43.3
Disposals of investment properties	−277.0	−37.7
Reclassifications to/from property, plant and equipment	4.2	−1.5
Reclassifications from trading properties	7.6	–
Other transfers	−1.9	0.8
Valuation gains and losses	92.9	26.2
Fair value of investment properties 31 Dec.	**2,534.9**	**2,455.1**

Investment properties are properties held by the company for the purpose of earning rental revenue or for capital appreciation. Sponda has chosen the fair value method to measure its investment properties, recognizing changes in their fair values in the income statement. The value of the properties is calculated by the company. Sponda's property portfolio was assessed in the final quarter by Catella Property Oy.

LOOKING AHEAD

There are no significant investment property issues on the IASB's agenda as this book goes to print. Because of the close relationship with some of the related IFRS, however, such as IAS 17 *Leases*, some change will likely occur. Please refer to the Looking Ahead feature at the end of each relevant chapter to determine the timing of expected changes in the related IFRS. In addition, the IASB's fair value measurement project, expected to result in the convergence of international and U.S. GAAP, may affect the measurement guidance in this standard. An Exposure Draft (ED/2009/5) was issued in May 2009, with the publication of final guidance expected in 2010.

END-OF-CHAPTER PRACTICE

11-1 IAS 16 *Property, Plant and Equipment* and IAS 40 *Investment Property* both provide a choice between using cost-based or fair value accounting.

Instructions

Prepare a comparison of the fair value model of IAS 40 and the revaluation model of IAS 16.

11-2 Saan Corp. (SC) is engaged in a variety of business ventures, including the following:
1. SC leases out the bottom two floors of its 10-floor office building under an operating lease. Within five years, SC expects to have grown to such an extent that it will need that space and will no longer rent it out.
2. Although SC is not a manufacturer, the company owns two manufacturing plants in a growing industrial park. SC signed a contract last year with a local food processing company to rent one of the plants under a five-year operating lease. SC maintains the outside of the building, the landscaping, and the parking lot. The other plant is not rented yet, but SC is actively searching for a tenant.
3. SC owns eight exclusive resorts across the country that are managed by a well-known hotel management company. The management company directs all day-to-day operations including advertising, food, maid and ancillary services, and routine maintenance. SC is responsible for all capital investment decisions related to the resorts and their financing. The management company guarantees SC a minimum fixed return each year, as well as 15% of its operating profit.

Instructions

Indicate whether the ventures described in (1) to (3) above are investment properties, and provide an explanation for your answer.

11-3 Cycol Inc. (CI) purchased a rental property as an investment in early January 2008 for $100. Legal costs to transfer title to the land and building were $2. A review of municipal records indicates that the property was appraised at a total of $75—$50 for the building and $25 for the land. The building is expected to have a useful life of 25 years and a residual value of $10, although the land value is expected to double every 10 years. In valuing the property, CI determines that the roof's fair value in its present condition is $8 and it will have to be replaced in another 8 years.

The rental property is appraised at the end of each December 31 fiscal period and the fair values of the property as a whole are determined to be $104, $110, and $111 respectively at December 31, 2008, 2009, and 2010.

Instructions
- (a) Assume CI applies the cost model in accounting for its investment property. Prepare all journal entries necessary to account for the acquisition of the property in 2008 and any adjusting entries required at December 31, 2008, 2009, and 2010.
- (b) Continuing with the assumption in part (a), prepare the entry required in January 2015 when the roof is replaced at a cost of $13.
- (c) Assume CI applies the fair value model in accounting for its investment property. Prepare all journal entries necessary to account for the acquisition of the property in 2008 and any adjusting entries required at December 31, 2008, 2009, and 2010.

(d) Continuing with the assumption in part (c), what entry would be required in January 2015 when the roof is replaced at a cost of $13? Comment on any choices that are available.

(e) Compare the amounts reported on CI's statement of financial position at December 31, 2008, 2009, and 2010 and the amounts and type of income and expenses reported on the income statements for each year under parts (a) and (c).

11-4 In this chapter, flag icons identify areas where there are GAAP differences between IFRS requirements and national standards.

Instructions

Access the websites(s) identified on the inside back cover of this book, and prepare a concise summary of the differences that are flagged throughout the chapter material.

Chapter 12

Exploration for and Evaluation of Mineral Resources: IFRS 6

U.S. GAAP References
FAS 144 Accounting for the Impairment or Disposal of Long-lived Assets
FAS 69 Disclosures about Oil and Gas Producing Activities
FAS 25 Amendment of FASB Statement No. 19
FAS 19 Financial Accounting by Oil and Gas Producing Companies

Related IFRS
IAS 8 Accounting Policies, Changes in Accounting Estimates and Errors
IAS 16 Property, Plant and Equipment
IAS 36 Impairment of Assets
IAS 37 Provisions, Contingent Liabilities and Contingent Assets
IAS 38 Intangible Assets

OBJECTIVE AND SCOPE

The objective of IFRS 6 is limited to setting out the financial reporting requirements for the exploration for and evaluation of mineral resources, two activities that are excluded from IAS 38 *Intangible Assets* and IAS 16 *Property, Plant and Equipment*.

The *exploration for and evaluation of mineral resources* is defined in Appendix A of IFRS 6 as the following:

The search for mineral resources, including minerals, oil, natural gas and similar non-regenerative resources after the entity has obtained legal rights to explore in a specific area, as well as the determination of the technical feasibility and commercial viability of extracting the mineral resource.

The only expenditures covered by the standard, therefore, are those incurred after exploration begins and before the technical feasibility and commercial viability of the resource are demonstrated.

IFRS 6 was issued as an interim measure until the major project on extractive activities that the IASB is currently working on is completed. This project is expected to take a number of years. The standard allows entities to continue with policies they applied before adopting IFRS, without specifically considering whether the policies comply with the IFRS *Framework*. In addition, IFRS 6 sets out requirements for impairment testing and disclosures to help financial statement users understand the cash flow implications of the exploration and evaluation assets recognized.

RECOGNITION AND MEASUREMENT OF EXPLORATION AND EVALUATION ASSETS

Recognition

The *Basis for Conclusions* document that accompanies IFRS 6 acknowledges that companies engaged in the exploration and evaluation of mineral resources follow a variety of accounting policies, from expensing all related costs to fully capitalizing the costs as assets. Rather than prescribe one treatment that may or may not be overturned when the current comprehensive project on extractive industries is finished, the standard allows entities to continue with their existing policies for the recognition and measurement of exploration and evaluation assets, provided the resulting information is relevant and reliable. IFRS 6 exempts them from the requirement of ensuring their policy is consistent with the *Framework*.[1]

This results in **exploration and evaluation assets** being defined in terms of the specific policy chosen by each entity.

Measurement at Recognition

At initial recognition and according to the policy adopted by the entity, exploration and evaluation assets are measured **at cost**.

Elements of Cost

Entities have to determine which costs are classified as exploration and evaluation expenditures; however, they are guided by the requirement that the expenditures must be incurred **before the technical feasibility and commercial viability of extracting the mineral resource are demonstrated**. After this point, the expenditures are development costs and are covered by IAS 38 *Intangible Assets*.

Examples of costs that may be capitalized as exploration and evaluation assets are provided in IFRS 6, with a clear indication that some entities **may not include** them and that other expenditures **may be included**. Some of the examples provided are the costs to acquire exploration rights, the costs of geological studies, of exploratory drilling, of sampling, and of evaluating the technical and commercial aspects of extraction. Obligations incurred for the restoration of the site as a result of exploration and evaluation activities are also recognized.

---

[1] Specifically, entities must comply with IAS 8.10 in their choice of policy, but not necessarily with IAS 8.11 and 8.12.

IFRS 6 does not specify whether administrative and overhead costs directly related to exploration and evaluation activities may be capitalized as exploration and evaluation assets.[2]

Classification of Exploration and Evaluation Assets and Measurement after Recognition

Exploration and evaluation assets are classified and measured after recognition as shown in Illustration 12-1.

Illustration 12-1
Classification and
Measurement
Standards

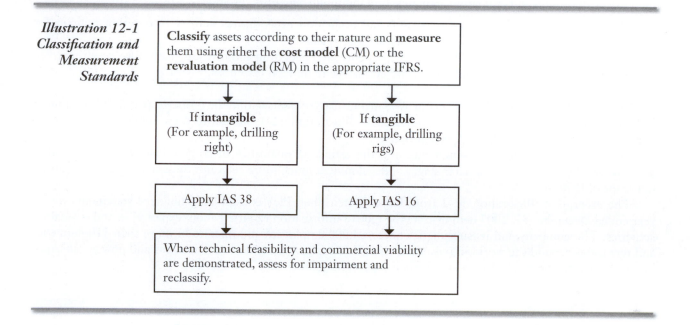

Classify assets according to their nature and **measure** them using either the **cost model** (CM) or the **revaluation model** (RM) in the appropriate IFRS.

If **intangible** (For example, drilling right)

If **tangible** (For example, drilling rigs)

Apply IAS 38

Apply IAS 16

When technical feasibility and commercial viability are demonstrated, assess for impairment and reclassify.

IMPAIRMENT

With exploration and evaluation assets, no impairment testing must be carried out until facts and circumstances suggest that their carrying amount may be more than their recoverable amount. Examples of situations that might suggest impairment include the following:

(a) The right to explore expires and is not expected to be renewed.
(b) No other substantial expenditures are planned for exploration or evaluation in the area.
(c) The entity decides to stop exploration and evaluation activities because viable quantities have not been found in the area.
(d) Although development is likely, the costs capitalized as exploration and evaluation assets exceed the amounts that are likely to be recovered.[3]

An impairment test is performed under IAS 36 *Impairment of Assets* if these or other factors suggest the assets may be impaired. The cash-generating unit used in assessing impairment cannot be larger than an **operating segment,** as defined in IFRS 8 *Operating Segments*.

---

[2] The *Basis for Conclusions* document indicates that there is an inconsistency in how these costs are accounted for under IAS 2 *Inventories*, IAS 38 *Intangible Assets*, and IAS 16 *Property, Plant and Equipment*. The IASB agreed that IFRS 6 was not the appropriate standard to resolve this issue.
[3] IASCF, IRFS 6.20.

Impairment losses are recognized as **an expense**. Like most asset impairments, these losses may be reversed.[4] Chapter 16, Impairment of Assets: IAS 36, covers impairment losses and their reversal in more detail.

DISCLOSURE

IFRS 6 identifies the underlying principle that entities should follow in disclosing information about their exploration and evaluation activities, rather than lists numerous specific disclosures. The principle is to provide information that **identifies and explains the amounts recognized** in the financial statements that result from an entity's exploration and evaluation activities. At a minimum, an entity discloses

(a) its accounting policies for exploration and evaluation expenditures and its recognition policies for capitalization as exploration and evaluation assets; and

(b) the amount of assets, liabilities, income, expense, and operating and investing cash flows resulting from activities related to the exploration and evaluation of mineral resources.[5]

Exploration and evaluation assets are set out as a separate class of assets within the property, plant, and equipment and intangible asset classifications. As indicated in Illustration 12-1, an entity then applies the disclosure requirements of IAS 16 and IAS 38, as appropriate.

Although users of financial statements find the estimated quantities of commercial reserves and other information about these assets at later stages of development much more relevant, these disclosures are outside the scope of IFRS 6.

The excerpts in Illustration 12-2 from Royal Dutch Shell Plc's consolidated financial statements for its year ended December 31, 2007 demonstrate the type of information reported about exploration and evaluation activities. The company and its subsidiaries have 104,000 employees and operate in more than 110 countries and territories around the world in businesses related to exploration and production, gas and power, oil sands, oil products, and chemicals. Royal Dutch Shell reports in millions of U.S. dollars.[6]

Illustration 12-2
Excerpts from
Royal Dutch
Shell's Financial
Statements

Notes to the Consolidated Financial Statements

2

ACCOUNTING POLICIES

PROPERTY, PLANT AND EQUIPMENT AND INTANGIBLE ASSETS

EXPLORATION COSTS

Shell follows the successful efforts method of accounting for oil and natural gas exploration costs. Exploration costs are charged to income when incurred, except that exploratory drilling costs are included in property, plant and equipment, pending determination of proved reserves. Exploration wells that are more than 12 months old are expensed unless (a) proved reserves are booked, or (b) (i) they have found commercially producible quantities of reserves, and (ii) they are subject to further exploration or appraisal activity in that either drilling of additional exploratory wells is under way or firmly planned for the near future or other activities are being undertaken to sufficiently progress the assessing of reserves and the economic and operating viability of the project.

---

[4] See IAS 36.109 to 36.123 for the specific requirements.

[5] IASCF, IFRS 6.23 and 24.

[6] http://www.static.shell.com/static/investor/downloads/financial_information/reports/2007/2007_annual_report.pdf

3

KEY ACCOUNTING ESTIMATES AND JUDGMENTS

EXPLORATION COSTS

Capitalized exploration drilling costs more than 12 months old are expensed unless (a) proved reserves are booked, or (b) (i) they have found commercially producible quantities of reserves and (ii) they are subject to further exploration or appraisal activity in that either drilling of additional exploratory wells is under way or firmly planned for the near future or other activities are being undertaken to sufficiently progress the assessing of reserves and the economic and operating viability of the project. In making decisions about whether to continue to capitalise exploration drilling costs for a period longer than 12 months, it is necessary to make judgments about the satisfaction of each of these conditions. If there is a change in one of these judgments in a subsequent period, then the related capitalized exploration drilling costs would be expensed in that period, resulting in a charge to income. Information on such costs is given in Note 12.

12

PROPERTY, PLANT AND EQUIPMENT

Exploration and evaluation assets, which mainly comprise unproved properties (rights and concessions) and capitalized exploration drilling costs, included within the amounts shown above for oil and gas properties are as follows:

		$ million
	2007	2006
Cost		
At January 1	8,963	4,386
Capital expenditure	2,947	4,649
Sales, retirements, currency translation differences and other movements	(430)	(72)
At December 31	11,480	8,963
Depreciation, depletion and amortization		
At January 1	1,633	1,439
Charge for the year	97	164
Sales, retirements, currency translation differences and other movements	(52)	30
At December 31	1,678	1,633
Net book amount at December 31	9,802	7,330

Capitalised exploration drilling costs are as follows:

CAPITALISED EXPLORATION DRILLING COSTS		$ million
	2007	2006
At January 1	1,708	832
Capital expenditure (additions pending determination of proved reserves)	1,606	1,182

Amounts charged to expense	(222)	(72)
Reclassifications to productive wells on determination of proved reserves	(593)	(228)
Other movements, including acquisitions, disposals and currency translation differences	1	(6)
At December 31	2,500	1,708

There were $1,044 million exploration drilling costs at December 31, 2007, capitalized for periods greater than one year, representing 136 wells. Information by year of expenditure is as follows:

	$ million	Number of wells
2000	21	1
2001	20	2
2002	66	6
2003	84	5
2004	100	8
2005	206	15
2006	547	99
Total	1,044	136

These costs remain capitalized for more than one year because, for the related projects, either (a) firm exploration/exploratory appraisal wells were executed in 2007 and/or are planned in the near future, and/or (b) firm development activities are being progressed with a final investment decision expected in the near future.

LOOKING AHEAD

The IASB has begun a comprehensive research project as the first step in developing an approach to resolving accounting issues unique to the upstream extractive activities undertaken by companies in the mining and oil and gas industries. Upstream extractive activities are much broader than the exploration and evaluation activities covered by IFRS 6. They include the search for, finding, and extraction of mineral and oil and gas reserves and resources. The project is concerned with the definition, recognition, measurement, and disclosure issues associated with all of these processes.

The IASB expects to publish a Discussion Paper (DP) containing the views of the project team in the second half of 2009, with a decision whether to add the project to its agenda coming about a year later.

This significant undertaking is a "modified joint" project with the FASB. The FASB will issue an Invitation to Comment containing the DP after the IASB releases it. Once it receives feedback on the document, the FASB will decide whether to add this issue to its agenda as a joint project. With these timelines, a replacement for IFRS 6 is not expected in the near future.[7]

---

[7] IASCF, IASB Extractive Activities Research Project Report, November 27, 2008, paras. 1 to 12.

END-OF-CHAPTER PRACTICE

12-1 In IFRS 6, paragraphs 6 and 7 make up a section entitled "Temporary exemption from IAS 8 paragraphs 11 and 12."

Instructions
 (a) Locate IAS 8 and read paragraphs 11 and 12. What do these paragraphs require?
 (b) Briefly explain the effect of the temporary exemption from these paragraphs on entities applying IFRS 6.

12-2 In North America, oil and gas exploration and development companies may choose either the successful efforts or the full cost method to account for their exploration and evaluation expenditures and assets.

Instructions
Write a short report suitable for presentation to your class that identifies how a company's financial statements will differ if it chooses a full cost accounting policy, instead of one that is based on successful efforts, for its exploration and evaluation activities. Identify what types of financial ratios will be affected by this choice.

12-3 In this chapter, flag icons identify areas where there are GAAP differences between IFRS requirements and national standards.

Instructions
Access the website(s) identified on the inside back cover of this book, and prepare a concise summary of the differences that are flagged throughout the chapter material.

Chapter 13

Borrowing Costs:
IAS 23

U.S. GAAP Reference
FAS 34 Capitalization of Interest Cost

Related IFRSs
IAS 2 Inventories
IAS 16 Property, Plant and Equipment
IAS 38 Intangible Assets
IAS 40 Investment Property

OBJECTIVE AND SCOPE

IAS 23 *Borrowing Costs* sets out the requirements for capitalizing financing costs related to the acquisition, construction, or production of a qualifying asset. The standard is based on the principle that the cost of an asset should include all costs incurred that are necessary to get it ready for its intended use.

Borrowing costs are defined as "interest and other costs that an entity incurs in connection with the borrowing of funds"; the cost of equity financing is specifically excluded.[1] Examples of borrowing costs include interest expense that results from applying the effective interest method (see IAS 39 *Financial Instruments: Recognition and Measurement*); finance charges on finance leases; and exchange adjustments on foreign currency borrowings to the extent they are viewed as interest cost adjustments.

Qualifying assets, assets that require substantial time to get ready for their intended use or sale, may be inventory; property, plant and equipment; intangible assets; or investment property. Qualifying assets that are measured at fair value and inventories that are produced in large quantities on a repetitive basis may, but are not required to, apply IAS 23.[2]

---

[1] IASCF, IAS 23.3 and 23.5. Dividends on preferred equity capital that is classified as a liability would qualify as a borrowing cost.
[2] IASCF, IAS 23.4, 23.5, and 23.7. For assets that are measured at fair value, the amount of financing costs during construction will not affect their fair value at the balance sheet date. Entities that manufacture large quantities of inventory items on a recurring basis may not find it cost effective to determine the borrowing costs associated with their production.

RECOGNITION

IAS 23 requires entities to include **borrowing costs** incurred during the acquisition, construction, or production of qualifying assets as **part of the cost** of those assets, provided it is probable they will result in future economic benefits and can be measured reliably. That is, if the costs meet the criteria to be an asset, they are capitalized; other borrowing costs are expensed as incurred.

Calculation of Avoidable Borrowing Costs

When a company borrows to finance a **specific** qualifying asset, it is relatively straightforward to determine the borrowing costs to capitalize. They are the avoidable costs—the actual borrowing costs that would not have been incurred if expenditures for the qualifying asset had not been made, reduced by the investment income earned on any temporary investment of these funds.

The **avoidable costs** are more difficult to calculate when an entity does not tie its financing to the development of specific assets. Some companies raise funds through a number of different debt instruments to support a variety of investments, so they have to determine how much of their borrowing costs are eligible to be capitalized. The following steps are taken:

1. Determine a **capitalization rate:**

$$\text{Capitalization \%} = \frac{\text{Borrowing costs during period}}{\text{Weighted average borrowings during period}}$$

2. Determine the **expenditures on the qualifying asset**, usually its **average** carrying amount.
3. Determine the costs to capitalize. For non-specific asset borrowing, apply the capitalization rate to the appropriate expenditures on the qualifying asset:

Costs to capitalize = Borrowing costs on asset-specific borrowing

+

Remaining average expenditures × Capitalization rate

The **borrowing costs** used to determine the capitalization rate are the total borrowing costs incurred on eligible debt reduced by the amount that is related to a specific qualifying asset. When the remaining amount is divided by the weighted average of the general debt outstanding during the period, the rate that results represents the average borrowing rate on that debt.

The **expenditures on the qualifying asset** are usually represented by the asset's (weighted) average carrying amount. It includes expenditures that were paid with cash or other assets, or the assumption of an interest-bearing liability, as well as previously capitalized borrowing costs. Any progress payments received from a customer decrease the "expenditures," as do grants received, such as those provided by various levels of government.

The **costs to capitalize** are limited by the actual borrowing costs incurred in the period. An entity begins capitalization on the **commencement date**; that is, when **all three** of the following conditions are **first met**:

- Expenditures are incurred for the asset.
- Borrowing costs are incurred.
- Activities needed to prepare the asset for its intended use or sale have begun.

Activities needed to prepare the asset include administrative and technical work in the phase leading up to construction. The holding of an asset while no development activities take place to change the asset's condition, however, are excluded. For example, borrowing costs associated with land acquired in the current year to be built on in a future year without any development activities currently taking place are not capitalized.[3] An example is provided to show how this is applied.

---

[3] IASCF, IAS 23.19.

Situation

In early February 2008, Huey Corp. began construction of an addition to its head office building that is expected to take 18 months to complete. The following 2008 expenditures relate to the addition:

February 1	1st payment to contractor	$120
March 1	Payment to architect	24
July 1	2nd payment to contractor	60
December 1	3rd payment to contractor	180
December 31	Asset carrying amount	$384

On February 1, Huey issued a $100 three-year note payable at a rate of 12% to finance most of the initial payment to the contractor. No other asset-specific debt was entered into. Details of other interest-bearing debt during the period are provided in the table below. **What amount of interest should be capitalized according to IAS 23?**

Analysis

Step 1. Determine the capitalization rate for 2008—the weighted average rate of the non-asset-specific debt borrowing costs.

Other debt instruments outstanding—2008	Principal amount	Weight	Weighted debt outstanding	Borrowing costs[4]
7% 10-year bonds, issued June 15, 2002	$500	12/12	$500	$35
6% 12-year bonds, issued May 1, 2008	$300	8/12	$200	12
9% 15-year bonds, issued May 1, 1993, matured May 1, 2008	$300	4/12	$100	9
			$800	$56
Capitalization rate: $56 / $800 = 7%				

Step 2. Determine the **expenditures on the qualifying asset**, usually its **average** carrying amount.

Date	Payment	Amount	Weight	Average Expenditures
February 1	1st payment to contractor	$120	11/12	$110
March 1	Payment to architect	24	10/12	20
July 1	2nd payment to contractor	60	6/12	30
December 1	3rd payment to contractor	180	1/12	15
		$384		$175

Step 3. Determine the costs to capitalize, applying the capitalization rate to the appropriate expenditures on the qualifying asset:

Costs to capitalize:

Borrowing costs on asset-specific borrowing:

Asset-specific borrowing (weighted)	$100 × 11/12 = $91.7	
Related borrowing costs	$91.7 × 12% =	$11.0

+ Borrowing costs on general borrowing:

Remaining average expenditures × Capitalization rate

Average expenditures – total	= $175.0	
Less financed through specific borrowing	= 91.7	
Financed through general borrowing	= $ 83.3	
Capitalization rate	× 7%	5.8

Borrowing costs to capitalize in Building cost, 2008	$16.8

---

[4] In this example, the borrowing costs are equal to the stated interest rate applied to the principal amount borrowed. This is a simplifying assumption. The interest expense that results from applying the effective interest method could also include amortization of discounts or premiums or other direct costs of borrowing.

Capitalization Suspended or Stopped

An entity **suspends** the capitalization of borrowing costs when development activities are suspended on the qualifying asset, and **stops** capitalizing when substantially all the activities needed to prepare the asset for its intended use are complete.

Suspension is required only when active development activities are clearly on hold, not when there is a temporary delay needed as part of the development process. An entity usually **ceases** capitalizing borrowing costs when the construction phase is complete, even though minor activities may still need to be completed. Applying the same principle, if a qualifying asset is finished in parts that can be used while construction continues on other parts, no additional borrowing costs are capitalized on the portion that is substantially complete. For example, if Huey Corp.'s building addition, described above, takes place in two stages, so that a portion of the office space is available for use when stage 1 is substantially complete, no further borrowing costs are added to the building costs for stage 1 after the stage 1 space is usable.

Disclosure

IAS 23 requires only two brief disclosures for capitalized borrowing costs:

(a) the amount capitalized during the period, and
(b) the capitalization rate used to determine the costs that are eligible for capitalization.

Although IAS 23 did not **require** capitalization of borrowing costs prior to its recent amendment (effective for annual periods beginning on or after January 1, 2009), Royal Dutch Shell Plc followed a policy of capitalization in its financial statements for the year ended December 31, 2007. Royal Dutch Shell is a vertically integrated energy giant with operations worldwide. Illustration 13-1 sets out excerpts from this company's financial statements, presented in millions of U.S. dollars, that comply with these disclosures.[5]

Illustration 13-1
Royal Dutch
Shell–Capitalized
Borrowing Costs
Disclosures

2

ACCOUNTING POLICIES: PROPERTY, PLANT AND EQUIPMENT AND INTANGIBLE ASSETS

[A] Recognition in the Consolidated Balance Sheet
Interest is capitalized, as an increase in property, plant and equipment, on major capital projects during construction.

5

INTEREST AND OTHER INCOME AND INTEREST EXPENSE

[B] INTEREST EXPENSE			$ million
	2007	2006	2005
Interest incurred	1,235	1,296	1,124
Accretion expense (see Note 22)	540	417	371
Less: interest capitalized	(667)	(564)	(427)
Total	1,108	1,149	1,068

The capitalization rate used to determine the amount of interest incurred eligible for capitalization in 2007 was 5.0% (2006: 4.0%; 2005: 3.0%).

---

[5] http://www-static.shell.com/static/investor/downloads/financial_information/reports/2007/2007_annual_report.pdf

LOOKING AHEAD

The accounting treatment for borrowing costs explained in this chapter represents a recent revision to IAS 23, effective for annual accounting periods beginning on or after January 1, 2009. The revisions were made as part of the short-term convergence project with the FASB, and this part of the project is now considered complete. The topic of borrowing costs is not included on the IASB project list going forward.

END-OF-CHAPTER PRACTICE

13-1 Alpha Inc. manufactures equipment for companies in the forestry and related sectors. During its year ended March 31, 2009 Alpha is engaged in the manufacture of the following, all of which require an extended time period to complete:

1. log-handling equipment produced routinely on a repetitive basis for inventory
2. a specialized machine, custom-ordered and designed by a major customer that made a $50 advance payment on its production
3. a new production facility for Alpha's own use

Except for a $100 loan arranged as interim financing on the new production facility, no specific debt was incurred to finance these activities.

Instructions

Prepare notes for a presentation to your class that address the following questions:

(a) Do the carrying costs on all three assets have to be capitalized under IAS 23?
(b) Are borrowing costs and interest payments the same thing?
(c) Does the $50 advance payment on the custom-ordered machine affect the calculation of borrowing costs to be capitalized? If it does, how?
(d) Explain briefly how the capitalization rate should be calculated.

13-2 Gamma Ltd. (GL) signed a contract on September 29, 2008 for the $200 construction of a state-of-the-art distribution complex for the company's Atlantic region. Gamma has a December 31 fiscal year end. On September 30, GL borrowed $120 from the bank at a rate of 10% to finance the first part of the construction. GL paid the contractor $40 on September 30 and $50 on December 2, 2008, investing the excess funds in short-term securities. As of December 31, 2008 GL earned $2 interest on the excess funds.

Instructions

(a) Determine the borrowing costs to be capitalized for GL's year ended December 31, 2008.
(b) If GL had paid the bank a fee of $3 on September 30 to enter into the loan agreement, how would this affect your calculation in part (a), if at all?

13-3 Epsilon Inc. (EI) is a franchisor that has been growing at a rate of 20% per year over the past three years. As part of EI's agreement with its franchisees, EI is responsible for the construction of the franchisees' outlets. The outlets are transferred to the individual franchisee at cost plus 10% shortly after completion of construction and final inspection.

In 2009, EI contracted with Ace Builders to construct five outlets in different parts of a growing municipality at a cost of $100 each, for a total cost of $500. In accordance with the contract, EI made the following payments in 2009:

March 1	$120
April 30	150
December 30	130
	$400

All five outlets were completed as of December 31, 2009 and ready for transfer to the franchisees on January 4, 2010. The franchisees paid for the outlets when invoiced in late January 2010, at which time EI made the final payment to Ace Builders.

EI did not enter into any new borrowing arrangements to finance this construction. The following interest-bearing liabilities were reported on EI's January 31, 2009 balance sheet at the end of its fiscal year:

- 8% 8-year $200 loan payable, dated April 1, 2008, interest payable each April 1
- 10% 12-year $300 bond payable, issued at face value on September 25, 2003, interest payable each September 25

Instructions

(a) Calculate the capitalization rate for determining the borrowing costs to be capitalized as part of the cost of the outlets.
(b) Calculate the amount of borrowing costs to be capitalized.
(c) What would be the appropriate accounting treatment for the borrowing costs incurred by the company during the year if EI had issued additional common shares to finance the construction? Explain.

13-4 In this chapter, flag icons identify areas where there are GAAP differences between IFRS requirements and national standards.

Instructions

Access the website(s) identified on the inside back cover of this book, and prepare a concise summary of the differences that are flagged throughout the chapter material.

Chapter 14

Accounting for Government Grants and Disclosure of Government Assistance: IAS 20

U.S. GAAP Reference
NA

Related IFRSs
IAS 41 Agriculture
IAS 37 Provisions, Contingent Liabilities and Contingent Assets

OBJECTIVE AND SCOPE

IAS 20 *Accounting for Government Grants and Disclosure of Government Assistance* sets out the current standards for recognizing, measuring, and disclosing government grants and for disclosures related to other forms of government assistance. Government, in this IFRS, includes local, national, and international governments and their agencies, and similar bodies.

Government assistance is an action taken by a government that is designed to generate an economic benefit specifically for an entity or entities that meet qualifying criteria. Government transactions undertaken to indirectly benefit general business activity, such as providing transportation infrastructure, is not considered government assistance.

A *government grant* is a form of government assistance. It is defined as a transfer of resources from a government to an entity that requires compliance (either in the past or future) with certain conditions relating to the operating activities of the entity. Transactions in the ordinary course of business between the government and the entity are excluded from the definition, as is government assistance that cannot be reasonably valued.

IAS 20's guidance does not apply to transactions and events relating to a government in its capacity as an owner, government grants covered in IAS 41 *Agriculture*, issues in accounting for grants in reports that deal with the effects of changing prices, or to benefits provided by adjusting taxable profit or loss or that are determined or limited on the basis of the income tax liability. This means that investment tax credits, income tax holidays, accelerated tax depreciation methods, and reduced income tax rates are excluded from the scope of this standard.[1]

ACCOUNTING FOR GOVERNMENT GRANTS

Recognition and Measurement

Government grants, whether in the form of cash or other assets or as a reduction of a liability, are recognized when there is reasonable assurance that

1. the grant will be received, and
2. the entity will comply with the conditions attached to the grant.

Judgment often has to be applied in determining whether there is reasonable assurance that the conditions will be met. For example, a forgivable loan may be received and recorded in the accounts, but it will be presented as a liability until there is sufficient assurance that the terms for forgiveness will be met. Then, and only then, is the loan accounted for as a grant.

After a government grant has been recognized, any contingent asset or contingent liability related to the grant is dealt with by applying IAS 37 *Provisions, Contingent Liabilities and Contingent Assets*. For example, an entity may receive cost-sharing grants that are repayable if a specific number of employees are not employed for a period of five years from the date of the first grant. The criteria in IAS 37 are used in each period to determine how this contingency is dealt with in the financial reports.

Two general approaches have been suggested to account for government grants—a capital approach and an income approach. The **capital approach** considers government grants as contributed capital financing, supporting an accounting treatment that credits the grants directly to equity. However, because these grants represent non-shareholder-related increases in net assets, the **income approach** is the method required by IAS 20. More consistent with the conceptual framework, this approach requires government grants to be recognized systematically in profit or loss in the same periods that the related expenses are recognized by the entity.

Grants may relate either to the acquisition of assets or to income. If received for depreciable assets, grants are usually recorded in profit or loss on the same basis as depreciation expense is recognized. If the assets are non-depreciable but require certain obligations to be met, recognition is tied to the costs associated with meeting those obligations. Grants that are directly related to incurring specific expenditures are recognized on the same basis as the expenditures. They are recognized in profit or loss when received only if there is no logical basis on which to allocate them to future periods or when they are received as compensation for expenses or losses that have already been incurred.

Situation

Assume four entities each receive a government grant.

Company 1 receives a cash contribution from a local government to apply against the purchase cost of its manufacturing plant. The grant is an inducement to locate in the area.

Company 2 receives annual grants for each of five years equal to 40% of the company's increase in its research and development expenditures. The government agency's objective is to promote increased levels of research and development activity.

---

[1] IASCF, IAS 20.1 to 20.3.

Company 3 is given land in a new industrial park to induce the company to locate in the area.

Company 4 is provided with an interest-free loan to help reduce the financing costs associated with the purchase of new manufacturing equipment.

How should the income approach be applied in each case?

Analysis

Company 1 is likely to recognize the grant in profit or loss on the same basis and over the same period as the depreciation expense on the plant is recognized. If the company is required to remain in the location for only a specified period of time to be eligible for the grant, for five years, for example, a case can be made for amortizing the grant over the shorter five-year period.

Company 2's annual grants are tied specifically to its increase in R&D spending. The grants are recognized as assets when the annual R&D expenditures exceed previous levels, and are recognized in profit or loss on the same basis.

Company 3 recognizes a grant receivable as soon as it has met the specific requirements to qualify for the grant. Because the land does not depreciate and its cost is not charged to expense over time, the grant may be recognized in profit or loss when it is received. However, if the land grant is conditional on the construction of a building on the property, it may be more appropriate to recognize the grant on the same basis as the depreciation on the building.

Company 4 is required to recognize the interest-free loan at its fair value under IAS 39 *Financial Instruments: Recognition and Measurement.* The difference between the cash received and the lower fair value (because it is discounted at the current market rate of interest) is a grant. Interest expense is recognized on the loan each period using the effective interest method, and the grant is taken into profit or loss on the same basis.

Grants that are received in the form of non-monetary assets are usually measured at their fair value, although entities may record both the asset and the grant at a nominal amount.

Presentation of Grants Related to Assets

Companies have a choice in how they present **grants related to assets**; that is, grants received with the condition that the entity must acquire or construct long-term assets.

One option is to recognize the grant as an item of **deferred income** that is reported with liabilities on the statement of financial position. The entity reduces the carrying amount of the deferred income account as the grant is systematically recognized in profit or loss. This offsets the regular amount of depreciation expense reported in profit or loss. A benefit of this option is that the assets continue to be reported according to measurement models required in their respective IFRSs. On the downside, however, this method results in companies reporting deferred income amounts as liabilities when no obligation may exist.

The second option is to recognize the grant as **a reduction of the carrying amount of the related asset.** With a smaller carrying amount, the depreciation expense is also reduced. While this approach eliminates the need to report a liability that is not an obligation and therefore is more consistent with the conceptual framework, the asset values reported are not representative of their value to the entity.

In a survey of 70 companies reporting government grants related to assets in their 2005 financial statements prepared under international standards, KPMG IFRG Limited found that 56% of the companies chose to deduct the grants from the carrying amount of the asset, and 44% recognized the grants as deferred income.[2] Based on this survey, there does not appear to be a very strong preference for one method over the other.

Regardless of which presentation method is used, the net effect on the income statement is exactly the same.

---

[2] Prof. Dr. Isabel von Keitz and KPMG IFRG Limited, *The Application of IFRS: Choices in Practice* (December 2006), p. 12.

Presentation of Grants Related to Income

For **grants related to income**, that is, all those that are not related to assets, companies also have a choice. The grants received may be reported separately on the income statement as "other income" items, or as reductions of the expenses they were designed to offset. Those who oppose the netting of income and expense items on the grounds that both end up misstated support the "other income" presentation, while others argue that netting is appropriate, especially when the expenses might not have been incurred if the grant had not been available.

Repayment of Government Grants

A government grant that becomes repayable is accounted for as a change in estimate, as described in IAS 8 *Accounting Policies, Changes in Accounting Estimates and Errors*, with no retroactive effect on incomes that were previously reported.

If the **grant was related to an asset**, the amount repayable is either paid or recognized as a liability, with a concurrent adjustment to the carrying amount of the asset or the deferred income account affected, depending on the balance sheet presentation option that was applied. The cumulative amount of additional depreciation that would have been recognized in profit or loss to date if the grant had not been received is recognized in the current period's profit or loss.

If a **grant related to income** must be repaid, the balance in any related unamortized deferred credit is eliminated. If there is no unamortized deferred credit associated with the grant, or if the amount repaid is greater than this account's balance, the repayment is recognized in the current year's profit or loss.

GOVERNMENT ASSISTANCE

At the beginning of this chapter, government grants were defined to exclude assistance that cannot reasonably be valued and transactions between a government and an entity that are in the normal course of business. If a government guarantees an entity's loan or its performance under a contract, for example, or if the government, as a customer, accounts for 30% of a company's sales, there is no question that the entity has received government assistance. Although the entity may not be able to measure the benefits, readers of its financial statements are likely to find this type of information useful in their assessment of the entity if the benefits are significant and recurring.

DISCLOSURE

Three types of disclosure are required by IAS 20:

1. The accounting policy applied for government grants, and the methods chosen for presentation on the financial statements.
2. The nature and extent of the grants recognized in the financial statements, and information about other forms of government assistance the entity has benefitted directly from.
3. Information about any contingencies outstanding or conditions that have not yet been met related to government assistance that has been recognized.

LOOKING AHEAD

IAS 20 *Accounting for Government Grants and Disclosure of Government Assistance* was identified by the IASB as part of its short-term convergence project with the FASB. The objective was to amend IAS 20 in two ways:

    (a)   to bring it into line with the conceptual framework (the *Framework*) by eliminating the recognition of deferred credits when the entity does not have a liability, and

    (b)   to eliminate options that understate an entity's assets and reduce the comparability of its financial statements.[3]

In addition, this standard's requirements are inconsistent with more recent pronouncements issued by other standard-setting bodies. These standard setters have developed accounting treatments for similar transactions that **are consistent** with the *Framework*.

    Grappling with these issues becomes very difficult when many of the underlying issues are being studied in other projects at the same time. The IASB is currently working on its conceptual framework project along with IAS 37 *Provisions, Contingent Liabilities and Contingent Assets*, and another project on revenue recognition, all of which are directly related to the deficiencies in IAS 20. Further work on amending IAS 20 has been deferred until progress is made on IAS 37 and the revenue recognition project. As this book goes to print, a final standard on IAS 37 is expected in late 2009 and an Exposure Draft on revenue recognition is expected in the first half of 2010.

END-OF-CHAPTER PRACTICE

14-1 Iota Inc. received a $100 government grant to be applied against the construction of a new building. The building is accounted for using the cost model, has an initial cost of $500, a useful life of 25 years, and $0 residual value.

Instructions
    (a)   Prepare entries to account for the acquisition of the building and receipt of the government grant on Day 1 assuming Iota presents the grant as deferred income, and then assuming Iota presents it as a reduction of the asset's cost.
    (b)   Prepare the entry to record depreciation expense at the end of the first year of operations, as well as any other adjusting entries required under each assumption in (a) above.
    (c)   In what respects will the statement of financial position and income statement differ under the two accounting presentations? Does it matter that they are different? Why?

14-2 Refer to 14-1 above. Assume that after four years of operating in the new building, Iota Inc. decides to transfer its operations to a larger municipality. The original $100 grant is required to be repaid if Iota does not remain in the building for a minimum of seven years.

Instructions
    (a)   Prepare the entry(ies) to recognize the grant repayment liability at the end of year 4 assuming Iota recognized the grant originally as deferred income.
    (b)   Prepare the entry(ies) to recognize the grant repayment liability at the end of year 4 assuming Iota recognized the grant originally as a reduction of the asset's cost.

14-3 Chi Corp. agreed to locate a new call center in an economically disadvantaged area in return for specific government assistance. The government provided $200 funding to a local college to bring the general education level of a number of residents to an acceptable minimum, $25 toward the cost of a four-week call center employee training program delivered by Chi Corp., and a $50 grant to offset the higher travel and administrative costs to be incurred by Chi over a five-year period.

---

[3] IASB Project Update, May 2008: Amendments to IAS 20 *Accounting for Government Grants and Disclosure of Government Assistance.*

This grant is repayable at the rate of $10 per year for each year less than five years that Chi does not operate in the area. In addition, Chi Corp. is eligible for a 10% wage rebate at the end of each year in which an average of 20 people or more are employed at the operation. The company expects to have more than 23 employees on staff at all times and to operate in this location for a minimum of eight years.

Assume the operation opens on July 2, 2009, at which time the $50 grant is received. The employee training program takes place from July 5 to August 3 and Chi receives the $25 grant in early September. The payroll for the first six months for the 27 full-time employees hired is $400.

Instructions

(a) Prepare all entries related to government assistance that Chi Corp. needs to make from July 1 to December 31, 2009, Chi's fiscal year end. Identify any situations where there are alternatives.

(b) Identify the government assistance disclosures that are required for Chi's December 31, 2009 financial statements.

14-4 In this chapter, flag icons identify areas where there are GAAP differences between IFRS requirements and national standards.

Instructions

Access the website(s) identified on the inside back cover of this book, and prepare a concise summary of the differences that are flagged throughout the chapter material.

Chapter 15

Intangible Assets:
IAS 38

U.S. GAAP References
FAS 142 Goodwill and Other Intangible Assets
FAS 141 Business Combinations
FAS 86 Accounting for the Costs of Computer Software to Be Sold, Leased, or Otherwise Marketed

Related IFRSs
IFRS 3 Business Combinations
IAS 36 Impairment of Assets
IAS 17 Leases
IFRS 4 Insurance Contracts
IFRS 5 Non-current Assets Held for Sale and Discontinued Operations
IFRS 6 Exploration for and Evaluation of Mineral Resources

OBJECTIVE AND SCOPE

IAS 38 sets out the accounting requirements for the recognition and measurement of intangible assets that are not covered in other IFRSs and for their related disclosures.

Standards on leases, inventories, financial instruments, business combinations, and others may deal with assets that are intangible in nature and that meet the definition of an intangible asset as described below. These standards should be applied if they prescribe the accounting for a specific type of intangible asset.

Sometimes it is difficult to tell whether a particular asset is tangible—and covered by IAS 16 *Property, Plant and Equipment*—or intangible and covered by IAS 38, so judgment often needs to be applied. Consider the example of computer software and licensing rights to films. What is the asset? Is it the intangible software and the licensing rights, or is it the tangible hardware and film that the intangibles reside in? IAS 38 suggests that if the software, for example, is necessary for the physical component to work, it should be treated as a physical asset. If the intangible component is not an integral part of the physical object, then it is accounted for as an intangible.

An entity may lease either a tangible or an intangible asset. While IAS 17 *Leases* determines whether the asset is initially recognized as a finance lease, IAS 38 sets the standards for how any intangible assets resulting from the lease are accounted for. A variety of rights under licensing agreements, such as patents, video recordings, and copyrights, for example, are guided by IAS 38, not IAS 17.[1]

An *intangible asset* is defined simply as "an identifiable non-monetary asset without physical substance."[2] Three aspects of this definition have to be looked at more closely. The first issue is **identifiability**, and the second and third aspects are carried forward from the definition of an asset: **control** by an entity, and the existence of **future economic benefits**.

An asset is considered **identifiable** if it meets **one** of the two following criteria:

1. It can be separated from the entity and sold, transferred, licensed, rented, or exchanged, either by itself or in conjunction with a related contract, identifiable asset, or liability, whether or not the entity intends to do so.
2. It is based on contractual or other legal rights, regardless of whether it is separable from the entity or other rights and obligations.[3]

Identifiability differentiates intangible assets from goodwill.

For an asset to be recognized, however, an entity has to be able to **control access** to the future benefits the asset is expected to provide. The entity must be able to benefit from them itself and to restrict others from doing so. Access is often controlled by being legally enforceable such as when patent rights are conferred on an entity. An example of a situation where control over the expected future benefits does not exist is company spending on employee training programs. Employees are free to leave the company, taking their enhanced skills with them. Therefore, the cost of such programs is not an intangible asset.

Future economic benefits usually refer to the increased revenues, cash flows, and productivity or reduced costs associated with expenditures on assets.

RECOGNITION AND MEASUREMENT

An item is **recognized as an intangible asset** when it meets the definition of one, and when the two following **recognition criteria** are met:

1. it is probable, using management's best estimates of conditions that will likely exist, that the expected future economic benefits will be realized; and
2. the cost of the asset can be reliably measured.

Intangible assets are **measured** initially **at cost**, and an expenditure on an intangible item that was initially recognized as an expense cannot be recognized retroactively as part of the asset's cost.

Intangible assets are acquired or developed in a variety of ways, and the accounting for them at acquisition depends on how they are acquired or developed. The chart in Illustration 15-1 provides a road map through this next section.

---

[1] IASCF, IAS 38.1-7.
[2] IASCF, IAS 38.8.
[3] IASCF, IAS 38.12.

Illustration 15-1
Recognition of
Intangible Assets

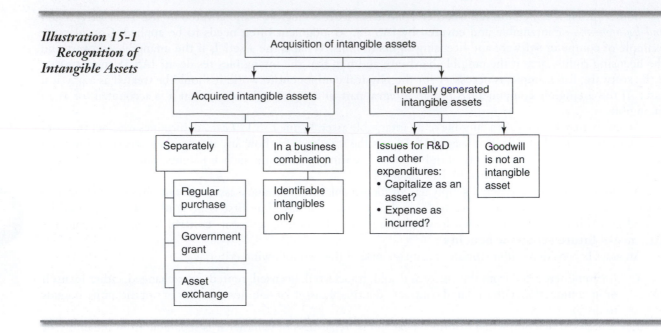

ACQUIRED INTANGIBLE ASSETS

Intangible Assets Acquired Separately

The cost of an intangible asset that is acquired on its own usually meets all the requirements for recognition: it is separable; the likelihood of future benefits flowing to the entity can be assessed; and its cost can be reasonably measured, particularly if it is acquired for cash or other monetary assets. Similar to other non-financial assets, **cost** is the cash equivalent price and **includes** the purchase price and duties and non-refundable purchase taxes, net of trade discounts and rebates. Direct costs of preparing the intangible asset and bringing it to an appropriate condition for its intended use are also capitalized. Examples of common intangibles that are purchased are franchises, trademarks, and customer lists.

Expenditures **not included in the cost** of an intangible asset include those for advertising, promotion, and training associated with new products, locations, or customers; and administrative and other general overhead costs. Once the asset is **ready for use as intended** no further costs and no early stage operating losses are capitalized.

Intangible Assets Acquired by Government Grant or through an Asset Exchange

Government Grants

If an entity acquires an intangible asset through a government grant, IAS 20 *Accounting for Government Grants and Disclosure of Government Assistance* is applied. IAS 20 allows a choice of amounts to recognize. The asset and the grant can be recognized at fair value or at only a nominal amount. If recognized at a nominal amount, the incremental costs to prepare the asset for its intended use are capitalized.

Asset Exchanges

What is the cost of an intangible asset if it is acquired by giving up non-monetary assets? When some portion of the consideration given is **non-monetary**, cost is measured at the fair value of what is given up.

There is an **exception,** however, to using fair value as the cost of an asset in a non-monetary exchange. If the transaction does not have commercial substance, or if the fair value of neither the asset received nor the one given up can be reliably measured, the cost of the asset acquired is the **carrying amount** or book value of the asset(s) given in exchange. What does it mean for a transaction to have, or not have, commercial substance?

In general, an exchange transaction has *commercial substance* if it has an economic effect on the entity, i.e., if the future cash flows of the entity are changed in some way. Commercial substance exists if

(a) the amount, timing, and risk of the future cash flows of the asset received differ from those of the asset(s) transferred out; or

(b) the after-tax cash flows of the part of the business affected by the transaction (**entity-specific value**) have changed as a result of the exchange; and

(c) the difference in (a) or (b) is significant relative to the fair values of the assets exchanged.[4]

Situation

A book publisher acquires copyrights to a portfolio of professional publications in exchange for $5 cash and copyrights to an educational book list with a carrying amount of $20 (cost $42) and a fair value of $50. What is the cost of the copyrights acquired assuming considerable savings are expected as a result of synergies between the new copyrights and the company's other titles? Would your answer change if the amount of the future cash flows is expected to be unchanged in the future as a result of this transaction?

Analysis

Under the first assumption, the exchange is expected to have an economic effect on the publisher. The new copyrights acquired have increased the specific value of the publisher due to synergies expected from its existing assets. Assuming that the effect is significant, the intangible asset acquired is recognized at the fair value of the assets given up: $5 cash + $50 copyrights given up = $55. The entry is as follows:

Copyrights, Professional Publications	55	
Accumulated Amortization, Copyrights Educational	22	
Cash		5
Copyrights, Educational List		42
Gain on Disposal ($50 − $20)		30

Under the second situation, if the amount, timing, and risk of the cash flows associated with the new copyrights are considered unchanged from before the transaction, if the entity-specific value of the publisher has not changed, or if the changes are considered insignificant, then the transaction does not have commercial substance. In this case, there is no reason to recognize a change in the value of the assets and the related gain. Therefore, the intangible asset acquired is recognized at the carrying amount of what is given up: $5 cash and $20 copyrights given up = $25. The entry is as follows:

Copyrights, Professional Publications	25	
Accumulated Amortization, Copyrights Educational	22	
Cash		5
Copyrights, Educational List		42

Although the amount of the future cash flow is expected to remain unchanged in the second situation, if the timing of the cash flows has changed, or operating in different markets has changed the risks, the publisher may be in a different economic position than before the exchange. If this is so, the transaction may have commercial substance and be accounted for as illustrated in the first scenario.

---

[4] IASCF, IAS 38.46.

Intangible Assets Acquired in a Business Combination

The cost of an intangible asset acquired as part of a business combination is its **fair value**. IFRS 3 *Business Combinations* and IAS 38 both require an entity to identify all intangible assets acquired as part of the combination, recognizing the identifiable intangibles separately from goodwill.

Intangible assets that were **not recorded in the accounts** of the business acquired may be recognized in a business combination transaction. One of the most common intangibles recognized in this way is in-process research and development. An in-process R&D project is recognized as an intangible asset if it meets the **definition** of an asset and is **identifiable**, as explained above. Any expenditure on the project after it is acquired, however, is accounted for in the same way as for internally generated intangibles, explained below.

Determining the fair value of an intangible asset often involves uncertainty. For example, if an asset is separable, but only when combined with other assets, the assets are grouped and the group's fair value is recognized as a single asset. This approach is also used for complementary intangible assets such as those making up a "brand."

If quoted market prices in an active market—the most reliable fair value measure—are not available, other methods are used to determine fair value. These range, in order, from relevant bid prices in a less active market, to prices determined in similar arm's-length transactions, and then to estimation techniques based on market transactions or discounted cash flows from the asset.

INTERNALLY GENERATED INTANGIBLES

Goodwill Generated Internally

Internally generated goodwill is **not recognized** as an asset. Although future economic benefits may be expected as entities incur a variety of costs, the costs do not create an intangible asset that meets the recognition criteria identified earlier: there is no identifiable resource controlled by the entity that can be measured reliably at cost.

Capitalize or Expense?

The same factors that prevent internally generated goodwill from being recognized have to be overcome before internally generated intangibles can be recognized as assets:

- Is there an identifiable asset that will generate expected future economic benefits?
- Can the cost of the asset be measured reliably and differentiated from ordinary operating costs or costs needed to maintain or add value to internally generated goodwill?

The first step in addressing these questions is to classify the costs incurred into one of two phases needed to generate an intangible asset—**a research phase** and a **development phase**.

Research Phase

Research is "original and planned investigation undertaken with the prospect of gaining new scientific or technical knowledge and understanding."[5] The **research phase** involves activities such as the search for alternatives for materials, devices, products, processes, systems, or services and their formulation, design, evaluation, and final selection; as well as activities at a more fundamental level searching for new knowledge and new applications of findings.

Expenditures on research or research activities are expensed as incurred. These activities on their own cannot result with enough certainty in an intangible asset that will generate probable future economic benefits.

---

[5] IASCF, IAS 38.8.

Development Phase

Development is "the application of research findings or other knowledge to a plan or design for the production of new or substantially improved materials, devices, products, processes, systems, or services before the start of commercial production." The **development phase**, therefore, takes over where the research phase leaves off. It includes activities such as

(a) the design, construction, and testing of pre-production prototypes and models;

(b) the design of tools, molds, and dies involving new technology;

(c) the design, construction, and operation of a pilot plant that is not economically feasible for full commercial production; and

(d) the design, construction, and testing of a chosen alternative for new or improved material, devices, products, processes, systems, or services.[6]

Because the development phase is further along in the process of generating an economically viable intangible asset, some development costs meet the recognition criteria and therefore are recognized as an internally generated intangible asset. In general, this happens only when the technical, economic, and financial viability of the product or process being developed is assured. **Development costs are recognized as intangible assets if, and only if, all six** of the following factors can be demonstrated:

1. the **technical feasibility** of completing the intangible asset for use or sale;
2. the **intention** to complete and use or sell it;
3. the **ability** to use or sell it;
4. how the intangible asset will generate probable **future economic benefits**;
5. the **availability** of adequate technical, financial, and other **resources** to complete and sell or use the intangible asset; and
6. the ability to **reliably measure** the expenditures related to the intangible asset during its development.[7]

The principles in IAS 36 *Impairment of Assets* provide guidance on how to determine the future economic benefits expected to be generated by an intangible asset.

If all six conditions are not met, the costs are expensed as incurred.

The standard specifically states that certain internally generated items are not recognized as assets. These are internally generated brands, mastheads, publishing titles, customer lists, and other items similar in nature that cannot be distinguished from the cost of developing the business as a whole. The blanket exclusion of these items is controversial in that a number of people contend that entities should apply the principles provided to determine the appropriate accounting treatment.

Costs of an Internally Generated Intangible Asset

What costs **are included** in the cost of an internally generated intangible asset? Again, as for most non-monetary assets, **cost includes** those costs that are directly associated with making the asset ready for use in the manner intended by management. These include costs of materials and services consumed, and employee benefit, depreciation, and amortization costs incurred in generating the intangible, as well as legal fees to register the related legal rights. For example, although most of the expenditures incurred to develop a patentable process are expensed as research, costs to register the patent after its asset value is established are capitalized.

Costs Recognized as Expense

As explained above, all research costs and the development costs incurred prior to the point at which all six criteria are met that support the feasibility and economic viability of the asset are expensed. The total amount of

---

[6] IASCF, IAS 38.8 and 38.59.
[7] IASCF, IAS 38.57.

all **research and development** expenditures recognized as **expense** in the period **is required to be disclosed** in the financial statements. **Once expensed, these costs cannot be retroactively capitalized**. Also expensed are indirect selling, administrative, and other general overhead costs; the costs of inefficiencies and operating losses before the asset is performing as planned; and costs to train staff to operate the asset.[8]

IAS 38 provides guidance on a variety of other expenditures on intangible items. In general, all expenditures are recognized as an expense unless they meet the requirements to be recognized as part of the cost of an intangible asset or are included in the goodwill recognized in a business combination.

More specifically, **as long as no intangible or other asset is acquired that can be recognized**, expenditures on intangibles are recognized as an expense **when incurred**. This means that an expense is recognized when an entity has the right to access goods supplied; that is, when the entity owns them, even if they have not been delivered. When services are acquired, an expense is recognized when the service is received. A **prepaid asset** can be recognized instead of an expense, but only when the payment for goods and services is made **before the goods are delivered** or the **services are rendered** to the entity.

Situation

Consider the following expenditures made by a retail organization. What accounting treatment should be applied in each case?

(a)   Expenditure 1 is the recognition of an account payable to a supplier for producing and delivering a mail-order catalog. The catalog will be used over the next 12-month period.

(b)   Expenditure 2 covers prepayments to an advertising production company for the production of a set of television and website advertisements.

(c)   Expenditure 3 is the payment of an invoice received from the caterers for food and beverage service in connection with the opening of the newest outlet store.

(d)   Expenditure 4 covers the cost of moving the retailer's administrative staff and offices to its new head office location.

Analysis

(a)   Expenditure 1 is an advertising and promotion cost that is charged to expense as incurred, i.e., when the catalogs are received. The catalogs do not meet the definition of an intangible asset, inventory, or a prepaid expense.

(b)   Expenditure 2 is also an advertising and promotion-related cost. It is a prepayment for services and is recognized as a prepaid asset. When the production company completes the advertisements and delivers them to or on behalf of the retail organization that contracted for them, the service is rendered and the total cost is recognized as an expense.

(c)   Expenditure 3 is a type of start-up cost. The costs associated with start-up activities are usually expensed as incurred unless they meet the definition of an item of property, plant, and equipment. In this case, it is a pre-opening cost that is expensed.

(d)   Expenditure 4 is a relocation cost. This and other types of costs related to reorganizing an entity are expensed as incurred.

IAS 38 provides a number of similar examples to illustrate what is meant by recognizing expenses as they are incurred. In general, pre-opening and pre-operating costs, training costs, advertising and promotional costs, and relocation costs are expensed.

MEASUREMENT AFTER RECOGNITION

Similar to accounting for property, plant, and equipment assets, entities have a choice of models they can apply to account for their intangible assets after initial recognition: the **cost model** or the **revaluation model**. A decision is made for each class of intangible assets, so that all assets of a similar nature and use to the entity are valued on the same basis. Examples of classes provided in IAS 38.119 are:

---

[8] IASCF, IAS 38.67.

- brand names
- mastheads and publishing titles
- computer software
- licences and franchises
- intangible assets under development
- recipes, formulas, models, designs, and prototypes
- copyrights, patents, and other industrial property rights, service and operating rights

Cost Model (CM)

Most entities choose to apply the cost model. This model states that an intangible asset is carried at its **cost** less any **accumulated amortization** and any **accumulated impairment losses**.

Revaluation Model (RM)

Under the revaluation model, an intangible asset is reported at its **fair value** at the date of the revaluation, less any **subsequent accumulated amortization** and **subsequent accumulated impairment losses**. Revaluations are carried out often enough that the carrying amount at the end of the period is not significantly different from the asset's fair value.

The RM cannot be used to pick up and recognize intangible assets that were not previously recognized, or to establish the initial "cost" of an asset.

All assets in a class using the revaluation model are revalued at the same time, and the **fair value measure** must be a value **determined in an active market**. This condition severely restricts the use of this model. Only intangible assets that are traded on a regular basis with active market prices, such as those for freely transferable licences or quotas, for example, qualify to apply the RM. This is likely the reason that a recent KPMG IFRG Limited study found no intangible assets that were accounted for under the revaluation option in its sample of 147 companies.[9]

How does the revaluation model work for intangible assets? This model is applied in the same way as it is for property, plant, and equipment assets. A summary of the key aspects of the model is provided below, but for a detailed example, please refer to the discussion and sample scenario in Chapter 10.

Summary of Key Aspects of the Revaluation Model (RM)

- If an asset is revalued, its carrying amount is adjusted to the revalued amount in one of two ways: either both the asset and the accumulated amortization are restated proportionately, or the accumulated amortization is eliminated against the asset's gross value and then this net amount is adjusted to the current fair value.
- An increase in the carrying amount is credited to other comprehensive income and accumulated in a revaluation surplus account in shareholders' equity. However, if the increase offsets a previous decrease in value that was recognized in profit or loss, the increase first offsets that previous charge.
- A decrease in the carrying amount is first applied against any previously recognized revaluation surplus in equity (i.e., through other comprehensive income), and any excess is charged against profit or loss.
- When the intangible is retired or disposed of, any remaining revaluation surplus is transferred directly to retained earnings. To the extent that the surplus is realized as the asset is used, transfers are made from revaluation surplus directly to retained earnings as the asset is used. The amount transferred is the difference between the amortization determined under the RM and the amount that would have been charged under the CM. No part of the revaluation surplus is adjusted through profit or loss.

---

[9] Prof. Dr. Isabel von Keitz and KPMG IFRG Limited, *The Application of IFRS: Choices in Practice* (December 2006), p. 11.

If there has never been an active market value for an asset in a class of assets using the RM, the asset is carried at its cost less accumulated amortization and impairment losses. However, if an active market no longer exists for an intangible asset that was previously fair valued, it is carried at its last revaluation amount, reduced by accumulated amortization and impairment losses since that revaluation.

Useful Life

Unlike property, plant, and equipment assets (with the exception of land), an intangible asset may have an **indefinite useful life** or a **finite**—limited—useful life.

Useful life refers to the period of time the asset is expected to be used or to the number of units of output expected from the asset **by the entity**. If there is no foreseeable limit to the period the asset is expected to generate net cash inflows, it is identified as having an **indefinite life** and it is **not amortized**. An intangible with a limited life **is amortized**.

When an intangible asset is based on contractual or legal rights, its useful life is usually limited by the period covered by those rights, although if the term can be renewed or extended at little cost, the renewal period is included in determining the maximum useful life. Of course, the useful life **to the entity** may be shorter than the life covered by law or contract. Other factors to consider in determining useful life include

(a) how long the entity expects to use the asset,
(b) technological and commercial or other obsolescence,
(c) industry factors such as the demand for and life cycle of its products or services,
(d) the expenditures needed and expected to be made to maintain its value, and
(e) dependency on the useful lives of other assets.

Any one of these factors can severely restrict an otherwise longer legal or contractual life.

Intangible Assets with Finite Useful Lives

To amortize an intangible asset with a limited useful life,

•   the cost or carrying amount of the asset less its residual value is allocated on a systematic basis over its useful life.
•   amortization begins when the asset is available for use as intended by management.
•   amortization stops at the earlier of when it is classified as held for sale or the asset is derecognized.
•   the method of amortization reflects the pattern in which the asset's benefits are expected to be consumed by the entity; if this cannot be determined, the straight-line method is used.
•   the amortization is recognized as an expense, unless another IFRS requires it to be included in the carrying amount of another asset.
•   the amortization period and method are reviewed at each fiscal year end at a minimum with any changes accounted for as a change in an accounting estimate.

The asset is assumed to have **no residual value** except under very restrictive conditions: unless a third party has made a commitment to purchase it at the end of its useful life, or the asset trades in a continuing active market that can be used to establish a residual value. In this case, the residual value is based on the expected proceeds from the sale of a similar asset that is at the end of its useful life, having been used in a manner similar to how the intangible asset will be used. Residual values are also reviewed at each fiscal year end at a minimum. If the estimate of residual value is higher than the asset's carrying amount, no amortization is charged.

IAS 36 *Impairment of Assets* provides guidance on assessing intangible assets with finite useful lives for impairment.

Intangible Assets with Indefinite Useful Lives

An intangible asset with an indefinite useful life **is not amortized**. Instead, and as required by IAS 36, the asset is tested for impairment at least annually and when there is any indication that it may be impaired. The assumption of an indefinite useful life is also reassessed annually.

RETIREMENTS AND DISPOSALS

An intangible asset is derecognized when it is disposed of or when an entity expects no further benefits from its use or disposal. The gain or loss on derecognition—the difference between the asset's carrying amount and the net proceeds on disposal—is recognized in profit or loss. Gains are not reported as revenue.

Other IFRSs may have to be applied on derecognition, depending on how the disposal is carried out and what form the proceeds take.

DISCLOSURES

General

A significant amount of information is required about each class of intangible assets, segregated between those that are internally generated and those that are not. The information requirements include the following:

(a) whether the useful lives are indefinite or finite, and if finite, the amortization rates used or the useful lives

(b) the amortization methods used, and the lines on the statement of comprehensive income that include any amortization

(c) the opening and closing balances of the gross carrying amount and the total of the accumulated amortization and accumulated impairment losses

(d) a complete reconciliation of the opening and ending carrying amounts, showing
- additions, separately indicating those internally generated, those acquired in business combinations, and those acquired separately;
- assets held for sale and other disposals;
- revaluation adjustments and impairment losses accounted for through other comprehensive income;
- impairment losses and any impairment reversals recognized in profit or loss;
- amortization during the period; and
- currency exchange adjustments and other changes

In addition to these disclosures and the amount of contractual commitments to acquire intangibles, the following information is required in specific cases:

- If an asset has an indefinite life—report its carrying amount and why its life was assessed as indefinite.
- If there is an individual asset that is material to the financial statements—describe it and report its carrying amount and remaining useful life.
- If assets were acquired through a government grant and recognized at fair value at acquisition—disclose their initial fair value, their current carrying amount, and whether the CM or RM is applied.
- For intangible assets with restricted title and those pledged as security for liabilities—report their carrying amounts.

Intangibles Accounted for Using the Revaluation Model

For each class of intangible assets that uses the RM, it is necessary to disclose the date of the revaluation, the carrying amount of revalued assets, and their carrying amount if the cost method had been used. In addition, the methods and assumptions used to determine fair values, a reconciliation of the balances and changes in the revaluation surplus account, and any restrictions on the distribution of the revaluation surplus are also reported.

Aside from providing basic intangible asset information on its December 31, 2007 balance sheet, Switzerland-based Nestlé Group presents related accounting policy disclosures in an appendix to its financial statements, and detailed supplementary disclosures in Note 13. Excerpts from these disclosures are set out in Illustrations 15-2 and 15-3. There is additional extensive disclosure relating to impairment testing of intangible assets along with goodwill in other notes that have not been reproduced. Note that Nestlé presents its financial statements in Swiss francs.[10]

Illustration 15-2
Nestlé Group
Excerpts from
Accounting
Policy Notes

Valuation methods and definitions
Intangible assets
This heading includes intangible assets that are acquired either separately or in a business combination when they are identifiable and can be reliably measured. Intangible assets are considered to be identifiable if they arise from contractual or other rights, or if they are separable i.e. they can be disposed of either individually or together with other assets. Intangible assets comprise indefinite life intangible assets and finite life intangible assets.

Indefinite life intangible assets are those for which there is no foreseeable limit to their useful economic life as they arise from contractual or other legal rights that can be renewed without significant cost and are the subject of continuous marketing support. They are not depreciated but tested for impairment annually or more frequently if an impairment indicator is triggered. They mainly comprise certain brands, trademarks and intellectual property rights. The assessment of the classification of intangible assets as indefinite is reviewed annually.

Finite life intangible assets are those for which there is an expectation of obsolescence that limits their useful economic life or where the useful life is limited by contractual or other terms. They are depreciated over the shorter of their contractual or useful economic lives. They comprise mainly management information systems, patents and rights to carry on an activity (i.e. exclusive rights to sell products or to perform a supply activity). Finite life intangible assets are depreciated on a straight-line basis assuming a zero residual value: management information systems over a period ranging from three to five years; and other finite life intangible assets over five to 20 years. The depreciation period and depreciation method are reviewed annually by taking into account the risk of obsolescence.

Depreciation of intangible assets is allocated to the appropriate headings of expenses by function in the income statement.

Internally generated intangible assets are capitalised, provided they generate future economic benefits and their costs are clearly identifiable.

Research and development
Research costs are charged to the income statement in the year in which they are incurred.

Development costs relating to new products are not capitalized because the expected future economic benefits cannot be reliably determined. As long as the products have not reached the market place, there is no reliable evidence that positive future cash flows would be obtained.

Other development costs (essentially management information system software) are capitalized provided that there is an identifiable asset that will be useful in generating future benefits in terms of savings, economies of scale, etc.

---

[10] http://www.nestle.com/Resource.axd?Id=24E5A5E2-93F8-43A3-956E-0F259448CB90

Impairment of property, plant and equipment and finite life intangible assets

Consideration is given at each balance sheet date to determine whether there is any indication of impairment of the carrying amounts of the Group's property, plant and equipment and finite life intangible assets. If any indication exists, an asset's recoverable amount is estimated. An impairment loss is recognized whenever the carrying amount of an asset exceeds its recoverable amount. The recoverable amount is the greater of the fair value less cost to sell and value in use. In assessing value in use, the estimated future cash flows are discounted to their present value based on the average borrowing rate of the country where the assets are located, adjusted for risks specific to the asset.

Illustration 15-3 Nestlé Group Excerpts from Intangible Assets Note

13. Intangible assets

In millions of CHF   2007

	Brands and intellectual property rights	Operating rights and others	Management information systems	Total
Gross value				
At 1 January	1 550	753	3 533	5 836
of which indefinite useful life	1 167	–	–	1 167
Currency retranslations	(153)	(38)	(24)	(215)
Expenditures	11	61	547	619
Disposals	(8)	(18)	(58)	(84)
Modification of the scope of consolidation	3 129	478	(6)	3 601
At 31 December	4 529	1 236	3 992	9 757
of which indefinite useful life [a]	4 133	–	–	4 133
Accumulated depreciation and impairments				
At 1 January	(224)	(521)	(1 318)	(2 063)
Currency retranslations	–	29	12	41
Depreciation	(16)	(90)	(485)	(591)
Impairments	(2)	(2)	(2)	(6)
Disposals	8	14	56	78
Modification of the scope of consolidation	–	1	–	1
At 31 December	(234)	(569)	(1 737)	(2 540)
Net at 31 December	4 295	667	2 255	7 217

[a] Yearly impairment test performed together with goodwill items (refer to Note 12)

Internally generated intangible assets consist mainly of management information systems.

LOOKING AHEAD

Whether recognized or not, intangible assets are an increasingly important aspect of what gives an entity value, and IAS 38 does not do an adequate job of reporting these assets to users of the financial statements. The current requirements of this standard significantly restrict the intangibles that can be recognized, and after initial recognition, allow only those with fair values determined in an active market to apply the revaluation model. In addition, there are inconsistent treatments of intangible assets developed internally and those acquired in a business combination, as well as for internally developed property, plant, and equipment assets.

The scope of a proposal for a comprehensive recognition-based project agreed to by both the FASB and IASB was recently considered by the IASB. The Board recognized the importance of the accounting issues, but decided not to add the project to its active agenda because of other projects competing for time and resources. Instead, the issues will continue to be researched. It is unlikely, therefore, that there will be significant changes in the accounting standards set out in IAS 38 in the short to medium term. However, the IASB's fair value measurement project, expected to result in the convergence of international and U.S. GAAP, may affect the measurement guidance in this standard. An Exposure Draft (ED/2009/5) was issued in May 2009, with the publication of final guidance expected in 2010.

END-OF-CHAPTER PRACTICE

15-1 The following is a list of expenditures made by Zorro Corp. (ZC) during its year ended May 31, 2008.
1. December 2007: cost of annual update on payroll software.
2. November 2007: training costs incurred for new product line.
3. December 2007: rent prepayment (six months paid in advance).
4. June 2007: payment for exclusive rights for national sports figure endorsement of ZC products for two years.
5. May 2008: payment for production of special advertisements to be run on television during world championship games in July 2008.

Instructions
Indicate whether ZC should report a related intangible or other asset on its May 31, 2008 balance sheet for each expenditure described above. Explain your answer in each case.

15-2 Three intangibles acquired by Hamm Ltd. (HL) in the current year are described below. HL, a progressive company with a variety of divisions and subsidiaries, has applied fair value measures on its balance sheet wherever permitted.

Intangible 1 is a license granted by the federal government to HL that allows the company to provide essential services to a key military installation overseas. The license expires every five years, but is renewable indefinitely at little cost. Because of the profitability associated with this license, HL fully expects to renew it continually. The license is very marketable and will generate cash flows indefinitely.

Intangible 2 is a non-competition covenant acquired by HL when the company bought out a major owner-managed competitor. The seller signed a contract in which she agreed not to set up or work for another business that is in direct or indirect competition with HL. The projected cash flows resulting from this agreement are expected to continue for at least 25 years.

Intangible 3 is medical files. One of HL's subsidiary companies owns several medical clinics. A recent purchase of a retiring doctor's practice required a significant payment for the practice's medical files and clients. HL believes that this base will benefit the business for as long as it exists, providing cash flows indefinitely.

Instructions
(a) Does each intangible as described above qualify to be recognized as an intangible asset? Explain briefly.
(b) Identify the appropriate method of accounting for each intangible described above after acquisition, and explain the decisions you have made.

15-3 The following research and development costs were incurred by Ordo Inc. (OI) during its most recent fiscal year:

Equipment acquired for use in various R&D projects (six-year life)	$90
Depreciation on the equipment above	5
Quality control costs during production, including routine product testing	30
Costs of efforts to refine, enrich, or otherwise improve the qualities of an existing product	25
Evaluation of potential new products	13
Costs of operating a lab to improve an existing formula	34
Materials cost for use in a pre-production pilot plant	9

Instructions

For each cost described above, indicate whether it should be capitalized as an intangible asset or whether it should be expensed. Explain briefly.

15-4 In this chapter, flag icons identify areas where there are GAAP differences between IFRS requirements and national standards.

Instructions

Access the website(s) identified on the inside back cover of this book, and prepare a concise summary of the differences that are flagged throughout the chapter material.

Chapter 16

Impairment of Assets:
IAS 36

U.S. GAAP References
FAS 157 Fair Value Measurements
FAS 144 Accounting for the Impairment or Disposal of Long-lived Assets
FAS 142 Goodwill and Other Intangible Assets
FAS 141 Business Combinations

Related IFRSs
IFRS 3 Business Combinations
IAS 16 Property, Plant and Equipment
IAS 17 Leases
IAS 27 Consolidated and Separate Financial Statements
IAS 28 Investments in Associates
IAS 31 Interests in Joint Ventures
IAS 38 Intangible Assets
IAS 40 Investment Property

OBJECTIVE AND SCOPE

An entity's economic resources are presented on its statement of financial position as key information for users. The assumption in evaluating these assets is that they are reported on this statement at no more than the amount the entity can recover from their use or sale. IAS 36 sets out the requirements to ensure this is the case: it specifies when an impairment loss is indicated, how to determine its amount, when and how much of it can be reversed, and what disclosures are necessary.

IAS 36 is a blanket standard on asset impairment that **applies to all assets** except for those specifically excluded, regardless of whether the assets are classified as current or non-current. The **exclusions**, covered by their own IFRSs, are inventories, assets arising from construction contracts and employee benefits, deferred tax assets, financial assets covered by IAS 39 *Financial Instruments: Recognition and Measurement*, non-current assets or disposal groups classified as held for sale, investment property and biological assets (agricultural activity) based on fair value measurements, and specific intangibles related to insurance contracts.

An *impairment loss* is defined as "the amount by which the carrying amount of an asset or a cash-generating unit exceeds its recoverable amount." Assets are grouped into cash-generating units when they do not generate independent cash flows on their own. A *cash-generating unit*, or *CGU*, is "the smallest identifiable group of assets that generates cash inflows that are largely independent of the cash flows from other assets or groups of assets."[1] Assessing assets in cash-generating units and goodwill is more complex than assessing individual assets so much of the standard is made up of special requirements for this type of situation. Illustration 16-1 provides a snapshot of how IAS 36 and this chapter are organized.

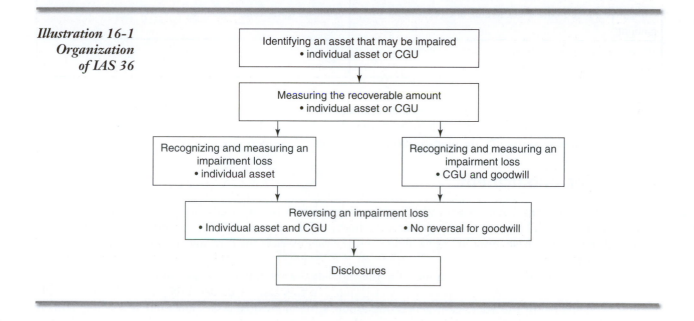

Illustration 16-1
Organization
of IAS 36

In general, an asset is considered impaired if its recoverable amount is less than its carrying amount, in which case an impairment loss is recognized. An impairment loss can be reversed if circumstances change. The remainder of the chapter takes you through the more detailed requirements of IAS 36.

---

[1] IASCF, IAS 36.6.

IDENTIFYING AN ASSET THAT MAY BE IMPAIRED

Assets are **assessed for indications of impairment** at the end of each reporting period, and **are tested** for impairment only when factors suggest that the assets might be impaired. A higher standard is applied to intangibles with indefinite lives, intangibles that are not yet ready for use, and goodwill acquired in a business combination. Regardless of whether there is any indication of impairment, these assets must be **tested for impairment annually**.[2] Note that all three of these types of assets have carrying amounts that involve some uncertainty and none is subject to amortization.

Indication of Impairment

The following indicators of impairment are required to be considered at a minimum.

External sources	Internal sources
There has been a significant reduction in the asset's market value.	There is evidence of obsolescence or physical damage of an asset.
A significant change in the technological, market, economic, or legal environment has affected or may adversely affect the entity.	Significant changes with adverse effects have taken place or are expected to take place in how the asset is used.
There has been an increase in market rates of return with a negative effect on the asset's value and recoverable amount.	Internal reports about the asset indicate its performance is or will be worse than expected.
The entity's net assets are greater than its market capitalization.	

There may be other factors that suggest that an asset's carrying amount is overstated. The objective is to be alert to conditions that may indicate an impairment in value. Even if a loss is not indicated, an entity may need to reassess the asset's useful life, the amortization method applied, or its residual value.

Testing for Impairment

If there is any indication that an asset or a cash-generating unit may be impaired, the entity needs to estimate its recoverable amount. The *recoverable amount* is the higher of the asset or CGU's **fair value less costs to sell** and its **value in use**. These terms are explained below. If either exceeds the carrying amount, the asset or CGU is not impaired.

The recoverable amount is determined for the individual asset unless its cash flows are not generated independently from those of other assets or asset groups. In this case, with two exceptions, the recoverable amount is calculated for the asset's cash-generating group. If the individual asset's fair value less selling costs is more than its carrying amount, or if this amount can be determined and the asset's value in use is estimated to be close to it, the asset can be assessed on its own.

When it is possible to determine only an asset's fair value less costs to sell **or** its value in use, the one that can be measured more reliably may be used as the recoverable amount. Fair value less costs to sell is the only relevant amount to use for assets held for disposal.

---

[2] IAS 36.24 indicates that an intangible with an indefinite life may not have to calculate the recoverable amount needed for the impairment test every period if certain conditions that indicate the recoverable amount is not likely to have changed are met. If they are met, the most recent calculation of recoverable amount from a prior period may be used.

Measuring the Recoverable Amount

Fair Value Less Costs to Sell

The *fair value less costs to sell* is the amount that can be obtained from the sale of an asset or cash-generating unit in an arm's-length transaction between knowledgeable, willing parties, less the incremental costs directly attributable to its disposal, excluding finance costs and income tax expense.[3]

The best basis for **fair value** is an arm's-length-bargained price in a binding sales agreement, but other market evidence may have to be substituted when this is not available. There is a hierarchy used for determining fair value, with active market prices being preferred to estimates of selling prices. The intent is to determine how much is recoverable in a bargained, rather than a forced, sale transaction. The **disposal costs** deducted from the asset's fair value are those directly attributable to disposal—legal costs, transaction taxes, removal costs, and direct incremental costs to put the asset into condition for sale.

Value in Use

Value in use is the present value of the future cash flows expected to be derived from an asset or cash-generating unit.[4] This discounted valuation reflects the following:

(a) the future cash flows expected to be derived from the asset or cash-generating unit,
(b) variations in the amount or timing of the expected cash flows,
(c) the time value of money or current market risk-free interest rate,
(d) the price for the asset-specific risks, and
(e) other factors the market is likely to factor into the pricing of the cash flows.

The asset or CGU's value in use is determined in a two-step process: (1) the future cash flows expected from its use and ultimate disposal are estimated, and (2) these are brought to their present value by applying the appropriate discount rate. There are two approaches to making these calculations and either one may be used. One way is to weight the possible cash flows for the probability that each will occur and then apply a discount rate incorporating the remaining uncertainties. The other method is to use the best, or most likely, estimate of the expected future cash flows and build the uncertainties into the discount rate used. The difference in the two approaches is explained in the following example.

Situation

An entity estimating future cash flows for an asset determines that there is a 40% probability that cash inflows will be $120 and a 60% probability that they will be $80. What are the cash flows expected from this asset?

Analysis

Under the first approach, the cash flows are adjusted. The expected value of the cash flows is ($120 × 40%) + ($80 × 60%) = $96.

Under the second approach, the discount rate is adjusted. Here, the best estimate of the cash flows is $80.[5]

The appropriate discount rate will differ, depending on the approach chosen. In either case, the objective is to reflect the weighted average of all possible outcomes—the present value of the future cash flows.

The IAS 36 standard provides considerable principles-based guidance on the bases to use in **estimating the future cash flows**. These include the use of reasonable and supportable assumptions related to the asset in its

---

[3] IASCF, IAS 36.6.
[4] IASCF, IAS 36.6.
[5] IASCF, Basis for Conclusions on IAS 36 *Impairment of Assets*, para. BCZ41.

current condition. Cash flows from the continued use and the disposal of the asset or CGU, reduced by the cash outflows needed to generate cash flows from their continued use, are all taken into account. Cash flows from financing activities and those associated with income taxes are excluded and the cash flows on disposal at the end of the asset's useful life are based on the amounts expected in an arm's-length transaction reduced by expected disposal costs. Foreign cash flows are all estimated and discounted in the currency in which they are expected to be generated, and then are translated at the spot rate when the value in use calculation is prepared.

A pre-tax **discount rate** is used that reflects current market assessments of the time value of money and the asset's specific risks not taken into account in the cash flow estimates. The estimate of this rate is based on current market transactions for similar assets, or the weighted average cost of capital for a listed entity with similar risks. Appendix A to IAS 36 provides additional guidance in applying present value techniques to measure value in use.

RECOGNIZING AND MEASURING AN IMPAIRMENT LOSS FOR AN INDIVIDUAL ASSET

If the recoverable amount of an asset (other than goodwill) as determined above is less than its carrying amount, the carrying amount or book value is written down to its recoverable amount: this reduction is the ***impairment loss***.[6] If the recoverable amount is a negative value, a liability is recognized only if required by another standard.

An impairment loss is usually **recognized immediately in profit and loss** as follows:

Impairment Loss	$	
Accumulated Impairment Losses		$

Because this changes the remaining depreciable/amortizable amount, the depreciation or amortization expense must be revised for future periods and the deferred tax balances need to be reviewed and adjusted.

If the asset is measured under the revaluation model in IAS 16 *Property, Plant and Equipment* or IAS 38 *Intangible Assets,* the applicable standard is applied instead. For IAS 16 and IAS 38, this means that the impairment loss is accounted for on the same basis as a revaluation decrease—it is charged first through other comprehensive income to any revaluation surplus that exists for that asset, and only the excess is recognized in profit or loss.

RECOGNIZING AND MEASURING AN IMPAIRMENT LOSS FOR CASH-GENERATING UNITS AND GOODWILL

Cash-Generating Units

When the recoverable amount of an individual asset cannot be determined, the entity instead calculates the recoverable amount of the cash-generating unit to which it belongs. As indicated above, this happens only when the asset does not generate cash flows that are largely independent of flows from other assets, or when its fair value less selling costs is not considered representative of its value in use. The allocation of assets to cash-generating units often involves judgment.

The cash flows considered are external flows and the dependence or independence of the cash flows from other assets is judged primarily on how management assesses operations and makes resource decisions. For products produced internally that are affected by internal transfer pricing, management uses its best estimates of the assets' fair values in external markets to determine the appropriate CGU and its value in use. Once assigned to a cash-generating unit, the asset or assets are consistently identified with that CGU in future periods.

---

[6] IASCF, IAS 36.59.

Situation

A forestry company owns significant standing timber in its northern territory. Included in the assets is a road system that was constructed to give company personnel access to the timber for maintenance and later logging activity. The road system cannot be sold independently. How should the road system's recoverable amount be determined?

Analysis

The road system's fair value less selling costs is almost negligible; certainly far less than its value in use. Because its recoverable value cannot be determined independently, the road system is assigned to the smallest identifiable group of assets that generate independent cash inflows. Its CGU is likely made up of the acreage of standing timber serviced by the road system along with any other site specific non-cash-generating assets. The CGU's recoverable amount can be determined because it is possible to estimate both its fair value less selling costs and its value in use.

Recoverable Amount and Carrying Amount of a CGU

The **recoverable amount of a CGU**, like an individual asset, is the greater of its fair value less costs to sell and its value in use. Because this recoverable amount is compared with the CGU's **carrying amount** to determine if there is an impairment loss, it is reasonable to include the same assets in both measures.

The CGU's carrying amount, therefore, **includes** the book value of only those assets that are used to generate the relevant stream of cash inflows. These can be assets that are directly involved, or that can be allocated to the CGU on a reasonable and consistent basis. Where liabilities are needed to calculate the recoverable amount, they are also deducted in determining the carrying amount of the CGU.

Allocating Goodwill to Cash-Generating Units

Goodwill is recognized only as a result of a business combination. It represents the future economic benefits an entity expects from assets acquired in the combination that are not identified and recognized as separate assets. Because of this, goodwill is assigned to a CGU or group of CGUs that is expected to benefit from the synergies of the combination. Goodwill is allocated to the lowest level in the organization that manages this asset. It is not allocated arbitrarily. The CGU chosen cannot be larger than an operating segment, as defined by IFRS 8 *Operating Segments*.

If part of the cash-generating unit that the goodwill is assigned to is disposed of, the goodwill has to be allocated between the portion sold and the portion of the CGU remaining. The carrying amount of the goodwill associated with the portion sold is included in calculating the gain or loss on disposal. This amount is usually based on the relative value of the portion of the CGU sold to the value of the part retained, unless there is a better method of associating the goodwill with that operation. Goodwill is reallocated on a similar relative value basis if there are changes in the composition of an entity's cash-generating units.

Situation

Acme Corp. allocated the goodwill acquired in a recent business combination to its entire Retail Products Division because allocating it to this Division's five product lines, each a CGU, would have been purely arbitrary. Acme sells all the assets associated with product line A for $25 at a time when the recoverable amount of lines B, C, D, and E is $100. The carrying amount of line A's identifiable assets is $15 and of the goodwill assigned to the Retail Products Division is $30. What amount of goodwill is included in the carrying amount of product line A?

Analysis

The goodwill is assigned to the product line sold based on relative values. Product line A has a value of $25, and the remaining CGUs in the Division have a recoverable amount of $100, for a total value of $125. The portion of the carrying amount of goodwill assigned to product line A is therefore 25/125, or 1/5 of $30, or $6.

Testing CGUs with Goodwill for Impairment[7]

CGUs **with related goodwill that has not been allocated to that unit** are tested for impairment when there is an indication that the unit may be impaired. In this case, the impairment loss is determined by comparing the carrying value of the unit, **excluding any goodwill**, with its recoverable amount.

A cash-generating unit **that has goodwill allocated to it** is tested at least **annually** for impairment. In this case, the recoverable amount of the unit is compared with its carrying amount, **including goodwill**, to determine if the unit and its goodwill are impaired.

Impairment Loss for a Cash-Generating Unit

When the recoverable amount of a CGU or group of units that goodwill has been allocated to is less than the CGU or group's carrying amount, an **impairment loss is recognized**. The loss is assigned in the following specific order:

1. the carrying amount of goodwill allocated to the CGU or group is reduced, and
2. any remaining amount is allocated to each asset in the unit or group of units on the basis of its relative carrying amount.

No asset, however, is written down below its recoverable amount, or zero, if higher.

The amount of the reduction in each asset's carrying amount is its impairment loss. The losses are accounted for in the same way as they were for individual assets explained earlier in the chapter—usually recognized in profit or loss. For property, plant, and equipment and intangible assets accounted for using the revaluation model, however, the losses are treated as if they were revaluation writedowns.

REVERSING AN IMPAIRMENT LOSS

At each reporting date, information that mirrors the original indicators of impairment is assessed to determine whether a previously recognized impairment loss still exists. If a reduction in the amount of the loss is indicated for an asset other than goodwill, the asset's recoverable amount is recalculated. If the **estimates used** to determine the recoverable amount **have changed**, an impairment loss can be reversed.[8]

Impairment losses for **goodwill** are **not reversed**. Any subsequent increase in value of goodwill is considered to be internally generated rather than a reversal of the previous impairment.

Reversing an Impairment Loss for an Individual Asset

In most cases the amount of the reversal is limited. For an individual asset it is limited to an increase in the asset's carrying amount to what it would have been, net of depreciation or amortization, if the impairment had not been recognized originally. This limitation does not apply if the asset is accounted for under the revaluation model, as applied in IAS 16 and IAS 38. The full reversal in this case is accounted for as a revaluation increase.

Again, the asset's remaining depreciable or amortizable amount changes with this adjustment; therefore, new rates of depreciation or amortization expense are determined and deferred tax balances are reviewed and adjusted.

---

[7] Corporate assets such as headquarter buildings, divisional head offices, centralized EDP (electronic data processing) equipment, and research facilities are similar to goodwill in that they do not generate cash flows independently of other assets or asset groups. Testing these assets for impairment is addressed in IAS 36.100 to 36.103.

[8] The increase in recoverable amount must reflect an increase in the asset's service potential, not merely the time value of money.

Reversing an Impairment Loss for a Cash-Generating Unit

The reversal of an impairment loss for a CGU is allocated to the assets of the unit, excluding goodwill, in proportion to the assets' relative carrying amounts. The loss reversal for each asset is usually recognized in profit or loss, unless considered a revaluation increase for assets accounted for under the revaluation model of IAS 16 or IAS 38.

The impairment loss reversal is limited in the same way as explained above for an individual asset. As with individual asset adjustments, new rates of depreciation or amortization are determined, and deferred tax balances are reviewed and adjusted.

DISCLOSURE

The next section provides a summary of the key elements of the significant disclosures required for an entity's impairment losses and loss reversals.

For each class of assets, the following information is reported. It is often provided in the reconciliation of asset opening and ending balances:

- the amount of impairment losses and the amount of impairment loss reversals recognized in profit or loss, along with the line item where each is located in the statement of comprehensive income; and
- the amount of impairment losses and impairment loss reversals on revalued assets recognized in other comprehensive income.

For each impairment loss or reversal that is **individually material**, descriptive information is needed that explains the events and circumstances leading to the adjustment, the nature of the asset or unit, and how its recoverable amount is determined, as well as the amount of the loss or reversal recognized. Similar information is provided in total about the events and circumstances and main classes of assets affected for the remainder of items that are not individually material.

Because goodwill and intangibles with indefinite lives are not amortized, users have to be given more information so they can assess the reliability of the impairment tests carried out on these assets. Extensive disclosures such as those summarized below attempt to meet this goal.

1. For **each** CGU or group of units with **significant amounts** of allocated goodwill or intangibles with indefinite lives:
   (a) the carrying amount of goodwill and of intangibles with indefinite lives allocated and whether the recoverable amount of the unit is based on value in use or fair value less selling costs;
   (b) if based on **value in use**, detailed descriptions of key assumptions underlying cash flow projections, along with how the assumptions were determined, information about the time horizon of the projections, growth rates used for extrapolation, and the discount rates used; and
   (c) if based on **fair value less selling costs**, an explanation of the methodology used to determine fair value, key assumptions and the approach used to make them, details about variables used in cash flow projections, and sensitivity information that might cause an impairment to be recognized.

2. If an entity has CGUs with allocated goodwill or intangibles assets with indefinite lives that are **individually insignificant** relative to the entity's total amount, this fact is disclosed along with the amounts allocated to these units. Where the recoverable amounts of any of these units are based on the same assumptions as in (1) above and the total of the allocated goodwill and unamortized intangibles to these units is significant, disclosures similar to those above are required.

Illustration 16-2 sets out impairment disclosures from the financial statements of the world's largest confectionery company, Cadbury Schweppes plc (now Cadbury plc).[9] The first excerpt is the company's accounting policy note on impairment, while the other notes provide information on the relatively minor, but

---

[9] http://www.cadbury.com/Reports/2007AnnualReport.pdf.

specific impairment losses recognized in Cadbury's year ended December 31, 2007, and where they have been reported. This company's reporting currency is U.K. pounds (£).

Illustration 16-2
Cadbury
Schweppes plc
Impairment
Notes

Impairment review

The Group carries out an impairment review of its tangible and definite life intangible assets when a change in circumstances or situation indicates that those assets may have suffered an impairment loss. Intangible assets with indefinite useful lives are tested for impairment at least annually and whenever there is an indication that the asset may be impaired. Impairment is measured by comparing the carrying amount of an asset or of a cash-generating unit with the 'recoverable amount', that is the higher of its fair value less costs to sell and its 'value in use'. 'Value in use' is calculated by discounting the expected future cash flows, using a discount rate based on an estimate of the rate that the market would expect on an investment of comparable risk.

3. Trading costs

(a) Trading costs analysis:

	2007	2006
	£m	£m
Impairment of goodwill	13	15

5. Non-trading items

(Loss)/profit on impairment/disposal of land and buildings	(12)	22

The impairment of land and buildings is the loss recognised on the write-down of property, plant and equipment in China.

14. Goodwill

	£m
Cost	
At 31 December 2006	2,502
Exchange differences	78
Recognised on acquisition of subsidiaries	257
Transferred to asset held for sale	(1)
Derecognised on disposal	(3)
At 31 December 2007	2,833
Impairment	
At 31 December 2006	(15)
Impairment charge in the year	(13)
At 31 December 2007	(28)
Net book value at 31 December 2007	2,805

The impairment charge recognized in 2007 relates to the Group's business in China. The Group's strategy relating to China was revised in the first half of 2007 with a change in focus to concentrate on key brands and streamline the distribution network which led to the impairment of goodwill historically recognized.

LOOKING AHEAD

IAS 36 *Impairment of Assets* has undergone two recent revisions, both as part of the IASB's project on business combinations. The most recent changes reflect decisions made in revised IFRS 3 *Business Combinations* and the amended version of IAS 27 *Consolidated and Separate Financial Statements*, both released in 2008. The major changes relate to the impairment test for goodwill.

Impairment has been identified by both the IASB and FASB as a topic for longer term convergence; however, as this book goes to print, it has not developed even to a project proposal stage. Therefore, no significant changes are likely in this area in the near future. However, the IASB's fair value measurement project, expected to result in the convergence of international and U.S. GAAP, may affect the measurement guidance in this standard. An Exposure Draft (ED/2009/5) was issued in May 2009, with the publication of final guidance expected in 2010.

END-OF-CHAPTER PRACTICE

16-1 Three years ago, Ace Airlines (AA) was granted permission to schedule flights on the popular and profitable Newalta to Oldsford route, provided it also serviced Remoteville, which is considerably further north than Oldsford. As a result, AA set up a facility in Oldsford and a small office and maintenance bay in Remoteville. Remoteville is sparsely populated and accessible only by air. AA's controller now wants to review the Remoteville assets for impairment due to the continuing losses on the Oldford-Remoteville route, but is not familiar with IAS 36.

Instructions
Write a short memo to AA's controller, identifying how he should proceed in determining whether the Remoteville assets are impaired.

16-2 Waix Ltd. (WL) is a manufacturer with a number of product lines, one of which is the production of parts for residential telephone sets. Recently there have been indications that the market for this product is likely to decline significantly, and WL is assessing various assets for impairment. The following assets are used specifically to manufacture these parts:

	Cost	Accumulated Depreciation
Tools and dies	$10	$ 6
Specialized equipment	50	35
General equipment	30	18

The tools and dies and specialized equipment have no resale value other than for scrap, although the general equipment could be sold or used profitably in one of WL's other product lines. WL plans on continuing production of these parts for two more years in order to fill its existing commitments. The present value of the net cash flows from the next two years' production of these parts is $26 and the estimated net amount that could be recovered if these assets were sold today is $15.

Instructions
(a) Briefly discuss whether these assets should be assessed for impairment individually or as part of a cash-generating unit.
(b) Assuming the assets are allocated to a CGU made up of the three types of assets identified, determine whether an impairment loss needs to be recognized, and if so, in what total amount.
(c) Prepare the entry needed to record any impairment loss indicated, assuming these assets are reported in separate asset classes.

16-3 Firstall Corp. (FC) acquired four divisions of a competitor eight years ago in a business combination transaction, paying $25 more than the fair value of the identifiable assets acquired. The goodwill was determined to be 100% attributable to the operations of the East Division and the South Division. Although these two divisions are cash-generating units in their own right, there was no basis on which to allocate the goodwill between them. FC has identified the combined divisions as one CGU for assessing goodwill impairment on an annual basis. At the end of the most recent year, the following information is available:

	Carrying Amount
East Division	$75
South Division	125
Goodwill	25

FC has determined that the estimated recoverable value of the two divisions together is $215.

Instructions
(a) Identify the asset, cash-generating unit, or group of CGUs that FC should use to test for impairment.
(b) Is there an impairment loss at the end of the current year? Explain how you determined your answer.
(c) If applicable, indicate how any impairment loss should be accounted for. Be specific.

16-4 In this chapter, flag icons identify areas where there are GAAP differences between IFRS requirements and national standards.

Instructions
Access the website(s) identified on the inside back cover of this book, and prepare a concise summary of the differences that are flagged throughout the chapter material.

Chapter 17

Basic Financial Instruments:
IAS 32, IAS 39, and IFRS 7

U.S. GAAP References
FAS 115 Accounting for Certain Investments in Debt and Equity Securities
FAS 130 Reporting Comprehensive Income
FAS 133 and 138 Accounting for Derivative Instruments and Hedging Activities
FAS 140 and 156 Accounting for the Transfer and Servicing of Financial Assets and Extinguishment of Financial Liabilities
FAS 150 Accounting for Certain Financial Instruments with Characteristics of Both Liabilities and Equity
FAS 155 Accounting for Certain Hybrid Financial Instruments
FAS 157 Fair Value Measurements
FAS 159 The Fair Value Option for Financial Assets and Financial Liabilities

Related IFRS
IAS 1 Presentation of Financial Statements

OBJECTIVE AND SCOPE

The framework for accounting for financial instruments is laid out in three standards as follows:

- IAS 32, which deals with presentation from the perspective of the issuer (only);
- IAS 39, which deals with measurement and recognition of financial assets and financial liabilities; and
- IFRS 7, which deals with disclosures.

IAS 1 deals with financial statement presentation (including comprehensive income). This chapter gives an overview of the standards while Chapters 18–20 go into more detail.

According to IAS 32.11,

"A *financial instrument* is any contract that gives rise to a financial asset of one entity and a financial liability or equity instrument of another entity."

The majority of items on the balance sheets of many companies are financial instruments. Some exceptions are inventories; prepaids; and property, plant, and equipment. Illustration 17-1 shows the accounting equation, along with the related IFRSs as they pertain to financial instruments.

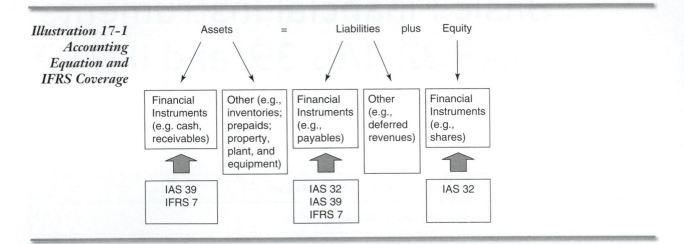

Illustration 17-1 Accounting Equation and IFRS Coverage

A defining attribute of a financial instrument is that it is a contract between two parties. It may be a financial asset to one party, while at the same time being a financial liability or equity instrument of the other party. For instance, an agreement to pay on credit is a financial asset to the supplier (accounts receivable) and a financial liability to the customer (accounts payable). IAS 32 and 39 do not change the fundamental accounting for items such as trade receivables and payables except for derecognition which will be covered later in the chapter. Financial assets, liabilities, and equity instruments are defined in IAS 32.11. The definitions are summarized as follows:

A *financial asset* is

(a) cash,
(b) an equity instrument (of another entity), or
(c) a contractual right to receive cash (or another financial asset) or to exchange financial assets or financial liabilities under conditions that are potentially favorable.

An *equity instrument* is a contract that represents a residual interest in the net assets of the company.

A *financial liability* is basically a contractual obligation to deliver cash (or another financial asset) or to exchange financial assets or financial liabilities under conditions that are potentially unfavorable.

(The definitions for financial assets and financial liabilities also include certain contracts that are settled in the entity's own equity instruments. These will be covered later in Chapter 19. The definitions above include definitions of derivatives, which will be dealt with in Chapter 18.)

Note that although many items on the average balance sheet are financial items, they may be excluded from IAS 32, IAS 39, and IFRS 7. This is because these items may be covered by other standards, are presently being reviewed by the IASB, or are residual in nature (for instance a company's own shares).[1] The financial instruments that are either completely or partially excluded from the standards are as follows:

IAS 32:[2]

- investments that are consolidated or equity accounted for under the following standards: IAS 27, 28, 31
- rights and obligations under employee benefit plans (IAS 19) and insurance contracts (IFRS 4)
- share-based payments (IFRS 2)

IAS 39:[3]
Those noted above as well as

- rights and obligations under leases covered under IAS 17 (may be partially covered by the financial instrument standards)
- equity instruments of the entity (issuer) that are classified as equity (IAS 32)
- contracts to buy/sell an acquiree at a future date
- some loan commitments (IAS 37) although all loan commitments are subject to derecognition provisions in IAS 39
- rights to payments to reimburse the entity for expenditures to settle a liability (previously recognized as a provision)

RECOGNITION AND DERECOGNITION

Initial Recognition

Financial instruments should be recognized when the entity becomes a party to the contract.[4] Therefore, when a company takes delivery of goods purchased on credit, it recognizes a financial liability (accounts payable). Commitments to purchase or sell items are generally not recognized until the items are delivered or received unless they meet the definition of a derivative or are onerous, in which case they might be recognized. As mentioned above, derivatives will be dealt with in Chapter 18. Onerous contracts were dealt with in Chapter 5.

When financial instruments are initially recognized, they must be classified as one of the following (which are defined in IAS 39.9):

1. financial assets at fair value through profit or loss (FVTPL)
2. held to maturity investments (HTM)
3. loans and receivables
4. available for sale financial assets (AFS)

The classification is important because it dictates how the asset/liability will be measured going forward and where the profits and losses will be booked. The definition for each of these classifications is discussed below. Subsequent measurement and what to do with gains/losses will be discussed later in the chapter.

Financial Assets at Fair Value through Profit or Loss (FVTPL)

Under IAS 39.9, **FVTPL** assets/liabilities are either held for trading (HFT) or designated as FVTPL by the entity. Instruments may be classified as HFT if they

- are acquired with the intent to sell or repurchase in the near term,
- are part of a portfolio of instruments that are managed together to maximize profits, or

---

[1] An entity's own shares are not covered by IAS 39 because they are valued (along with related equity accounts) at the difference between assets and liabilities as per the accounting equation. Income taxes are not covered either since they are not financial instruments (no contractual relationship).
[2] IASCF, IAS 32.4.
[3] IASCF, IAS 39.2.
[4] IASCF, IAS 39.14.

- are derivatives (other than financial guarantee contracts or designated and effective hedging instruments.) Hedge accounting will be discussed in Chapter 18.

In other words, the instruments are traded for profit ("active and frequent buying and selling"[5]). Not all companies would engage in this type of activity since significant expertise is normally required to trade instruments. Banks and investment dealers are examples of entities that would engage in trading activities. Conversely a manufacturing company would normally direct its energies toward manufacturing activities and not be trading in securities.

An entity may, as an accounting policy choice, designate assets as FVTPL. This option is available to, among other things, encourage the use of fair value and to reduce the need for having to use hedge accounting (which can be fairly complex). Under the standard, entities are allowed to use this option when doing so results in more relevant information.[6] Where there is no market value (quoted in an active market) and fair value is not reliably measurable, equity instruments may not be classified as FVTPL.

Once an item is classified as FVTPL, it may not be reclassified to another category.

Held to Maturity Investments (HTM)

HTM investments have the following characteristics:

- They are not derivatives.
- They have fixed and determinable payments and fixed maturity dates.

Therefore, only debt instruments that are not derivatives can be classified as HTM (equity instruments such as shares do not have maturity dates). It is still acceptable to classify an investment as HTM even if there is a significant risk that the issuer will not make the payments.[7] HTM investments are meant to be held to maturity (hence the name), and the entity must demonstrate positive intent and ability to do so. These investments may be disposed of or reclassified prior to maturity only in very limited circumstances. If the entity disposes of or reclassifies more than an insignificant amount of investments prior to maturity in the current year or in the previous two years, it will not be allowed to use the HTM category going forward.[8]

Does this mean that the entity may never dispose of these investments even if they become bad investments? The standard does not handcuff the entity entirely. It is acceptable, under the standard, to dispose of the investment under the following situations:

- the investment is very close to maturity;
- the entity has collected substantially all of the amounts under the terms of the debt; or
- circumstances exist that are attributable to an isolated event beyond the entity's control, which is non-recurring and could not have been anticipated.

Thus, there may be some unanticipated, one-time situations where it is acceptable under the standard to dispose of the instrument prior to maturity. For instance, a decline in the credit rating of the issuer may cause the entity to rethink its intent to hold the investment to maturity. Presumably, the entity would not have invested in the instrument if it thought there was too much risk.

---

[5] IASCF, IAS 39, AG14.

[6] More relevant information would result where, for instance, the use of fair value eliminates or reduces inconsistencies in accounting or where fair value provides better information to users because the entity manages its resources on a fair value basis. For example, if management bonuses are paid based on the fair value of the investment portfolio, then it might make sense to measure the investment portfolio at fair value.

[7] IASCF, IAS.39, AG17.

[8] In other words, there is a punishment if an entity reclassifies or disposes of these investments prior to maturity. This is a bit of an anomaly since accounting standards generally do not include punitive clauses.

Other acceptable situations include but are not limited to the following:[9]

- changes in tax laws regarding the deductibility of interest;
- major business combinations/dispositions; or
- changes in regulatory requirements regarding the investment allowed/required to be held (for instance, in the banking and insurance industries, the government mandates certain levels of and types of investments).

This restriction on reclassification exists because HTM investments are measured at amortized cost, so reclassification would potentially trigger a gain or loss and may lead to manipulation of income. Using amortized costs makes sense only if the investment is held to the end of the contract and the contractual cash flows are collected. If there is intent to dispose of the investment prior to this then using fair value makes more sense.

How does an entity demonstrate positive intent and ability? Positive intent and ability can be shown by many factors. These factors must be assessed upon initial recognition and subsequently.

The following chart looks at some specific factors dealing with the characteristics of HTM investments and the criteria that must be met before investments may be classified as HTM.[10]

Illustration 17-2
HTM
Investments

Situation	Accounting
The entity stands ready to sell in response to changes in market conditions (interest rates/ yields, risk, foreign currency risks).	Not HTM because there is no positive intent displayed to hold the investment for the longer term. The entity is ready to sell if general market conditions change.
The issuer of the debt has the right to settle the debt at significantly less than the amortized costs.	Not HTM since it would appear likely that the entity will not recover its full investment and therefore might consider earlier disposition (no positive intent and ability to hold to maturity). If the issuer can settle the debt by paying less, it will likely take this option.
The entity has the right to require the issuer to redeem or repay the instrument early (this feature is referred to as "puttable").	Not HTM since the entity would have paid extra for this right and therefore, from an economic perspective, would not have paid for the right unless it thought it might use it.
Common shares.	Not HTM since they have no maturity date.
The entity has sold or reclassified HTM in past.	Not HTM if the entity has disposed of or reclassified more than an insignificant amount of HTM investment in the current or previous two years. This past behavior provides evidence of the lack of intent to hold to maturity.
Perpetual debt.	Not HTM since there is no maturity date.
The issuer has the right to redeem the debt early.	May classify as HTM. The early redemption feature (if triggered) is seen to accelerate the maturity date.
The creditworthiness of the issuer declines significantly for an investment initially classified as HTM.	The entity may dispose of the investment prior to maturity without being barred from using the HTM classification in the future.
The entity does not have sufficient cash flow and may have to sell some of its investments.	Not HTM because the entity does not have the demonstrated ability to hold the investment to maturity.

---

[9] IASCF, IAS 39, AG22.

[10] Many of these are discussed in the Application Guidance to the standard IAS 39, AG16-25.

Loans and Receivables

Loans and receivables have the following characteristics:[11]
- They are non-derivative.
- They have fixed and determinable payments.
- They are not quoted in an active market.

Therefore, this category includes loan assets, trade receivables, and investments in debt instruments.

Available for Sale Financial Assets

Available for sale financial assets are those that are not classified as one of the others, i.e., FVTPL, HTM, or loans and receivables. This category is therefore a default category, i.e., instruments are presented here if they do not meet the definitions of the other categories (either due to the nature of the instrument, management intent or other).

Derecognition of a Financial Asset

Derecognition is the process of removing an item from the balance sheet (statement of financial position). Financial assets are derecognized when

- the contractual rights to the cash flows related to the asset expire, or
- the rights are transferred and certain derecognition criteria are met.[12]

For instance, a loan receivable might be derecognized when the company that owes the money goes bankrupt. At that point, the entity may have no further rights to the cash flows. Therefore, the asset would be removed, which might trigger a gain or loss. In addition, when all cash flows have been paid under the terms of the loan, the entity would derecognize the asset because the rights to receive cash have expired. The situation gets more complex with transfers since the transaction must be examined to determine if a transfer occurs and then the transactions must pass certain derecogition criteria.

Transfers

Many companies transfer their financial assets to other companies. An example is a factoring arrangement whereby receivables might be transferred—often for an amount below their carrying value. This allows the entity (transferor) to free up capital. Many entities in the retail business factor their receivables. In general, the act of transferring the asset qualifies the asset for derecognition as long as the risks and rewards of ownership are passed to the transferee. Chapter 18 examines this in greater detail.

Derecognition of a Financial Liability

Liabilities are removed from the balance sheet when the obligation is extinguished (i.e., it is discharged or cancelled, or it expires). For instance, when the entity has paid out all principal and interest, then it would derecognize the liability. Things get complicated when an entity extinguishes an obligation earlier than required or modifies the obligation. These scenarios will be further examined in Chapter 18.

---

[11] IASCF, IAS 39.9.
[12] IASCF, IAS 39.17.

MEASUREMENT

Initial Measurement of Financial Assets and Financial Liabilities

Financial assets/liabilities are initially recognized at fair value. Transaction costs that are directly attributable to the transaction should be added to the carrying value unless the asset is classified as FVTPL.[13]

Subsequent Measurement of Financial Assets and Liabilities

Subsequent measurement depends on the classification upon initial recognition. The chart in Illustration 17-3 explains how to measure the financial instruments and where the resulting gains/losses are booked.

Illustration 17-3 Subsequent Measurement of Financial Instruments

Classification	Subsequent measurement	Gains/losses
FVTPL	Fair value	Profit or loss
HTM	Amortized cost using the effective interest method	NA
Loans/receivables	Amortized cost using the effective interest method	NA
AFS	Fair value	Other comprehensive income except that for debt instruments, any premium/discount must be amortized to profit or loss using the effective interest method
Other (equity instruments that do not have a quoted price in an active market and whose fair value cannot be reliably measured)	Cost	NA
Financial liabilities (as long as they are not classified as FVTPL)[14]	Amortized cost using the effective interest method	NA

It is important to note that debt instruments classified as AFS investments pose additional complexities in accounting. Subsequent to initial recognition, the assets are continually revalued to fair value. The unrealized gains/losses are booked to other comprehensive income except for amounts that are realized though amortization of a premium/discount using the effective interest method. Changes in fair value of debt instruments due to changes in exchange rates are booked through profit or loss. In addition, any impairments are booked through profit or loss. Impairments will be discussed later in the chapter.

---

[13] IASCF, IAS 39.43.
[14] Chapter 18 will discuss additional exceptions to accounting for financial liabilities.

Situation

Jenkins Limited purchases some common shares of Galliano Limited, which trade on the national stock market. Jenkins pays $100 plus purchase commissions of $10. At the end of the year, the shares are worth $105. Prepare the journal entries illustrating the accounting initially and at year end assuming classification as AFS and FVTPL.

Analysis

Assuming AFS classification:

		AFS Classification	FVTPL Classification
Purchase date	Dr. Investment	$110	100
	Dr. Expense	0	10
	Cr. Cash	110	110
Year end	Dr. Other comprehensive income	5	
	Cr. Investment	5	
	Dr. Investment		5
	Cr. Gain		5

Fair Value Measurement Considerations

Fair value is defined as[15]

"the amount for which an asset could be exchanged, or a liability settled between knowledgeable, willing parties in an arm's length transaction."

How do you determine fair value? There is a significant amount of evidence that may be gathered to support fair value, but the best evidence is quoted prices in an active market.[16]

A market is active if the prices are readily and regularly available and reflect actual arm's-length transactions.[17] According to the standard, market inputs should be used as much as possible, with less reliance on inputs that are specific to the entity (entity-specific inputs). In other words, the fair value should reflect what the market perceives the instrument to be worth and not the entity.

As a secondary choice, the entity would use a valuation technique. The objective of a valuation is to arrive at a value that would have been paid "in an arm's length exchange motivated by normal business considerations."[18] Valuation techniques should use whatever market data are available. Examples of valuation techniques include researching recent transactions, making reference to current fair values of similar instruments, discounted cash flows, and options pricing models. Following are examples of inputs:[19]

- time value of money
- credit risk
- foreign exchange rates
- commodity prices
- equity prices
- volatility (variability in value)

---

[15] IASCF, IAS 32.11.
[16] IASCF, IAS 39.48.
[17] IASCF, IAS 39, AG71.
[18] IASCF, IAS 39, AG75.
[19] IASCF, IAS 39, AG82.

- prepayment risks
- other

Instruments that carry below-market interest rates are discounted using the prevailing interest rates for similar instruments with similar credit and other risks.

Reclassifications

As previously noted, once an instrument has been classified as FVTPL, it may not be subsequently reclassified. Similarly, instruments may not be subsequently reclassified into the FVTPL category. If it is no longer appropriate to classify an item as HTM, it is classified as AFS.

Impairment and Uncollectibility of Financial Assets

If there is objective evidence of impairment, the asset should be written down through profit or loss. Illustration 17-4 shows how the impairments would be accounted for in the various classifications.

Illustration 17-4 Accounting for Impairments

Classification	Measurement	Impairment Loss
FVTPL	Fair value with gains/losses through profit or loss	NA—Losses are all booked through profit or loss already.
HTM	Amortized cost	• Assess individual assets first and then, if there is no impairment, assess in a group with similar risk. • May subsequently reverse loss.
Loans/receivables	Amortized cost	See above.
AFS	Fair value with gains/losses though other comprehensive income	• Reclassify loss from other comprehensive income to profit or loss. • May reverse loss for debt instrument only (it is too difficult to differentiate between reversals of impairment losses and other changes in fair value for equity instruments).

For financial assets carried at cost (e.g., because fair value is not reliably measurable), impairments are not subsequently reversed.

In assessing whether there is objective evidence of impairment, the standard focuses on the existence of events (referred to as loss events) such as financial difficulty of the issuer, breach of contract, disappearances of an active market, bankruptcy and other.

PRESENTATION

Liabilities and Equity

Financial instruments should be classified as debt or equity according to their economic substance.[20] Often financial instruments contain both debt and equity components (referred to as compound instruments). These

---

[20] IASCF, IAS 32.15.

instruments should be divided into their respective debt and equity components and presented as part debt and part equity. In making these assessments, the definitions of financial liability and equity instruments discussed earlier should be used in the analysis.

In addition, the instrument is an equity instrument if both the following conditions are met:[21]

- the instrument contains no contractual obligation, and
- the instrument may be settled in a fixed number of the issuer's own equity instruments.

Care should be taken to review the legal form and economic substance of financial instruments. The economic substance, as noted above, should dictate the accounting. The chart in Illustration 17-5 looks at some instruments and their accounting. Where an instrument contains both liabilities and equity, the liability would generally be measured at the present value of the future cash flows with any remaining consideration exchanged for the instrument being booked as equity. This topic will be discussed further in Chapter 19.

Illustration 17-5
Debt and Equity
Instruments
and Issuer
Accounting

Instrument	Classification
Mandatorily redeemable preferred shares	Even though these are equity in terms of legal form, the substance is that the instrument contains a liability due to the contractual obligation to repay (redemption is mandatory).
Shares where the holder has the right to sell them back to the company for a fixed amount ("puttable")	Even though these are equity in terms of legal form, the substance is that the instrument contains a liability due to the contractual obligation to repay if the holder presents the shares. Therefore, a liability exists unless certain restrictive criteria are met. This will be discussed further in Chapter 19.
Liability that may be repaid in cash or a variable number of shares, which will approximate the face value of the amount owing	Even though the amount can be repaid with shares, the number of shares vary depending on the amount owed and the share value. The entity is therefore locked into repaying a certain value and this is a liability.
Financial instrument may require the entity to repay if a certain event occurs (such as a decline in the entity's shares below a benchmark)	Due to the fact that there is uncertainty which is beyond the control of the entity, this is treated as a liability.

Interest, Dividends, Losses, and Gains

Interest, dividends, losses, and gains are accounted for consistently with the economic substance of the underlying financial instrument (not the legal form).

For instance, term-preferred shares are debt in substance and therefore the dividends would be accounted for as interest and deducted from profit or loss.

Offsetting a Financial Asset and a Financial Liability

Offsetting is the process of netting financial assets and liabilities. It is different from derecognition, which removes the assets and liabilities completely from the balance sheet. With offsetting, the balances remain;

---

[21] IASCF, IAS 32.16.

they are just netted. Derecognition criteria must be met before an entity can derecognize assets and liabilities.

Financial assets and liabilities may be offset when there is a legally enforceable right to offset (upon eventual cash flow payments) and where there is intent to settle on a net basis.

DISCLOSURES

IFRS requires additional disclosures including information about fair and carrying values, use of FVTPL, reclassifications, derecognition, collateral, compound instruments, defaults, breach, hedges, risks, gains and losses. In general, the disclosures give information about the significance of the financial instruments and the nature and extent of related risks. This will be discussed further in Chapter 20.

Illustration 17-6 provides a sample disclosure of the accounting policies related to financial instruments for Del Monte Pacific Limited.

Illustration 17-6 Excerpt from the Financial Statements of Del Monte Pacific Ltd.	**2 Summary of Significant Accounting Policies (Cont'd)** **2.6 Financial instruments** ***Non-derivative financial instruments*** Non-derivative financial instruments comprise trade and other receivables, cash and cash equivalents, financial liabilities, and trade and other payables. Non-derivative financial instruments are recognized initially at fair value. Subsequent to initial recognition, non-derivative financial instruments are measured at amortized cost using the effective interest method, less any impairment losses. A financial instrument is recognised if the Group becomes a party to the contractual provisions of the instrument. Financial assets are derecognized if the Group's contractual rights to the cash flows from the financial assets expire or if the Group transfers the financial asset to another party without retaining control or transfers substantially all the risks and rewards of the asset. Regular way purchases and sales of financial assets are accounted for at trade date, i.e., the date that the Group commits itself to purchase or sell the asset. Financial liabilities are derecognized if the Group's obligations specified in the contract expire or are discharged or cancelled. Cash and cash equivalents comprise cash balances and bank deposits and represent short-term, highly liquid investments which are readily convertible into known amounts of cash and are subject to an insignificant risk of changes in value.

LOOKING AHEAD

Due to the complexity of accounting for financial instruments, the IASB and FASB are working on a project to simplify the accounting. Following are the main principles:
- All financial instruments are measured at fair value with gains/losses to net income.
- Simplify or eliminate hedge accounting.
- Provide new standards for derecognition.

END-OF-CHAPTER PRACTICE

17-1 IAS 32, IAS 39, and IFRS 7 allow various classifications of financial assets.

Instructions
Explain what each classification is, how the items are measured, and where the gains and losses are booked. How are impairments handled? Are reclassifications allowed subsequent to initial recognition? Why/why not?

17-2 During the chapter, reference has been made to the term "puttable instruments."

Instructions
Explain what a puttable instrument is and how the feature affects the accounting.

17-3 Acorn Inc. issued some 1% five-year notes with a face value of $1,000. The current market interest rate for similar notes is 10%.

Instructions
Calculate the carrying value of these notes upon initial recognition. How might these notes be classified if they are purchased by Chestnut Inc.?

17-4 Buyer Limited recently entered into transactions that resulted in the following financial instruments:

- Investments in equity instruments
- Investments in marketable notes receivables
- Trade accounts receivables
- Derivatives
- Term preferred shares
- Debt issued by the entity that is repayable in a variable number of the entity's own shares
- Debt issued by the entity that is repayable in a fixed number of the entity's own shares

Instructions
How should these instruments be classified in the statement of financial position? Discuss, noting any alternative treatments.

17-5 Firenze Inc. has transferred its portfolio of receivables to Uffizi Limited for $800. The receivables have a carrying value of $850 and will be serviced by Uffizi.

Instructions
How should these be accounted for? How would this change if the assets were still collected by Firenze, but Firenze agreed to pay all amounts collected to Uffizi? Are there any additional criteria that must be met?

17-6 In this chapter, flag icons identify areas where there are GAAP differences between IFRS requirements and national standards.

Instructions
Access the website(s) identified on the inside back cover of this book, and prepare a concise summary of the differences that are flagged throughout the chapter material.

Chapter 18

Financial Instruments–Recognition and Measurement: IAS 39

U.S. GAAP References
FAS 115 Accounting for Certain Investments in Debt and Equity Securities
FAS 130 Reporting Comprehensive Income
FAS 133 Accounting for Derivative Instruments and Hedging Activities
FAS 138 Accounting for Certain Derivative Instruments and Certain Hedging Activities—an amendment of FASB Statement No. 133
FAS 140 and 156 Accounting for Transfers and Servicing of Financial Assets and Extinguishments of Liabilities—a replacement of FASB Statement No. 125
FAS 155 Accounting for Certain Hybrid Financial Instruments
FAS 157 Fair Value Measurements
FAS 159 The Fair Value Option for Financial Assets and Financial Liabilities
FIN 45 Guarantor's Accounting and Disclosure Requirements for Guarantees, Including Indirect Guarantees of Indebtedness of Others

Related IFRSs
IFRS 7 Financial Instruments: Disclosures
IAS 1 Presentation of Financial Statements
IAS 32 Financial Instruments: Presentation

OBJECTIVE AND SCOPE

As mentioned in Chapter 17, this standard deals with recognition and measurement of financial assets and liabilities and is part of a suite of standards dealing with financial instruments. While Chapter 17 presents an overview of the standards, this chapter will go into a bit more depth on some of the more complex areas such as derivatives (including embedded derivatives), guarantees, loan commitments, expected use contracts, derecognition, and hedging.

DERIVATIVES

A **derivative** has three essential characteristics:[1]

- Its value changes in response to the change in an underlying primary instrument/index exchange rate or other, called an "underlying." The underlying may not be specific to a party to the contract if it relates to a non-financial variable.
- There is little or no initial investment.
- It is settled (or may be settled) in the future.

Typical examples of derivatives are options, forwards, futures, and swaps. Options may be purchased or written (issued), transferring the right to do something to the holder of the option. Call options give the right to buy something, whereas put options give the right to sell something. Chapter 19 discusses written options dealing with the company's own equity instruments. Following are examples of options:

- purchased or written options to buy shares at a fixed price (referred to as the exercise price or strike price)
- purchased or written options to sell shares at a fixed price
- options to extend contracts
- options to repay liabilities in another currency
- options to pay interest in a commodity (instead of cash)

Options are priced using options pricing models such as the Black Scholes and binomial tree models.

Forward contracts lock the parties to the contract into buying or selling something in the future (unlike the option, where only the writer/issuer has an obligation if the option is exercised). Futures are just standardized forwards. The most common example of forward/futures contracts is a contract to buy and sell foreign exchange in the future at a fixed price (known as the forward price). Futures also include contracts to buy and sell non-financial commodities such as wheat, oil, gold, and butter. Non-financial futures will be discussed later in the chapter.

Forward contracts are normally priced so that the forward price equals the current spot price plus carrying costs (sometimes referred to as cost of carry or cost of capital).[2]

Finally, many companies enter into contracts known as swaps. Swaps are a series of forward contracts to exchange currencies or interest payments (fixed interest payment for variable interest—for example, prime plus 1%—or vice versa).

When calculating the fair value of derivatives, generally two components make up the value—the intrinsic value (relating to the current spot price of the underlying) and a time value (relating to the fact that the contract will be settled in the future).

The following three scenarios illustrate typical derivatives.

---

[1] IASCF, IAS 39.9.

[2] The contracts are priced to replicate a situation whereby the entity would borrow money upfront, buy the underlying (for example, US$), and then enter into a contract to sell the underlying (the US$) at a price at the end of the period that will allow it to repay the loan plus interest. If the forward price is higher (allowing the company to make a profit), then investors will want to borrow more money and buy more US$ today. This will drive up the spot price until it again equalled the present value of the spot price plus cost of carry.

Situation

Options Limited purchased an option to buy one share of Investment Limited for $10 within 30 days (purchased call option). It paid $1 for this right. Why is this a derivative?

Analysis

The option is a purchased call option. It meets the definition of a derivative as noted below:

1. The value of the option changes with the market value of the shares of Investment Limited. The price of the shares of Investment Limited is the "underlying."
2. The options cost only $1, which is a small fraction of the value of the shares of Investment Limited.
3. The option may be settled or exercised in the future. Note that the option gives the company the right (but not the obligation) to purchase the shares for $10. If the company exercises the option, the writer of the option must sell them one share for $10. The company may choose not to exercise the option, for instance, if the price of the Investment Limited shares declines below $9 (the exercise price less the option premium).

Situation

Forex Limited enters into a forward contract to buy US$100 in 30 days for Cdn$105. Why is this a derivative?

Analysis

The foreign exchange forward contract is a derivative for the following reasons:

1. The value of the forward changes with the US$/Cdn$ exchange rate. If the US dollar appreciates, the contract is more valuable since it allows the company to purchase the US$100 for Cdn$105. The exchange rate is the "underlying."
2. The forward contract is priced such that there is no premium and therefore there is no initial investment.
3. The forward must be exercised in 30 days. At the end of 30 days, the company will pay Cdn$105 and get US$100. Note that this is different from the option above since the purchased option gives the holder the right to buy the shares but does not obligate them to do so. Under the forward contract, the company must purchase the US$100 or sell the contract to someone else who must settle at the end of the 30-day period.

Situation

Swap Limited has 5% fixed rate debt outstanding with the bank (principal amount $100, five-year loan). It would like to switch this to variable rate debt because it thinks interest rates will fall. The bank charges a significant penalty for early repayment and so Swap does not want to repay early. Instead, it enters into a five-year swap contract to receive $5, which is the amount of the interest that it owes on the loan—$100 X 5%, and to pay the equivalent of $100 X prime. Why is this a derivative?

Analysis

The swap contract is a derivative for the following reasons:

1. The value of the swap will change depending on the prime interest rate.
2. There is no money paid at the beginning of the contract. The first payment will be at the end of the first year.
3. The contract will be settled in the future. Under the contract, the company is locked into paying the interest at prime and receiving $5 for five years. Hence this is a series of forward contracts.

Derivatives are accounted for as follows:

1. They are recognized in the financial statements.
2. They are presented as fair value through profit and loss.
3. They are measured and remeasured at fair value with related gains/losses being booked through profit or loss.

Derivatives Versus Insurance Contracts

Rights and obligations under most insurance contracts are excluded from the standards partially because they are covered by IFRS 4 (the IFRS for insurance companies) and also because the IASB is planning to study the issue further (including the IFRS for policy holders). How do insurance contracts differ from derivatives? As noted above, derivatives may be used for instance to lock in a price of a share/foreign currency (sometimes to guarantee against a loss). This is very similar to insurance contracts that are entered into to guarantee against a loss. The main difference is that insurance contracts usually deal with non-financial assets such as buildings and machinery **that are owned by the insured (assets are specific to the insured party)**.

As noted in the definition of a derivative, the value of a derivative varies with an "underlying." Examples of "underlyings" are share prices, interest rates, foreign exchange rates, indices, and credit ratings. The definition of an underlying excludes **non-financial variables where the variable is specific to one of the parties to the contract**. An example is the change in the physical condition of a building owned by one of the parties to the contract. Depending on the specifics of the contract, insurance contracts often meet the definition of a derivative except for the fact that they usually relate to this exclusion. The example below illustrates this.

Situation

Jenkins Limited is in the photography business. Its employees attend local events and take pictures, which they sell onsite. The company enters into a contract whereby Crandall Inc. will pay it $100 if one of its cameras is lost or stolen (the approximate value of the camera is $100). It pays a premium of $1 for this. Discuss whether this meets the definition of a derivative.

Analysis

From a legal perspective, the contract may be structured as an insurance contract. Jenkins will suffer no loss if the camera is stolen or lost. Thus there is a guarantee on the value and Jenkins has paid $1 for this guarantee/insurance.

The contract meets the definition of a derivative (except for one aspect, which is discussed below) as follows:

1. The value of the contract varies with the value of the camera.
2. The initial investment is only $1, which is very small compared with the value of the camera.
3. The contract will be settled in the future (if there is a theft or loss).

In this case, however, because we are dealing with a non-financial variable (the physical condition of the camera) and since the camera is owned by the company (is specific to one of the parties to the contract—Jenkins), the contract is not a derivative and is instead accounted for as an insurance contract.[3]

Judgment must be used to determine whether the substance of the contract indicates it is more like insurance.[4]

Derivatives Versus Insurance Versus Financial Guarantee Contracts

Financial guarantee contracts also add complexity to any accounting analysis because they are very much like insurance contracts. Should a financial guarantee contract be accounted for as an insurance contract, as a derivative, or in some other manner? A *financial guarantee contract* is defined as follows:

---

[3] The reason that the camera is worth less than $100 may be due to its physical condition (damaged/lost/stolen) or because the technology has changed and all cameras of that nature are therefore worth less. The former is a non-financial variable and the latter—the market price of the cameras in general—a financial variable. The contract deals only with the non-financial variables, i.e., loss or theft. It covers Jenkins if the camera is lost or stolen, which is a physical condition that is specific to that particular camera.

[4] This area gets much more complex and goes beyond the scope of the book.

a contract that requires the issuer to make specified payments to reimburse the holder for a loss it incurs because a specified debtor fails to make payment when due in accordance with the original or modified terms of a debt instrument.[5]

Examples of financial guarantee contracts are identified in the following scenarios:

1. Bank guarantee by vendor. A vendor might guarantee the bank loan of a customer (to facilitate the sale of inventory to the customer).
2. Guarantee by unrelated party. An unrelated third party might guarantee the same customer's bank loan (for a fee).
3. Standby letters of credit. A bank might guarantee payment of a specific financial obligation if the customer does not pay. The standby letter of credit may be cashed on demand if the customer fails to pay.[6]

There are four ways to account for financial guarantee contracts depending on the nature of the contract and the business of the entity. The substance of the transaction must be analyzed to determine if it is an insurance contract. The four options for accounting for financial guarantees are as follows:

1. Under IAS 39—fair value through profit and loss (FVTPL), if more relevant.
2. Under IFRS 4—as an insurance contract if the contract represents insurance in substance and the entity has accounted for it as insurance in the past.
3. Under IAS 39—where the transfer of a financial asset/liability does not qualify for derecognition because substantially all of the risks and rewards are retained or there is continuing involvement.
4. Under IAS 39—all other financial guarantee contracts.

A financial guarantee contract may be classified as FVTPL if this classification results in more relevant information in the financial statements. If it is classified as such, it would be measured at fair value and gains/losses would be booked to income.

An entity can elect to account for financial guarantee contracts as insurance contracts under IFRS 4 if it has previously concluded that the contract is an insurance contract and it has previously used insurance accounting to account for similar contracts. This is a transition measure or temporary solution to ensure that appropriate accounting treatment is given while the IASB studies the issue further. The liability would be carried at the estimate of the amount payable under IFRS 4.

If the guarantee is as a result of a transfer of financial instruments where the derecognition criteria are not met because substantially all of the risks and rewards are retained or there is continuing involvement, the guarantee would be measured at the amount of funds received (in a transfer) or an amount that best reflects the entity's obligations.[7]

Finally, all other financial guarantees would be measured at the higher of the amount determined under IAS 37 *Provisions, Contingent Liabilities and Contingent Assets* and the amount initially recognized less any amortization booked in accordance with IAS 18 *Revenues*.[8]

Illustration 18-1 shows how guarantees are accounted for. Note that there is no specific GAAP for holders of guarantee contracts and guarantees that do not meet the definition of financial guarantee under IAS 39 are accounted for under IAS 37 or IFRS 4.

---

[5] IASCF, IAS 39.9.

[6] This is different from a commercial letter of credit, which is a primary payment mechanism to facilitate payment for foreign customers/suppliers because they operate in different countries. The commercial letter of credit allows the supplier to present evidence of shipment of the goods to a financial institution and to receive payment before the customer receives the goods. The standby letter of credit is a secondary/default payment mechanism (a backup if the customer does not pay).

[7] IASCF, IAS 39.29 and 39.31.

[8] IASCF, IAS 39.47c.

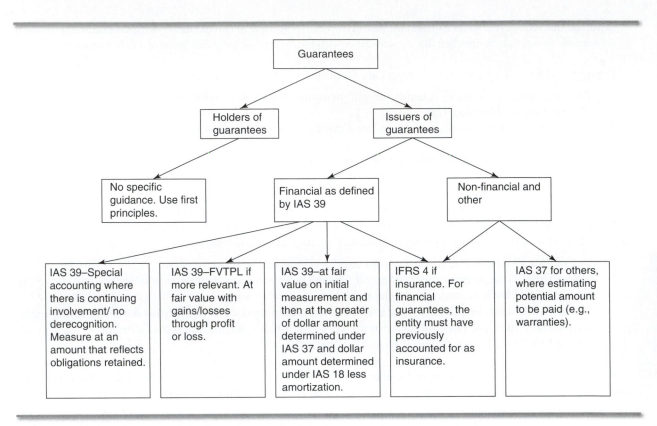

Illustration 18-1 Accounting for Guarantees

Below is an example of a financial guarantee contract.

Situation

Guarantor Inc. enters into a contract with Banker Inc. to guarantee the debt of Needy Limited on December 31, 2008. At that point, Needy Limited is financially solvent and fully intends to repay the debt. At December 31, 2009, Needy Limited is in financial distress and it is probable that Guarantor will have to step in and honor the guarantee. The likely payout is $100. How should Guarantor account for the financial guarantee?

Analysis

First, this is a financial guarantee because it meets the definition as outlined in IAS 39.9. Guarantor may be required to cover any losses that Banker might incur if Needy does not repay amounts owing to Banker. This type of contract is very similar to insurance. Guarantor probably charged a fee to take on this risk just like an insurance premium and may have to cover any losses that Banker may incur relating to the loan (similar to an insurance contract where the insurer would have to cover any losses to assets insured by the entity). If Guarantor can prove that it has treated these types of contracts as insurance in past, it may use IFRS 4 to account for the contract. Otherwise, because the contract meets the definition of a financial guarantee, it will be covered by IAS 39. Under IAS 39, Guarantor has two choices. It can treat the guarantee as a FVTPL, in which case, the contract would be continuously measured at fair value with gains/losses booked to Net Income, or it could record the contract at fair value initially and then remeasure it at the higher of the amount determined under IAS 37 and the original amount less any amortization under IAS 18.

In this case, assuming that $100 is greater than any original fee received, the contract would be measured at $100, which is the best estimate of the amount owed (the most likely outcome).

Derivatives Versus Loan Commitments

Loan commitments are agreements to provide loans in the future. Are loan commitments derivatives? Some are and some are not.

Loan commitments that can be settled net in cash (or other financial assets) are derivatives and treated as such. Other loan commitments that extend a loan at below market interest rates are onerous contracts and should be measured at the higher of the amount determined in accordance with IAS 37 and the initial amount less amortization under IAS 18 *Revenues*. Finally, any loan commitment that is classified as FVTPL is covered by IAS 39. Having stated that, all loan commitments are subject to the derecognition standards in IAS 39.[9]

Non-financial Derivatives

The standard covers financial derivatives (dealing with interest rates, foreign exchange rates, share prices, and others) but many derivative contracts deal with non-financial underlyings such as commodities (wheat, oil, gold). Should these contracts be covered by the standard? Because the accounting issues are the same and because derivatives relating to non-financial underlyings often trade in very liquid markets, the IASB decided to include these, and therefore they are covered by IAS 39 when the contracts can be settled net in cash or other financial instruments. In general then, commodities derivatives such as futures and options are recognized when the contract is entered into, are measured at fair value (and continually remeasured), and the resulting gains and losses are booked to profit and loss.

Where the derivatives are entered into for trading purposes, this accounting makes sense. But what if the company is using a derivative or a derivative-like contract to lock in a supply of raw materials for its own use or to lock in the selling price for its own inventory? Should the accounting be the same? To take this one step further, should purchase commitments be treated as derivatives? Let's examine whether a purchase commitment to lock in the price of oil that the entity plans to use in production of its inventory is a derivative or not. Consider the following provisions of the contract:

1. The value of the contract will change if the price of oil changes.
2. There is no initial payment required to enter into the contract, just a signature.
3. The contract will be settled in the future when the entity takes delivery of the oil.

Therefore, the contract appears to meet the definition of a derivative. However, IAS 39 specifically excludes this type of transaction unless the entity is able to settle the contract net in cash (i.e., the entity can get out of the contract without taking delivery of the underlying by paying cash). Even if it is able to settle the contract net in cash, as long as the entity can prove that it intends to use the commodity for its own expected use (e.g., to lock in a supply of raw material or lock in a selling price for its products) then the contract is excluded from the standard. These are called "expected use" contracts.

Following are the various ways that an entity may settle a contract net in cash:[10]

1. Where the terms of the contract allow either party to get out of the contract by paying the net difference between the contract price and the market price of the underlying.
2. Where the terms of the contract do not explicitly allow net settlement but the entity has a past practice of settling similar contracts net.
3. Where the entity has a past practice of taking delivery of the underlying and then immediately reselling it for profit as opposed to using it.[11]
4. Where the underlying is readily convertible to cash.

---

[9] IASCF, IAS 39.2 and 39.4.
[10] IASCF, IAS 39.6.
[11] This does not include companies that buy wholesale and sell retail.

Situation

Breadco Limited makes bread. To ensure that it has a good supply of high quality wheat to make the bread, it enters into purchase commitments with its suppliers. Under the terms of the purchase commitments, it locks in the amounts (100 bushels), the delivery dates, and the prices for wheat ($10 per bushel). The contracts are non-cancellable and the entity plans to take delivery. How should the contracts be accounted for?

Analysis

The purchase commitments meet the definition of a derivative because

1. the value of the contracts will vary with the price of the wheat, i.e., the company is locked in to pay $10 per bushel and if the price of wheat rises above that, then the contract has greater value;
2. there is no initial investment/fee to enter into the contracts; and
3. the company plans to take delivery of the wheat in future.

However, because there is no net settlement option, this is not a derivative. The contract would not be recognized at all until the entity takes delivery of the wheat. If the price of wheat falls below the $10 noted in the contract, the entity would treat the contract as an onerous contract and record a potential loss and liability (dr. loss, cr. liability).

If there were a net settlement provision in the contract (that is, the entity could settle the contract in cash on a net basis without taking delivery of the wheat), the entity would not treat this as a derivative either, because the contract meets the expected use criteria. Either way, the entity can still use the fair value option and classify the contract as FVTPL if it results in more relevant information. Sometimes this latter option is used to avoid having to use the more complex hedge accounting. Hedge accounting will be discussed later in the chapter.

Embedded Derivatives

An *embedded derivative* is defined as

> a component of a hybrid (combined) instrument that also includes a non-derivative host contract—with the effect that some of the cash flows of the combined instrument vary in a way similar to a stand-alone derivative.[12]

Some contracts contain derivatives within the contract. They essentially have two components—the host non-derivative contract and the embedded derivative. Should the derivative contract be bifurcated (separated) from the host contract and accounted for as a derivative? The IASB intended for all derivatives that are within the scope of IAS 39 to be accounted for as derivatives and therefore deals with the special case of derivatives that are included within other contracts.

In general, according to IAS 39.11, embedded derivatives are separated from the host instrument and accounted for as derivatives if all of the following conditions are met:

*   The economic characteristics and risks of the derivatives are not closely related to those of the host.
*   If the embedded derivative were stand-alone, it would meet the definition of a derivative.
*   The combined instrument is not already accounted for as FVTPL (in which case there would be no need to separate the embedded derivative).

An entity can avoid having to do this analysis, which can be quite complex, if it accounts for the combined instrument as FVTPL. In addition, if it is required to bifurcate the embedded derivative but is unable to measure it, the standard requires that the combined instrument be accounted for as FVTPL.

In determining whether the economic characteristics are closely related, the following should be considered:

---

[12] IASCF, IAS 39.10.

- Debt and equity instruments have economic characteristics that are not closely related (equity is often more risky; debt has a more stable return (interest) that is tied to the principal amount and is often secured).
- Any option that allows the entity to participate in risks that are not germane to the contract would not be closely related. For instance, if an entity buys raw materials in Europe, it would expect to pay the suppliers in euros. However, if the contract allows the entity to pay in another currency that is not the normal reporting currency of the entity or a currency in which the raw materials are normally traded, then this option would not be closely related to the contract and would have to be separated.
- Any option that allows the entity to use leverage to earn significantly higher returns or exposes it to significant loss might be seen to be an embedded derivative and not closely related to the host contract.[13]

Convertible debt is a hybrid instrument. The debt is the host instrument and the option to convert to shares is the embedded derivative. The option is not closely related to the debt because it is an equity feature that allows the holder of the instrument to participate in the risks and rewards of owning shares. A purchased option to buy shares would be accounted for as a derivative if it were a stand-alone instrument. Therefore, investments in convertible debt would therefore be bifurcated where the investment is not already classified as FVTPL.[14]

Regular Way Purchase or Sale of a Financial Asset

When shares are bought and sold, it normally takes a day or two to settle the deal. In the meantime, these contracts meet the definition of a derivative. However, they are accounted for using trade date accounting (where a receivable and payable are booked the minute the trade is entered into) or settlement date accounting (where only the net position is booked until the shares actually change hands).[15]

DERECOGNITION

Transfers Revisited

The issue of how to account for transfers was introduced in Chapter 17 and will be expanded upon here. Transfers of receivables, whether they are called factoring, discounting, or other, are fairly common transactions. Entities enter into these transactions often to generate cash flows. Where substantially all of the risks and rewards of ownership are transferred and there is no continuing involvement, derecognition of the receivable takes place and often a gain or loss is recognized.

This analysis is not always so clear cut. Sometimes it is difficult to determine whether substantially all risks are retained or transferred, in which case the entity must determine whether it has retained control over the asset. Determining whether the entity has retained control is a matter of judgment and depends on whether the entity can sell the asset or not. If the transferee is able to sell the asset (without involving other parties) and without imposing any restrictions on the transfer, then control has passed from the entity (transferor) to the other party (transferee).

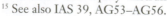

[13] This analysis is fairly complex and beyond the scope of the book. See IAS 39, AG 30–AG 33 for additional examples.
[14] From the perspective of the issuer, convertible debt would be accounted for a bit differently because IAS 39 does not cover most "own equity" instruments. This will be covered in Chapter 19.
[15] See also IAS 39, AG53–AG56.

Illustration 18-2 shows how to account for transfers.

Risks and rewards	Derecognize?	Accounting
Substantially all transferred	Yes	Remove and recognize gain/loss
Substantially all retained	No	Continue to recognize
Neither of the above, but no control retained	Yes	Remove from books and recognize gain/loss. Recognize any assets or liabilities created by the arrangement or retained.
Neither of the above and control retained	No	Continue to recognize to the extent of continuing involvement

Illustration 18-2
Accounting for
Transfers

In certain cases, the contractual rights to receive cash flows may be retained but the company assumes a contractual obligation to pay those cash flows to another party. Is this type of transaction a transfer? The asset is retained; however, because a liability is assumed, the transaction must be examined to determine its economic substance. It may be a transfer in substance.

If the following criteria are met, this type of transaction would be accounted for as a transfer and may also qualify for derecognition:

- there is no requirement for the entity to pay the contractual obligation unless it collects equivalent amounts from the original asset,
- the entity is prohibited from selling the original asset, and
- any cash flows collected on behalf of the eventual recipient must be remitted to the eventual recipient without material delay.

Situation

Transferor Limited has a portfolio of receivables with a carrying value of $1,000. On January 1, Transferor entered into a transaction with Tranferee Inc. Under the terms of the deal, Transferor will receive $950 from Transferee on January 1 and agrees to pay the money that it collects from the receivables to Transferee. If some of the receivables are not collected, Transferor has no obligation to pay. Transferor is not allowed to sell the receivables.

Analysis

Even though the asset has not been physically transferred, the transaction would be accounted for as a transfer and assessed for derecognition. These types of transactions are often referred to as "pass-through" arrangements since the money is just passing through the transferor. In this case, all of the criteria listed above are met: Transferor does not need to pay anything unless it receives the cash flows from the assets; it cannot sell the assets; and any cash flows received must be remitted to Transferee. Therefore, this is a transfer and must be further assessed to see if substantially all of the risks and rewards of ownership have been transferred.

When collateral is pledged under the arrangement, then care should be taken to determine how to account for the collateral. In general, the transferor carries the collateral as an asset except as noted below.

If the transferee can sell or repledge the asset, the collateral will be accounted for as shown in Illustration 18-3.[16]

---

[16] IASCF, IAS 39.37.

	Transaction/arrangement	Accounting
Illustration 18-3 Accounting for Collateral	Transferee has the right to sell or pledge.	Transferor presents the asset separately from other assets.
	Transferee sells/repledges.	Transferee recognizes proceeds from the sale and the liability for the obligation to Transferor. Transferor may change the description of the asset (e.g., from pledged equity instrument to receivable).
	Transferor defaults and is no longer allowed to redeem collateral.	Transferor derecognizes collateral. Transferee recognizes collateral as an asset or derecognizes the liability (if the collateral is already sold).

Debt Extinguishment Versus Debt Modification

When an entity repays its debt, the liability is extinguished and the debt derecognized. However, what about when it refinances the debt? Is the refinancing an extinguishment of the old debt and an issuance of new debt? Or is it a modification of the old debt?

If the new debt is substantially different, it is treated as an extinguishment. In terms of a benchmark, per IAS 39, AG62 the new debt is substantially different when the present value of the cash flows under the new debt is different by more than 10% of the present value of the cash flows under the old debt (using the original effective rate).

HEDGING

IAS 39 includes the following definitions with respect to hedge accounting:[17]

> *Hedge effectiveness* is the degree to which changes in the fair value or cash flows of the hedged item that are attributable to a hedged risk are offset by changes in the fair value or cash flows of the hedging instrument.

Hedges must be viewed through an economic lens as well as an accounting lens. Entities enter into hedges to protect themselves from economic losses (or to reduce uncertainty). Hedging therefore changes the risk profile of the entity by reducing certain risks that are targeted for hedging. In a perfect hedge, gains/losses on the item/risk hedged are offset by the gains/losses on the item used to effect the hedge. Thus earnings are insulated from changes in value of the hedged item.

Hedge accounting, on the other hand, is a special type of accounting that is optional. It may be applied or not. This is an accounting policy choice. Hedge accounting may be used when the entity has economic hedges to ensure that there is no mismatch in the bookkeeping when an economic hedge exists (that is, that the gains and losses on the hedged and hedging items are offset in the financial statements). It may be necessary because the IFRS is currently based on a mixed measurement model (some assets and liabilities are carried at cost and some at fair value). Hedge accounting steps in to "fix" this.

When hedging from an economic perspective, an entity must first determine which risks it would like to hedge (interest rate risk, foreign exchange risk, credit risk, etc.)[18] and in which transactions. It then designs a hedge

---

[17] IASCF, IAS 39.9.
[18] IFRS 7 has a more extensive list of risks with definitions (Appendix A).

by identifying which additional transactions it would like to enter into in order to modify the risk profile of the transactions. This is referred to as a hedging relationship. Derivatives are most often used to modify the risks.

For instance, if an entity has a receivable in a foreign currency, there is a foreign exchange risk. If the exchange rate changes, the entity will end up collecting more or less from that receivable once it converts to the local currency. In order to offset that risk, the entity might consider buying a forward contract to sell the foreign currency in the future. Thus, the entity locks in the amount of local currency that it will be able to receive. This would be an economic hedge. The entity must now decide whether it would like to or need to use special hedge accounting to ensure that the gains/losses from restating the receivable offset the gains/losses from the forward contract (which, as a derivative, will be recognized in the statements and valued at fair value).

The standard states that if there is a designated hedging relationship between hedging instruments and a hedged item, then hedge accounting may be used.[19]

Hedging Instruments

A *hedging instrument* is defined in IAS 39.9 as follows:

> . . . a designated derivative or (for a hedge of the risk of changes in foreign currency exchange rates only) a designated non-derivative financial asset or non-derivative financial liability whose fair value or cash flows are expected to offset changes in the fair value or cash flows of a designated hedged item.

Most hedging instruments are derivatives such as forwards, options, futures, or swaps but, as noted above, when hedging changes in foreign currency exchange rates, non-derivative financial instruments may be used such as an existing receivable or payable that is denominated in a foreign currency. For instance, in the example above, where there is a receivable outstanding that is denominated in a foreign currency, the entity might designate an already existing liability that is payable in the same foreign currency as the hedging item. If the exchange rate appreciates, the receivable will increase in value and trigger a gain. However, at the same time, the payable will also increase in amount and trigger a loss. These gains and losses will offset each other and a hedge exists from an economic perspective.

An entity may designate as a hedging item the whole financial instrument, a portion of it (for instance, 50% of the balance, but not a portion of the time period), or a group of financial instruments.

Hedged Items

A *hedged item* is defined in IAS 39.9 as follows:

> . . . an asset, liability, firm commitment, highly probable forecast transaction or net investment in a foreign operation that (a) exposes the entity to risk of changes in fair value or future cash flows and (b) is designated as being hedged.

A hedged item is the item that is exposing the entity to some unwanted risk where the entity chooses to get rid of that risk. It can be an asset or liability already recognized on the balance sheet, or it can be an item that is not yet recognized but is an unrecognized firm commitment or a highly probable forecasted transaction. The standard further defines these terms in IAS 39.9 as follows:

> A *firm commitment* is a binding agreement for the exchange of a specified quantity of resources at a specified price on a specified future date or dates.

> A *forecast transaction* is an uncommitted but anticipated future transaction.

An example of a typical firm commitment is a purchase commitment.

---

[19] IASCF, IAS 39.71.

Hedge Accounting

Hedge accounting is special accounting that is optional and recognizes the offsetting profits and losses on hedging relationships in the statement of profit and loss in the same period. This is transparent because if an economic hedge exists, the gains and losses on the hedged and hedging items offset each other. Therefore, if the pre- "hedge accounting" is such that the gains and losses do not otherwise offset each other, the entity must decide whether it wants to use the special hedge accounting to correct this. Hedge accounting is complex and costly and so a cost-benefit analysis should be done before deciding to use hedge accounting.

There are three types of hedging relationships under hedge accounting. They are identified in IAS 39.9 as follows:

(a) *fair value hedge*: a hedge of the exposure to changes in fair value of a recognised asset or liability or an unrecognised firm commitment, or an identified portion of such an asset, liability or firm commitment, that is attributable to a particular risk and could affect profit or loss.

(b) *cash flow hedge:* a hedge of the exposure to variability in cash flows that (i) is attributable to a particular risk associated with a recognised asset or liability (such as all or some future interest payments on variable rate debt) or a highly probable forecast transaction and (ii) could affect profit or loss.

(c) *hedge of a net investment in a foreign operation*[20]

Fair Value Hedges

A fair value hedge is accounted for as follows:[21]

• Gains/losses from the hedging item are recognized in profit and loss.
• Gains/losses on the hedged item are recognized (by adjusting the carrying value of the hedged item) and are recognized through profit and loss.

This way the gains and losses on both the hedged and hedging items are booked through profit and loss at the same time and are therefore matched. If the firm commitment is not otherwise recognized on the balance sheet, hedge accounting requires it to be recognized.

Situation

Invictus Inc. has inventory on its books that is for sale (carrying value $50). There is a price risk associated with this inventory, i.e., while it holds the inventory, the price will vary. In order to ensure that it locks in a selling price that will be realized, it enters into a forward contract to sell the inventory for $100. How would this be accounted for using hedge accounting?

Analysis

This is a fair value hedge since the entity is hedging the price risk related to the inventory, which is recognized on the balance sheet. The inventory (specifically the price risk associated with it) is the hedged item. The forward contract to sell the inventory is the hedging item.

Normally the forward will be recognized and measured at fair value with gains/losses booked to income (as a derivative). Because the inventory is valued at historical cost, any related gains/losses will not be reflected in the statements. Therefore, there will be a mismatch—the gains/losses on the derivative will be booked, but the gains/losses related to changes in the value of inventory will not. Therefore, the entity may choose to use hedge accounting.

If hedge accounting is used, the derivative is accounted for as usual (recognized, measured at fair value, and gains/losses recognized in profit/loss) but the inventory is revalued to fair value with the gains and losses booked to income.

---

[20] A hedge of a net investment in a foreign operation is a hedge of the exposure to variability in the cash flows related to an investment in a foreign operation.

[21] IASCF, IAS 39.89.

Cash Flow Hedges

Cash flow hedges are a bit different because the hedged item may not yet be on the balance sheet. It may relate to a future transaction.

Cash flow hedges are accounted for as follows:[22]

- Gains/losses on the hedging instrument are booked to other comprehensive income.

Normally the gains/losses on the hedging item would be booked through profit and loss; however, since the hedged item is not recognized on the balance sheet (it does not meet the recognition criteria because the transaction has not yet happened), the gains/losses on the hedged item are not recognized either. This creates a mismatch. Therefore, as a compromise, the gains/losses on the hedging item are booked through other comprehensive income in the short run so that profit and loss is not affected.

When the forecasted transaction actually occurs, it is subsequently recognized on the balance sheet (e.g., inventory is acquired and booked as inventory). What happens to the gains/losses sitting in other comprehensive income? They are reclassified from other comprehensive income to profit and loss when the inventory is sold. Thus the gains/losses are matched and booked through inventory at the same time. The entity may choose to reclassify these gains/losses from other comprehensive income and book against the asset/liability itself, if the asset/liability remains on the balance sheet at year end. This achieves the same objective.

Situation

Buyer Inc. projects that it will probably purchase $100 worth of inventory in 30 days for 100 euros. Buyer is concerned about the cash flow risk associated with having to pay 100 euros and so wants to hedge this. It enters into a forward contract to buy 100 euros for Cdn$150. How would this be accounted for using hedge accounting?

Analysis

This is a cash flow hedge because the entity is hedging the cash flow risk related to a future transaction that is not yet recognized on the balance sheet. The probable future purchase is the hedged item. It is exposing the company to cash flow risk because it is denominated in a foreign currency. The derivative is the hedging items. By entering into a forward contract to buy euros, the entity is locking in the cash flows. Now it will cost only Cdn$150 to purchase the inventory.

Because the future inventory purchase is not recognized on the balance sheet, any related gains/losses will not be recognized either. Because the forward is a derivative instrument, it would normally be recognized and valued at fair value with gains/losses booked to profit and loss. Therefore, unless hedge accounting is used, there will be a mismatch of gains/losses and the economic substance of the hedge (which gets rid of the volatility) is not reflected. If hedge accounting is used, the gains/losses on the periodic remeasurement of the forward contract are booked to other comprehensive income (instead of profit and loss).

When the entity takes delivery of the inventory, the entity has the option to transfer the gains/losses from other comprehensive income and book them as part of the carrying value of the inventory. Alternatively, it can wait until the inventory is sold and transfer the gains/losses to the cost of sales at that point.

Hedges of a Net Investment

These hedges are essentially cash flow hedges and the accounting is therefore the same (gains and losses on the hedged item are booked through other comprehensive income).

---

[22] IASCF, IAS 39.95.

Formalization of Hedging Relationship

In order to qualify for hedge accounting, an entity must formalize and document the analysis regarding the existence of a hedging relationship. The following hedging relationship conditions/criteria must be met:

1. The hedging relationship must be designated and documented at the inception of the hedge. This includes the objective and strategy regarding the hedge, identification of the hedged and hedging items, the nature of the risks being hedged, and how the entity will assess whether the hedge is effective in offsetting gains/losses on the hedged item.
2. The hedge is expected to be highly effective in offsetting the changes in cash flows/fair values of the hedged item.
3. For cash flow hedges, the forecasted transaction must be highly probable and must present an exposure to cash flows that will affect the profit and loss statement.
4. The effectiveness of the hedge must be reliably measurable.
5. The hedge must be assessed on an ongoing basis and must be highly effective throughout the hedge period.

A hedge will be considered highly effective if the following can be demonstrated (by projecting forward or by looking at past history). The actual results of the hedge must be within an 80–120% range (e.g., as calculated by taking the dollar amount of the gain/loss on hedged item divided by the dollar amount of the gain/loss on hedging item).

Hedge accounting has significantly more complexity and is thus beyond the scope of this book.

LOOKING AHEAD

As discussed in Chapter 17, there is an overall move to simplify the accounting for financial instruments—especially for derivatives and hedges. The IASB and FASB are currently working on this project.

END-OF-CHAPTER PRACTICE

18-1 Investico Limited has the following transactions and is not sure how to account for them:

- a forward contract to buy euros
- a future contract to buy oil
- options to sell shares of Franko Inc.
- a loan commitment to lend funds to another company
- a guarantee contract under which it has guaranteed the value of an asset for an unrelated company

Instructions
How should each of these be accounted for?

18-2 Feller Furniture Limited has a significant amount of its cash tied up in receivables from its customers. It would like to free up this cash and has decided to sell its receivables. Under the terms of the deal, it will receive 95% of the carrying value of the receivables as at December 1. Feller will continue to collect the receivables and will pass the funds on to the other company as soon as they are received.

Instructions
How should this be accounted for?

18-3 Hedge Co. has a payable denominated in euros (100 euros) in 30 days. It has entered into a contract to buy 100 euros in 30 days for $140.

Instructions

From an economic perspective, is this a hedge? Does a hedging relationship exist? Discuss. What is the hedged item (identify the specific risk being hedged)? What is the hedging item?

From an accounting perspective, what type of hedge is this? How will the items be accounted for if hedge accounting is not used? How will they be accounted for if hedge accounting is used? Is there a need for hedge accounting in this case?

18-4 Many companies enter into economic hedges but not all use hedge accounting.

Instructions

Explain the difference between economic hedges and hedge accounting. Why is hedge accounting used by some companies and not others?

18-5 In this chapter, flag icons identify areas where there are GAAP differences between IFRS requirements and national standards.

Instructions

Access the website(s) identified on the inside back cover of this book, and prepare a concise summary of the differences that are flagged throughout the chapter.

Chapter 19

Financial Instruments–Presentation: IAS 32

U.S. GAAP References
FAS 133 Accounting for Derivative Instruments and Hedging Activities
FAS 138 Accounting for Certain Derivative Instruments and Certain Hedging Activities—an amendment of FASB Statement No. 133
FAS 150 Accounting for Certain Financial Instruments with Characteristics of both Liabilities and Equity
FAS 155 Accounting for Certain Hybrid Financial Instruments—an amendment of FASB Statements No. 133 and 140
FAS 157 Fair Value Measurements

Related IFRSs
IFRS 7 Financial Instruments: Disclosures
IAS 1 Presentation of Financial Statements
IAS 39 Financial Instruments: Recognition and Measurement

OBJECTIVE AND SCOPE

This standard deals with financial liabilities and equity instruments from the perspective of the issuer. It also provides guidance on how to present compound (hybrid) instruments, where the instrument contains both debt and equity components, including some guidance on how to measure and bifurcate compound instruments. Finally, it gives significant guidance on and examples of how to account for derivatives that deal with the entity's own equity instruments.

Chapter 17 reviews issues related to basic financial instruments. This chapter will look at some of the more complex issues from an issuer perspective. The exclusions from the standard are noted in Chapter 17. Chapter 17 also lists the relevant definitions; however, as noted in Chapter 17, the definitions for financial assets and liabilities include one additional element that was not covered in that chapter. The definitions will therefore be repeated here with the additional element added that deals with accounting for the entity's own equity instruments.[1]

A *financial asset* is any asset that is

    (a)   cash;

    (b)   an equity instrument of another entity;

    (c)   a contractual right

        (i)   to receive cash or another financial asset from another entity, or

        (ii) to exchange financial assets or financial liabilities with another entity under conditions that are potentially favorable to the entity; or

    (d)   a contract that will or may be settled in the entity's own equity instruments and is

        (i)   a non-derivative for which the entity is or may be obliged to receive a variable number of the entity's own equity instruments, or

        (ii) a derivative that will or may be settled other than by the exchange of a fixed amount of cash or another financial asset for a fixed number of the entity's own equity instruments. For this purpose, the entity's own equity instruments do not include puttable financial instruments classified as equity instruments . . . or instruments that are contracts for the future receipt or delivery of the entity's own equity instruments.

A *financial liability* is any liability that is

    (a)   a contractual obligation

        (i)   to deliver cash or another financial asset to another entity, or

        (ii) to exchange financial assets or financial liabilities with another entity under conditions that are potentially unfavorable to the entity; or

    (b)   a contract that will or may be settled in the entity's own equity instruments and is

        (i)   a non-derivative for which the entity is or may be obliged to deliver a variable number of the entity's own equity instruments, or

        (ii) a derivative that will or may be settled other than by the exchange of a fixed amount of cash or another financial asset for a fixed number of the entity's own equity instruments. For this purpose, the entity's own equity instruments do not include puttable financial instruments that are classified as equity instruments . . . or instruments that are themselves contracts for the future receipt or delivery of the entity's own equity instruments. . . .

As an exception, puttable instruments that meet the definition of a financial liability may be classified as an equity instrument if certain conditions are met. Puttable instruments will be defined and discussed below.

Recall that financial instruments represent contracts or arrangements between two parties where there are clear economic consequences for non-performance.

PRESENTATION

At this point, it is worthwhile to revisit the concept of equity. Because equity is residual in nature, it is generally not measured separately. According to the accounting equation, equity is measured at the residual value of assets less liabilities. Therefore, it is important to measure assets and liabilities properly and then the equity is the plug or difference between the two.

---

[1] IASCF, IAS 32.11.

An instrument is an *equity instrument* if it is residual in nature and both of the following conditions are met:[2]

(a) The instrument includes no contractual obligation

    (i) to deliver cash or another financial asset to another entity, or

    (ii) to exchange financial assets or financial liabilities with another entity under conditions that are potentially unfavorable to the issuer.

(b) If the instrument will or may be settled in the issuer's own equity instruments, it is

    (i) a non-derivative that includes no contractual obligation for the issuer to deliver a variable number of its own equity instruments, or

    (ii) a derivative that will be settled only by the issuer exchanging a fixed amount of cash or another financial asset for a fixed number of its own equity instruments . . .

The most common example of an equity instrument is a common share. Certain options dealing with an entity's own shares are also covered such as written call options or purchased put/call options, as long as they do not contain net settlement provisions. In addition, as an exception, certain puttable instruments discussed below are included as equity instruments.

Puttable Instruments

Puttable instruments are defined as follows:[3]

A *puttable instrument* is a financial instrument that gives the holder the right to put the instrument back to the issuer for cash or another financial asset or is automatically put back to the issuer on the occurrence of an uncertain future event or the death or retirement of the instrument holder.

If an instrument is puttable, it has an embedded put option and may be presented to the entity (issuer) for payment. In general, the put option represents an obligation on the part of the entity and is therefore presented as a financial liability. As indicated in the definition of a liability, it is a contractual obligation to deliver cash or other assets.

However, certain instruments are puttable only in very restrictive circumstances such as when an entity ceases to exist (windup). It is inevitable that all companies will eventually end (wind up). Therefore, the standard allows an exception to the general treatment as a liability where the following conditions are met:[4]

(a) The instrument entitles the holder or another entity to a share of the entity's net assets upon liquidation.

(b) The instrument is in a class of instruments that is subordinate to all other instruments and is residual in nature (e.g., common shares).

(c) All instruments in the class have the same features including the put option.

(d) The instrument otherwise does not meet the definition of a liability.

(e) The expected cash flows of the instrument relate to the earnings of the entity.

Thus, if the instruments are otherwise common shares (legally or in substance) except for the put option, they may be treated as equity. As a final caveat, the entity may have no other instruments that would be subordinate to the puttable instruments (i.e., other common or ordinary shares). The puttable instruments must represent the residual ownership interest.

---

[2] IASCF, IAS 32.16.

[3] IASCF, IAS 32.11.

[4] IASCF, IAS 32.16A.

Situation

Habanero Inc. has two classes of shares. The shares are closely held by members of the Habanero family. Class A shares carry a dividend of $1 per share (cumulative) and rank in preference upon windup. Class B shares are residual, have voting rights, and pay dividends if profits/cash are available. On windup of the entity, which is triggered if one of the shareholders dies, the shares are redeemable by the company for an amount equal to the net assets available on a liquidation basis after Class A shares have been paid out. How should the Class B shares be presented?

Analysis

As a starting point, the Class B shares are residual in nature and therefore in substance they are equity. They carry voting rights and share in the profits and net asset growth of the company. However, the redemption feature represents a liability. The company has a contractual obligation to settle the shares on the death of a shareholder, which is inevitable. Should the shares be treated as debt or equity? The standard allows these shares to be treated as equity as long as certain criteria are met. In this case, the criteria are met since the payout is triggered only upon liquidation, the shares are residual, all shares in the class have the same characteristics, and the shares otherwise do not meet the definition of a liability. In conclusion, the shares are presented as equity.

A financial instrument may change in status after initial recognition and the presentation should reflect this. For instance, if an entity has three classes of shares—preferred shares, common shares, and puttable shares (as described above)—the puttable shares would be treated as liabilities initially, given that the common shares exist (and therefore the common shares are the most subordinated). If the entity redeems all of its common shares, the puttable financial instruments become the most subordinated and are therefore reclassified as equity as long as the criteria noted above are met.

If the puttable instruments are originally classified as equity because they meet the criteria and then cease to meet the criteria, they would be reclassified as liabilities.

If reclassified, the instruments are valued as follows:[5]

- if reclassified from equity to liability, at fair value at the date of reclassification with the difference being booked as equity
- if reclassified from liability to equity, at the carrying value of the liability

No Contractual Obligation to Deliver Cash

As discussed in Chapter 17, the economic substance determines the accounting. In addition, the instrument must be analyzed to determine whether there is a contractual obligation to deliver cash or other financial assets (and thus a financial liability). Following are examples of instruments that meet the definition of liabilities:

- mandatorily redeemable shares. These must be redeemed by the entity and so a liability exists.
- puttable instruments unless they meet certain criteria. These are redeemable at the option of the holder, which is beyond the control of the entity, and so a liability exists.

Per IAS 32.19 the instrument is or contains a liability if the entity does not have the unconditional right to avoid delivering cash or other financial assets to settle the instrument. This may be explicit or implicit. In some cases an obligation is implied in the contract. For instance an entity might be economically compelled to settle the instrument in cash or other assets. As an example, assume the instrument is settleable at the option of the entity in cash or equity instruments whose value substantially exceed the cash settlement amount. In this case, the entity would be economically compelled to settled in cash and therefore a liability exists.

---

[5] IASCF, IAS 32.16F.

Settlement in the Entity's Own Equity Instruments: Non-derivatives

Fixed Versus Variable Number of Shares

As noted in the definition, non-derivative contracts, such as debt, may include a contractual obligation to deliver shares when settled. Does this make the instrument an equity instrument? As long as it is a fixed number of shares, the economic substance is that the instrument is equity. The holder of the instrument will receive a fixed number of shares on settlement (versus a variable number) and therefore essentially has a residual interest in the entity. If the company increases in value, the holder will benefit. Conversely, if the company decreases in value, the holder will lose.

To summarize, a contract is not an equity instrument just because it may or will be settled in the entity's own equity instruments. As long as it is to be settled or can be settled in a **fixed amount of shares** it meets the definition of an equity instrument. If it can be settled in a **variable number of shares** then it is more like a liability. This is because a fixed value is needed to settle it. The entity must give whatever number of shares is needed (depending on the market value of the shares) to settle the fixed value. The following scenario illustrates this.

Situation

Francis Limited has $100 of one-year debt outstanding that pays 10% interest. It will settle the $110 debt by issuing 10 shares. The shares have a market value of $5 on the repayment date. How would this be accounted for? How would the accounting change if the entity was obligated to settle the debt with a variable number of shares equal to $110?

Analysis

Is the instrument debt in substance or equity?
  Fixed number of shares:
  Because the debt will be repaid in a fixed number of shares, it is equity.
  Variable number of shares:
  If the debt were to be settled by issuing a variable number of shares equal to the principal plus interest = $110/5 = 22 shares, this is more like debt. The entity has a contractual obligation to pay $110 and so this is presented as a liability.

Settlement in the Entity's Own Equity Instruments: Derivatives

Entities may enter into forward contracts or options (written or purchased) to buy or sell their own shares. Are these equity instruments?

Net Settlement Provisions

Derivatives settled in the entity's own equity instrument are treated as such and accounted for under IAS 39 if the contract includes a net settlement provision; that is, the contract will be settled net in cash or shares.[6] If the contract is settled **net in cash**, the substance is that the entity is trading for profit using its own shares as the underlying. Thus, this is more like an operating transaction than a capital transaction since the entity is not buying or selling its own shares.

Where the instruments may be settled **net in shares**, the number of shares would vary with the settlement amount and, therefore, this does not meet the definition of an equity instrument, which must be settled for a fixed number of shares.

In both cases above, the instruments are recognized in the financial statements, measured and remeasured at fair value, and gains/losses are booked to net income.

---

[6] IASCF, IAS 32.26 and 32.27.

Gross Settlement Provisions

Some contracts do not have net settlement provisions in them; they require that the entity deliver or take delivery of the shares. Are these equity instruments?

Obligations to purchase own equity instruments: written put options or forwards. Where the entity is locked into purchasing a fixed amount of its own shares for cash, a financial liability exists. The liability is measured at the present value of the redemption amount and credited to a liability account.[7] The corresponding debit is booked to equity since this is also an equity instrument (under the contract, the entity will deliver a fixed amount of cash for a fixed number of shares). This is due to the unique nature of a forward contract. It creates both a liability (obligation to deliver something) and an asset (right to receive something) at the same time. In this case, because the right is a right to receive the entity's own shares, it is not an asset but rather a debit to equity (like treasury shares).

Obligations to sell own equity instruments: written call options or forwards. When the entity agrees to sell its own shares, this is an equity instrument. If the contract is structured as an option, the entity writing the option receives a premium upfront. The premium received on the option issue is recorded as a credit to equity and debit to cash. If the contract is structured as a forward contract, there is no entry since no cash changes hands (forwards are generally priced so that their value at inception is $0).

Purchased options. An entity may choose to purchase options on its own shares for a premium. Where these are settled gross (by delivery of shares if settled), they are equity instruments and are recorded as a deduction from equity as opposed to an asset.[8] The premium is therefore booked as a debit to equity and credit to cash.

Illustration 19-1 summarizes the accounting.

	Derivative	Accounting Treatment	
Illustration 19-1 Accounting for Derivatives Involving Own Equity Instruments[9]		Will be settled net in cash or a variable number of shares; accounted for as derivatives[10]	Will be settled by physical delivery of shares; accounted for as equity instruments or compound instruments[11]
	Forward contract to buy own shares	No entry upfront since forward valued at zero and no premium paid	Dr. Equity Cr. Financial liability (present value of forward rate)
	Forward contract to sell own shares	No entry upfront since forward valued at zero and no premium paid	No entry until settlement since no $$ exchanged upfront and no contractual obligation to deliver cash
	Written call options	Dr. Cash Cr. Financial liability (equal to option premium which represents fair value)	Dr. Cash Cr. Equity (equal to the option premium)

---

[7] IASCF, IAS 32.23.

[8] IASCF, IAS 32, AG14.

[9] The illustrative examples in IAS 32 are an excellent source for journal entries and examples relating to these instruments.

[10] Initially recorded at premium (zero for forwards). Subsequently measured at fair value with gains/losses to net income.

[11] Initially recorded at the premium paid except for the forward to buy own shares/written put options. This is measured at the amount of the obligation to pay cash.

Derivative	Accounting Treatment	
Written put options	Dr. Cash Cr. Financial liability (equal to option premium)	Dr. Cash Cr. Equity (amount of premium) Dr. Equity Cr. Liability (present value of liability) (The net amount booked to equity represents the cost to repurchase the shares net of the premium)
Purchased call options	Dr. Financial asset Cr. Cash (equal to option premium)	Dr. Equity Cr. Cash (equal to the option premium)
Purchased put options	Dr. Financial asset Cr. Cash (equal to option premium)	Dr. Equity Cr. Cash (equal to the option premium)

Where the contract has a choice regarding settlement, it is treated as a derivative unless all options result in it meeting the definition of an equity instrument.

Compound Financial Instruments

Compound financial instruments contain both debt and equity components. For instance, convertible debt contains both a debt component plus an option to convert to common shares. Accounting for financial instruments that include several components is more complex. If the entity holds the instruments as an investment, they are covered by IAS 39. Accounting for these types of investments was covered in Chapters 17 and 18 (embedded derivatives). Recall that embedded derivatives that are not closely related to the host instruments are bifurcated and measured at fair value with gains and losses subsequently booked to profit and loss.

If the entity is the issuer, however, the starting point for the analysis is IAS 32. The equity component is stripped out and then any financial liability is accounted for under IAS 39.

Illustration 19-2 illustrates how to deal with financial instruments that are compound instruments from the perspective of the issuer. It is important to identify the equity instruments first and strip them out because they are not covered by IAS 39.

As noted in the illustration, compound instruments are separated into liability and equity components. The equity component is accounted for under IAS 32 as a residual interest in the entity, while the financial liability component is then covered by IAS 39. The liability might contain embedded derivatives and therefore further analysis as to whether embedded derivative exists within a financial liability would be done under IAS 39. Recall the earlier discussion regarding derivative instruments dealing with the entity's own equity instruments. If settled on a net basis, these would be further analyzed under IAS 39.

In terms of allocating an amount to the debt and equity components, the debt is measured first. In general, the entity measures the liability at fair value; that is, the value of a similar instrument without the equity feature, which might be approximated by doing a discounted cash flow calculation.[12]

---

[12] IASCF, IAS 32.31.

*Illustration 19-2
Dealing with
Compound/Hybrid
Instruments from
the Perspective of
the Issuer*

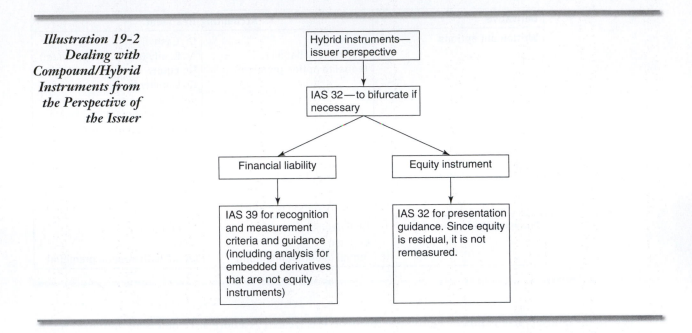

The following situation illustrates how to deal with a compound instrument from the perspective of the issuer.

Situation

Dela Limited has $100 of one-year debt outstanding (10% interest). The holder has the right to convert the instrument into 10 common shares. The discount rate is 10% and the debt was issued for $102. How would this be accounted for?

Analysis

This is a compound instrument. It contains both a debt and equity component and the equity component must be bifurcated and presented as equity upon initial recognition. The option to convert to a fixed amount of shares is, by definition, equity. The choice of settlement options is beyond the entity's control and so the fixed obligation to repay the debt meets the definition of a liability.

   The equity is separated and measured at the residual after deducting the fair value of the obligation. The fair value of the obligation is $100 (present value of the $100 principal and $10 interest discounted at the market rate of 10%). This means that the equity is valued at $102−100 = 2.

```
Dr. Cash           $102
     Cr. Liabilities        100
     Cr. Equity               2
```

Once classified as debt or equity, a financial instrument is not subsequently changed as a result of a change in likelihood of conversion.

Contingent Settlement Provisions

Where the entity may be required to deliver cash or other financial assets upon the occurrence or non-occurrence of a future event, and that event is beyond the control of the entity (e.g., a change in the share price), this would generally be treated as a financial liability.

Settlement Options

According to IAS 32.26, when the issuer or holder has a choice as to how to settle a derivative (net or by exchanging shares for cash), it is a financial asset/liability unless all of the settlement options result in it being an equity instrument.

Treasury Shares

Treasury shares are shares acquired or reacquired by the entity. They are presented as a deduction from equity with no gains/losses recognized in profit and loss. These are capital transactions.

LOOKING AHEAD

Determining what is a liability versus equity is a very controversial topic which will have far reaching implications for many IFRS standards. As mentioned earlier, FASB and IASB are currently studying this issue and have a Discussion Paper out.

END-OF-CHAPTER PRACTICE

19-1 Puttable instruments allow the holder to sell the instruments back to the entity for a fixed price.

Instructions

In theory, how should these be accounted for (use the definitions of liabilities and equity)? Why does IAS 32 allow these to be treated differently?

19-2 Kanga Limited has a $1,000 10-year debt outstanding at 5% interest. The debt will be settled by issuing 100 common shares.

Instructions

Prepare the journal entry to record the debt upon issuance. Discuss why it is accounted for this way. How would this change and why, if the debt were to be settled in with a variable number of shares?

19-3 Roo Inc. entered into the following contracts during the year:

- A written put option. The option allows the holder to sell 100 common shares of Roo back to the company for $100. The company received $5 for writing this option.

- The same option as above but this option has a net settlement provision.

- Issued convertible 10 year debt for $505. The debt carries interest at 5% and is convertible at the option of the holder to 100 common shares of Roo. Market interest rates for similar debt are 5%.

- Purchased option. The option was purchased for $6 and allows Roo to buy 100 common shares of Roo for $101.

- A forward contract under which Roo will repurchase 100 Roo shares in one year for $110.

Instructions

Prepare the journal entries to record these transactions in the financial statement. Explain why they are accounted for this way.

19-4 In this chapter, flag icons identify areas where there are GAAP differences between IFRS requirements and national standards.

Instructions

Access the website(s) identified on the inside back cover of this book, and prepare a concise summary of the differences that are flagged throughout the chapter.

Chapter 20

Financial Instruments–Disclosure: IFRS 7

U.S. GAAP References
Various FAS—see Chapters 17–19
FAS 161 Disclosures about Derivative Instruments and Hedging Activities—an amendment of FASB Statement No. 133

Related IFRSs
IAS 1 Presentation of Financial Statements
IAS 32 Financial Instruments: Presentation
IAS 39 Financial Instruments: Recognition and Measurement

OBJECTIVE AND SCOPE

This standard contains very detailed prescriptive guidance on required disclosures that are meant to assist users in assessing

1. the significance of financial instruments, in terms of financial performance and position, and
2. the nature and extent of risks related to financial instruments.

IFRS 7 applies to all entitles and all financial instruments except the following:[1]

- interests in subsidiaries, associates, and joint ventures accounted for under standards other than IAS 32 and 39;
- employers' rights and obligations;
- insurance contracts; and
- contracts related to share-based payments.

---

[1] IASCF, IFRS 7.3.

In addition, it applies to those instruments covered by IAS 39 and to some unrecognized financial instruments that are outside the scope of IAS 39 (for example, some loan commitments). The standard includes mandatory application guidance in Appendix B and non-mandatory implementation guidance.

This chapter walks through the lengthy list of required disclosures and should be read in conjunction with Chapters 17-19. The following is a brief overview and recap of the provisions and requirements in IFRS 7.

CLASSES OF FINANCIAL INSTRUMENTS AND LEVEL OF DISCLOSURE

IFRS 7 groups financial instruments into classes for some disclosure requirements. Instruments should be grouped taking into account their nature and characteristics.

SIGNIFICANCE OF FINANCIAL INSTRUMENTS FOR FINANCIAL POSITION AND PERFORMANCE

Statement of Financial Position

Since the use of fair value can be subjective and has a significant impact on earnings, information about fair value and carrying amounts is required.

Carrying amounts for the following should be presented in the balance sheet or the notes:

- financial assets and liabilities classified as fair value through profit and loss (FVTPL)
    - o   show those that are initially classified as such as those that are held for trading (HFT)
- held to maturity investments (HTM)
- loans and receivables
- available for sale assets (AFS)
- financial liabilities measured at amortized cost.

FVTPL

For loans and receivables classified as FVTPL, the following should be disclosed:

- the maximum exposure to credit risk (the maximum exposure may be seen to be the varying amount or the cash loss that is the amount owed),
- the amount by which a derivative or other instrument mitigates credit risk,
- the change in fair value during the period (and cumulatively) attributable to changes in credit risk, and
- the change in fair value during the period (and cumulatively) of related credit derivatives or other instruments that mitigate credit risk.

For financial liabilities designated as FVTPL, the following should be disclosed:

- the change in fair value during the period (and cumulatively) attributable to credit risk, and
- the difference between the carrying amount and the amount of contractual obligation at maturity.

For the above, the entity needs to disclose the methods used to determine disclosures concerning changes in fair value related to credit risk. If the entity believes that the fair value amounts relating to credit risk do not faithfully represent the changes due to credit risks, the entity needs to disclose the reasons why, including relevant factors.

Note that as an entity's creditworthiness deteriorates, the fair value of the debt decreases, resulting in gains being recognized. This would appear to be counterintuitive, i.e., the entity is worse off if its creditworthiness deteriorates. The disclosures are meant to help explain and clarify this.

Determining the fair value change attributable to credit risk may be difficult only because other risks will affect the fair value and be reflected in market prices.

Reclassification

If an entity has reclassified an instrument between categories measured at fair value and amortized costs respectively, the amount and reasons for reclassification need to be disclosed. The classification of instruments is partly based on management intent and so it is important to show the reasons why instruments are reclassified.

Derecognition

Where an entity has transferred financial assets and they do not qualify for derecognition, the following should be disclosed:

- the nature of the assets,
- the nature of risks and rewards exposed to,
- the carrying amounts, and
- the carrying amount of original assets and any remaining assets/liabilities where there is continuing involvement.

It is important for users to be able to determine how the risks and rewards that are retained affect the entity.

Collateral

Where an entity has pledged assets as collateral, the following should be disclosed:

- the carrying amounts, and
- conditions and terms.

Where it holds collateral and is able to sell or repledge it, the entity should disclose

- the fair value of the collateral,
- the fair value of the collateral sold or repledged, and
- the terms associated with the use of the collateral.

Allowance Account for Credit Losses

When assets are impaired due to credit losses and the amounts are recorded in an allowance account, a reconciliation between the opening and closing balances should be disclosed.

Compound Financial Instruments and Multiple Embedded Derivatives

The entity should disclose the existence of compound instruments with multiple embedded derivatives whose values are interdependent.

Defaults and Breaches

Where an entity has loans payable at the end of the period, it should disclose the following:

- details of the defaults,
- carrying amounts of loans in default, and
- whether the defaults were remedied.

The same information should be disclosed for a breach of a loan agreement during the period if the breach allows the lender to accelerate repayment.

Statement of Comprehensive Income

Items of Income, Expense, Gains, or Losses

The following should be disclosed:

- net gains/losses on

  - financial assets/liabilities at FVTPL,
  - AFS (showing the amount in other comprehensive income and profit and loss),
  - HTM,
  - loans and receivables, or
  - financial liabilities measured at cost;

- interest income and expenses;
- fee income and expenses;
- interest income on impaired financial assets; and
- impairment loss.

Other Disclosures

Hedge Accounting

The entity should disclose the following:
For each type of hedge,

- a description of each hedge,
- a description of hedging instruments and their fair values, and
- the nature of risks being hedged.

For cash flow hedges,

- the periods when the cash flows are expected to occur,
- a description of forecasted transactions,
- the amount recognized in other comprehensive income during the period,
- the amount reclassified to profit and loss during the period, and
- the amount removed from equity and included in the initial cost or carrying value of the hedged item.

For fair value hedges,

- gains/losses on the hedging instrument, and
- gains/losses on the hedged risk.

The entity should also disclose the amount of ineffectiveness recognized in profit and loss from cash flow hedges and hedges of net investment in foreign operations.

Fair Value

An entity should disclose

- the fair values of each class of financial assets/liabilities in such a way to allow them to be compared with carrying values;
- the methods and assumptions used to calculate fair value;
- where fair values are based on published price quotations in an active market or valuation techniques;
- where valuation techniques are used and fair value is based on assumptions that are not supported by prices from observable market transactions or observable market data; and

- where changing assumptions will change the value significantly. This should be stated along with the effect of these changes.

If there is no active market for a financial instrument and an entity uses a valuation technique on initial recognition, there could be a difference between this value and the transaction value. An entity should disclose the following:

- the accounting policy for recognizing these differences, and
- the aggregate difference to be recognized in profit and loss at the beginning and end of period and a reconciliation between the two.

Fair value disclosures are not required

- when the carrying amount is a reasonable approximation of the fair value,
- for equity instruments that do not have quoted market prices in an active market because the fair value cannot be measured reliably, or
- in other situations where the fair value cannot be measured reliably.

In these cases, the entity should disclose information to assist users in making their own judgments, including the fact that fair values are not disclosed, a description of the instruments, information about the markets, information about intent to dispose of the instruments, and details about where these instruments are derecognized during the period.

NATURE AND EXTENT OF RISKS ARISING FROM FINANCIAL INSTRUMENTS

Qualitative Disclosures

An entity shall disclose for each type of risk

- exposures to risks and how they arise;
- objectives, policies, and processes for managing risks and methods used to measure them; and
- any changes during the period.

Illustration 20-1 shows an excerpt from the financial statements of Del Monte Pacific Ltd. relating to key risks.[2]

Illustration 20-1 Excerpt from Del Monte Pacific Ltd. Financial Statements

Risk related to agricultural activities

As an integrated producer of processed pineapple and mixed tropical fruit products for the world market, the Group's earnings are inevitably subjected to certain risk factors, which include general economic and business conditions, change in business strategy or development plans, weather conditions, crop yields, raw material costs and availability, competition, market acceptance of new products, industry trends, and changes in government regulations, including, without limitation, environmental regulations.

The Group is exposed to financial risks arising from changes in cost and volume of fruits harvested from the growing crops which is influenced by natural phenomenon such as weather patterns and volume of rainfall. The level of harvest is also affected by field performance and market changes. The cost of growing crops is also exposed to the change in cost and supply of agricultural supplies and labour which are determined by constantly changing market forces of supply and demand.

---

[2] http://www.delmontepacific.com/ir/media/ar_ipo/AR2007.pdf.

The Group is subject to risk relating to its ability to maintain the physical condition of its fruit crops. Plant diseases could adversely impact production and consumer confidence.

The Group is subject to risks affecting the food industry generally, including risks posed by food spoilage and contamination. Specifically, the production of canned pineapple and other food related products is regulated by environmental, health and food safety organisations and regulatory bodies from local and international markets. These authorities conduct operational audits to assess the Group's compliance with food processing standards. The Group has put into place systems to monitor food safety risks throughout all stages of manufacturing and processing to mitigate these risks. Despite the precaution taken by the Group, the authorities and food safety organizations may impose additional regulatory requirements that may require significant capital investment at notice.

The Group's overall earnings from its trading activities with international customers are primarily affected by movements in the worldwide consumption, demand and prices of its products. However, the demand and supply risk associated with the Group's international business is minimized by the nature of its long-term supply agreements, five of which are with various Del Monte brand owners around the world. These contracts have various mechanisms with regard to pricing and volume off-take that help limit the downside risk of the Group's international business.

In some cases, the Group is protected by the existence of price floors whereby the Group is able to recover its production costs. In other instances, the Group has the right of first refusal to supply additional quantities at prices no worse than those from alternative sources.

The Group's exposure to the operational risks is managed through the following processes, among others:

- Development and execution of a realistic long-term strategic plan and annual operating plan;
- Securing long-term land leases with staggered maturity terms;
- Increasing production and packaging capacity;
- Pursuit of productivity-enhancing and efficiency-generating work practices and capital projects;
- Focus on consumption-driven marketing strategies;
- Continuous introduction of new products and line extensions with emphasis on innovation, quality, competitiveness and consumer appeal;
- Increased penetration of high-growth distribution channels;
- Building on closer working relationships with business partners; and
- Close monitoring of changes in legislation and government regulations affecting the Group's business.

Fair Values

The notional amounts of financial assets and liabilities with a maturity of less than one year (including trade and other receivables, cash and cash equivalents, financial liabilities and trade and other payables) are assumed to approximate their fair values because of the short period to maturity. All other financial assets and liabilities are discounted to determine their fair values.

Quantitative Disclosures

For each of the risks noted above, the entity should disclose

- summary quantitative data about the exposures at the end of the reporting period (based on information provided internally to management), and
- concentrations of risks.

If the end-of-period exposures are not representative of exposures during the period, additional disclosures should be given.

Credit Risk

An entity should disclose the following by class of financial instrument:

- the maximum exposure to credit risk,
- a description of collateral held,
- information about credit quality of financial assets, and
- carrying amounts of renegotiated financial assets that would otherwise be past due or impaired.

Illustration 20-2 is an example of disclosures related to credit risk for Del Monte Pacific Ltd.

Illustration 20-2 Disclosures Related to Credit Risk—Del Monte Pacific Ltd.

Credit risk

The Group sells its products through major distributors in various geographical regions. For the year ended 31 December 2007, the Group's major customers collectively accounted for 24% (2006: 33%) of its total revenue. Management has a credit risk policy which includes, among others, the requirement of certain securities to be posted to secure prompt observance and performance of the obligations of its distributors and other buyers from time to time. The Group monitors its outstanding trade receivables on an on-going basis.

Apart from the above, the Company and the Group have no significant concentration of credit risk with any single counterparty or group counterparties. The maximum exposure to credit risk is represented by the carrying amount of each financial asset in the balance sheets.

Where financial assets are past due or impaired, the following disclosures are required:

- an analysis of the aging;
- an analysis of individual assets that are impaired, including factors the entity considered in making the determination; and
- a description of any collateral held.

Where the entity obtained collateral during the period, it should disclose

- the nature and carrying value of collateral and other assets obtained; and
- where the collateral is not readily convertible to cash, the policy for disposition.

Liquidity Risk

The entity should disclose

- a maturity analysis for financial liabilities that shows the remaining contractual maturities, and
- a description of how it manages the liquidity risk.

Market Risk

An entity shall disclose a sensitivity analysis for each type of market risk, including methods and assumptions used to calculate the risk and any changes from the previous period.

The various market risks are defined in Appendix A to IFRS 7.

Currency risk is the risk that future cash flows or fair values will fluctuate due to foreign currency changes.

Interest rate risk is the risk that fair values or the cash flow will change due to changes in interest rates.

Other price risks include the risks that fair value and prices will fluctuate due to changes in other market prices, for example, share prices.

In order to complete the sensitivity analysis, the following steps might be taken:

1. Identify risks.
2. Identify exposures at the balance sheet date.
3. Determine which financial statement balances might change and why.
4. Determine the appropriate level of aggregation for the analysis.
5. Calculate and present the sensitivity analysis.

Illustration 20-3 shows an example of sensitivity analysis disclosures for Del Monte Pacific Ltd.

Illustration 20-3 Sensitivity Analysis Disclosures—Del Monte Pacific Ltd.	**Sensitivity analysis** A 10% strengthening of US dollar against the following currencies at the reporting date would increase/(decrease) the income statement by the amounts shown below. This analysis assumes that all other variables, in particular interest rates, remain constant.

	Group	
	2007 **US$'000**	**2006** **US$'000**
Philippine pesos	2,978	3,047
Chinese renminbi	1,033	863

A 10% weakening of the US dollar against the above currencies would have had the equal but opposite effect on the above currencies to the amounts shown above, on the basis that all other variables remain constant.

Sensitivity analysis

A 1% general increase in interest rates at the reporting date would increase/(decrease) equity and profit or loss by the amounts shown below. This analysis assumes that all other variables, in particular, foreign currency rates, remain constant.

	Group	
	Equity **US$'000**	**Profit or Loss** **US$'000**
2006		
Group		
Short-term deposits	–	491
Unsecured short-term borrowings	–	(437)
Obligations under finance leases	–	(18)
	–	36
2007		
Group		
Short-term deposits	–	109
Unsecured short-term borrowings	–	(342)
Obligations under finance leases	–	(8)
		(241)

A 1% general decrease in interest rates would have the equal but opposite effect on the amounts shown above, on the basis that all other variables remain constant.

LOOKING AHEAD

The IASB is currently studying the area of financial instruments and hedging as noted in Chapter 17. Additional disclosures provide useful information; however, there reaches a point where too much disclosure results in information overload. The IASB has a goal to simplify financial reporting as it relates to financial instruments and the nature and extent of disclosures is part of this issue.

END-OF-CHAPTER PRACTICE

20-1 IFRS requires a sensitivity analysis for key risks.

Instructions
Find the statements for L'Oreal and identify the main risks that the company faces. Review the disclosures regarding risks. Discuss whether they meet the overall objective of IFRS 7.

20-2 The standard requires significant disclosures about fair values.

Instructions
Why are these additional disclosures important? Write a short essay.

20-3 IFRS 7 is a fairly lengthy standard requiring a significant number of detailed disclosures.

Instructions
Discuss the pros and cons of mandating such detailed and voluminous disclosures.

20-4 Sensitivity analysis requires a significant amount of judgments.

Instructions
Discuss what judgments go into providing a sensitivity analysis. Do they add value to the statements? How easy are these types of disclosures to understand? How easy are they to audit?

20-5 In this chapter, flag icons identify areas where there are GAAP differences between IFRS requirements and national standards.

Instructions
Access the website(s) identified on the inside back cover of this book, and prepare a concise summary of the differences that are flagged throughout the chapter.

Chapter 21

Accounting Policies, Changes in Accounting Estimates and Errors: IAS 8

U.S. GAAP References
FAS 162 The Hierarchy of Generally Accepted Accounting Principles
FAS 154 Accounting Changes and Error Corrections—A replacement of APB Opinion No. 20 and FAS 3

Related IFRSs
IAS 1 Presentation of Financial Statements
Framework for the Preparation and Presentation of Financial Statements
IAS 12 Income Taxes

OBJECTIVE AND SCOPE

Accounting choices and changes have a direct effect on the comparability of financial statements between accounting entities and, in the case of a single entity, from one reporting period to the next. Yet change is a constant in financial reporting, estimates are a fundamental part of accounting measurements, and errors are occasionally made. The objective of IAS 8, therefore, is to provide guidance on four major areas: how an entity chooses the accounting policies to apply, the accounting and disclosure requirements for changes in accounting policies, changes in accounting estimates, and the correction of prior period errors.

IAS 12 *Income Taxes* sets out how to account for and report the tax effects of any adjustments to prior period financial statements.

SELECTION AND APPLICATION OF ACCOUNTING POLICIES

The GAAP Hierarchy

IAS 8 sets out how an entity should choose the accounting policies it applies and identifies *accounting policies* as the "specific principles, bases, conventions, rules and practices applied by an entity in preparing and presenting financial statements." The **first step** in answering the question **"what is GAAP?"** in a particular situation is to determine if there is an IFRS that specifically applies to the transaction or event. **If so, GAAP is made up of the policies in the applicable IFRS**. These policies are the highest level in the **GAAP hierarchy**.

International Financial Reporting Standards or *IFRS* are the Standards and Interpretations adopted by the IASB. They are made up of the following:

- International Financial Reporting Standards,
- International Accounting Standards, and
- Interpretations developed by the International Financial Reporting Interpretations Committee (IFRIC) or its predecessor, the Standing Interpretations Committee (SIC).[1]

Because standards and interpretations often have additional material such as appendices and implementation guidance attached to them, IAS 8 makes it clear that only the guidance that states it is an **integral part** of the standard or interpretation is included in the IFRS.

When the appropriate IFRS is applied, the resulting information is assumed to be **relevant and reliable**. Any deviation from the IFRS requirements is assumed to result in information that does not have these qualities, unless the effect is **immaterial**.[2] These terms are used in IAS 8 the same way they are in the *Framework for the Preparation and Presentation of Financial Statements*.

What if there is no specific IFRS that applies to a particular event or situation? In this case, management has to use judgment in developing and applying a policy that is **relevant and reliable**. The standard identifies a hierarchy of sources for management to use in exercising judgment:

- The requirements in other IFRSs that deal with similar situations and issues are looked to first.
- The basic components of the conceptual *Framework*—the definitions; recognition and measurement criteria; and concepts for assets, liabilities, income, and expenses—are applied next.
- A third level of other sources may be considered as long as they do not conflict with those in the first two levels. Examples include recent pronouncements of other standard-setting bodies with similar conceptual frameworks, the accounting literature, and accepted industry practices.

Consistency of Accounting Policies

In general, the same accounting policies must be used for similar transactions and events. However, a specific IFRS may allow or require similar items to be categorized and different policies to be applied to each, such as for inventory or plant and equipment. In each case and for each category, the policies chosen are applied consistently.

---

[1] IASCF, IAS 8.5.
[2] IAS 8.5 explains that omissions or misstatements are **material** if they could, either on their own or collectively, influence the economic decisions that users make on the basis of the financial statements. Materiality depends on the size and/or nature of an omission or error and has to be judged in light of the surrounding circumstances. The requirements in IAS 8 complement the IAS 1 statement that IFRS-required disclosures are not necessary if the information is immaterial.

CHANGES IN ACCOUNTING POLICIES

What Is a Change in Accounting Policy?

The most common reason for an entity to change an accounting policy or the way in which it is applied is the issuance by the IASB of new or revised accounting standards. The only other acceptable reason for a change is that a different policy results in financial statements that provide "reliable and more relevant information about the effects of transactions, other events or conditions on the entity's financial position, financial performance or cash flows."[3] An example of such a voluntary change is a move from the weighted average cost formula for establishing inventory cost to the FIFO method in a period of rapidly escalating costs. In this situation, the FIFO formula assigns more recent costs to period-end inventory, therefore providing reliable and more relevant financial position information to users.

Sometimes an entity changes an accounting policy because economic conditions have changed or a policy is needed to account for new events or conditions or for items that were previously immaterial. **These are not considered changes in accounting policy**. Consider the following examples.

Situation

1. An entity that previously amortized product development costs over four years changes to a two-year amortization period because of the effect of technology in reducing product life cycles.
2. An entity uses straight-line depreciation on all of its property, plant, and equipment assets because they provide benefits based on the passage of time. On acquiring a new machine that provides economic benefits as it is used to produce goods, the entity chooses the units of production method to depreciate the machine.
3. An entity begins to capitalize interest during construction of an extension to its plant. In the past, interest was always expensed directly to profit or loss because the entity had only engaged in minor construction activities previously.

Which of these three situations, if any, should be accounted for as a change in accounting policy?

Analysis

In situation 1, the four-year policy was appropriate for the conditions that existed in the past and the two-year policy is appropriate for current conditions. In situation 2, the type of asset and the pattern in which it delivers benefits to the entity are different. In situation 3, the expensing of interest costs instead of capitalizing them did not result in a material difference in the financial statements. Therefore, none of the three situations presented is considered a change in an accounting policy.

IAS 8 specifically indicates that if an entity begins to apply a policy of revaluing property, plant, and equipment assets or intangible assets under IAS 16 or IAS 38, the change in policy is dealt with under those IFRSs.

Accounting for a Change in Accounting Policy

Illustration 21-1 summarizes the accounting requirements for a change in policy.

When a new IFRS is issued or revised, the standard often indicates how the change is to be accounted for. If it does not, or if an entity changes a policy voluntarily, it uses retroactive or *retrospective application*. This means the new accounting policy is applied to transactions, other events, and conditions as if that policy has always been applied.[4]

---

[3] IASCF, IAS 8.4(b).

[4] IAS 8.20 and 21 indicate that early application of an IFRS is not considered a voluntary change in accounting policy. However, if an entity applies a pronouncement of another standard setter because there is no relevant IFRS, and this pronouncement is amended, the change in policy is considered a voluntary change.

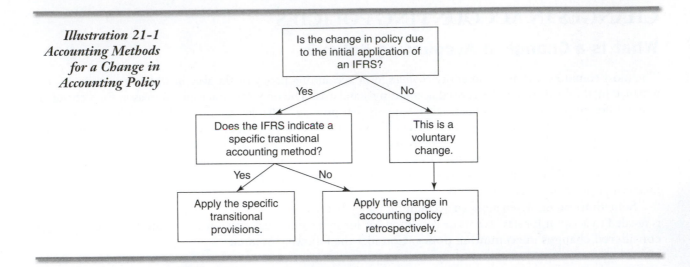

Illustration 21-1
Accounting Methods
for a Change in
Accounting Policy

Retrospective Application

In most situations, an entity applies a change in accounting policy by adjusting the opening balance of each component of equity that is affected, along with the opening balance of other comparative amounts disclosed, **for the earliest prior period presented.** As indicated, the objective is to present the financial statements as if the new policy had always been in effect. There is **one exception** to applying retrospective or retroactive treatment in this way. The exception applies when it is **impracticable** to determine either the effects on specific prior periods or the cumulative effect of the change.

Impracticable does not mean that the process might take too much time or use too many resources. It means that an entity is not able to determine the adjustments needed for retrospective treatment even after making a reasonable effort to do so. That is,

(a) the effects of the retrospective changes cannot be determined;
(b) assumptions are needed about what management's intentions were in that prior period; or
(c) significant estimates must be made that need to take into account circumstances that existed in that prior period, and it is no longer possible to do this, i.e., it is not appropriate to use hindsight to determine the effects on prior periods.

For example, assume that retrospective application requires measuring an asset at its fair value at the balance sheet date for each of the past three years. If the asset is a financial instrument that is traded on the stock exchange, the fair value numbers can be easily obtained. However, if determining fair value requires estimating future cash flows that were expected from the asset, discounted at risk-adjusted interest rates appropriate at each balance sheet date, it may not be possible to do so without the use of hindsight and making assumptions about management's intentions in those prior years.

In order to apply an accounting policy back to specific prior periods, the cumulative effect on the opening and closing balance sheets of each prior period must be known. An adjustment is then made to the appropriate item of equity—usually retained earnings—for the cumulative effect of the change at the beginning of the earliest period presented.

When full retroactive application is impracticable **because the effects on specific prior periods cannot be determined,** the change in policy is applied to the assets, liabilities, and appropriate equity account at the beginning of the earliest possible period for which the entity knows the effects. This could be as recent as the current period.

When it is impracticable to determine the cumulative effect even on the current year's opening balances, the new accounting policy is applied **prospectively.** This method applies the effects of the new policy only to transactions, events, and conditions that occur after the date the policy is changed.

Disclosures for a Change in Accounting Policy

The disclosures set out in IAS 8 are meant to help readers understand the effect of any accounting policy change on the current, prior, and future period financial statements. When an entity **initially applies the requirements of an IFRS** and there is an effect on past, present, or future periods, it is required to disclose the following:

(a) the title of the IFRS, that the change is made under its transitional provisions, and a description of the transitional provisions, as well as information about any provisions that are likely to affect future periods, if applicable;

(b) the nature of the change in the accounting policy;

(c) the amounts of the adjustments to each financial statement line item affected and to basic and diluted earnings per share for the current period for each past period presented, and where practicable, the amount of the adjustment relating to periods prior to these; and

(d) when retrospective application is judged to be impracticable, an explanation of why this is and a description of how the change in policy has been applied.

When the change in policy is considered **a voluntary change**, the disclosures identified above in (b), (c), and (d) are all required. In addition, management must explain why the new policy provides reliable and more relevant information than before.

Other disclosures are added when a **new IFRS has been released but is not yet effective**. Entities are required to alert their financial statement readers to the existence of the new standard, what the upcoming changes are, and the timing of its application with some indication of the possible effects it might have on their financial statements in the period it is first applied, if practicable to determine.

CHANGES IN ACCOUNTING ESTIMATES

What Is a Change in an Accounting Estimate?

Estimates are a fundamental and necessary input to many accounting measurements. Examples of estimates include the fair values of some financial instruments, the net realizable value of accounts receivable, the useful lives of property, plant, and equipment and intangible assets, the patterns in which the benefits associated with depreciable assets are consumed, and the obsolescence of inventory. All estimates are subject to change as new information becomes available and events and conditions become clearer with time. A change in an estimate, therefore, is an expected, essential, and recurring aspect of financial accounting and reporting.

IAS 8.5 defines a *change in an accounting estimate* as an adjustment of either the carrying amount of an asset or liability or the amount of an asset consumed in a period that results from assessing its present status and the expected future benefits and obligations associated with it. Changes in accounting estimates are not corrections of errors in prior periods; they result instead from new information or new developments.

Sometimes when a change has characteristics of both a change in policy and a change in estimate, it is difficult to determine which it is. In this case, IAS 8 indicates that if uncertain, the change is accounted for as a change in estimate.

Accounting for a Change in Estimate

It is not reasonable to go back and change prior period results whenever an estimate changes. Instead, adjustments are made prospectively. *Prospective application* of a change in accounting estimate means that the effect of the change is recognized in the current and future periods affected by the change. If the change relates to an asset, liability, or equity item, such as the estimate of the allowance for doubtful account, for example, the carrying amount is adjusted in the period of change. A change in estimate that affects the current period only is included immediately in profit or loss. A change that affects the current and future periods, such as a change in the estimated useful life of a tangible asset, is recognized over the periods affected.

Disclosures for a Change in Accounting Estimate

For a change in estimate that affects the current period or is expected to affect future periods, an entity discloses

    (a) the nature of the change in estimate; and
    (b) the amount of the change, unless the effect of the change on future periods is impracticable to estimate. If impracticable to estimate, this fact is reported.

CORRECTIONS OF ERRORS

What Is an Accounting Error?

When material errors are made and not discovered until a later accounting period, they have to be corrected. How does an error differ from a change in policy or estimate? A *prior period error* is an omission from or a misstatement in an entity's previously reported financial statements from failing to use, or the misuse of, reliable information that

    (a) was available when those financial statements were authorized to be issued, and
    (b) could reasonably be expected to have been collected and used in preparing those statements.

    Errors generally result from arithmetic mistakes, mistakes in applying accounting policies, oversights or misinterpretation of facts, or fraud.[5]

Accounting for Prior Period Errors

Material accounting errors are corrected by **retrospective restatement** in the first financial statements issued after the error is discovered. This means that all prior periods are restated to reflect what would have been reported if the error had not occurred. If the error took place further back than the earliest financial statements presented, the assets, liabilities, and equity balances on the earliest statements are restated.

    If it is impracticable to determine the period-specific or cumulative effects of the error, **limited retrospective restatement** or even **prospective treatment** is applied, similar to the equivalent situations for a change in accounting policy explained earlier in the chapter.

Disclosures for Prior Period Errors

The objective of disclosure related to the correction of a prior period error is to ensure the statement reader can assess the effect of the error on the prior period financial statements previously issued. In the period of correction only, an entity therefore discloses

    (a) the nature of the error;
    (b) the amount of the correction for each financial statement line item affected and to basic and diluted earnings per share, if applicable, for each past period presented, and the amount of the correction at the beginning of the earliest period presented; and
    (c) if retrospective restatement is judged to be impracticable, an explanation of why this is, and a description of how and the date from which the error has been corrected.[6]

---

[5] IASCF, IAS 8.5.
[6] IASCF, IAS 8.49.

LOOKING AHEAD

IAS 8 *Accounting Policies, Changes in Accounting Estimates and Errors* is not currently on the IASB's project agenda.

END-OF-CHAPTER PRACTICE

21-1 The Braker Division of Hoy Co. (HC) has consistently shown an increasing profit over each of the past four years. On closer examination of the division's operating reports, HC's controller noticed that the bad debt expense and inventory obsolescence charges are not in line with the level of activity or with other divisions. In discussing this with the divisional accountant, the controller learned that the accountant used estimates related to the write off of receivables and inventory to manage the division's bottom line and the amount of profit reported.

Instructions

Discuss what HC's controller should do. Explain whether any type of accounting change is needed and, if so, how it should be accounted for.

21-2 At a recent conference on financial accounting and reporting, three participants provided examples of similar accounting changes they had just encountered. They all relate to changes involving the accounting for development costs.

The first participant explained that it had recently come to her attention that capitalized product development costs incurred three years ago had not been adjusted or amortized since they were incurred. These costs should have been amortized over three years, but had been incorrectly coded and were missed in the annual adjustment process.

The second participant explained that his company was switching to a policy of expensing development costs as incurred because changing technologies were making the product life cycles so short. Previously, the company had amortized these costs over a 24-month period.

The third participant also reported a change in accounting for development costs. In this case, instead of amortizing development costs on a straight-line basis over the estimated product life as in the past, her company was changing to an activity-based method. The new method charges an equal amount of development cost amortization to each inventory item produced. The change was made because the new approach better represents the benefits received from the development cost assets.

Instructions

1. Advise each participant whether the situation described is a change in accounting policy, a change in accounting estimate, a correction of a prior period error, or none of these. Explain your choice briefly.
2. Describe how each participant's situation should be accounted for and reported according to IAS 8.

21-3 In 2007, Kohl Co. recognized a $100 loss due to a lawsuit that it appeared the company would lose. In 2009, when the judge ruled in favor of Kohl's position, Kohl's accountant made the following entry:

Estimated Lawsuit Liability	100	
Retained Earnings		100
To correct 2007's profit due to the outcome of the lawsuit.		

Instruction

Briefly discuss the accountant's treatment of the lawsuit.

21-4 In this chapter, flag icons identify areas where there are GAAP differences between IFRS requirements and national standards.

Instructions

Access the website(s) identified on the inside back cover of this book, and prepare a concise summary of the differences that are flagged throughout the chapter material.

Chapter 22

Events After the Reporting Period: IAS 10

U.S. GAAP References
SAS 1 Codification of Auditing Standards and Procedures
SEC staff pronouncements

Related IFRSs
IFRS 5 Non-current Assets Held for Sale and Discontinued Operations
IAS 36 Impairment of Assets
IAS 37 Provisions, Contingent Liabilities and Contingent Assets

OBJECTIVE AND SCOPE

This standard assists in the determination of when to recognize transactions that occur after the reporting period. Furthermore, it dictates when additional disclosures should be made regarding these events.

Events after the reporting period are defined as follows:[1]

. . . those events, favorable and unfavorable, that occur between the end of the reporting period and the date when the financial statements are authorised for issue. Two types of events can be identified:

(a) those that provide evidence of conditions that existed at the end of the reporting period (**adjusting events after the reporting period**); and

(b) those that are indicative of conditions that arose after the reporting period (**non-adjusting events after the reporting period**).

Thus, transactions that occur after year end are divided into two types.

---

[1] IASCF, IAS 10.3.

RECOGNITION AND MEASUREMENT

Adjusting events are recognized in the statements of financial position and profit or loss if they occur prior to the statements being authorized.

Illustration 22-1 shows the dividing line between which transactions are recognized in the current financial statements and which ones are recognized in the financial statements for the following year.

Illustration 22-1
Accounting
for Adjusting
Events that
Occur After
the End of the
Reporting Period

year end	statements authorized	statement released

Transaction recognized this year/statements adjusted	Transactions not recognized this year

Determining when the statements are authorized is a matter of judgment but depends on the structure of management, statutory requirements, and an entity's governance and procedures. For instance, if the board of directors must formally approve the financial statements before issue, then this is the point that divides the transactions between those recognized this year and those that are not.

The chart below includes examples of both types of events. In most cases, deciding what type an event is requires judgment.

Illustration 22-2
Examples of
Various Types
of Subsequent
Events and
their Proposed
Accounting
Treatment

Examples of events	Adjusting events[2]	Non-adjusting events
Lawsuits	Settlement of lawsuit that existed at year end—the settlement provides additional information that helps measure the impact on the financial statements.	Settlement of lawsuit that arose after year end. The lawsuit was not a condition that existed at year end.
Impairments	Bankruptcy of a customer/investee where a receivable/investment existed at year end (and there was evidence of financial distress). Normally a period of financial distress precedes the actual bankruptcy whether that financial distress is openly evident or not.	Bankruptcy of a customer where no receivable existed at year end or where a receivable existed but was fully provided for or due to an event such as an uninsured fire that occurs after year end.

[2] Taken from examples given in IASCF, IAS 10.9.

Examples of events	Adjusting events	Non-adjusting events
	Decline in value of inventory after year end where a decline in price is due to a condition that existed at year end but had not yet been incorporated into the price (oversupply, new competitor product).	Decline in value of inventory after year end where inventory is a commodity that trades on a commodities market. Decline in market value of an investment reflecting events that arose subsequent to the reporting period. Destruction of an asset by fire after year end.
Purchased assets	Additional evidence becomes available regarding the cost or value of assets purchased before year end.	Additional evidence becomes available regarding the cost of assets purchased after year end.
Profit-sharing/bonus	Determination of profit-sharing/ bonus after year end where a present legal or constructive obligation existed at year end.	Determination of profit-sharing/bonus after year end where a present legal or constructive obligation did not exist at year end.
Fraud/errors	Discovery of fraud/errors that prove that the financial statements are incorrect.	Discovery of fraud or errors that do not change the numbers.
Dividends	Declaration of dividend before the reporting period but based on information that is clarified after year end (e.g., dividend in kind where the value of assets is clarified after the end of the reporting period). This is a present obligation where the measurement is later clarified.	Declaration of dividend after the reporting period. This is a present obligation of the subsequent period.
Going concern	Management makes a determination (either before year end or after) that it intends to liquidate the entity or cease trading (or has no other realistic alternative). If the entity is no longer considered to be a going concern, management would consider restating the whole set of statements using a different basis of accounting.	Management determines that the entity is running out of cash. If the entity is still considered to be a going concern, management would not adjust the basis of accounting.
Refinancing	A contract to refinance short-term loans is signed after year end but agreements are reached prior to year end.	A contract to refinance short-term loans is signed after year end for agreements finalized after year end.

DISCLOSURE

The following disclosures are required to be presented in the financial statements:[3]

- the date when the statements were authorized, including who gave the authorization;
- where adjusting events occur, related disclosures should be updated, as well; and
- where non-adjusting events occur and are material, the nature of the event and an estimate of its financial effect (or a statement that the financial effect cannot be determined).

The following examples are excerpted from the financial statements of Royal Dutch Shell and L'Oreal.

Illustration 22-3
Excerpt from the Statements of Royal Dutch Shell

36 POST BALANCE SHEET EVENTS

Since December 31, 2007, additional purchases of shares have been made under the Company's buyback program. At February 26, 2008, a further 21,280,000 Class A shares (representing 0.3% of Royal Dutch Shell's issued share capital at December 31, 2007) had been purchased for cancellation at a total cost of $796 million including expenses, at an average price of €25.23 and 1,892.73 pence per Class A share.

Illustration 22-4
Excerpt from the Statements of L'Oreal

5. POST-BALANCE SHEET EVENTS

In November 2007, L'Oreal signed an agreement to acquire 100% of the share capital of Canan Kozmetik, Canan Pazarlama and Seda Plastik, which are Turkish haircare product companies. The acquisition was finalised in January 2008 having obtained the necessary authorizations.

On 23rd January 2008, L'Oreal made a firm offer to PPR:

- acquire the share of YSL Beauté Holding, including the Roger & Gallet brand, for an enterprise value price of €1,150 million,
- obtain an exclusive and very long-term worldwide operating licence for the use of the Yves Saint Laurent and Boucheron brands, in the category of perfumes and cosmetics, under conditions conforming to usual market practice,
- take over the licences for the Stella McCartney, Oscar de la Renta and Ermenegildo Zegna brands in the category of perfumes and cosmetics.

The acquisition should be concluded after consultation of the employee representative bodies of the PPR group and subject to the approval of the appropriate authorities notably those relating to antitrust law.

LOOKING AHEAD

IASB currently does not have this topic on its agenda; however, it is part of the Memorandum of Understanding between IASB and FASB and is on the agenda for short-term convergence. FASB is working on incorporating guidance provided in auditing standards (AICPA) into U.S. GAAP (codifying existing standards). In addition, FASB is looking at minor differences between IFRSs and U.S. GAAP to see if they can be eliminated.

---

[3] IASCF, IAS 10.17-.22.

There are two differences between IFRS and U.S. GAAP that will not be addressed in the short term. These relate to the following:
- refinancing of short-term obligations and
- curing (recitifying) breaches of borrowing covenants.

END-OF-CHAPTER PRACTICE

22-1 Owemoney Inc. has some 10-year bonds payable that are due in the coming year (2009). Just after the balance sheet date, the company entered into an agreement with a large well-known bank to refinance the debt with a new 10-year loan. The agreement has been signed and the company is not in default of any of the provisions. The financial statements for the year ended December 31, 2008 have not yet been finalized.

Instructions
Discuss how the debt would be presented in the December 31, 2008 balance sheet (provide support for your answer). How would this differ under U.S. GAAP?

22-2 Early Bird Limited (EBL) recently released its preliminary fourth-quarter EPS numbers. In the process of finalizing the year-end financial statements, the company received information that one of its major customers had gone bankrupt. EBL had made a small provision for bad debt at year end (due to concerns about the customer's ability to pay).

Instructions
How should EBL account for the bankruptcy, if at all?

22-3 GC Limited has a significant amount of long-term debt. In addition, there is no working capital. The company is in the process of finalizing its year-end statements and has just received notification from the bank that it will not extend any further credit. This is a serious problem for GC since the payroll is due at the end of the month and there are insufficient funds.

Instructions
How should this be reflected in the financial statements, if at all?

22-4 In this chapter, flag icons identify areas where there are GAAP differences between IFRS requirements and national standards.

Instructions
Access the website(s) identified on the inside back cover of this book, and prepare a concise summary of the differences that are flagged throughout the chapter material.

Chapter 23

Income Taxes: IAS 12

U.S. GAAP Reference
FAS 109 Accounting for Income Taxes

Related IFRSs
IAS 1 Presentation of Financial Statements
IAS 8 Accounting Policies, Changes in Accounting Estimates and Errors
IAS 37 Provisions, Contingent Liabilities and Contingent Assets
IFRS 3 Business Combinations

OBJECTIVE AND SCOPE

IAS 12 prescribes the accounting treatment for income taxes, their presentation in the financial statements, and the disclosures that are needed.

The accounting issues relate primarily to accounting for the tax effects of transactions and events of the current period, of unused tax losses or tax credits, and the tax consequences when the carrying amounts of assets and liabilities reported differ from their tax values.

Income taxes in this standard refer to all domestic and foreign taxes based on taxable profits and to withholding taxes payable by associated entities on distributions to the reporting entity. Accounting for government grants—covered by IAS 20 *Accounting for Government Grants and Disclosure of Government Assistance*—and investment tax credits are outside the scope of IAS 12.

As discussed in the Looking Ahead section at the end of this chapter, the IASB has agreed to a number of changes to the requirements of IAS 12 as a result of its Memorandum of Understanding with the FASB. None of these changes affects the principles underlying income tax accounting; however, they reduce a number of the exceptions that now exist in applying the basic concepts. This chapter does not cover all the technical requirements in depth.

RECOGNITION OF CURRENT TAX LIABILITIES AND ASSETS

Entities prepare tax returns each year to determine the amount of tax that is currently payable on their taxable profits. If the tax payable is more than the amount of tax paid to the balance sheet date, a **liability** is recognized. Alternatively, if the amount paid is greater than the amount due, an **asset** is recognized.

Current tax is a defined term that means the amount of income taxes payable or recoverable on the taxable profit or loss for the period.[1]

When an entity incurs a tax loss in the year that can be carried back to recover current taxes of prior periods, this benefit is also recognized as an **asset**. The benefit is recognized in the period of the loss because it is probable that the benefit will be received and is measurable.

RECOGNITION OF DEFERRED TAX LIABILITIES AND ASSETS

An underlying assumption in the accounting model we use is that entities will recover the carrying amount of the assets they report and that they will settle the liabilities reported at their carrying amounts. If the recovery of an asset at an amount equal to its carrying value results in the entity having to pay additional tax, this effect must be captured on the statement of financial position. And if the settlement of a liability at its carrying amount results in a reduction in the tax that would otherwise be payable, this effect should also be reported. That is, the future or deferred tax consequence of the recovery or settlement has to be recognized. It is recognized as a deferred tax liability if future tax payments will be larger, and as a deferred tax asset if future tax payments will be smaller.

Temporary Differences

Why might there be future tax consequences? The future tax consequences occur because the carrying amounts of some assets and liabilities are not the same as their tax amounts or tax base. The difference between the carrying amount of an asset or liability in the statement of financial position and its tax base is known as a *temporary difference*. A temporary difference may result in increased taxable amounts in determining the taxable profit or loss of a future period when the carrying amount of the asset or liability is recovered or settled. This is known as a *taxable temporary difference*. Alternatively, a *deductible temporary difference* results in amounts that can be deducted in determining the taxable profit or loss of the future period when the carrying amount of the asset or liability is recovered or settled.

Tax Base

These differences exist when the tax base of the asset or liability differs from its carrying amount. Illustration 23-1 gives a fuller explanation of the *tax base*; that is, the amount attributed to the asset or liability for tax purposes.

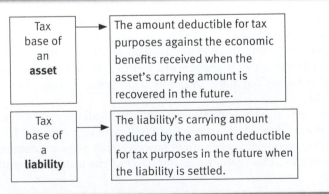

Illustration 23-1
Tax Base of
an Asset and
Liability

| Tax base of an **asset** | → | The amount deductible for tax purposes against the economic benefits received when the asset's carrying amount is recovered in the future. |

| Tax base of a **liability** | → | The liability's carrying amount reduced by the amount deductible for tax purposes in the future when the liability is settled. |

---

[1] IASCF, IAS 12.5.

Some examples will illustrate how these are determined.

Situation

An entity has the following assets and liabilities on its statement of financial position at the carrying amounts indicated:

1. Dividend receivable, $100. Dividends are not taxable in this entity's jurisdiction.
2. Equipment, $40 net (cost of $90, accumulated depreciation of $50). For tax purposes, tax depreciation of $75 has been deducted in determining taxable profit to date, leaving an undepreciated amount of $15 for tax purposes.
3. Installment account receivable, $40. The associated revenues are taxed on a cash basis.
4. Warranty obligations payable, $90. Payments under warranties are deductible expenses for tax purposes only when the entity makes good under the warranty.
5. Unearned service revenue, $100. This type of income is taxed on a cash basis as it is received.
6. Environmental liability payable, $57. The liability relates to a fine that is not a deductible cost for tax purposes.

Using the definitions of tax base in Illustration 23-1, determine the tax base of each asset and liability listed.

Analysis

1. When the $100 carrying amount of the dividend receivable is recovered by the entity in the future, no part of it is taxable. That is the whole $100 can be deducted for tax purposes. Its tax base is therefore $100.
2. When the $40 carrying amount of the equipment is recovered through operations or sale in the future, the entity can deduct only $15 of its cost for tax purposes. Therefore, its tax base is $15.
3. As the $40 receivable is collected, it is taxable in full. No amount is deductible from the $40 in the future. Its tax base is $0.
4. When the warranty obligations of $90 are paid and the liability is reduced, the entity will deduct $90 in determining its taxable profit. This liability's tax base is therefore $90 − $90 = $0.
5. When the service revenue is taken into income and the liability is reduced in the future, $100 is deductible for tax purposes because it was all taxed earlier as received. The tax base of this account is $100 − $100 = $0.
6. When the environmental liability of $57 is paid, no amount is deductible for tax purposes. Its tax base therefore is $57 − $0 = $57.

Some items have a tax base even though they do not appear as an asset or liability. For example, research costs of $10 that were expensed as incurred in the accounts may not be deductible for tax purposes until a future year. Their carrying amount is $0, but, according to the definition, their tax base is $10. This is the amount deductible in the future.

When working with consolidated financial statements, temporary differences are determined by comparing the consolidated carrying amounts with the tax base of the individual assets and liabilities.

Taxable Temporary Differences and Deferred Tax Liabilities

As indicated above, temporary differences have future tax consequences. When the temporary difference is a **taxable temporary difference**, future taxes will be higher than they would have been otherwise, so a related **deferred tax liability** must be recognized.

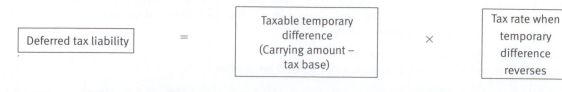

Simply put, a ***deferred tax liability*** is the amount of income tax payable in future periods in respect of taxable temporary differences.[2] An example is provided below.

---

[2] IASCF, IAS 12.5.

Situation

Consider Situation 2 in the previous Applications Box, in which an entity reports equipment of $40 on its balance sheet. The asset's cost is $90 and its accumulated depreciation is $50. For tax purposes, tax depreciation of $75 has been deducted in determining taxable profit to date, leaving an undepreciated amount of only $15 for tax purposes. If the entity pays taxes at a rate of 40%, what is the amount of the deferred tax liability that should be reported?

Analysis

The **taxable temporary difference** is $40 − $15 = $25, the difference between the carrying amount and the tax base or tax value of the asset. When the $40 carrying amount of the equipment is recovered through operations or sale in the future, the entity can deduct only $15 of its cost for tax purposes, leaving an amount of $25 that is taxable. If the entity's tax rate is 40%, the entity will increase its taxes payable in the future by $25 × 40%, or $10. This is the amount of the **deferred tax liability**.

Many temporary differences originate when an income or expense is reported in GAAP profit or loss in one period and on the tax return in another. That is, the income or expense is included in *accounting profit*—the profit or loss for a period before deducting tax expense. However, the income or expense is included in *taxable profit*—the profit or loss determined using the rules established by the tax authorities and upon which income taxes are payable or recoverable—**in a different period**.[3] These are often referred to as **timing differences**, and they are closely related to temporary differences. For example, if an entity recognizes depreciation expense of $10 in accounting income in each of four years and deducts tax depreciation of $15 in each of the same four years, the timing difference each period is $5. The temporary difference at the end of Year 4 is $20, the difference between the carrying amount of the asset and its tax base at that time. Deferred tax liabilities (and assets) are based on the accumulated differences.

Temporary differences also arise in other circumstances, such as the following:

1. In a business combination, assets and liabilities are acquired and reported on consolidated financial statements at amounts based on their fair values at acquisition. Often there is no equivalent change in their tax base.
2. Assets are revalued for financial reporting purposes with no concurrent adjustment of their tax values.
3. Goodwill is acquired in a business combination and the tax treatment usually differs from its accounting treatment.
4. The tax base of an asset or liability may differ from its carrying amount on initial recognition, such as when a non-taxable government grant is provided for the acquisition of equipment.
5. The carrying amount of investments in subsidiaries, associates, or joint ventures becomes different from their tax bases.

Deferred Tax Assets

As previously indicated, temporary differences have future tax consequences. When the temporary difference is a **deductible temporary difference**, future taxes will be lower than they otherwise would be and a related **deferred tax asset** is recognized. This situation may also occur when an entity has **unused tax losses and unused tax credits** that it can carry forward and deduct in the future. A *deferred tax asset* then is the amount of income tax recoverable in future periods from:

(a) a deductible temporary difference, and
(b) the carry-forward of unused tax losses and unused tax credits.[4]

---

[3] IASCF, IAS 12.5.
[4] IASCF, IAS 12.5.

Because the benefit—the future reduction in tax—is dependent on having taxable profit in the future, the deferred tax asset is recognized only if it is **probable** that taxable profit will be available. The IASB defines **probable** as more likely than not; that is, with a probability of greater than 50%.

We will look at each of these sources of deferred tax assets in turn.

Deferred Tax Assets and Deductible Temporary Differences

Deferred tax assets are a function of deductible future amounts and the future tax rate.

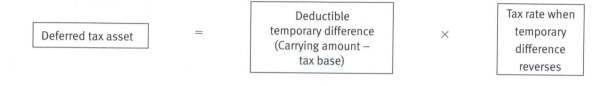

| Deferred tax asset | = | Deductible temporary difference (Carrying amount − tax base) | × | Tax rate when temporary difference reverses |

An example of the calculation of a deferred tax asset is provided below.

Situation

Consider Situation 4 in the first Applications Box, in which an entity recognizes a $90 warranty obligation payable on its statement of financial position. Warranty expenses are deductible in this jurisdiction only when the entity makes good on its obligation under the warranty. If the entity's tax rate is 40%, what is the amount of the deferred tax asset that should be reported?

Analysis

The **deductible temporary difference** is $90 − $0 = $90, the carrying amount of the liability less its tax base. When the $90 obligation is met in the future, the entity can deduct the full $90 for tax purposes. With a 40% tax rate, the entity will benefit in the future by paying $90 × 40%, or $36, less tax than it otherwise would have. This is the amount of the **deferred tax asset**.

Deductible differences may originate in other situations, such as the following:

1. A liability is recognized at the acquisition date in a business combination and the related costs are deductible in determining taxable profit in a later period. Therefore, a deferred tax asset is recognized. A deferred tax asset is also recognized if an acquired asset in a business combination is taken on at a fair value that is less than its tax base.
2. Assets carried at fair value with no corresponding adjustment to its tax value will give rise to a deferred tax asset when the tax value exceeds its carrying amount.

Because future taxable profit is needed in order to benefit from future deductible amounts, the entity has to assess whether taxable profits are probable. Because taxable profit can be created or increased by reversing taxable temporary differences, IAS 12 assumes that it is probable that taxable profit will be available in the future when an entity has sufficient taxable temporary differences that are expected to reverse either

(a) in the same period as the deductible difference is expected to reverse, or
(b) in periods when a tax loss resulting in the deferred tax asset can be carried back or forward.[5]

---

[5] Note that the taxable differences must relate to the same taxation jurisdiction and taxable entity.

If so, the deferred tax asset is **recognized** in the **same period** as the deductible temporary difference is generated.

If the entity does not meet this test, the deferred tax asset can still be recognized if it is probable that the entity will have enough taxable profit in that future period or there is a potential for tax planning opportunities that will create taxable profit at the appropriate time.[6] IAS 12 includes guidance on what is meant by tax planning opportunities.

Deferred Tax Assets from Unused Tax Losses and Unused Tax Credits

If an entity has unused tax losses and unused tax credits available to carry forward, it can recognize an associated deferred tax asset and benefit if it is probable that future taxable profit will be available so the deductions can be used. This deferred tax asset is very similar to a deferred tax asset arising from deductible temporary differences. An entity with a history of recent losses, however, may find it more difficult to justify the likelihood of future taxable profits. Because of this, the deferred tax asset is recognized **only to the extent** the entity has sufficient taxable temporary differences or there is other convincing evidence that enough taxable profit will be available.

Reassessment of Unrecognized Deferred Tax Assets

The income tax standard sets out criteria useful in assessing the likelihood of sufficient taxable profit and requires that deferred tax assets be recognized only **to the extent** that this profit will be available. Because of this limitation, entities often have **unrecognized deferred tax assets**; that is, deductible temporary differences or unused tax losses or credits for which no tax asset has been booked. The economic situation and the degree of probability are always subject to change, so at each balance sheet date entities are required to reassess the likelihood of benefiting from these differences in the future.

Temporary Differences and Goodwill

Because goodwill is measured as a residual and recognizing a deferred tax liability has the effect of increasing the carrying amount of goodwill, IAS 12 does not permit the recognition of the deferred tax liability related to any taxable temporary difference that arises on the initial recognition of goodwill.

If goodwill is acquired in a business combination and its carrying amount is less than its tax base, a deferred tax asset may be recognized, but only if it is probable that the entity will benefit from the temporary difference.

Temporary Differences and the Initial Recognition of Assets and Liabilities

Related deferred tax assets and liabilities are recognized for the temporary differences on assets and liabilities acquired in a business combination and on assets and liabilities acquired in a transaction that affects accounting or taxable profit. However, when assets and liabilities are acquired in other circumstances and there are temporary differences, **no deferred tax assets or liabilities are recognized**. For example, if an asset is acquired and a government grant is either deducted from its cost or is recognized as deferred income and the grant is not taxable, a deductible temporary difference exists. In this situation, no deferred tax asset is recognized.

Temporary Differences and Investments in Subsidiaries, Branches, Associates, and Joint Ventures

The tax base of an investment is usually its acquisition cost. After acquisition, the carrying amounts of subsidiaries and other strategic investments change as a result of such circumstances as:

---

[6] See note 5.

(a)   the existence of undistributed profits,
(b)   changes in exchange rates, and
(c)   writedowns to lower recoverable amounts.

To what extent should deferred tax accounts be recognized for these temporary differences?

IAS 12 recognizes that it is often impracticable for entities to determine the amount of future income tax for such temporary differences. The standard therefore states that **deferred tax liabilities** should be recognized for all taxable temporary differences related to these investments **except when both of the following conditions are met:**

1.   the investor can control the timing of the reversal of the temporary difference, and
2.   it is probable that the temporary difference will not reverse in the foreseeable future.

Deferred tax assets are recognized for all deductible temporary differences resulting from these investments **only to the extent that it is probable** that

1.   the temporary difference will reverse in the foreseeable future, and
2.   taxable profit will be available so that the tax benefit can be realized.[7]

MEASUREMENT

Current Tax Liabilities and Assets

The measurement of current tax liabilities and assets is relatively straightforward, at least from an accounting standards perspective! These accounts represent the amount expected to be paid to or recovered from the tax authorities, and are measured using the tax rates and tax laws that have been **enacted** or **substantially enacted** by the end of the reporting period. In some jurisdictions, the conditions surrounding an announcement of a change in law or rate prior to the passing of legislation is substantive enough that the planned rate or law can be used as if it were an actual change.

Deferred Tax Assets and Liabilities

A number of general principles govern the measurement of future tax amounts. These include the following:

*   Use the tax rates expected to apply to the period when the asset is expected to be realized or the liability settled based on the rates and laws enacted or substantively enacted by the end of the reporting period.
*   If different tax rates apply to different levels of taxable income, use the average rates expected to apply to the taxable profit or loss in the period in which the temporary difference is expected to reverse.
*   If the tax differs depending on how the asset is recovered or liability is settled, apply the tax consequences from the entity's expected course of action.
*   Do not discount deferred tax assets and liabilities, even when the underlying carrying amount of the related asset or liability is discounted.
*   If income tax rates differ based on whether earnings are retained or paid out as dividends, use the tax rate that applies to undistributed profits when calculating current and deferred tax assets and liabilities. When a dividend is declared and recognized as a liability, then recognize the tax consequences in current profit or loss.
*   Review the carrying amount of deferred tax assets at the end of each reporting period, decreasing or increasing its carrying amount depending on the probability that sufficient taxable income will be available.[8]

---

[7] IASCF, IAS 12.38 to 45.
[8] IASCF, IAS 12.47 to 56.

Some of these requirements are applied in the following examples.

Situation

A. Company X has an asset with a carrying amount of $80 and a tax base of $60 at the end of Year 2. At the end of Year 1, the carrying amount and tax value were $88 and $72 respectively. At the end of Year 2, the tax rate for all future years remains unchanged at 25%.

B. Assume the same asset and situation as in A, but now the tax rate for all future years changed at the end of Year 2 to 30%.

C. Company Y earns $100 profit in Year 5 and declares no dividends. The tax rate on income is 30%, reduced to 20% for any income paid out by way of dividends. Company Y declares a dividend of $40 from previous profits six months later in Year 6.

D. Assume the same situation as in C, but in this case, the $40 dividend is declared at December 31 of Year 5.

E. Company Z has unused tax losses of $100 available to carry forward at the end of Year 4 when the tax rate for the current and future years is 25%. At this time, it is probable that $80 of the losses will be able to be used. At the end of Year 5, none of these losses has been used, but now the company will likely be able to benefit from only $50 of them. The future tax rate at the end of Year 5 is 30%.

In each situation, what entry is required to recognize deferred tax assets or liabilities in the year indicated?

Analysis

A. Company X has a deferred tax liability because there is a taxable temporary difference. The balance of the deferred tax liability at the end of Year 2 is ($80 − $60) × 25% = $5. Before adjusting to this correct Year 2 balance, the account stands at the balance from the end of Year 1: ($88 − $72) × 25% = $4. The following entry is made:

Deferred tax expense	$1	
Deferred tax liability		$1

B. The correct balance of the deferred tax liability account at the end of Year 2 is ($80 − $60) × 30% = $6. Before adjustment, the account is $4 as calculated above. The following entry is needed:

Deferred tax expense	$2	
Deferred tax liability		$2

C. In Year 5, the current tax expense and amount payable is calculated at the rate of 30%, as would any deferred tax assets or liabilities that needed to be recognized or adjusted in Year 5. No asset is recognized for dividends that may be declared in the future. In Year 6, when the dividend is declared, Company X recognizes the recovery of income taxes of $4 (10% of the $40 recognized as a liability) as a current tax asset and current tax benefit for Year 6.

D. Again, the tax reduction for the dividends declared is recognized as a current tax item. Current tax expense in Year 5 is $26 ($60 × 30% + $40 × 20%). No deferred taxes are recognized.

E. The deferred tax asset that Company Z reports for the tax losses at the end of Year 5 is $15 ($50 × 30%). Before adjustment, the deferred tax asset has a balance of $20 ($80 × 25%). The following entry is needed:

Deferred tax expense	$5	
Deferred tax asset		$5

RECOGNITION OF CURRENT AND DEFERRED TAX

The accounts explained so far in this chapter relate primarily to accounts on the statement of financial position. Now we shift to the effect on profit or loss, other comprehensive income, and equity.

Items Recognized in Profit or Loss

Current and deferred taxes are recognized as income or expense and are included in profit or loss for the current period **except** in two circumstances:

1. when the transaction or event the tax relates to is recognized (either in the current period or other period) outside of profit or loss, i.e., in other comprehensive income, or directly in equity; or
2. when the tax results from a business combination.

Most tax transactions and events are recognized in profit or loss, even if they are not recognized as taxable or deductible in the same period in which they are recognized as income and expense for financial reporting purposes. The carrying amount of deferred tax assets and liabilities can change even if the underlying temporary differences do not. This happens, for example, when tax rates or tax laws change or when deferred tax assets are reassessed for recoverability. These changes are also recognized in profit or loss **unless they relate to items previously recognized elsewhere in the financial statements**.

Items Recognized Outside Profit or Loss

When a current or deferred tax relates to items that are recognized outside profit or loss, **in the same or a different period**, the tax is recognized where the related item is or was recognized. If a revaluation adjustment on property, plant, and equipment is recognized in other comprehensive income, the related tax is recognized there as well. If a correction of a prior period error results in an adjustment to opening retained earnings, any related current or deferred tax adjustments are recognized there as well. In effect, the tax follows whatever gives rise to it, **both when it originates and when it reverses**.

Deferred Tax Arising from a Business Combination

Although deferred tax assets and liabilities are recognized on the identifiable assets and liabilities acquired in a business combination, none is usually recognized on the initial recognition of goodwill. After a combination, an acquirer may reassess the probability of realizing benefits from the acquired business's unused tax losses or deferred tax assets that were previously not recognized. In this situation, the acquired deferred tax benefits are recognized in profit or loss (unless attributable to other comprehensive income or another equity item). An exception to this treatment is made if the reassessment is completed within the measurement period allowed for new information about circumstances that existed at the acquisition date. If this is the case, the reassessed benefits are accounted for by reducing the carrying amount of goodwill to zero if needed, and any excess benefit is recognized in profit or loss.

Current and Deferred Tax Arising from Share-based Payment Transactions

Entities in some jurisdictions are allowed a tax deduction for employee remuneration paid in shares, options, or other equity instruments of the entity. The amount of the deduction may differ from the expense recognized and it may not be deductible until a later period, perhaps when the share options are exercised. A few problems may arise in accounting for the associated income taxes.

First, the deductible temporary difference that results may be difficult to measure if the deduction allowed in the future, for example, is based on future share prices that are not known at the balance sheet date. The recommendation is to estimate the deferred tax benefit using the share price at the period end as a surrogate. Another issue arises if the future deduction is actually larger than the expense recognized as remuneration expense. In this case, the assumption is that the future deduction relates in part to equity. Therefore, the excess of the associated current and deferred tax is recognized directly in equity.

PRESENTATION

Classification

IAS 1 *Presentation of Financial Statements* sets out where the deferred tax asset and deferred tax liabilities are presented on the statement of financial position. This standard indicates that if an entity classifies its assets and liabilities as current and noncurrent, deferred tax assets and liabilities are **not reported in the current category**.[9]

Offsetting of Assets and Liabilities

A **current** tax payable and **current** tax recoverable normally can only offset one another if they relate to the same taxation authority. For this reason, an entity can present its current tax liabilities and current tax assets on a net basis only if the entity

(a) has a legally enforceable right to offset the recognized amounts, and
(b) intends to settle on a net basis or to realize the amounts simultaneously.

The same problem arises when accounting for **deferred** tax asset and **deferred** tax liability accounts. To what extent can these accounts be netted and presented as one net amount? Similar to the requirements for current tax amounts, deferred tax accounts can be offset only if

(a) the entity has a legally enforceable right to set off current tax accounts; and
(b) the deferred tax accounts relate to income taxes levied by the same tax authority on the same taxable entity, or on different taxable entities intending to settle current tax items on a net basis or to realize the assets and settle the liabilities in the future at the same time, if material.[10]

Tax Expense

Regardless of whether an entity prepares a separate income statement or one statement of comprehensive income, the tax expense related to ordinary activities is presented separately in each. *Tax expense* is a defined term that means the total of current and deferred tax expense included in determining profit or loss for the period.[11]

IAS 12 also indicates that when exchange differences on deferred foreign tax liabilities or assets are recognized in the statement of comprehensive income, they may be reported as deferred tax expense or income if this is considered useful to users.

DISCLOSURES

A significant amount of information is disclosed about the effects of income taxes—some relating to what is reported in profit or loss, other comprehensive income, or directly in equity; some to balance sheet amounts; and the remainder to items that have not been recognized.

It is necessary to disclose separately the **major components making up tax expense or income**. Examples of these components include current tax expense or income; current period adjustments for current tax of prior periods; deferred tax expense or income resulting from each type of originating and reversing temporary differences or from changes in tax rates or new taxes; and the benefits recognized in the current period that reduce current tax expense or that reduce deferred tax expense due to previously unrecognized tax losses, tax credits, or other temporary differences.

In addition, an entity is required to disclose the amount of tax expense recognized directly in equity and in each component of other comprehensive income, and to provide a reconciliation of the expected tax rate to the

---

[9] IASCF, IAS 1.56. This requirement was moved to IAS 1 in 2007.
[10] IASCF, IAS 12.71 and 74.
[11] IASCF, IAS 12.5.

effective tax rate experienced. For discontinued operations, the expense is disclosed separately for the gain or loss and the results of operations for the period.

Illustration 23-2 presents the Nestlé Group's disclosures for its year ended December 31, 2007 that address some of these requirements. Switzerland-based Nestlé reports its financial statements in Swiss francs.[12]

Illustration 23-2 Income Tax Disclosures The Nestlé Group

5. Taxes

In millions of CHF	2007	2006
Components of taxes		
Current taxes	3 400	2 845
Deferred taxes	229	647
Taxes reclassified to equity	(213)	(230)
Taxes reclassifed to discontinued operations	–	31
	3 416	**3 293**
Deferred taxes by types		
Property, plant and equipment	3	82
Goodwill and intangible assets	(36)	(43)
Employee benefits	266	261
Inventories, receivables, payables and provisions	(31)	(6)
Unused tax losses and unused tax credits	14	194
Other	13	159
	229	**647**
Reconciliation of taxes		
Taxes at the theoretical domestic rates applicable to profits of taxable entities in the countries concerned [a]	3 134	3 051
Tax effect of non-deductible or non-taxable items	(225)	(152)
Prior years' taxes	(58)	(105)
Transfers to unrecognised deferred tax assets	62	42
Transfers from unrecognised deferred tax assets	(46)	(80)
Changes in tax rates	–	46
Withholding taxes levied on transfers of income	403	312
Other [b]	146	179
	3 416	**3 293**

[a] The applicable Group tax rate varies from one year to the other depending on the weight of each individual company in the taxable Group profit.

[b] Include taxes on capital.

---

[12] http://www.nestle.com/Resource.axd?Id524E5A5E2-93F8-43A3-956E-0F259448CB90.

Other disclosures relate more closely to amounts reported on the statement of financial position. These include the amount of the deferred tax assets and liabilities recognized for each type of temporary difference and information about the deductible temporary differences and other balances for which no deferred tax asset has been recognized. Additional information about the nature of the evidence that supports the recognition of a deferred tax asset is required in situations where the amount of future taxable profits may be uncertain.

Illustration 23-3 provides an example of how the Nestlé Group, referred to above, meets some of these requirements.

Illustration 23-3
Deferred Tax
Disclosures
The Nestlé
Group

16. Deferred taxes

In millions of CHF	2007	2006
Tax assets by types of temporary difference		
Property, plant and equipment	277	317
Goodwill and intangible assets	285	297
Employee benefits	1 823	1 905
Inventories, receivables, payables and provisions	962	997
Unused tax losses and unused tax credits	278	288
Other	608	565
	4 233	**4 369**
Tax liabilities by types of temporary difference		
Property, plant and equipment	1 168	1 239
Goodwill and intangible assets	1 342	952
Employee benefits	241	52
Inventories, receivables, payables and provisions	71	99
Other	585	300
	3 407	**2 642**
Net assets	**826**	**1 727**
Reflected in the balance sheet as follows:		
Deferred tax assets	2 224	2 433
Deferred tax liabilities	(1 398)	(706)
Net assets	826	1 727
Temporary differences for which no deferred tax is recognized:		
on investments in affiliated companies (taxable temporary difference)	22 270	19 436
on unused tax losses, tax credits and other items [a]	1 743	2 175

[a] Of which CHF 115 million (2006: CHF 223 million) expire within one year, CHF 739 million (2006: CHF 930 million) between one and five years and CHF 890 million (2006: CHF 1022 million) in more than five years.

The disclosures identified above are not complete, but are indicative of the type of information required. Other disclosures are needed that address taxes related to business combinations, a variety of investments, and undistributed earnings.

Appendix A that accompanies, but is not part of, IAS 12 provides examples of a variety of temporary differences and illustrative calculations that help to clarify the standard.

LOOKING AHEAD

Because of the number of income tax-related reconciling differences for U.S.-listed foreign registrants applying IFRS, accounting for income taxes was included in the list of topics covered by the IASB-FASB short-term convergence project. The project summary indicates that the basic approach in both IAS 12 and FAS 109 is similar, and that the differences tend to relate to the numerous exceptions to the general principles. The approach in this project then was to work on eliminating the exceptions rather than to review and change the underlying concepts.[13]

As part of the project, the major areas of difference were identified and discussed. In some cases, the FASB has tentatively decided on changes to FAS 109, and in others, the IASB has agreed to change its standard. Since mid-2008, however, the FASB suspended further work on the project and does not plan to amend FAS 109 at this time. They may reactivate it, however, after the IASB has completed the process of issuing a replacement to IAS 12. The IASB issued an Exposure Draft (ED/2009/2) in early 2009 and expects to issue a replacement to IAS 12 *Income Taxes* in 2010.

What changes are likely to be seen in the replacement to IAS 12? The following is a summary of some of the key changes incorporated in the 2009 Exposure Draft. Until due process is completed, however, these changes are not certain.

Definition of tax basis. The tax basis is elevated to a measurement attribute defined as "the measurement under applicable substantively enacted tax law of an asset, liability or other item." The tax basis of an asset is based on the tax deductions available to the entity if the carrying amount is recovered by sale.

Exceptions to the temporary difference approach. The following exceptions are eliminated and replaced with less limiting restrictions: (i) that deferred tax liabilities or assets are not recognized for temporary differences arising from the initial recognition of an asset or liability in a transaction that is not a business combination and affects neither accounting nor taxable profit is eliminated; and (ii) that a deferred tax liability for temporary differences relating to investments in subsidiaries, branches, associates, and joint ventures is not recognized.

Measurement of deferred tax assets and liabilities. There is a clarification that a "substantively enacted" means when future events in the enactment process historically have not changed the outcome and are not likely to do so. In addition, instead of using the tax rate applicable to undistributed profits, current and deferred tax assets and liabilities will be measured using the rate expected to apply when the tax asset or liability is realized or settled, including the effect of expected future distributions.

Recognition of deferred tax assets. Deferred tax assets will be recognized in full, and an offsetting valuation allowance will be recognized separately to reduce the deferred tax asset to the amount that is "more likely than not" to be realizable.

Allocation of tax expense. IAS 12 currently requires entities to recognize in equity the tax effects of items that are credited or charged directly to equity, **both** for the current year **and** for any subsequent changes in these amounts. The Exposure Draft allows some of the changes in tax effects initially recognized outside continuing operations to be recognized on reversal within continuing operations.

Balance sheet classification of deferred tax assets and liabilities. The classification of deferred tax assets and liabilities as current or non-current is changed from the present non-current classification to one based on the classification of the related non-tax asset or liability for financial reporting purposes.

Uncertain tax positions. IAS 12 does not address the issue of uncertain tax positions, i.e., measurement uncertainty in the amounts underlying current and deferred tax. The IASB has decided to move to an expected outcome measure (a probability weighted average of the possible outcomes).

---

[13] IASCF, IASB Project Update: Short-term convergence: income taxes (December 2008).

END-OF-CHAPTER PRACTICE

23-1 IAS 12 provides much more guidance on the recognition and measurement of the tax effects derived from deductible temporary differences than for the tax effects from taxable temporary differences.

Instructions
Write a short paragraph to explain this situation.

23-2 Listed below are a number of situations that affect the financial statements.
1. Development costs have been capitalized on the statement of financial position and are being amortized to profit or loss over three years, but deducted as an expense for tax purposes as incurred.
2. Revenue is recognized as goods are delivered for financial reporting purposes, but on a cash basis for tax purposes.
3. An entity borrows money and pays a transaction fee on the amount borrowed. The transaction costs are added to the debt and amortized using the effective interest method for financial reporting purposes, although they were deducted when they were paid for tax purposes.
4. Pension expense is charged to profit or loss each period although tax legislation allows entities to deduct only the contributions to the pension trustee for tax purposes. Expenses have always exceeded the contributions.
5. Investment property is measured according to the revaluation model for financial reporting purposes, resulting in valuations in excess of the original cost. This method is not permitted for tax purposes.

Instructions
For each situation described above, indicate whether the company has a deductible or a taxable temporary difference and whether it will result in the recognition of a deferred tax asset or a tax liability. Explain each briefly.

23-3 A company buys equipment for $1,000, uses it in the manufacturing of goods for resale, and depreciates it on a straight-line basis over its five-year expected useful life. For tax purposes, the equipment is depreciated at 25% a year on a straight-line basis. Tax losses may be carried back against taxable profit of the previous five years. The tax rate for all years is 40%, and in 2004 the company's taxable profit was $500. In each year from 2005 to 2009, the company reported profits **before depreciation expense and taxes** of $200.

Instructions
(a) For each year from 2005 to 2009, determine the company's taxable profit or loss and the current tax expense recognized.
(b) For each year from 2005 to 2009, determine the amount of any year-end taxable or deductible temporary difference and the related balance of the deferred tax asset or liability account reported on the balance sheet, and the deferred tax expense reported for the year.
(c) To the extent possible with the information provided and the results of (a) and (b), prepare a partial statement of comprehensive income for each year from 2005 to 2009.

(adapted from Appendix B of IAS 12)

23-4 In this chapter, flag icons identify areas where there are GAAP differences between IFRS requirements and national standards.

Instructions
Access the website(s) identified on the inside back cover of this book, and prepare a concise summary of the differences that are flagged throughout the chapter material.

Chapter 24

Leases: IAS 17

U.S. GAAP Reference
FAS 13 Accounting for Leases

Related IFRSs
IAS 16 Property, Plant and Equipment
IAS 36 Impairment of Assets
IAS 38 Intangible Assets
IAS 40 Investment Property
IAS 41 Agriculture

OBJECTIVE AND SCOPE

Some leases result in significant amounts of assets and liabilities being reported on an entity's statement of financial position, while others result in disclosure treatment only. IAS 17 sets out the appropriate accounting and disclosure policies for leases, for both lessees and lessors. It excludes leases associated with the exploration for and use of non-renewable natural resources and, with licensing agreements, for a variety of intangible assets such as movies, video recordings, plays, manuscripts, patents, and copyrights. IFRIC 4 *Determining Whether an Arrangement Contains a Lease* and other IFRS interpretations provide further guidance on the legal and economic substance of a variety of potential lease arrangements.

Although the following properties fall within the scope of IAS 17, the **measurement basis** for each is provided by the standard more closely related to the specific assets involved. Investment properties held by lessees and those provided under operating leases by lessors look to IAS 40 *Investment Property* for measurement guidance; biological assets held by lessees under finance leases and those provided by lessors under operating leases apply IAS 41 *Agriculture*.

CLASSIFICATION OF LEASES

A *lease* is defined in IAS 17.4 as "an agreement whereby the lessor conveys to the lessee in return for a payment or series of payments the right to use an asset for an agreed period of time." It is classified for accounting purposes as either a **finance** lease or an **operating** lease. The classification decision, for both the lessor and the lessee, is governed by the extent to which the risks and rewards of ownership remain with the lessor or are transferred to the lessee.

A lease that transfers substantially all the risks and rewards incidental to ownership is a *finance lease*. One that does not is an *operating lease*. The lessee and the lessor each must evaluate its own specific circumstances, and it is possible for a particular agreement to be classified as an operating lease by one party and a finance lease by the other.

What conditions or circumstances might support a decision to classify a lease as a finance lease? Examples that **normally support** classification as a **finance lease** include any one or more of the following situations:

- Ownership of the asset is transferred to the lessee by the end of the lease term. This may happen either as a condition in the lease or because the lessee has an option to purchase the asset at a price that is so much lower than the expected fair value of the property at the exercise date that it is reasonably certain the option will be exercised and ownership transferred (a bargain purchase).
- The lease term covers the major part of the asset's economic life, i.e., the lessee will receive most of the economic benefits the asset has to offer.
- At the beginning of the lease, the present value of the minimum lease payments covers substantially all the fair value of the leased property, thereby providing the lessor with a return **of** its investment in the property and a return **on** the investment.
- The asset leased is so specific to the lessee's needs that significant modifications would have to be made to make it useful to another party.

In addition, other conditions may exist that **might lead** to classification as a finance lease:

- A lessor's losses from cancellation of the lease by the lessee are borne by the lessee.
- Gains and losses from changes in the asset's fair value accrue to the lessee at the end of the lease.
- The lessee is able to extend the lease for another period at considerably less than market rent at that time.

In order to apply the first group of criteria, financial statement preparers have to be familiar with terminology specific to lease accounting. The *lease term*, for example, refers to the non-cancellable period over which the lessee has agreed to lease the asset, plus any additional terms where the lessee has an option to continue the lease and it is reasonably certain the option will be exercised.

Minimum lease payments is a critical term—not only in helping to determine whether a lease is finance or operating in nature, but also when measuring the amount to recognize in the accounts if it is a finance lease. The *minimum lease payments* are defined in IAS 17.4 as:

(a) the payments over the lease term that the lessee is or can be required to make, excluding contingent rent, costs for services, and taxes to be paid by and reimbursed to the lessor;

(b) if applicable, the payment required to exercise a "bargain purchase" option; and

(c) for the **lessee**, any amounts guaranteed by the lessee or party related to the lessee; or for the **lessor**, any residual value guaranteed by a party not related to the lessor.

The classification decision often requires the use of professional judgment, exercised in light of the overriding principle of whether or not the risks and rewards of ownership are transferred. When it is determined that there is no transfer, the lease is classified as an **operating lease**.

A special problem arises when land and buildings are leased together and title to the land is not later transferred to the lessee. Because land tends to have an indefinite life, it is unlikely that the risks and rewards of ownership can be judged as transferred to the lessee; therefore, the land lease is usually classified as operating. When land and buildings are leased together, the two assets are split into separate elements for classification purposes. The minimum lease payments are allocated between land and building in proportion to the relative fair values of the leased interests in each element. An exception is permitted if the amount allocated to the land is immaterial, in which case the land and building are treated as one unit for classification purposes.

RECOGNITION AND MEASUREMENT BY THE LESSEE
Finance Leases

The lessee recognizes a finance lease as the acquisition of an asset and as a liability on its statement of financial position when its right to use the leased asset begins, i.e., on the lease's **commencement date**. This accounting treatment reflects the economic substance of the lease transaction—the lessee has acquired the use of economic resources and has taken on an obligation to make future lease payments.

The amount capitalized as an asset and recognized as a liability is the lower of the fair value of the leased asset and the present value of the minimum lease payments when the major provisions of the lease were agreed on, i.e., at the **inception of the lease**. The lessee uses the interest rate implied in the lease to discount the future cash flows if it is known or can be reasonably determined. Otherwise, the lessee uses its incremental borrowing rate. In addition, any incremental **initial direct costs** incurred by the lessee directly attributable to negotiating and arranging the lease are added to the asset's cost.

After initial recognition, leased assets are accounted for in each period in accordance with the depreciation policies in IAS 16 *Property, Plant and Equipment* or IAS 38 *Intangible Assets*, if depreciable, and with IAS 36 *Impairment of Assets*.

The minimum lease payments are accounted for in the same way as any payment on a liability: the portion representing interest, applying the effective interest method, is reported as a period expense; and the portion representing principal is reported as a reduction of the liability. Contingent rentals—incremental lease payments that change with a variable other than time, such as total sales—are recognized as an expense in the period incurred.

Lessees disclose the following information about their finance leases, in addition to disclosures required under related IFRSs:

(a) the net carrying amount at the balance sheet date, by class of asset;

(b) the future minimum lease payments and their present value that are due within one year, those due between the end of year one and the end of year five, and those due beyond year five, and a reconciliation of the total minimum lease payments outstanding at the balance sheet date to their present value;

(c) contingent rents recognized as an expense in the period;

(d) total minimum sublease payments expected to be received in the future on non-cancellable subleases; and

(e) significant information about its leasing arrangements, such as how contingent rentals are determined, information about renewal or purchase options and escalation clauses, and details about any restrictions imposed as part of the lease agreements.

Operating Leases

Operating leases are treated very differently for accounting purposes. The lease payments are recognized as an expense over the term of the lease on a systematic basis that relates to the time pattern of the benefits received, usually on a straight-line basis. This principle is applied even if the lease payments themselves are not uniform amounts.

Because the **unrecognized** agreement to make operating lease payments is similar to the **recognized** lease obligation for finance leases, many of the disclosure requirements are the same. Lessees disclose the following information for their operating leases:

(a) the total future minimum lease payments that are due within one year, those due between the end of year one and the end of year five, and those due beyond year five;

(b) total minimum sublease payments expected to be received in the future on non-cancellable subleases;

(c) each of the minimum lease payments, contingent rents, and sublease payments recognized in expense in the period; and

(d) significant information about the entity's leasing arrangements, such as how contingent rentals are determined, information about renewal or purchase options and escalation clauses, and details about any restrictions in the lease agreements.

The Nestlé Group, reporting in millions of Swiss francs in its 2007 financial statements, includes information related to its finance and operating leases in Illustration 24-1. It is interesting to note that the off-balance sheet operating lease obligations are almost four times that of the company's recognized liability under finance leases!

Illustration 24-1
Nestlé Group
Finance and
Operating Lease
Disclosures

Accounting policies

Valuation methods and definitions

Leased assets

Assets acquired under finance leases are capitalized and depreciated in accordance with the Group's policy on property, plant and equipment unless the lease term is shorter. Land and building leases are recognized separately provided an allocation of the lease payments between these categories is reliable.

The associated obligations are included under financial liabilities.

Rentals payable under operating leases are expensed.

The costs of the agreements that do not take the legal form of a lease but convey the right to use an asset are separated into lease payments and other payments if the entity has the control of the use or of the access to the asset or takes essentially all the output of the asset. Then the entity determines whether the lease component of the agreement is a finance or an operating lease.

11. Property, plant and equipment

At 31 December 2007, property, plant and equipment include CHF 1178 million of assets under construction. Net property, plant and equipment held under finance leases amount to CHF

354 million. Net property, plant and equipment of CHF 117 million are pledged as security for financial liabilities. Fire risks, reasonably estimated, are insured in accordance with domestic requirements.

28. Lease commitments

Operating leases

In millions of CHF	2007	2006
	Minimum lease payments	
	Future value	
Within one year	559	480
In the second year	425	389
In the third to the fifth year inclusive	859	702
After the fifth year	571	555
	2 414	**2 126**

Finance leases

In millions of CHF	2007		2006	
	Minimum lease payments			
	Present value	Future value	Present value	Future value
Within one year	78	88	78	87
In the second year	100	120	81	97
In the third to the fifth year inclusive	146	208	166	229
After the fifth year	122	264	159	331
	446	**680**	**484**	**744**

RECOGNITION AND MEASUREMENT BY THE LESSOR

Finance Leases

A lessor classifies its leases by applying the same criteria as the lessee, except that the definition of minimum lease payments is applied from the lessor's perspective. Because a lease is classified as a finance lease only if the risks and rewards associated with legal ownership have been transferred, it is reasonable to remove the leased asset from the lessor's balance sheet and to recognize instead its **net investment** in the lease arrangement. The net investment is made up of a receivable and its contra unearned finance (interest) income account.

Lessors who are manufacturers or dealers and who offer their customers a choice of whether to buy or lease the asset record the lease arrangement as a sale. In general, these lessors are interested in recovering the sale price (fair value) through the lease, and this is the basis for the amount of their net investment. These lessors recognize the profit on the sale of their inventory when the lease begins, and the finance or interest income over the term of the lease as shown in Illustration 24-2.

Illustration 24-2
Finance Lease:
Manufacturer
or Dealer Lessor
Accounting

At beginning of lease term			Throughout lease term		
Lease Receivable	X		Cash	X	
Sales		X	Lease Receivable		X
Unearned Finance Income		X	To record lease payment received.		
Cost of Goods Sold	X		Unearned Finance Income	X	
Inventory		X	Finance Income		X
To record the lease transaction.			To recognize finance income earned in period.		

Lessors whose business model is primarily financing the acquisition of assets by others look to recover the costs they incur to acquire the asset for the lessee and this is the basis for their net investment. There is no sale in this situation. The lessor earns and recognizes finance income over the term of the lease as shown in Illustration 24-3.

Illustration 24-3
Finance Lease:
Financing
Lessor
Accounting

At beginning of lease term			Throughout lease term		
Lease Receivable	X		Cash	X	
Unearned Finance Income		X	Lease Receivable		X
Assets Purchased to Lease		X	To record lease payment received.		
To record the lease transaction.			Unearned Finance Income	X	
			Finance Income		X
			To recognize finance income earned in period.		

The next step is the measurement of the amounts recognized in these two finance lease situations.

In both Illustrations 24-2 and 24-3, the Lease Receivable is the *gross investment in the lease*. It is the undiscounted total of the minimum lease payments plus any unguaranteed residual value that accrues to the lessor. Because the minimum lease payments by definition include any **guaranteed** residual values, the gross investment includes both guaranteed and unguaranteed residuals. If a bargain purchase option is part of the agreement, it is included instead of any residual values.

If the lessor is a manufacturer or dealer, the Sales account is credited with the fair value of the leased asset and Cost of Goods Sold is debited with the carrying amount of the leased property. (An exception to this measurement of the sales and cost of sales amounts is discussed below.) The inventory's carrying amount is removed from the accounts.

In order to determine the amount of unearned finance income under both types of finance leases, the net investment in the lease must be calculated. The *net investment in the lease* is the present value of the **gross investment in the lease** discounted at the interest rate implicit in the lease. The difference between the gross and net investment is the unearned finance income—the interest to be earned and recognized over the lease term.

The **undiscounted** lease payments received are credited directly to the Lease Receivable account, reducing both the gross investment and the net investment in the lease. The finance income earned is recognized using the **effective interest method**, whereby interest income is recognized at a constant rate based on the carrying amount of the remaining net investment.

The following situations may affect one or more numbers in the measurements explained above:

1. Incremental **initial direct costs** incurred by **manufacturer or dealer lessors** to negotiate and arrange the lease are recognized as an expense in the period the sale is recognized.

2. Similar **initial direct costs** incurred for finance leases by **other types of lessors** are added to the carrying amount of the asset acquired by the lessor. This requires the *interest rate implicit in the lease* to be recalculated. The recalculated rate is the internal rate of return that equates the present value of the total of the minimum lease payments and any unguaranteed residual value, if applicable, with the total of the fair value of the leased asset plus any initial direct costs of the lessor. This results in a lower discount rate and a reduced amount of finance income recognized in each period over the lease term. In this way, the initial direct costs are spread over the lease term.

3. When a **manufacturer or dealer lessor enters into a finance lease that includes an unguaranteed residual value**, the amounts recognized as Sales and Cost of Goods Sold are both reduced by an equal amount—the present value of the unguaranteed residual. These accounts are the only ones affected. The gross investment, net investment, and unearned finance income continue to be calculated as described above.

4. If a manufacturer or dealer uses an **artificially low rate of interest**, perhaps to entice a customer into the arrangement, the gross profit on the sale is limited to the amount that would result if a market rate of interest had been used.

5. The estimated unguaranteed residual value included in the gross investment is reviewed on a regular basis. The effect of any reduction in this value is recognized in profit or loss in the current period.

The lessor meets the disclosure requirements of IFRS 7 *Financial Instruments: Disclosures* as well as the following, some of which mirror the lessee's disclosures:

(a) the gross investment in the lease and the present value of the minimum lease payments that are receivable within one year, those receivable between the end of year one and the end of year five, and those receivable beyond year five and a reconciliation between the gross investment in the lease and the present value of the minimum lease payments receivable at the balance sheet date;

(b) unearned finance income;

(c) unguaranteed residual values accruing to the lessor;

(d) the allowance for uncollectible minimum lease payments receivable;

(e) contingent rents recognized as income in the period; and

(f) general information about its material leasing arrangements.

Operating Leases

Accounting for operating leases is relatively straightforward:

- The **leased assets** continue to be reported on the statement of financial position.
- **Lease income** is recognized on a straight-line basis over the term of the lease unless another systematic basis is a better fit for the time pattern by which the benefits are received from the asset.
- **Initial direct costs** incurred in negotiating and arranging the lease are added to the carrying amount of the leased asset and depreciated over the lease term on the same basis as the lease income is recognized.
- Depreciation of the leased asset is determined by applying IAS 16 *Property, Plant and Equipment* or IAS 38 *Intangible Assets*.
- Impairment of the leased asset is governed by applying IAS 36 *Impairment of Assets*.

As well as applying the disclosure requirements of IFRS 7 *Financial Instruments: Disclosures*, lessors with operating leases also report

- the total minimum lease payments due in the future, broken down by those due within one year, between the end of year one and the end of year five, and beyond year five;
- contingent rents recognized in income in the period, and
- a general description of the entity's leasing arrangements.

In addition, the disclosure requirements of all related IFRSs identified at the beginning of the chapter apply to operating lease assets.

SALE AND LEASEBACK TRANSACTIONS

It is not unusual for entities that own specific assets to sell them and then lease them back. This is known as a *sale and leaseback*, and the same criteria as identified earlier in the chapter apply in classifying the lease portion of the transaction. Because the amount of the minimum lease payments on the lease portion of the transaction may be related to the sales price agreed to by the buyer and seller, the two parts of the transaction are considered interdependent for accounting purposes.

If the **leaseback is a finance lease**, the seller-lessee defers any profit it would otherwise recognize on the sale, and amortizes it to income over the term of the lease. It is not appropriate to recognize a gain as a result of a financing transaction.

If the **leaseback is an operating lease** and **the sale was made at fair value,** any profit or loss on the sale is recognized immediately. The accounting treatment differs in this case, because classification as an operating lease indicates that the risks and rewards of ownership have been transferred to the buyer-lessor and the transaction is a normal sale. If the **sale amount is less than fair value** without lower-than-fair-value lease payments, the loss again is recognized immediately. However, if the future lease payments are lower to compensate for the less-than-fair-value selling price, the loss is deferred and amortized on the same basis as the lease payments. If the **sale amount is greater than fair value**, the excess over fair value is deferred and amortized over the period the asset is expected to be used. If the **fair value is less than the asset's carrying amount**—indicating an impairment—this loss is recognized immediately.

LOOKING AHEAD

The IASB and the FASB have been working on a joint project on lease accounting since 2006, with the objective of agreeing on a common standard that requires balance sheet recognition of the assets and liabilities arising from lease contracts. A joint Discussion Paper, *Leases: Preliminary Views* (DP/2009/1), was released in 2009, with the expectation of an Exposure Draft in 2010 and final standard in 2011.`

Standard setters are moving away from the "transfer of risks and rewards associated with ownership" criterion that underlies current standards. Instead, the Discussion Paper supports a "right-of-use" approach to identifying the lease asset and the performance obligation to make lease payments over the lease term as a lease liability. This has the effect of also giving balance sheet recognition to most agreements that are now treated as operating leases. The Discussion Paper also presents preliminary views on accounting for lease contracts that contain options to renew or terminate the lease, options to purchase the asset, residual value guarantees, and contingent rentals. Different approaches to the measurement of these as part of the asset and liability are set out, with the two Boards agreeing on some preferred methods and differing on others.

The FASB and the IASB deferred an analysis of accounting issues related to the lessor in order to focus on lessee-related problems. The Discussion Paper, therefore, does not go into any detail on lessor accounting except to identify some of the issues that need to be discussed and resolved before a new lessor standard could be issued. By limiting the scope to the lessee, a new standard with a significant impact is likely to be released by 2011.

END-OF-CHAPTER PRACTICE

24-1 Lessee Corp. entered into a non-cancellable agreement with Lessor Corp. on May 15, 2008 to lease equipment manufactured by Lessor according to Lessee's specifications. If Lessee had purchased the equipment outright from Lessor, it would have cost Lessee $100, although Lessor's cost was only $80. The following information is available:

Lease term	May 15, 2008–May 14, 2012
Economic life of equipment	6 years
Annual rental payment	$25.8
1st payment due	May 15, 2008
Estimated residual value, unguaranteed	$13
Interest rate implied in lease	10%
Title transfer in lease?	No
$n = 4$, $i = 10$:	
PV factor, lump sum	0.68301
PV factor, annuity due	3.48685
Lessee and Lessor Corp. year ends	December 31

Instructions (round all amounts to one decimal place)
- (a) Discuss the nature of this lease to Lessee Corp.
- (b) Discuss the nature of this lease to Lessor Corp.
- (c) Prepare Lessee Corp.'s entries for 2008 and 2009 assuming the lease is classified as
  - (i) a finance lease
  - (ii) an operating lease

(d) Prepare Lessor Corp.'s entries for 2008 and 2009 assuming the lease is classified as
   (i)   a finance lease
   (ii) an operating lease
(e) Explain how your answers to parts (a) and (b) above would change, if at all, if the following features were added to this lease agreement. Assume each feature is an independent case. In addition, explain how any entries in parts (c) and (d) would differ, if at all, from those prepared above.
   (i)   The lessee's incremental borrowing rate is 12%.
   (ii) The residual value is guaranteed by Lessee Corp.
   (iii) The residual value is guaranteed by a third party not related to Lessee Corp.
   (iv) The agreement contains an option permitting Lessee Corp. to purchase the leased asset on May 14, 2012 for $4.
   (v)   The equipment is so specialized to Lessee Corp.'s needs that Lessor Corp.'s only option at the end of the lease term is to sell off the component parts for the estimated residual value.

24-2 Prepare a decision chart or diagram to accompany IAS 17 that can be used by seller-lessees to determine the correct accounting for gains and losses on disposal of an asset that is sold and leased back. Write a brief explanation of why the standard provides a reasonable treatment in each situation.

24-3 Jamal Corp. enters into a four-year operating lease for the rental of two floors of a new building, and makes a payment of $2 in advance to hold the space. The monthly rental is $10 and Jamal qualifies for a special promotion, getting the last four months of the lease rent-free.

Instructions
   (a)   Determine the rent expense to be recognized each year of the four-year lease.
   (b)   Prepare the journal entries to record the $2 payment, the $10 rental payment for months 1 and 2 of the lease, and any entries required in each of months 45, 46, 47, and 48. Round the monthly rent expense to one decimal place.

24-4 On June 30, 2008, Lor Ltd., a lessor, enters into a six-year non-cancellable finance lease that requires annual rental payments of $100 beginning June 30, 2008. In addition, the lessee is required to make payments in advance of $12 each year to Lor Ltd. to cover a maintenance agreement on the equipment. The equipment has an estimated residual value of $40 at the end of the lease term. Lor Ltd. is a dealer that ordinarily sells this equipment inventory, which costs $450, for $524.50. Lor Ltd. expects to earn an 8% return on any delayed payment terms.

Instructions
   (a)   Assuming the lessee has guaranteed the residual value, prepare Lor Ltd.'s entries on June 30, 2008, December 31, 2008 (its year end), and June 30, 2009. Identify the lessor's gross investment in the lease and the net investment in the lease on December 31, 2008, and the profit or loss reported on the lease arrangement for the year that just ended.
   (b)   Assuming the residual value is not guaranteed, prepare Lor Ltd.'s entries on June 30, 2008, December 31, 2008 (its year end), and June 30, 2009. Identify the lessor's gross investment in the lease and the net investment in the lease on December 31, 2008, and the profit or loss reported on the lease arrangement for the year that just ended. Comment on your results in this part compared with your results in part (a).
   (c)   Explain briefly how the initial direct costs of negotiating the lease of $10 would be accounted for on June 30, 2008, and how this would affect any subsequent entries. You are not required to make any calculations.

24-5 In this chapter, flag icons identify areas where there are GAAP differences between IFRS requirements and national standards.

Instructions
Access the website(s) identified on the inside back cover of this book, and prepare a concise summary of the differences that are flagged throughout the chapter material.

Chapter 25

Employee Benefits: IAS 19

U.S. GAAP References
FAS 87 Employers' Accounting for Pensions
FAS 88 Employers' Accounting for Settlements and Curtailments
FAS 106 Employers' Accounting for Postretirement Benefits Other than Pensions
FAS 112 Employers' Accounting for Postemployment Benefits
FAS 158 Employers' Accounting for Defined Benefit Pension and Other Postretirement plans

Related IFRSs
IFRS 2 Share-based Payment
IAS 24 Related Party Disclosures

OBJECTIVE AND SCOPE

IAS 19 sets out the accounting and disclosure requirements for the wide range of employee benefits that are provided under formal plans or agreements, legislative requirements and industry arrangements, and informal practices that result in a constructive obligation.[1] *Employee benefits,* "all forms of consideration given by an entity in exchange for services rendered by employees," include the following categories:

- short-term employee benefits,
- post-employment benefits,
- other long-term employee benefits, and
- termination benefits.[2]

---

[1] IASCF, IAS 19.3. A constructive obligation is one evidenced by past practice where the entity has no realistic choice but to meet the obligation. Constructive obligations are recognized as liabilities.

[2] IASCF, IAS 19.4 and 19.7.

Employees include full-time, part-time, permanent, casual, or temporary workers, as well as directors and management personnel.

Accounting **by employee benefit plans** is covered by IAS 26 *Accounting and Reporting by Retirement Benefit Plans*.

SHORT-TERM EMPLOYEE BENEFITS

Short-term employee benefits are benefits other than termination benefits that are **due to be settled within 12 months after the end of the period in which the related service is rendered** by the employee. The following are examples of this type of benefit:

(a) salaries, wages, and social security contributions;
(b) short-term compensated absences such as paid vacation and sick leaves;
(c) profit-sharing and bonuses; and
(d) non-monetary benefits such as medical care, housing, cars, and free or subsidized goods or services.

Because the associated obligations are normally met in the short term, the accounting for this type of benefit is relatively straightforward. IAS 19 does not require any specific disclosures for short-term benefits, although IAS 24 *Related Party Disclosures* requires benefit information for key management personnel and IAS 1 *Presentation of Financial Statements* requires the employee benefits expense to be reported.

Recognition and Measurement

In general, an entity recognizes the undiscounted amount of benefits expected to be paid as a liability and an associated cost. If the payments made exceed the benefits, an asset is recognized provided future payments are reduced or a cash refund is expected. The benefit cost is recognized as an expense, unless another IFRS allows or requires it to be capitalized, such as part of production overhead costs for inventory or property, plant, and equipment.

Short-term Compensated Absences

There are two types of short-term compensated absence—accumulating and non-accumulating—and the costs for each are recognized differently.

An example of an employee's right to a benefit that **accumulates** as the employee provides additional service is the entitlement to compensated vacation. In this situation, the entity makes an accrual for the additional amount that it expects to pay as a result of the unused entitlement that has accumulated at the balance sheet date. On the other hand, if the entitlement does **not accumulate**, such as with parental leave, the liability and cost are not recognized until the event occurs that obligates the entity, i.e., when the employee absence occurs.

Situation

Company A's employees are entitled to five paid sick days for each year they work. If these days are not used in the year, they can be carried forward and used in the following year if needed; however, employees are required to use the current year's sick days before those carried forward. During 2008, the company's 100 employees took an average of three days paid sick leave, leaving two days per employee to carry forward to 2009. Based on past experience, Company A estimates that 95 of the employees will not use their full five days of annual entitlement in 2009, and that 5 employees are likely to take an average of seven days each.

Company B's situation is the same as Company A's except that its employees are entitled to five paid sick days for each year they work, but there is no provision for carrying forward unused days.

Company C's employees are entitled to nine months parental leave. In early October 2008, one employee left on a nine-month paid leave.

Discuss each company's accounting requirements in respect of these short-term benefits.

Analysis

At December 31, 2008, Company A estimates the expected additional amount it expects to pay as a result of any unused entitlement that has accumulated to this date. Because only five employees are expected to use an average of two days each, Company A recognizes a liability and related expense equal to the cost of 10 days of sick leave.

Company B does not recognize any cost or liability relating to the unused days at the reporting date because it will not make any future payments related to them.

Company C recognizes an expense and liability for the full nine months of parental leave when the employee begins the leave. Because the employee benefit does not increase with the amount of service provided, it is not reasonable to accrue the cost and obligation as the employee provides service. The full cost is expensed when the leave begins because no benefits accrue to the company during the leave.

Profit-sharing and Bonus Plans

An entity recognizes the cost and liability under profit-sharing and bonus plans only when a **legal or constructive obligation** exists and the amount can be **reliably estimated**. If the payments are not all due within 12 months from the end of the period that the employees render the related services, they are accounted for as other long-term employee benefits.

The estimate of the obligation is the amount expected to be paid out, and, in order to make a reliable estimate as required to support recognition as a liability, one of the following conditions must exist:

(a) The plan has formal terms that contain a formula for calculating the amount of the benefit.
(b) The amount is determined before the financial statements are authorized to be issued.
(c) Past practice provides clear evidence of the amount of the constructive obligation.

POST-EMPLOYMENT BENEFIT PLANS

Post-employment benefit plans are among the most complex employee benefits. These formal or informal arrangements to provide employee benefits (other than termination benefits) after employment cover retirement pension benefits and other benefits such as post-employment life insurance and medical care.

There are two types of post-employment benefit plans: defined contribution plans and defined benefit plans. *Defined contribution plans* are relatively straightforward in that the employer pays fixed contributions into a separate entity known as a fund, after which the employer has no legal or constructive obligations to make further payments, even if the assets that accumulate are insufficient to pay all the benefits. A *defined benefit plan* is a post-employment benefit plan that is not a defined contribution plan.

Illustration 25-1 indicates that a key difference between these two types of plan is the party that assumes the primary risks.

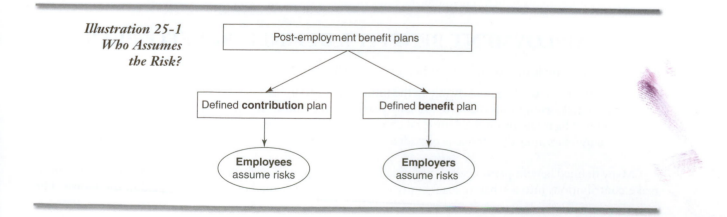

Illustration 25-1 Who Assumes the Risk?

When an employer is obligated only to make specified contributions into the plan, the risk that the benefits will be less than expected in the future—the **actuarial risk**—and the risk that the assets invested will not earn a large enough return and therefore not be enough to meet the expected benefits—**investment risk**—fall on the employee. However, if the employer is obligated to provide a specified benefit to the employee after employment, the employer absorbs these risks. This also happens when the plan calls for benefits in addition to the amount of the contributions, when the employer has guaranteed a specific return on the contributions, or when the employer has voluntarily taken on responsibility in the past for minimum levels of benefits, i.e., has taken on a constructive obligation.

If a number of **unrelated** employers sponsor a plan by pooling their contributions and use the assets to provide benefits to all their employees, this is a **multi-employer plan**. A multi-employer plan can be accounted for either as a defined benefit plan or a defined contribution plan, depending on the specific agreement and terms of the plan. Sometimes such a plan is a defined benefit plan but not enough information is available to allow it to be accounted for in this way by the employer. In this case, it is treated as if it were a defined contribution plan, and additional disclosures are required. A **state plan** that is established by legislation to cover all entities and that is controlled by a government or other body not under the employer's influence or control is accounted for in the same way as a multi-employer plan. If an entity **insures employee benefits** by paying insurance premiums to cover the future benefits it promises, this is accounted for as if it were a defined contribution plan unless the entity takes on other obligations. IAS 19 contains more details on the accounting requirements for these plans.

POST-EMPLOYMENT BENEFITS: DEFINED CONTRIBUTION PLANS

Accounting for defined contribution plans is not complicated because the obligation for the period is limited to the contributions required in the period. As long as unpaid amounts are due within a year from the end of the period the services were provided, they are not discounted.

Recognition and Measurement

The recognition and measurement criteria for the liability and costs related to defined contribution plans are the same as those for short-term employee benefits discussed above.

The entity recognizes a **liability** associated with employee service during the period that is unpaid at the reporting date. An asset is recognized if the entity has paid more than the contributions due as long as this leads to a cash refund or a reduction in the amounts otherwise payable in the future. The contributions are expensed in the same period the related services are provided.

Disclosures

Other IFRSs require disclosure of the expense for defined contribution plans and the contributions made to these plans for key management personnel.

POST-EMPLOYMENT BENEFITS: DEFINED BENEFIT PLANS

Two issues add complexity to the accounting for defined benefit plans:

1. Estimates of the benefits payable in the future that need to be recorded in the current period depend on actuarial assumptions that extend many years into the future and that change over time.
2. The obligations recognized must take the time value of money into account as they are usually settled many years after the service is provided by the employee.

Many defined benefit plans need to be funded, i.e., the employer, or both the employer and employee, must make contributions into a separate legal entity or fund from which the benefits will be paid in the future. The ability to pay the benefits depends on both the financial position and investment performance of the fund and on the ability of the employer entity to make up any deficiency in the fund's assets. Thus the employer underwrites the plan's actuarial and investment risks.[3]

To account for defined benefit plans the preparer of financial statements has to be familiar with a number of terms and concepts. The next sections explain the basic building blocks needed to account for these plans.

Present Value of a Defined Benefit Obligation

The *present value of a defined benefit obligation* (DBO) is the discounted present value of the expected future payments required to settle the obligation resulting from employee service in the current and prior periods.[4] It is an accumulated amount and the present value of the obligation reported at the end of each reporting period should approximate its present value at that time.

The present value of an entity's defined benefit obligation and the current service cost for a specific period are based on the following:

- using projected salaries rather than those earned in the period when the service is provided,
- applying the projected unit credit actuarial method, and
- attributing the benefits to the periods of service under the plan's benefit formula.[5]

Major factors in determining the present value of the obligation are the **actuarial assumptions**—demographic assumptions about the employees' mortality, turnover, dependants, etc.—and **financial assumptions**—the discount rate, future salary and benefit levels, future medical cost, and the expected rate of return on benefit plan assets. Illustration 25-2 indicates what causes this measure to change from one period to the next.

Illustration 25-2		
Changes in the		Present value of the obligation at the beginning of the period
Present Value	+	Current period's service cost
of the Defined	+	Interest cost on the outstanding obligation for the period
Benefit	+/−	Past service costs from plan amendments in the period
Obligation	−	Benefits paid under the plan in the period
	+/−	Actuarial gains (−) and losses (+) in the period
	=	Present value of the obligation at the end of the period

The rate used to **discount** the obligations is the end-of-period market yield on high-quality corporate bonds with terms corresponding to the obligations. The **interest cost** is calculated using the beginning-of-period interest rate applied to the weighted-average balance of the obligation during the period. Similar to any discounted liability, interest costs increase the amount of the outstanding obligation. *Past service cost* is the change in the present value of the defined benefit obligation from introducing a defined benefit plan that attributes benefits to past service, or from changing the benefits payable for past service under an existing plan. Past service cost can increase or decrease the obligation, depending on whether the benefits were increased or decreased. The **benefits paid** to former employees under the plan, like any liability that is paid, reduces the

---

[3] IASCF, IAS 19.49.
[4] IASCF, IAS 19.7.
[5] The projected unit credit method is explained in IAS 19.65 as an actuarial method that "sees each period of service as giving rise to an additional unit of benefit entitlement and measures each unit separately to build up the final obligation." This method is also known as the accrued benefit method pro-rated on service.

obligation. Lastly, the balance of the obligation is affected by *actuarial gains and losses,* made up of the effects of changes in the actuarial assumptions and experience adjustments recognizing the differences between the previous actuarial estimates and what has actually occurred.[6]

Plan Assets

The other key variable in accounting for defined benefit plans is the plan assets that have accumulated under the plan. *Plan assets* are assets held by the long-term employee benefit fund as well as qualifying insurance policies. The assets held must be legally separate from the reporting entity, exist solely to pay or fund employee benefits, and are not available to the reporting entity's creditors even in bankruptcy.[7] These are made up of investments in financial and non-financial assets. The plan assets are measured at fair value and, like the present value of the benefit obligation, must be representative of their end-of-period values. Illustration 25-3 explains how this pool of assets changes from one period to the next.

Illustration 25-3		Fair value of plan assets at the beginning of the period
Changes in the		
Fair Value of	+	Contributions from employer/employees in the period
Plan Assets	+/−	Actual return on plan assets in the period
	−	Benefits paid under the plan in the period
	=	Fair value of plan assets at the end of the period

The **contributions** from employers and employees, if applicable, increase the pool of funds available for investment, while the **benefits paid** to former employees under the plan reduce the assets. The **actual return** on the assets is made up of interest, dividends, other types of revenue from the assets invested, as well as realized and unrealized gains and losses on the assets during the period, all reduced by the costs of plan administration. Because the actual return on plan assets can be highly variable from one period to the next, pension accounting uses the **expected return** on the plan assets for some of its calculations instead of the actual return. The relationship between the two returns is as follows:

Actual return − expected return on plan assets = actuarial gain or loss

or

Expected return +/− actuarial gain or loss   = actual return on plan assets

Actuarial gains and losses are explained in more detail below.

Other Changes

In addition to the changes to the benefit obligation identified in Illustration 25-2 and to the plan assets in Illustration 25-3, plan settlements and curtailments also affect these two amounts, as might an adjustment

---

[6] IASCF, IAS 19.7.
[7] IASCF, IAS 19.7. A qualifying insurance policy is subject to the same limitations as the other plan assets.

limiting the amount of the benefit asset reported.[8] Although these three items affect the accounting for defined benefit plans, a fuller discussion of these complexities is outside the scope of this book.

A discussion of the calculation of the benefit cost recognized in profit or loss (or added to the production cost of inventory or plant and equipment under IAS 2 and IAS 16) follows. This cost is based on the events and transactions that affect the defined benefit obligation and plan assets as identified above.

Benefit Cost Recognized in Profit or Loss

Illustration 25-4 sets out the benefit cost to recognize during a period.

Illustration 25-4 *Calculation of Benefit Cost*		
		Current service cost for the period
	+	Interest cost for the period
	−	Expected return on plan assets for the period
	+/−	Actuarial gain (−) or loss (+) amortized in the period
	+/−	Past service cost recognized in the period
	=	Post-employment benefit cost to profit or loss

The same variables that go into determining the defined benefit obligation—the actuarial valuation method used and demographic and financial actuarial assumptions—as well as how the benefits are attributed to the periods of service, also affect the current service cost. The *current service cost* represents the increase in the present value of the defined benefit obligation that results from employee service in the current period.[9]

The **interest cost** is the same interest that increases the benefit obligation. As explained above, the **expected return on assets** is included instead of the actual return. The expected return is always a positive number, whereas the actual return could actually be negative.

Because changes in actuarial estimates and the difference between expected and actual experience result in **actuarial gains and losses** that are likely to offset each other over time, the standards do not require these gains and losses to be included in the calculation of the benefit expense **when they occur**. However, if the gains or losses accumulate to a significant amount, they must be amortized into expense. What is considered significant? Under IAS 19, if the net accumulated unrecognized actuarial gains and losses **at the end of the preceding period** is more than 10% of the larger of the present value of the benefit obligation and the fund assets, then some amortization must be recognized in the post-employment benefit cost. The minimum amortization is the amount of the net gains or losses in excess of the 10% corridor, divided by the expected average remaining working lives of the employees participating in the plan. Other systematic amortization methods may be used to amortize the net gain or loss, not just the excess, at a faster rate.

Entities also have an **option** to recognize all actuarial gains and losses **in other comprehensive income** in the period they occur and take them directly to retained earnings. If they choose this option, they must apply it for all defined benefit plans and for all actuarial gains and losses.

---

[8] **Curtailments**, often associated with restructurings, occur when there is a significant reduction in the number of employees covered by a plan or when the plan's terms are amended so that current employees' future service will no longer qualify in a significant way for benefits under the plan. A **settlement**, as its name suggests, occurs when the employer's obligation under the plan is eliminated, usually through a lump-sum cash payment to plan participants in exchange for their rights under the plan.

[9] IASCF, IAS 19.7.

The last component of the periodic cost relates to *past service costs.* On the assumption that the changes in the benefits for past service are given (or taken away) in return for employee service over the period until those benefits are vested in the employee, past service costs are taken into expense on a straight-line basis over the average period until the benefits become vested. If the changes in the benefits are vested immediately, then past service costs are recognized in expense immediately as well.[10]

As indicated above, the effects of settlements and curtailments and adjustments to the benefit asset recognized in the statement of financial position may also affect the employee benefit expense recognized in profit or loss.

Recognition and Measurement

It is important to note that neither the present value of the defined benefit obligation nor the fair value of the plan assets are reported directly on the statement of financial position. Instead, the entries made in the accounts are as shown below, the first to recognize the expense and set up a **defined benefit liability**, and the second to record the entity's contributions into the fund during the period, reducing the recognized liability.

Employee benefit expense	$X	
Defined benefit liability		$X
Defined benefit liability	$Y	
Cash		$Y

The liability on the balance sheet, therefore, represents the accumulated amounts charged to expense in excess of contributions made into the fund. The balance in the account can also be explained as indicated in Illustration 25-5.

Illustration 25-5		Present value of the defined benefit obligation
Defined Benefit	−	Fair value of the plan assets
Liability	=	Funded status of the plan
	+/−	Net unrecognized actuarial gains (+) or losses (−)
	−	Unrecognized past service costs
	=	Defined benefit liability

If the total contributions made are more than the accumulated expenses recognized, the balance sheet account indicated in Illustration 25-5 will be reported as an asset. Similar to all assets, a **defined benefit asset** cannot be reported at more than the benefits expected to be realized. IAS 19 sets out limitations and circumstances that may require an adjustment to the asset reported, the employee benefit expense for the period, or other comprehensive income.

Profit or Loss

The total employee benefit expense made up of the components shown in Illustration 25-4 is recognized in profit or loss for the period, unless another IAS requires or allows some portion to be included in the cost of an asset.

---

[10] IASCF, IAS 19.96. IAS 19.7 defines vested employee benefits as "employee benefits that are not conditional on future employment."

Recognition and Measurement: Other

IAS 19 sets out numerous requirements for the recognition and measurement of the defined benefit obligation and current service cost, including the actuarial valuation method to be used, the basis on which to attribute the benefits to the periods of service, and the actuarial and financial assumptions underlying actuarial estimates. Other measurement and recognition guidance relates specifically to the plan assets, business combinations, and curtailments and settlements.

Presentation

Entities often have more than one defined benefit plan so IAS 19 contains specific requirements similar to the guidance in IAS 32 *Financial Instruments: Presentation* for the **netting of plan asset and liability balances**. An entity offsets one plan's asset against another plan's liability only when it has a legally enforceable right to use the surplus in one to settle obligations in the other and it intends to do this simultaneously or to settle the obligations on a net basis.

The standard is silent on whether an entity should present the benefit liability or asset as a **current or non-current** amount on the balance sheet and whether the components of the employee benefit cost are reported as a **single item** in the statement of comprehensive income.

Disclosure

The objective of the many disclosures required for post-employment defined benefit plans is to allow users to evaluate the plans' nature and their financial effects on the entity during the period. The following is a summary of the major types of information required:

1. A description of the type of plan and the accounting policy for recognizing actuarial gains and losses.
2. A reconciliation of the opening balance of the present value of the defined benefit obligation to the closing balance showing each item that affected it separately.
3. A reconciliation of the opening balance of the fair value of the plan assets to the closing balance showing each item that affected it separately.
4. A reconciliation of the difference between the employee benefit liability or asset reported on the statement of financial position to the funded status of the plans (the difference between the obligation and the plan assets).
5. The total expense reported in profit or loss, the components making up the expense, and the line item where it is included.
6. Amounts recognized in other comprehensive income, particularly for actuarial gains and losses.
7. Information about the types of investments held as plan assets, the actual return on the plan assets, and a narrative about how the expected rate of return is determined.
8. Details of the principal actuarial assumptions used, a sensitivity analysis related to 1% changes in key estimates, and historical information about experience adjustments.
9. The entity's best estimate of the expected contributions in the annual period after the balance sheet date.

OTHER LONG-TERM EMPLOYEE BENEFITS

Entities also provide employees with benefits other than those discussed above and that are not all due within a year after the end of the period in which employees earn them. These are known as *other long-term employee benefits*. Those that accrue with service such as long-term disability benefits, long-service or sabbatical leaves, and deferred compensation paid 12 months or more after the period in which it was earned have characteristics similar to post-employment benefit plans.[11]

---

[11] IASCF, IAS 19.7 and 19.126. Note that long-term disability benefits available to all employees equally do not accrue with service. In this case, the liability and cost are recognized when the event occurs that gives rise to the obligation.

Recognition and Measurement

Although these benefits are similar to the post-employment benefits discussed in the previous section of this chapter, there is less uncertainty about the measurement of these benefits. Therefore, although the general approach is the same, actuarial gains and losses and past service costs are all recognized immediately in **expense**.

> **Other long-term employee benefits expense** = current service cost + interest cost − expected return on any plan assets + all actuarial gains and losses + all past service costs

Because there is no deferred recognition of actuarial gains and losses and past service costs, the liability for other long-term employee benefits reported on the statement of financial position usually differs from the **liability for post-employment** described above.

> **Other long-term employee benefits liability** = the present value of the defined benefit obligation − the fair value of the plan assets

Disclosure

This standard does not require any specific disclosures for other long-term employee benefits, although IAS 1 *Presentation of Financial Statements* requires disclosure if the amount is material and IAS 24 *Related Party Disclosures* sets out requirements for these benefits for key management personnel.

TERMINATION BENEFITS

Recognition

Termination benefits are employee benefits payable that result either from an entity's decision to end an individual's employment before the normal retirement date or an employee's decision to accept voluntary termination in exchange for those benefits.[12]

A liability and expense are reported only when the entity is demonstrably committed to the termination of an employee or group of employees or an offer to provide benefits to encourage voluntary withdrawal from the entity. Recognition hinges on what is meant by being **demonstrably committed**. IAS 19 explains that this means that the entity has a detailed formal plan for the termination that it cannot reasonably withdraw. The plan must set out

(a) the location, function, and approximate number of employees being terminated;
(b) the termination benefits to be provided for each job classification or function; and
(c) when the plan will be implemented.[13]

The benefits may be paid all in lump-sum amounts or may include enhanced retirement benefits or continued salary for a period of time. Because there are no future benefits accruing to the entity from employee service after termination, the entire cost is expensed when the entity is committed to the plan as explained above.

---

[12] IASCF, IAS 19.7.
[13] IASCF, IAS 19.134.

Measurement

When a plan is confirmed and the entity offers benefits to encourage voluntary termination, the entity does not know how many employees will accept the offer. In this case, it uses the number of employees expected to accept the offer to measure the expense and the liability. If termination benefits are due beyond 12 months from the balance sheet date, the entity discounts them using the same discount rate as determined for defined benefit post-employment plans.

Disclosure

As explained above for other long-term employee benefits, there are no specific disclosures required for terminations although IAS 1 and 24 may apply.

LOOKING AHEAD

IAS 19 *Employee Benefits* is currently on the IASB active agenda and work plan, specifically in relation to post-employment benefits, including pensions. The present project was added to the agenda in 2006, with the aim of issuing a standard to significantly improve pension accounting relatively quickly pending a more comprehensive review of issues associated with post-employment benefit accounting.

The IASB issued a Discussion Paper, *Preliminary Views on Amendments to IAS 19 Employee Benefits*, in 2008. The project was separated into two parts in 2009 so that the Board can focus on the more immediate issues. These include recognition and presentation matters associated with changes in the defined benefit obligation and plan assets, and with disclosures. The other issues – primarily associated with contribution-based promises – will be part of a later, second Exposure Draft and standard, perhaps in conjunction with a broader review of post-employment benefit accounting. An Exposure Draft on the first set of issues is scheduled for late in 2009. While the tentative decisions made by the Board to date are open to change before the Exposure Draft and final standard stages, they indicate the direction likely to be taken. Some of the tentative decisions reached that affect recognition and presentation are:

- All changes in the value of plan assets and the post-employment benefit obligation are recognized when they occur.
- Unvested past service costs are recognized when a plan is amended.
- Changes in the net benefit asset or liability are classified as one of three components: service cost, interest cost on the defined benefit obligation, or a remeasurements component (from other changes, gains and losses on settlement, and the effect of the asset ceiling).
- The service cost and interest cost are disclosed separately on the income statement or in the notes, with the interest presented similar to other financing costs.[14]

The remeasurements component is reported separately in the income statement and reported net of tax.

The tentative decisions made that are likely to be incorporated in the late 2009 Exposure Draft go a long way to ensuring more faithful representation of balance sheet amounts and an improvement in intercompany comparability. The IASB will then decide on the timing of Phase 2 of this long-term project. Although there is no certainty as this book goes to print about what the ultimate changes will be, it is clear that considerable change lies ahead.

---

[14] IASCF, *IASB Project Update: Post-employment benefits* (June 2009).

END-OF-CHAPTER PRACTICE

25-1 IAS 19 applies to employee benefits including short-term employee benefits, post-employment benefits, other long-term employee benefits, and termination benefits.

Instructions

    (a) What differentiates each type of employee benefit that IAS 19 applies to?

    (b) Identify the general principles evident in IAS 19 that underlie accounting for employee benefits.

25-2 Quayot Corp. (QC) is provided with the following information related to its defined benefit pension plan for the current year.

	$
Defined benefit obligation, Jan. 1	80
Plan assets, Jan. 1	64
Contribution to the plan assets	11
Current service cost	9
Actual return on plan assets	2
Expected return on plan assets	6
Past service cost recognized (amortized)	5
Pension benefits paid	4
Discount rate	10%
Net actuarial losses in current year, benefit obligation	1
Net actuarial losses in current year, plan assets	4

QC follows a policy of amortizing (i.e., recognizing) the minimum amount of actuarial gains and losses allowed under IAS 19 in determining pension benefit expense. There were no accumulated actuarial gains or losses at the beginning of the current year. The cost of past service benefits granted early in the current year was $8, of which $5 is recognized. To simplify, assume all other transactions and events affecting the obligation and plan assets take place at the end of the period.

Instructions

    (a) Prepare a reconciliation of the opening to closing balances for the current year for the pension benefit obligation and for the plan assets.

    (b) Determine the pension benefit expense for the current year.

    (c) If the balance in the pension benefit liability account is $16 at the beginning of the year, what is its ending balance?

    (d) If QC had chosen different, but acceptable, GAAP policies for calculating its pension expense and liability, what pension expense would have been reported?

    (e) If the changes proposed in the IASB Discussion Paper issued in 2008 are accepted and IAS 19 is amended, identify how your answers to (a) and (b) above would differ.

25-3 In this chapter, flag icons identify areas where there are GAAP differences between IFRS requirements and national standards.

Instructions

Access the website(s) identified on the inside back cover of this book, and prepare a concise summary of the differences that are flagged throughout the chapter material.

Chapter 26

Related Party Disclosures: IAS 24

U.S. GAAP Reference
FAS 57 Related Party Disclosures

Related IFRS
NA

OBJECTIVE AND SCOPE

Related-party transactions are different from other types of transactions. In general, where an arm's-length transaction exists, users may assume that the transaction reflects fair value and that the transaction would be entered into during the normal course of business or with valid business reason from the entity's perspective. This may not be the case with related-party transactions. These types of transactions may be entered into for other reasons and may be transacted at amounts other than fair value. Therefore, at a minimum, users must be made aware of the existence of these transactions. IAS 24 identifies mandatory disclosures as well as provides guidance on what a **related party** is.

Parties are related if[1]

- (a) directly, or indirectly through one or more intermediaries, the party:
    - (i) controls, is controlled by, or is under common control with, the entity (this includes parents, subsidiaries and fellow subsidiaries);
    - (ii) has an interest in the entity that gives it significant influence over the entity; or
    - (iii) has joint control over the entity;
- (b) the party is an associate (as defined in IAS 28 *Investments in Associates*) of the entity;
- (c) the party is a joint venture in which the entity is a venturer (see IAS 31 *Interests in Joint Ventures*);
- (d) the party is a member of the key management personnel of the entity or its parent;
- (e) the party is a close member of the family of any individual referred to in (a) or (d);

---

[1] IASCF, IAS 24.9.

(f)   the party is an entity that is controlled, jointly controlled or significantly influenced by, or for which significant voting power in such entity resides with, directly or indirectly, any individual referred to in (d) or (e); or

(g)   the party is a post-employment benefit plan for the benefit of employees of the entity, or of any entity that is a related party of the entity.

According to IAS 24.9, related-party transactions include transfers of resources, services, or obligations whether a price is charged or not. Close family members include a domestic partner and children/dependents. Key management members include those who have the authority and responsibility for planning, directing, and controlling the activities of the entity.

It is worthwhile to spend a bit of time looking at the definitions of control, joint control, and significant influence. IAS 24.9 provides the following definitions:

Control is the power to govern the financial and operating policies of an entity so as to obtain benefits from its activities.

Joint control is the contractually agreed sharing of control over an economic activity.

Significant influence is the power to participate in the financial and operating policy decisions of an entity, but is not control over those policies. Significant influence may be gained by share ownership, statute or agreement.

Situation

Consider the following situations:

1.   Parent company A owns 100% of subsidiary B.
2.   Parent company C owns 70% of subsidiary D.
3.   Parent company E owns 100% of both subsidiary F and G.
4.   Investor H has significant influence over investee I.
5.   J is the CEO of Company K.
6.   L is married to J.
7.   K and L are venturers who jointly control M.

Analysis

1.   A is related to B since A controls B.
2.   C is related to D even though C owns only 70% of the company. The ownership still gives C control over D.
3.   F and G are related because they are under common control. E is related to F and G because E controls both F and G.
4.   H is related to I because significant influence exists (I is an associate).
5.   J is related to K because J is a key management person who has the authority and responsibility for planning, directing, and controlling the activities of the entity.
6.   L is related to J and K because L is a close member of the family of J.
7.   Although K is related to M and L is related to M, K and L are not otherwise related.

Once the related party is identified, the next step is to determine what if any disclosures need to be made to help users understand the impact that the related-party transactions have on the company's performance and financial position.

DISCLOSURE

Parent-subsidiary Relationships

IAS 24 requires that details about the relationship between the parent and subsidiaries be disclosed, including

•   the name of the parent;
•   the name of the ultimate controlling party (if different from the parent); and

- if neither of the above produce financial statements that are available, the name of the next most senior parent.

This is disclosed even where no transactions exist.

Management Compensation

In addition, the standard requires that compensation for key management personnel be disclosed. Compensation includes short-term employee benefits (wages, salaries, bonuses, etc.), post-employment benefits (pensions, life insurance, etc.), other long-term benefits (sabbatical, disability, etc.), terminations, and share-based payments.[2] Total compensation benefits and subtotals for each of these categories should be disclosed.

Related-party Transactions

Where related-party transactions have occurred, the entity must disclose the relationship between the related parties and information about the transaction and any outstanding balances, including:[3]

- the amount;
- the amount of balances still outstanding (including terms and conditions, whether secured, the nature of consideration upon settlement, and details of any guarantees); and
- provisions for doubtful debt and any related expense recognized during the period.

According to IAS 24, these disclosures should be made separately for the parent, entities with joint control/significant influence over the entity, subsidiaries, associates, joint ventures, key management personnel, and other related parties. An entity may only disclose that the transaction was made based on arm's-length terms if this claim can be substantiated. Substantiation might, for instance, be made by benchmarking against other similar but arm's-length transactions.

Following are examples of related-party transactions that would be disclosed:

- purchase or sales of goods or property,
- leases,
- loans,
- guarantees, and
- others.

Illustration 26-1 shows a related-party note from Heineken.[4] Heineken is one of the world's largest brewers of beer and is based in the Amsterdam, the Netherlands. It reports in euros.

Illustration 26-1 *Related-party* *Note from* *Heineken*	**33. Related parties** **Identity of related parties** Heineken has a related party relationship with its associates (refer note 16 and 33), joint ventures (refer note 33 and 35), Heineken Holding N.V., Heineken pension funds (refer note 26) and with its key management personnel (Executive Board and the Supervisory Board).

Key management remuneration

In millions of EUR	2007	2006
Executive Board	4.1	6.0
Supervisory Board	0.4	0.4
	4.5	6.4

[2] IASCF, IAS 24.9.
[3] IASCF, IAS 24.17.
[4] http://www.annualreport.heineken.com/downloads/Heineken_AnnualReport_EN_07.pdf

Executive Board

The remuneration of the members of the Executive Board comprises a fixed component and a variable component. The variable component is made up of a Short-Term Incentive Plan and a Long-Term Incentive Plan. The Short-Term Incentive Plan is based on an organic profit growth target and specific year targets as set by the Supervisory Board. For the Long-Term Incentive Plan we refer to note 27. The separate remuneration report is stated on page 62.

As at 31 December 2007 and as at 31 December 2006, the members of the Executive Board did not hold any of the Company's shares, bonds or option rights, other than under the Long-Term Incentive Plan aforementioned. D.R. Hooft Graafland held 3,052 shares of Heineken Holding N.V. as at 31 December 2007 (2006: 3,052 shares).

Executive Board

In thousands of EUR	Fixed Salary		Short-Term Incentive Plan		Long-Term Incentive Plan		Other Deferred Benefits		Pension Plan		Total	
	2007	2006	2007	2006	2007	2006	2007	2006	2007	2006[*]	2007	2006
J.F.M.L. van Boxmeer	750	680	1,125	592	207	93	–	–	395	192	2,477	1,557
D.R. Hooft Graafland	550	525	619	455	143	86	–	–	311	238	1,623	1,304
M.J. Bolland[1]	–	306	–	189	–	50	–	2,550	–	82	–	3,177
Total	**1,300**	1,511	**1,744**	1,236	**350**	229	–	2,550	**706**	512	**4,100**	6,038

[1] Stepped down from the Executive Board on 1 August 2006. Mr. Bolland was compensated with an amount of €2,550,000.

[*] Comparatives have been adjusted to include pension entitlements related to the Short-Term Incentive Plan.

Supervisory Board

The individual members of the Supervisory Board received the following remuneration:

In thousands of EUR	2007	2006
C.J.A. van Lede	66	66
J.M. de Jong	52	52
M. Das	52	52
M.R. de Carvalho	50	50
A.H.J. Risseeuw[1]	13	50
J.M. Hessels	50	50
I.C. MacLaurin	50	33
A.M. Fentener van Vlissingen	50	33
Total	**383**	**386**

Only M.R. de Carvalho held 8 shares of Heineken N.V. as at 31 December 2007 (2006: 8 shares). As at 31 December 2007 and 2006, the Supervisory Board members did not hold any of the Company's bonds or option rights. C.J.A. van Lede and M.R. de Carvalho (2006: three Supervisory Board members) together held 2,664 shares of Heineken Holding N.V. as at 31 December 2007 (2006: 9,508 shares).

[1] Stepped down from the Supervisory Board on 19 April 2007.

Other related party transactions

In millions of EUR	Transaction value		Balance outstanding as at 31 December	
	2007	2006	**2007**	2006
Sale of products and services				
Joint ventures	**44**	26	**4**	1
Associates	**17**	20	**–**	–
	61	46	**4**	1
Raw materials, consumables and services				
Goods for resale—joint ventures	**4**	–	**1**	–
Other expenses—joint ventures	**1**	–	**1**	–
	5	–	**2**	–

Heineken Holding N.V.

In 2007 an amount of €572,000 (2006: €551,000) was paid to Heineken Holding N.V. for management services for the Heineken Group.

This payment is based on an agreement of 1977 as amended in 2001, providing that Heineken N.V. reimburses Heineken Holding N.V. for its administration costs. Best practice provision III.6.4 of the Dutch Corporate Governance Code of 9 December 2003 has been observed in this regard.

LOOKING AHEAD

Since the U.S. and international standards are largely converged, there are no plans to fundamentally change this standard in the near future. There is a project underway to address the requirements for state-controlled entities and study the definition of related parties further for associates and subsidiaries of the associate's significant investor.

END-OF-CHAPTER PRACTICE

26-1 Related Limited entered into the following transactions:
1. Sold inventory to a subsidiary.
2. Purchased land from the CEO's wife.
3. Borrowed funds from the bank.
4. Guaranteed loans for its subsidiary.
5. Paid its top management salary and bonuses.
6. Paid pension amounts to its former president.

Instructions

Identify whether these are related–party transactions under IAS 24. How should these transactions be presented in Related Limited's financial statements?

26-2 Under GAAP in other countries (Canada for instance), related-party transactions are remeasured either to fair value, exchange value, or as a default carrying value. The IFRS deals only with disclosures (there are no requirements to remeasure).

Instructions

Discuss the pros and cons of both approaches.

26-3 A Limited entered into a joint venture agreement with B Limited. Together they formed AB Inc., which will be jointly controlled by A and B.

Instructions

Identify which parties are related and discuss why/why not for each relationship.

26-4 In this chapter, flag icons identify areas where there are GAAP differences between IFRS requirements and national standards.

Instructions

Access the website(s) identified on the inside back cover of this book, and prepare a concise summary of the differences that are flagged throughout the chapter.

Chapter 27

Earnings per Share: IAS 33

U.S. GAAP Reference
FAS 128 Earnings per Share

Related IFRS
NA

OBJECTIVE AND SCOPE

The amount of earnings that is attributable to each common or ordinary shareholder is represented by the earnings per share (EPS) numbers. This standard seeks to provide guidance on

- how earnings per share should be accounted for,
- when diluted EPS should be presented, and
- what information should be disclosed.

Because the calculations can be fairly complex, the IASB has provided numerous illustrative examples that accompany but are not part of the standard.

Ordinary shares are defined by IAS 33.5 as "equity instruments that are subordinate to all other classes of equity instruments. Ordinary shares are also referred to as common shares."

The EPS calculations focus on these shares as they are residual in nature. For example, upon liquidation, the debt holders get paid out first, and then the preferred/senior shareholders, and finally the ordinary or common shareholders get whatever is left. In addition, the ordinary or common shareholders share in the residual earnings (after operating expenses and dividends on preferred shares). Thus, EPS provides useful information to these shareholders about the amount of earnings that will eventually go to them. The terms "ordinary" and "common" shares will be used interchangeably in this chapter.

IAS 33 covers financial statements of

- entities that have ordinary shares or potential ordinary shares traded in a public market, or
- entities that are in the process of filing their statements with a securities commission for the purpose of going public.

IAS 33.5 defines the following additional terms:

Potential ordinary shares are financial instruments (or other contracts) that may entitle the holder to ordinary shares. Examples are convertible debt, convertible preferred shares, options, warrants, and contingently issuable shares.

Contingently issuable shares are issuable under the terms of a contingent share agreement and are defined by the standard as shares that will be issued for little or no cash when certain conditions in the agreement are met.

Public markets include not only formal stock exchanges like the New York stock exchange, but also what are known as over-the-counter markets, which are less formal markets where trading is not as heavily regulated. Basically, if there are numerous public shareholders and the entity files financial statements with a securities regulator, such as the SEC, then EPS is calculated and presented. Other companies that elect to provide EPS disclosures must follow the standard. If both consolidated and non-consolidated statements are prepared, then the EPS disclosures need be presented only in the consolidated statements.[1]

Illustration 27-1 shows which companies must/may follow IAS 33.

Illustration 27-1 Entities Covered by IAS 33

	EPS	Notes
Shares publicly traded—consolidated statements	Required	If the entity produces both consolidated and non-consolidated statements, it may choose to present EPS only in the consolidated statements. If the entity chooses to also present EPS information in its non-consolidated statements, it must present it in the statement of comprehensive income and may not present the non-consolidated EPS in the consolidated statements.
Shares publicly traded—separate or individual statements (legal entity statements)	Required, unless presented in the consolidated statements	See above.
Private company	Not required, but may choose to present	If EPS information is presented, the entity must follow IAS 33.

MEASUREMENT

There are two types of EPS—basic (BEPS) and diluted (DEPS). BEPS is based on existing earnings and outstanding common/ordinary shares. DEPS is a "what-if" calculation. It illustrates what EPS would be if all the potential ordinary shares were actually ordinary shares (i.e., the instruments were actually converted into shares or options were exercised, resulting in additional shares being issued).

---

[1] IASCF, IAS 33.4.

Basic Earnings per Share (BEPS)

BEPS is calculated as follows:

The profit or loss attributable to ordinary equity holders is divided by the weighted average number of ordinary shares outstanding.[2]

The calculation should also be done for income from continuing operations as well (if this number is presented in the profit and loss statement).

Earnings

Profit or loss attributable to ordinary shareholders (the numerator) begins with

- profit or loss from continuing operations (if separately presented), and
- profit or loss.

Two separate calculations are done where profit or loss from continuing operations is presented separately on the profit and loss statement.

It is then adjusted for[3]

- dividends on preferred shares, and
- gains/losses on settlement/repurchase/early conversion of preferred shares.

Only declared dividends relating to non-cumulative preferred shares are deducted. This is because they are not owed unless they are declared. All dividends (declared or not) relating to cumulative preferred shares are deducted. This is because they are owed whether declared or not, so the EPS is always adjusted for them. Where shares are settled/repurchased/converted early during the year, any related gains/losses are added to/deducted from earnings in calculating EPS.

Shares

The denominator uses the weighted average number of ordinary shares outstanding during the period. This gives the best indicator of the earnings based on the average outstanding equity. The calculation looks at the number of shares outstanding each day although a "reasonable approximation of the weighted average"[4] may be used. In general, the shares are assumed to be issued on the date that the consideration is receivable, although there are several situations that may need clarifying:[5]

- When shares are issued on conversion of debt, the shares are assumed to be issued on the date that interest ceases to accrue.
- When shares are issued upon rendering of services, the shares are assumed to be issued as the services are rendered.
- When shares are issued in a business combination, the shares are assumed to be issued on the acquisition date.
- Contingently issuable shares are included from the date that all conditions are met (events have occurred).
- Where the number of shares issued and outstanding has changed without a corresponding change in resources (e.g., stock split, reverse split, or stock dividend), the number of shares is adjusted for all periods presented.

---

[2] IASCF, IAS 33.10.
[3] IASCF, IAS 33.16–33.18. Paragraph 33.15 also refers to preferred shares issued at a premium/discount (from par value). Many jurisdictions do not allow for shares with par value.
[4] IASCF, IAS 33.20.
[5] IASCF, IAS 33.21–33.29.

- Where the financial instrument is mandatorily convertible, it is treated as ordinary shares from the date that the contract is entered into (since it is seen to be a de facto ordinary share).

Situation

Early Limited has profit of $100. At the beginning of the year there were 100 ordinary shares outstanding. During the year, the following transactions occurred:

- On June 30, 100 additional shares were issued for cash.
- On July 31, 10 additional shares were issued on conversion of debt. The interest was paid up to (and ceased accruing on) June 30.
- On September 30, 10 shares were issued for services rendered. The services were rendered by June 30.
- On December 31, a two-for-one stock split occurred.

Calculate the denominator for the current year EPS.

Analysis

The weighted average of ordinary shares equals the following:

100 shares $\times$ 6/12	= 50
220 shares $\times$ 6/12	= 110
	= 160
$\times$ 2	= 320

The shares issued on conversion are assumed to be issued at the point interest stops accruing (June 30). In addition, where the shares were issued in exchange for services rendered, the shares are assumed to be issued when the services are rendered, which is June 30. Since a stock split occurred at the end of the year (the number of shares increased but there were no additional resources for the firm), all share numbers are adjusted. For every one old share, there are now two new shares.

Diluted Earnings per Share

As previously noted, DEPS shows earnings available to ordinary shareholders, assuming all potential common shares are now issued, and outstanding ordinary shares. Like BEPS, it is calculated based on profit and loss as well as profit or loss from continuing operations (if presented). Both the numerator (earnings) and the denominator (number of shares) are adjusted for the "what if" assumption. For instance, if convertible debt is assumed to be converted at the beginning of the year, interest would have been avoided and additional shares would have been issued.

Earnings

Profit or loss attributable to ordinary shareholders is adjusted for the following:

- after-tax interest/dividends that would be avoided if the convertible instruments had been converted at the beginning of the period; and
- any other changes in profit or loss that would result from the conversion of the convertible instruments (for instance, discount/premium amortization or changes in things such as bonuses that are based on profit or loss).[6]

---

[6] IASCF, IAS 33.33 and 33.34.

Note that no adjustment is made to the numerator for options and warrants. This has to do with the assumptions made in calculating DEPS. In doing the DEPS calculation, it is assumed that either

- funds received are used to buy back shares (rather than investing them), or
- shares are issued to generate sufficient cash to buy back the shares under option. The specific calculations will be discussed further below.

Shares

The weighted average number of ordinary shares as calculated for BEPS would be adjusted for additional ordinary shares that will be issued on conversion or exercise of potential ordinary shares. The potential ordinary shares are assumed to be issued at the beginning of the year or the date of issue of the potential ordinary shares if later. Similarly, if conversion or exercise options lapse during the period, the number of shares would be pro-rated for the part of the year that the potential common shares were outstanding. The dilutive weighted average common shares are calculated independently for each period presented (interim versus annual).[7]

Where more than one basis of conversion exists within the terms of the potential common shares, the entity would use the one that is most advantageous to the holder.[8]

Dilutive Potential Ordinary Shares

Most holders of ordinary shares are more concerned if there is the potential for their EPS to decline and therefore, in calculating DEPS, only those potential common shares that result in lower DEPS are included in the calculations; in other words, only those that are dilutive. Those potential common shares that would result in a DEPS that is higher than the BEPS are referred to as anti-dilutive and are not included in the calculations or final reported DEPS.

The entity must therefore determine whether potential common shares are dilutive or anti-dilutive. In doing so, the entity considers the incremental impact of each potential common share individually and then each potentially dilutive security in sequence from the most dilutive to the least dilutive. Options and warrants are always considered to be the most dilutive since the incremental impact to the numerator is assumed to be zero.[9]

Illustration 27-2 show the steps that an entity might take in calculating DEPS.

Illustration 27-2
Steps to Calculate
DEPS

When calculating DEPS, the entity might take the following steps:

1. Identify potential ordinary shares.
2. Assume that they will be converted/exercised at the beginning of the period.
3. Calculate the incremental impact of conversion/exercise.
4. Rank from most dilutive to least dilutive.
5. Starting with earnings and weighted average shares from BEPS, add back the incremental impact of each individual potential common share starting with the most dilutive. Recalculate the interim DEPS after each add back to see if it is still less than BEPS and declining.
6. DEPS should be the lowest number if profits exist (or highest if losses exist).

---

[7] IASCF, IAS 33.37.
[8] IASCF, IAS 33.39.
[9] IASCF, IAS 33.44.

Written Call Options/Warrants

When the entity writes a call option or issues a warrant, it gives the holder the right to buy/obtain shares for a predetermined price (exercise price). When that price is lower than market price, the option is said to be "in the money." Because the purchase price for the shares under the option is less than the market price, there would be an economic incentive for the holder to exercise the option and it would be dilutive to the company.

Illustration 27-3 shows the steps the entity might take when calculating the impact on DEPS of written call options.

Illustration 27-3 *Steps for Calculating the Impact on DEPS of Written Call Options*	When calculating the impact on DEPS of written call options, the entity performs the following steps: 1. Determine whether the option is "in the money." In general, if the exercise price is less than the average market price of the shares over the period, then it will be "in the money." An average price is used in the calculation.[10] If it is "in the money," then it is dilutive. 2. Assume that the option will be exercised at the beginning of the year (or later if the option is issued later). 3. Assume that the cash from the exercise of the option (exercise price multiplied by the number of shares to be purchased) is received at the beginning of the period (or later if the option is issued later). 4. Assume that the cash from number 3 is used to buy back shares in the open market to reduce the dilutive impact of the exercise. Because the market price is higher, the entity will not be able to buy back the same number of shares. 5. Adjust the denominator for the net change in shares.

Note that employee share options are treated as options for the purposes of the DEPS calculation.

Written Put Options and Forward Purchase Contracts

When the entity writes a put option or enters into a forward contract to sell shares, it gives the holder the right to sell the shares to the entity for a predetermined price (exercise price). When the price is higher than the market price, the option is "in the money." Because the exercise price is higher than the market price, there would be an economic incentive to exercise the option and sell the share to the entity at the higher price. This would be dilutive to the entity.

Illustration 27-4 shows the steps the entity might take when calculating the impact on DEPS of written put options.

Illustration 27-4 *Steps for Calculating the Impact on DEPS of Written Put Options*	1. Determine whether the option is "in the money." In general, if the exercise price is greater than the average market price of the shares over the period, then it will be "in the money." An average price is used in the calculation.[10] If it is "in the money," then it is dilutive. 2. Assume that the option will be exercised at the beginning of the year (or later if the option is issued later). 3. Assume that the entity must issue shares at the beginning of the period (or later if the option/forward contract is entered into later) in the market at the average price in order to raise the capital needed to buy back the shares under the put option/forward. Because the

---

[10] The standard allows for a simple average using weekly or monthly closing prices, unless prices fluctuate widely, in which case an average of the high and low prices may be more representative.

market price is lower, the entity will have to issue more shares to get sufficient funds to buy the shares under the put/forward contract.

4. Assume that the cash from number 3 is used to buy back shares under the put option.
5. Adjust the denominator for the net change in shares.

Convertible Instruments

Convertible instruments are included in the DEPS calculation when they are dilutive. For convertible preferred shares, they are assumed to be anti-dilutive if the related dividend per ordinary share is greater than BEPS. Similarly, convertible debt is anti-dilutive whenever the after-tax interest (and other related items) per ordinary share is greater than BEPS.[11] The following illustration identifies the steps in calculating the impact of convertible instruments on DEPS.

Illustration 27-5
Steps for Calculating the Impact on DEPS of Convertible Instruments

1. Determine whether the instruments are dilutive or not.
2. Assume that conversion would take place at the beginning of the year (or later if the convertible instrument was issued later).
3. Adjust the numerator—add back the after-tax amounts (e.g., after-tax interest) that would have been avoided had the instruments been converted at the beginning of the year.
4. Adjust the denominator—add back the number of shares that would have been issued on conversion.

Contingently Issuable Shares

According to IAS 33.52–33.57, contingently issuable shares are included from the beginning of the period (or later if the related contract was issued later) if the conditions are satisfied by year end. The conditions often relate to either earnings levels, share prices (or both), or other factors such as store openings. For instance, the contract might stipulate that additional shares will be issued if the earnings, share price, or both exceed a certain level within a certain time frame (which might or might not extend beyond the current period).

If the conditions are not satisfied by year end (e.g., the contingency might relate to the amount of earnings over a two-year period that extends beyond the current year end), then the calculation is based on the number of shares that would be issued if the end of the current period were the end of the evaluation period. If the issuance of additional shares is based on the market price of the ordinary shares over a two-year period, the calculation would assume the current year-end price of the shares. If the issuance of shares depends on earnings level and share prices, the number of ordinary shares included in the calculation would be based on both the earning levels and the share price (both conditions must be met).

Contracts that May Be Settled in Ordinary Shares or Cash

According to IAS 33.58, where the entity has an option to settle a contract in ordinary shares or cash, it is assumed that shares will be used. If this is dilutive, it would be included in the DEPS calculations.[12] If the holder has the option, then the entity would consider the more dilutive of the two and use that in the calculations.

---

[11] IASCF, IAS 33.50.

[12] According to IAS 33.59, where the instrument was initially classified as a financial asset or liability, the numerator is adjusted for any change in earnings that would have occurred if the instrument had been classified as equity.

Purchased Options

Purchased call and put options are not included in the DEPS calculations because they are anti-dilutive. When purchased, the entity is the holder and has the right but not the obligation to exercise the options. If the options are call options, they are "in the money" (for the entity/holder) when the exercise price is less than the market price. In this case, from an economic perspective, the entity would exercise the option and be better off. Similarly, if the options are put options, they are "in the money" when the exercise price exceeds the market price because the entity would be able to sell its shares for higher than market.

Retrospective Adjustments

As previously noted, where the number of shares increases but there is no corresponding change in resources (e.g., stock split or reverse split) and this occurs during or after the reporting period but before the statements are authorized for issue, all EPS numbers are adjusted.

In addition, all EPS numbers are also adjusted for any effects or errors or changes in accounting policies accounted for retrospectively.[13]

Situation

The following information pertains to Devlin Inc.
  Profit and loss for the year: $100
  Average market price of share during the year: $20
  Outstanding:

- 10 preferred convertible cumulative shares with $5 dividend rights per share per annum. The shares are convertible to 105 ordinary shares
- 50 preferred shares, non-cumulative dividend rights of $1 per share, not declared
- 100 ordinary shares outstanding all year
- 10 purchased options to buy 10 shares for $10 each
- 10 written options to buy 10 shares for $10 each

Calculate BEPS and DEPS.

Analysis

BEPS:
  Earnings = $100 − $50 = $50
  The non-cumulative dividends are ignored because they have not yet been declared.
  Weighted average common shares = 100
  BEPS = $50/100 = $.50

DEPS:

1. Identify potential ordinary shares.

  Convertible preferred shares
  Purchased options—although these are potential common shares, they are not included in the analysis since they are anti-dilutive by definition.
  Written options

2. Assume that the potential ordinary shares will be converted/exercised at the beginning of the period.

---

[13] IASCF, IAS 33.64 and 33.65.

Since the preferred shares and options were outstanding all year, there is no need to pro-rate the calculation.

3. Calculate the incremental impact of conversion/exercise.

Convertible preferred shares: $50 dividends avoided divided by 105 additional shares = $.48 and therefore potentially dilutive since it is less than BEPS.
Options: $0 impact on numerator divided by 10 additional shares = dilutive.

4. Rank from most dilutive to least dilutive

Options are the most dilutive and preferred shares are the least dilutive.

5. Starting with earnings and weighted average shares from BEPS, add back the incremental impact of each individual potential common share starting with the most dilutive. Recalculate the interim DEPS after each add back to see if it is still less than BEPS and declining.

	Income available to ordinary shareholders	Weighted average ordinary shares	EPS
BEPS	$50	100	$.50
Options	0	10	
Subtotal	$50	110	.45
Preferred shares	50	105	
Subtotal	$100	215	.48

6. DEPS should be the lowest number if profits exist (or highest if losses exist).

DEPS is therefore $.45 and the preferred shares are anti-dilutive in the end.

PRESENTATION

According to IAS 33, the entity must disclose the EPS numbers (with comparatives) in the statement of comprehensive income. If a separate profit and loss statement is presented, the EPS numbers are presented there. If discontinued operations are reported, the BEPS and DEPS for discontinued operations may be presented on the statement of comprehensive income or in the notes. Illustration 27-6 is an excerpt from the financial statements of Heineken NV.[14]

Heineken is a leading international brewery that is headquartered in the Netherlands. The company reports in euros.

Illustration 27-6 Presentation of EPS Information in the 2007 Financial Statements of Heineken NV	Weighted average number of shares – basic	23	489,353,315	489,712,594
	Weighted average number of shares – diluted	23	489,974,594	489,974,594
	Basic earnings per share €	23	1.65	2.47
	Diluted earnings per share €	23	1.65	2.47

[14] http://www.annualreport.heineken.com/downloads/Heineken_AnnualReport_EN_07.pdf

DISCLOSURE

IAS 33 requires the following additional disclosures:

- numerators in the calculations, including a reconciliation to reported profit or loss;
- the weighted average number of ordinary shares;
- any potentially dilutive instruments that were not included in the calculation; and
- a description of any transactions occurring after the reporting period that could affect the calculations, such as the issue or redemption of shares.

In some cases, an entity may decide to include additional per share amounts using other reported components from the statement of comprehensive income. Additional disclosures are required in this case, according to IAS 33.73 and 33.73A.

Illustration 27-7 is an excerpt from the financial statements of Heineken NV showing how EPS might be disclosed under the standard.

*Illustration 27-7
Disclosures
Related to EPS
Information
in the 2007
Financial
Statements of
Heineken NV*

23. Earnings per share
Basic earnings per share
The calculation of basic earnings per share as at 31 December 2007 is based on the profit attributable to ordinary shareholders of the Company (net profit) of €807 million (2006: €1,211 million) and a weighted average number of ordinary shares – basic outstanding during the year ended 31 December 2007 of 489,353,315 (2006: 489,712,594).

Basic earnings per share for the year amounts to €1.65 (2006: €2.47).

Weighted average number of shares – basic

In thousands of shares	2007	2006
Number of shares – basic – as at 1 January	489,564,594	489,974,594
Effect of own shares held	(211,279)	(262,000)
Weighted average number of shares – basic – as at 31 December	**489,353,315**	489,712,594

Diluted earnings per share
The calculation of diluted earnings per share as at 31 December 2007 was based on the profit attributable to ordinary shareholders of the Company (net profit) of €807 million (2006: €1,211 million) and a weighted average number of ordinary shares – basic outstanding after adjustment for the effects of all dilutive potential ordinary shares of 489,974,594 (2006: 489,974,594). Diluted earnings per share for the year amounted to €1.65 (2006: €2.47).

LOOKING AHEAD

The IASB and FASB are currently studying EPS as part of their joint convergence project. The objective of the work being done on EPS is to converge and simplify the accounting. As a result, discussions have taken place and the following have been proposed:

- the use of end of period market prices in calculating DEPS, as well as the carrying amount of any liabilities not remeasured at fair value; and

> - in calculating DEPS, and regarding financial instruments accounted for at fair value through profit or loss, that the profit or loss from changes in fair value remain in the numerator and that the denominator not include the incremental impact of additional shares.
>
> An Exposure Draft is expected to be issued in late 2008 to allow for discussion of the above and other alternatives that could lead to convergence and harmonization.

END-OF-CHAPTER PRACTICE

27-1 EPS numbers are generally based on profit and loss. An alternative would be to base the EPS calculations on comprehensive income.

Instructions

Discuss.

27-2 EPS Limited has 1,000 ordinary shares at the beginning of the year. During the year, the following transactions occur:

- The entity acquired another entity in return for issuing 100 shares. The shares were issued on July 15 and the date of acquisition is June 30.
- The entity entered into a side agreement related to the above under which the entity would issue an additional 10 shares if the earnings of the acquired company exceeded $100 in each of the two subsequent years. It is now the end of the first year and the earnings of the acquired company are $105.
- The entity repurchased and retired 15 of its ordinary shares on September 30.

Instructions

Calculate the weighted average number of common shares.

27-3 Assume the same information as in 27-2, as well as the following:

EPS Limited had earnings of $10,000 during the year. There are preferred shares outstanding with cumulative dividend rights. The dividends for the year are $1,100 and have not yet been declared. In addition, the entity has financial instruments outstanding with non-cumulative dividends of $700 (declared). These instruments were presented as financial liabilities in the financial statements.

The company purchased put options allowing it to sell 100 of its shares for $12 per share. The average market price of the shares during the year is $10. In addition, it also issued 100 call options giving the holder the right to buy shares for $7.

Under the terms of convertible debt, the holder of the debt can convert the debt into 150 ordinary shares. If converted, approximately $1,000 worth of after-tax interest would be avoided.

Instructions

Calculate the BEPS and DEPS.

27-4 In this chapter, flag icons identify areas where there are GAAP differences between IFRS requirements and national standards.

Instructions

Access the website(s) identified on the inside back cover of this book, and prepare a concise summary of the differences that are flagged throughout the chapter.

Chapter 28

Interim Financial Reporting: IAS 34

U.S. GAAP Reference
APB 28 Interim Financial Reporting

Related IFRS
NA

OBJECTIVE AND SCOPE

Annual reports are often supplemented with interim or quarterly reports, which provide more relevant and timely information. IAS 34 does not address how often nor how soon after the period entities should produce interim reports. Interim reporting is often mandated by securities regulators, governments, and stock exchanges. Having said this, the IASB encourages entities whose shares are publicly traded to provide interim information in accordance with IAS 34 at least as of the end of the first half of the year and issue it within 60 days of this date.[1]

The entity may choose not to prepare interim financial statements at all or in accordance with IFRSs, but if they do and they describe the financial statements to be in compliance with IFRSs, the standard would apply.

According to IAS 34.4, an *interim financial report* is defined as follows:

. . . a financial report containing either a complete set of financial statements (as described in IAS 1 *Presentation of Financial Statements* [as revised in 2007]) or a set of condensed financial statements (as described in this Standard) for an interim period.

Appendices A, B, and C, which accompany the standard, give numerous examples and clarifications; however, they are not technically part of the standard itself.

---

[1] IASCF, IAS 34.1.

CONTENT OF AN INTERIM FINANCIAL REPORT

The goal of interim reporting is to provide information about new events and circumstances and other changes, not to replicate the information given in the annual financial statements. Therefore, although the standard does not prohibit including a complete set of financial statements, the goal is to focus on incremental and updated information.[2] It is assumed that users will also have access to the most recent annual statements. The minimum requirements mandated by the standard are noted below.

Minimum Components of an Interim Financial Report

At a minimum, IAS 34 requires the following condensed statements:

- statement of financial position
- statement of comprehensive income (This may be presented as a single statement or a separate income statement plus a statement of comprehensive income. If the latter is presented in the annual statements, then it would be presented in the interim statements as well.)
- statement of changes in equity
- statement of cash flows

In addition, selected explanatory notes must accompany the above.

Form and Content of Interim Financial Statements

Under IAS 34, if the entity presents a full set of statements, it follows IAS 1.[3] If it presents condensed statements, the entity must present at a minimum the headings and subtotals that were presented in the annual statements.[4] Basic and diluted earnings per share are presented when the entity is covered by IAS 33. To promote comparability, the interim financial statements are based on consolidated statements where the most recent annual statements were prepared on a consolidated basis.

Selected Explanatory Notes

Given the emphasis on new and changing information, the explanatory notes should focus on this as well. Notes that are still relevant but have not changed from the annual report are not included since this is repetitive and will tend to obscure the new and more relevant information. Information is normally presented on a year-to-date basis. The following information would normally be disclosed if it is material:[5]

- A statement that the same accounting policies and method of computation as the annual report are followed.
- Explanatory comments about the seasonality/cyclicality of the business.
- Any unusual items (unusual due to nature, size, or incidence).
- Nature and amount of changes in estimates.
- Changes in debt and equity securities (issue, repurchase, repayment).
- Dividends paid.
- Segmented information including
  - revenues from external customers;
  - intersegment revenues;

---

[2] IASCF, IAS 34.6 and 34.7.
[3] IASCF, IAS 34.9.
[4] IASCF, IAS 34.10.
[5] IASCF, IAS 34.16.

     o segment profit/loss;
     o total assets, where there has been a material change;
     o a description of differences in the basis of segmentation/measurement;
     o reconciliation of segments' profit/loss to total profit/loss before discontinued operations and taxes. Material reconciling items should be listed.

- Material subsequent events.
- Effect of changes due to business combinations, changes in ownership of subsidiaries, long-term investments, discontinued operations, restructurings, and others.
- Changes in contingent assets/liabilities

Disclosure of Compliance with IFRSs

If the financial statements are prepared in compliance with IFRSs, this should be stated and the interim statements must also be in compliance with all IFRSs.

Periods for Which Interim Financial Statements Are Required to Be Presented

Which statements are required to be presented? Illustration 28-1 outlines which statements are presented under the standard.

Illustration 28-1 Interim Financial Statements to Be Presented Under IAS 34	**Statement**	**As at /for current interim period plus comparatives**	**Cumulative from beginning of year plus comparatives**[6]
	Financial Position	Yes (prior year end comparative)	NA
	Comprehensive Income (may present a single statement or two separate statements, including a separate statement of profit or loss)	Yes	Yes
	Changes in Equity	No	Yes
	Cash Flows	No	Yes

Materiality

Materiality is discussed in IAS 1 and 8, although there is no specific quantitative guidance. In addition to references in these standards, IAS 34 notes that materiality for interim statements should be assessed based on the interim period. Note that interim financials statements may have additional estimates and therefore the numbers may be a bit softer.

---

[6] Where the business is highly seasonal, it may present 12-month cumulative statements and/or additional information that expresses the seasonal/cyclical nature.

DISCLOSURE IN ANNUAL FINANCIAL STATEMENTS

Situations may arise where estimates are changed in the last quarter or final interim period. Where final interim period statements are not separately presented and where the change is significant, the nature and amount of change in estimate should be disclosed in the annual statements. The standard goes on to cross reference and link this to IAS 8, which requires disclosure of the nature and amount of material changes in estimates.

RECOGNITION AND MEASUREMENT

Same Accounting Policies as Annual

In order to encourage consistency, the entity is required to use the same accounting policies as in the year-end statements. Where there has been a subsequent change in accounting policies, the entity would use the newer policy. In general, each period is viewed as a discrete period with some exceptions, which take the view that the period is an integral period. The discrete approach treats the interim period as a separate and self-standing period. The integral approach treats it as part of the annual period (i.e., as a portion of a larger period). This has implications for recognition and measurement. For instance, if the interim period is seen as part of the annual period, it might make sense to allocate the annual costs to each period. However, if it is seen as a discrete period, the entity would recognize only costs incurred during that period.

Illustration 28-2 summarizes this somewhat dispersed view of the approach.

	Discrete	Integral
Illustration 28-2 Discrete Versus Integral Approach?	IAS 34.36 does not allow subsequent restatements of interim periods. Each period must stand on its own.	The interim statements are viewed as part of a larger time frame.
	Assets, liabilities, income, and expenses must all meet the definitions as articulated in IFRSs as at the end of the interim period. Only information at that date is used to make the decision. There is no "looking forward" to see if the definitions will be met at year end. A cost that does not meet the definition of an asset is not treated as one in the interim period.	IAS 34.28 notes that the annual financial statements should not be different just because of the frequency of interim reporting.
	No smoothing of costs is allowed (IAS 34.30).	The tax rate looks to the 12-month period (best estimate of weighted average annual rate expected for the year) as per IAS 34.30.
		Year-to-date estimates are continually revised as per IAS 34.29.

Thus the statement has a bit of a mixed approach.

Applying the Recognition and Measurement Principles

Appendix B to the standard includes numerous examples, which provide some additional guidance. Illustration 28-3 recaps some of these examples.

Illustration 28-3
Examples of
Applying IAS 34

Transaction	Accounting treatment	Approach
Employer taxes	If they are assessed on an annual basis, estimate the average annual rate and allocate it (even though they may be paid in the early part of the year).	Integral
Planned maintenance or overhaul	Do not accrue unless a legal or constructive obligation exists.	Discrete
Provisions	Do not accrue unless a legal or constructive obligation exists.	Discrete
Bonuses	Do not accrue unless a legal or constructive obligation exists.	Discrete
Contingent lease payments, e.g., based on sales	May have to accrue. If it is probable that certain sales levels will be met by the end of the year, resulting in additional lease payments, a legal or constructive obligation may exist.	Discrete (obligation must exist)/Integral (consider annual sales)
Expenditures that may result in intangibles	Do not capitalize unless the definition of an asset is met at the end of the interim period.	Discrete
Discretionary costs, e.g., charitable donations	Do not accrue unless a legal or constructive obligation exists. An entity is not allowed to allocate expected costs.	Discrete

Revenues Received Seasonally, Cyclically, or Occasionally

Revenues are recognized when they occur or are earned, notwithstanding their cyclical or seasonal nature. This may result in more revenues being recognized in one period than in another, but that reflects the underlying reality. This supports the discrete approach.

Costs Incurred Unevenly During the Financial Year

Costs are recognized when incurred as previously discussed and only capitalized when they meet the definition of an asset. This also supports the discrete approach.

Use of Estimates

It is important to note that out of necessity, more estimates need to be made in an interim period (the shorter the period, the more estimates). An entity needs to communicate this. In addition, it must take care to ensure that the information is relevant and reliable. What is a reasonable estimate for an interim period? What evidence is needed to support these estimates? Illustration 28-4 takes a look at these issues. These and other examples are outlined in Appendix C to the standard.

Illustration 28-4
Use of Estimates and Evidence to Support Them

Financial statement element	Best evidence	Acceptable evidence for interim reporting
Inventory	Inventory count and valuation	Estimates based on sales margins
Provisions	Outside experts/specialists	Update/roll forward from annual estimate
Pension obligations	Measured by actuary	Extrapolation of the most recent actuarial valuation
Taxes payable/receivable	Calculate by looking at rates and amounts for each separate jurisdiction	Use the weighted average rate across jurisdictions or categories of income as long as the rate is a reasonable approximation of the actual rates
Legal liabilities	Legal counsel/formal reports	Formal reports/counsel may not be needed

Note the amount of judgment required in assessing the quality and amount of evidence to ensure reliable and relevant reporting.

RESTATEMENT OF PREVIOUSLY REPORTED INTERIM PERIODS

Where there is a change in accounting policy, the comparative interim information must be restated or, where it is impracticable to determine the cumulative impact, the change would be applied from the earliest date practicable.[7]

LOOKING AHEAD

This topic will be dealt with in Phase C of the Financial Statement Presentation project, which has not yet begun. According to the FASB website, topics include the following:

1. Which, if any, financial statements should be required in an interim financial report.
2. Whether entities should be allowed to present the financial statements in an interim financial report in a condensed format; if so, whether the Boards should provide guidance on how to condense the information.
3. What comparative periods, if any, should be required or allowed in interim financial reports, and when, if ever, should 12-month-to-date financial statements be required or allowed in interim financial reports.
4. Whether guidance for non-public companies should differ from guidance for public companies.

---

[7] IASCF 34.43.

END-OF-CHAPTER PRACTICE

28-1 Two approaches for dealing with interim financial reporting are introduced in this chapter—discrete and integral.

Instructions
Do some research and discuss the relative merits of each. Which approach/approaches does the IFRS take? Discuss.

28-2 Interim Inc. has the following outstanding at the end of the interim period:
- The company is being sued. At this point, the company has been served legal papers but has not yet incurred any costs. Management has not yet discussed the status with the company's lawyers.
- The company has a pension plan outstanding. An actuarial evaluation of the liability was done at year end. It is now the end of the second quarter.
- A major overhaul of fixed assets is planned for the third quarter. The company has engaged outside engineers to do this, but a contract with them has not yet been signed.

Instructions
Discuss the issues related to preparing the interim financial statements.

28-3 Green and Green Accountants is retraining its entire staff to bring them up to speed with IFRSs. The costs are substantial and are incurred in the first quarter. It would like to spread the costs over the year since they will benefit the entire year.

Instructions
Assuming that the entity prepares first quarter statements, discuss the issues.

28-4 In this chapter, flag icons identify areas where there are GAAP differences between IFRS requirements and national standards.

Instructions
Access the website(s) identified on the inside back cover of this book, and prepare a concise summary of the differences that are flagged throughout the chapter.

Chapter 29

Share-based Payment: IFRS 2

U.S. GAAP Reference
FAS 123 Share-based Payment

Related IFRS
NA

OBJECTIVE AND SCOPE

IFRS 2 deals with transactions where equity instruments are used as consideration. The issue is one of recognition as well as measurement. Entities must recognize these types of transactions, and if they create liabilities, the liabilities must be remeasured after the transaction date. Appendix A is an integral part of the standard and contains definitions. Appendix B is also an integral part of the standard and contains application guidance. The Basis for Conclusion document is substantial, which speaks not only to the complexity of the standard itself and related issues in application, but also to the nature of the transactions. The standard also includes a significant number of illustrative examples. Much of this complexity is beyond the scope of this book. This chapter seeks to present an overview of the issues and basic calculations.

Examples of share-based payment transactions include

- remunerative option plans such as employee stock options plans,
- acquisitions where shares are used as consideration, and
- situations where services are paid for with equity instruments.

Accounting for employee remuneration plans is where much of the complexity arises. These plans often span numerous reporting periods and the cost to the entity may be very difficult to measure depending on the terms of the plans.

The standard puts all share-based transactions into three categories. The definitions for the first two categories follow:[1]

equity-settled share-based payment transaction	"A share-based payment transaction in which the entity receives goods or services as consideration for equity instruments of the entity (including shares or share options)."
cash-settled share-based payment transaction	"A share-based payment transaction in which the entity acquires goods or services by incurring a liability to transfer cash or other assets to the supplier of those goods or services for amounts that are based on the price (or value) of the entity's shares or other equity instruments of the entity."

The third category is a share-based payment transaction where there is a choice to settle in cash or equity. Either the entity has the option to determine whether to settle the transaction in cash or equity, or the counterparty (the other party to the contract) has this option. The third category is therefore subdivided into two parts.

Share-based payment transactions are defined as follows:

A transaction in which the entity receives goods or services as consideration for equity instruments of the entity (including shares or share options), or acquires goods or services by incurring liabilities to the supplier of those goods or services for amounts that are based on the price of the entity's shares or other equity instruments of the entity.

Transactions with employees are treated a bit differently. Situations where the employee is dealing with the entity in his/her role as a shareholder (i.e., buying and selling equity instruments) would not be covered by IFRS 2.[2] Furthermore, when the transaction in question is a business combination, it is covered by IFRS 3. Contracts to buy or sell non-financial items that can be settled net are covered by IAS 32 and IAS 39. Equity instruments were previously defined in earlier chapters and include common shares and certain options.

Illustration 29-1 provides an overview of the various categories of share-based payment transactions. Each of these categories has its own challenges for accounting purposes.

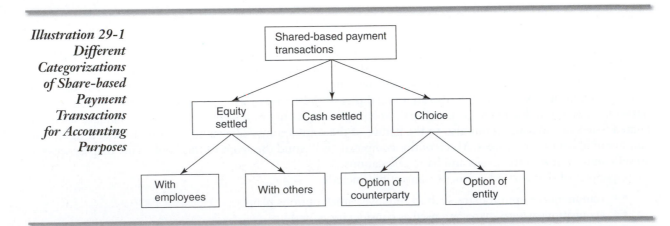

Illustration 29-1 Different Categorizations of Share-based Payment Transactions for Accounting Purposes

---

[1] IASCF, IFRS 2, Appendix A.
[2] IASCF, IFRS 2.4.

This chapter will walk through the various categories identifying the accounting issues and the accounting.

RECOGNITION

In general, the standard requires that the transaction be recognized when the goods are received or services rendered.[3] The credit is booked to equity in an equity-settled transaction and the liability in a cash-settled transaction. The debit is booked to expense or asset (if the definition of an asset is met).

EQUITY-SETTLED SHARE-BASED PAYMENT TRANSACTIONS

Overview

For equity-settled transactions, the transaction is measured at the fair value of the goods or services received. If the fair value cannot be reliably measured, then the fair value of the equity instrument is used.[4] In general, there is a rebuttable presumption that the fair value of the goods and services may be reliably measured.[5] This means that in most cases, the fair value of the equity instruments would not be used.

An exception to this is where the transaction involves employees rendering services. These transactions are measured by reference to the fair value of the equity instruments since it may be too difficult to measure the services, especially if the equity instruments are given to the employee as part of the compensation/remuneration package for services normally rendered as an employee.

Transactions in Which Services Are Received

The accounting might be affected by the vesting provisions. Many share-based transactions such as options have conditions attached to them, which must be met before the counterparty has legal entitlement to them. Legal entitlement is referred to as **vesting.**

If the equity instruments vest upfront (i.e., the counterparty is legally entitled to the equity instruments) when the contract is entered into, then the entity assumes that the services have already been provided and recognizes the full amount of the transaction at that date. If the equity instruments vest over time, the transaction is accrued and recognized over time.

> **Situation**
>
> Alice Feng has been granted stock options as part of her remuneration package (in lieu of salary). The options allow Alice to acquire 100 shares of the company for a fixed amount. The options are worth $100 and vest immediately. The options may not be net settled. How would the entity granting these options account for them?
>
> **Analysis**
>
> The options meet the definitions of share-based payment transactions. Under the terms of the arrangement, the entity will issue equity instruments and the employees will provide services for this right. For Alice, since the options vest immediately, she has earned them, and the entity will recognize the full amount at the fair value of the equity

---

[3] IASCF, IFRS 2.7.
[4] IFRS 2.10 actually says the transaction is measured indirectly by reference to the fair value of the equity instruments granted (which is essentially the same thing).
[5] IASCF, IFRS 2.13.

> instruments, or $100. Since the options do not have a net settlement feature, they are not accounted for as derivatives under IAS 32 and 39. The following journal entry would be booked.
>
>   Dr. Expense $100
>   Cr. Equity—stock options $100
>
> The options are measured at the grant date and not subsequently remeasured.

Where the options are granted conditional upon the employee achieving certain goals (or there are other conditions attached to the transactions) and the vesting period is also conditional upon achieving those goals, the entity must estimate the vesting period in order to calculate the amount of expense to recognize in each period.

This estimate may be revised in a subsequent period as a change in estimate. However, there is one exception if the condition is a market condition (such as the shares reaching a certain price), in which case no subsequent revision is allowed. This is because the market would have already included expectations about the future share price into the current share price.[6]

Transactions Measured by Reference to the Fair Value of the Equity Instruments Granted

Determining the Fair Value of Equity Instruments Granted

The fair value is estimated as at the measurement date based on market conditions and prices. The measurement date is generally the grant date, as defined below for transactions with employees. The grant date is generally the date that the contract is agreed to by both parties. For other transactions, the measurement date is the date that the goods are received or the services rendered.

The standard defines measurement and grant dates as follows:

measurement date	The date at which the fair value of the equity instruments granted is measured for the purposes of this IFRS. For transactions with employees and others providing similar services, the measurement date is grant date. For transactions with parties other than employees (and those providing similar services), the measurement date is the date the entity obtains the goods or the counterparty renders service.
grant date	The date at which the entity and another party (including an employee) agree to a share-based payment arrangement, being when the entity and the counterparty have a shared understanding of the terms and conditions of the arrangement. At grant date the entity confers on the counterparty the right to cash, other assets, or equity instruments of the entity, provided the specified vesting conditions, if any, are met. If that agreement is subject to an approval process (for example, by shareholders), grant date is the date when that approval is obtained.

If market prices are not available, then an entity may use a valuation technique/method.[7]

---

[6] IFRS 2.15(b).
[7] IFRS 2.17 goes on to say that the technique should be generally accepted and consistent with pricing financial instruments. An options pricing model would suffice where options are involved. Appendix B to the standard goes into a significant amount of detail regarding measurement.

If the equity instruments are publicly traded shares, then market values are available. If they are stock options, market values may or may not be available. For instance, options granted to employees often have more favorable terms than those granted to others and therefore may not be directly comparable to regular options that are available to all investors. Options pricing models are valuation techniques that are often used. Examples include the Black Scholes and binomial models. Monte Carlo simulations are also used to estimate the value. These models/simulations are explained in Finance texts. An entity may choose the model that provides the most useful information and does not need to use the same model for different transactions. These models should take into account at least the following inputs:[8]

(a) exercise price,
(b) life of the option,
(c) current price of the shares,
(d) expected volatility of the share price,
(e) dividends expected on the shares, and
(f) risk-free interest rate.

The volatility of the shares refers to how much the share price fluctuates in the marketplace. A problem arises when dealing with instruments that are not market-traded and this adds additional measurement uncertainty. In this case, entities would take into account other factors including volatility of similar instruments or similar entities.

Treatment of Vesting Conditions

As previously mentioned, there may be certain conditions attached to the transaction that must be met before the counterparty or employee has legal entitlement (i.e., before the instruments vest). An example of this is where employees have to remain with the entity for a predetermined period before they are entitled to exercise their stock options. Another example is where additional shares/options may be issued if certain performance criteria are met (e.g., target sales numbers). At the grant date, the transaction is recognized and measured but the vesting conditions are not factored into the measurement. After the grant date, the transaction is remeasured for the change in the number of equity instruments due to the conditions being met/not met, but not for the fair value of the equity instrument itself. Subsequent remeasurements are treated as a change in estimate in subsequent periods.

Where the vesting condition is a market condition, e.g., a target share price, this is taken into account at the measurement date and the transaction is not subsequently remeasured, as previously noted.[9]

Situation

Assume that a separate group of employees has also been granted the same options as Alice (in the earlier situation). Their options vest over the next 10 years. In other words, there is a condition attached to these options that states the employees must remain with the entity in order to have legal entitlement to the options. The fair value at inception is $1,000.

Analysis

At the end of the first year, the entity would recognize only an expense of $100. The transaction is measured based on the fair value of the options at the grant date. Subsequently, the entity may adjust the numbers but only for forfeitures (number of share/options). At the end of 10 years, the transaction reflects only the number of instruments actually issued/settled. For instance, at the end of year 2, if the entity assumes that only 90% of the employees will stay, the expense in the second year will be $1,000 × 90% × 2/10 years = 180. Since it has already recognized $100, it would recognize only $80 as expense in year 2.

---

[8] IASCF, IFRS 2, B6.
[9] IASCF, IFRS 2.19–2.21. This approach whereby some transactions are remeasured and some are not (depending on market conditions) is sometimes referred to as the modified grant date method.

Treatment of Non-vesting Conditions

Uncertainty might also be introduced with non-vesting conditions, e.g., the equity instrument might already be vested; however, the number of equity instruments to be issued might vary depending on some future event. In these cases, the transaction is recognized and measured at the grant date, as in the situation above, and the uncertainty is factored in at that point. There is no remeasurement after the vesting date.

Treatment of a Reload Feature

The contract may allow the entity to automatically issue new options when an old one is exercised using shares to satisfy the exercise price. These are treated as new option grants and reload features are not taken into account when estimating fair value.[10]

After Vesting Date

After initial recognition upon vesting (in accordance with the above), equity-settled transactions are not remeasured even if the equity instruments are forfeited. However, the entity may transfer amounts from one category of equity to another.

If the Fair Value of the Equity Instrument Cannot Be Reliably Estimated

Where the entity is required to measure the transaction at the fair value of the equity instruments but is unable to because the fair value is not reliably measurable, it may use the intrinsic value. The *intrinsic value* is defined in IFRS 2 Appendix A as follows:

> The difference between the fair value of the shares to which the counterparty has the (conditional or unconditional) right to subscribe or which it has the right to receive, and the price (if any) the counterparty is (or will be) required to pay for those shares. For example, a share option with an exercise price of CU15, on a share with a fair value of CU20, has an intrinsic value of CU5.

In this case, the transaction continues to be remeasured until the equity instrument is settled/exercised (or forfeited or lapses/expires). Costs related to forfeitures after the vesting date would be reversed. This is different from where fair value is used to value the instruments. As previously noted, the estimated fair value (used to measure the transaction) would already take into account the expected forfeitures. The intrinsic method does not take this into account upfront and therefore the transaction must be subsequently adjusted.

Modifications to the Terms and Conditions

If the equity instrument is modified afterwards (for instance, the entity changes the exercise price on an employee stock option plan), and the total fair value of the transaction is increased, then this additional amount is recognized. If the entity cancels or settles the grant of the equity instrument during the vesting period, it treats this as an acceleration of the vesting period and, thus, recognizes all remaining amounts.

Any cash payments are treated as a repurchase of equity (deducted from equity). The only exception is where the payment is greater than the fair value of the equity instruments granted; this excess is charged to expense. Additional guidance is provided where new or replacement equity instruments are granted.[11]

---

[10] IASCF, IFRS 2.22.
[11] IASCF, IFRS 2.28.

CASH-SETTLED SHARE-BASED PAYMENT TRANSACTIONS

Where the transaction will eventually be settled in cash, a liability is recognized and the transaction is measured at the fair value of the liability at the measurement date (grant date or the date that the entity receives the goods/services). For transactions involving options/share appreciation rights (SARs) the fair value of the liability is measured at the fair value of the options/SAR.[12]

The liability is subsequently remeasured at every reporting date.[13] Additional expenses/income due to the remeasurement are booked to profit and loss. They are not linked to the cost of goods or services, i.e., the cost of goods or services themselves are not remeasured. For example, if the transaction is related to the acquisition of inventory, the carrying value of the inventory would not be adjusted when the liability is remeasured.[14]

SARs are an example of cash-settled share-based transactions. Under this type of contract, an employee is granted a certain number of rights as remuneration for services. The rights allow the employee to be paid the excess of the market value of a share over a certain base price. The excess may be paid in cash (which is most often the case) or in shares.

Situation

Jason Pueblo works for Passo Limited and was recently granted 10 SARs as part of his remuneration package. Under the terms of the agreement, for each SAR, Jason has the right to receive cash equal to the difference between the market value of an ordinary share of Passo and $10 (the base price used to calculate the payout under the SAR). At the grant date, the SARs are valued at $21 using an option pricing model. The SARs vest over a three-year period.

Analysis

At the end of the year, the SARs are measured at the fair value of the SAR. Since the SARs are unique to the company and the employees, a market value may not be available and therefore a valuation technique such as an option pricing model may be used. Since the SARs vest over three years, only one third would be booked. The following entry would be booked at the grant date:

Dr. Expense	$7	
Cr. Liability		7

At the end of subsequent years, the liability would be continued to be remeasured to reflect the fair value of the SARs and the difference would be expensed over the remaining period. If the SARs vested upon grant date, the full amount would be booked at grant date and revised until paid out ($21 would be booked by the end of year 1).

This accounting may be inconsistent with IAS 32 in cases where the SAR may be settled in shares (according to the terms of the SAR).[15] Under IFRS 2, if the SAR is to be settled with shares (i.e., a variable number of shares), it is accounted for as equity (it is categorized as an equity-settled share-based transaction). As an equity-settled share-based transaction, the SAR would be accounted for under IFRS 2 as follows:

- measured at the fair value of the SAR at the grant date,
- credited to equity, and
- not subsequently remeasured after vesting date.

Under IAS 32, if the number of shares is variable, the instrument would be accounted for as a liability.

---

[12] IASCF, IFRS 2.33.
[13] IASCF, IFRS 2.30.
[14] IASCF, IFRS 2.IG19.
[15] IASB concluded that this was part of the larger issue of defining liabilities versus equities and would be studied further with the project on financial instruments.

SHARE-BASED PAYMENT TRANSACTIONS WITH CASH ALTERNATIVES

If the transaction creates a liability by definition, then the transaction is accounted for as a cash-settled transaction. Otherwise, it is measured as an equity-settled transaction. The accounting depends on who has the option to determine how it will be settled—the counterparty or the entity. This will be examined below.

Share-based Payment Transactions in Which the Terms of the Arrangement Provide the Counterparty with a Choice of Settlement

Where the counterparty has the option to dictate settlement, it is beyond the control of the entity and therefore a liability may exist. In reality, this is a compound instrument—part debt (the right to demand payment in cash) and part equity (the right to demand payment in shares).[16]

For transactions other than with employees and where the entire transaction is measured at fair value of the goods/services, the equity component is the difference between the total transaction value and fair value of the debt component.[17]

For other transactions, where the equity instrument is used to value the transaction, the following steps are taken:[18]

- measure fair value of debt component; and
- measure the equity component (considering that the entity must forfeit the right to the shares if the counterparty exercises the option to be paid in cash).

As an added complexity, the entity must split the transaction into two parts—the debt part and the equity part. The debit side of the journal entry, i.e., the expense, is also split into two parts. The debt part is accounted for as a cash-settled transaction and the equity part as an equity-settled transaction.[19]

Share-based Payment Transactions in Which the Terms of the Arrangement Provide the Entity with a Choice of Settlement

Where the entity has the choice of settlement options, the entity determines whether it has a liability (a present obligation to settle in cash). Where the choice has no commercial substance (e.g., the entity may not issue shares, or has a history of settling these transactions in cash, or there is no market for the shares so the entity has a history of buying the shares back), then a liability exists. The transaction is accounted for as a cash-settled transaction. Otherwise, it is accounted for as an equity-settled transaction.[20]

If the entity assumes equity settlement and subsequently settles in cash, this is treated as a share buyback or repurchase of an equity interest (debit equity), unless the settlement alternative is the one with the higher fair value, in which case the excess is booked as expense.

---

[16] IAS 32 describes instruments that are puttable (i.e., where the holder has the right to put the instruments to the entity for cash or other assets) as liabilities. In reality, as discussed in IAS 32, AG 25, the instrument contains a liability and therefore may also contain an equity component. This is the view taken by IFRS 2.

[17] IASCF, IFRS 2.35.

[18] IASCF, IFRS 2.37.

[19] IASCF, IFRS 2.37–2.40.

[20] IASCF, IFRS 2.41 and 2.42.

SUMMARY

Illustration 29-2 summarizes these complex rules and principles.

Illustration 29-2
Summary of
Accounting
Treatment for
Share-based
Payment
Transactions

Type of instrument	Equity-settled	Cash-settled	Choice (option of entity or counterparty)
Measurement	Fair value of goods/ services unless not reliably estimable, then fair value of equity instruments.	Fair value of equity instrument (e.g., an option or SAR). Must be continuously remeasured.	If liability exists, see cash-settled column. If there is no liability, see equity-settled column. A compound instrument, part debt and part equity, must be bifurcated and accounted for as such.
Exceptions	Where services are provided by employees, measure considering the fair value of equity instrument.	SARs that are settled in a variable number of shares are accounted for as equity-settled.	See equity- and cash-settled columns.
Fair value	The fair value of equity instruments granted is based on market prices. If no market prices are available, use the valuation method.	The fair value is based on the market value of the equity instrument, which should approximate the cash-settled value of the liability at settlement date. The entity may need to use valuation method.	See equity- and cash-settled columns.
Measurement date	At the date the entity obtains goods or the counterparty renders service for others. At the grant date for employees. However, where non-market vesting conditions exist, the entity may continue to remeasure for the number of equity instruments until fully vested.	At the date the entity obtains goods or the counterparty renders service for others. At the grant date for employees. However, where non-market vesting conditions exist, the entity may continue to remeasure for the number of equity instruments until fully vested. See also below.	See equity- and cash-settled columns.

Type of instrument	Equity-settled	Cash-settled	Choice (option of entity or counterparty)
Subsequent remeasurement?	No remeasurement after vested.	The entity must continue to remeasure until the instrument is settled since a liability exists. The income/expense is recognized in the profit or loss statement.	See equity- and cash-settled columns.

DISCLOSURES

In general, the entity must disclose sufficient information for the users to understand the nature and extent of these transactions and the impact on the profit or loss statement. Specifically, IFRS 2.45 requires the following:

(a) a description of each type of share-based payment arrangement that existed at any time during the period, including the general terms and conditions of each arrangement, such as vesting requirements, the maximum term of options granted, and the method of settlement (e.g., whether in cash or equity). An entity with substantially similar types of share-based payment arrangements may aggregate this information, unless separate disclosure of each arrangement is necessary to satisfy the principle in paragraph 44.

(b) the number and weighted average exercise prices of share options for each of the following groups of options:

    (i)   outstanding at the beginning of the period,
    (ii)   granted during the period,
    (iii) forfeited during the period,
    (iv) exercised during the period,
    (v)   expired during the period,
    (vi) outstanding at the end of the period, and
    (vii) exercisable at the end of the period.

(c) for share options exercised during the period, the weighted average share price at the date of exercise. If options were exercised on a regular basis throughout the period, the entity may instead disclose the weighted average share price during the period.

(d) for share options outstanding at the end of the period, the range of exercise prices and weighted average remaining contractual life. If the range of exercise prices is wide, the outstanding options shall be divided into ranges that are meaningful for assessing the number and timing of additional shares that may be issued and the cash that may be received upon exercise of those options.

Additional disclosures relating to fair value measurements and the impact on the profit or loss statement are required.

LOOKING AHEAD

Because the standard is fairly new and largely converged with North American GAAP, there are no plans to alter or amend this standard in the near future.

END-OF-CHAPTER PRACTICE

29-1 Historically, employee stock option plans (where no cash was exchanged when the options were granted) were not recognized in the financial statements at all until the options were exercised. IFRS 2 was issued in 2004 and proposed full recognition. There was a considerable amount of discussion relating to this "controversy."

Instructions

Discuss the pros and cons of full recognition. Hint: The IFRS 2 Basis for Conclusion document has some excellent discussion points on this matter.

29-2 IFRS 2 has a measurement hierarchy of sorts, i.e., it stipulates how the transactions should be measured including default measures.

Instructions

Identify the various measurement options noting which are the primary ones and which are the default ones. Discuss the merits of each.

29-3 Accounting for SARs is covered by IFRS 2 (not IAS 32). Treatment of equity-settled SARs would differ, however, if one applied IFRS 2 versus IAS 32 (for SARs that are settled in a variable number of equity instruments).

Instructions

Discuss the two treatments providing support for both. Why does this difference exist? Should it be allowed to remain?

29-4 Hannibal Limited has two employee remuneration plans as follows:

Stock option plan—500 options granted in the current year. The options give the holder the right to purchase a share of the company for $10. The options vest over the next three years. The fair value at the grant date is $60.

SARs—400 SARs granted this year. The SARs give the holder the right to receive in cash the difference between the fair value of the shares at the exercise date and $5 (the base price). The fair value of the SARs is $1900 at grant date and $2000 at year-end. They vest over the next five years.

Instructions

Prepare the journal entries required for year 1. How would the plans be accounted for in subsequent years?

29-5 In this chapter, flag icons identify areas where there are GAAP differences between IFRS requirements and national standards.

Instructions

Access the website(s) identified on the inside back cover of this book, and prepare a concise summary of the differences that are flagged throughout the chapter.

Chapter 30

Investments in Associates: IAS 28

U.S. GAAP References
APB 18 The Equity Method of Accounting for Investments in Common Stock
FAS 159 The Fair Value Option for Financial Assets and Financial Liabilities

Related IFRSs
IAS 27 Consolidated and Separate Financial Statements
IAS 36 Impairment of Assets
IAS 39 Financial Instruments: Recognition and Measurement

OBJECTIVE AND SCOPE

IAS 28 sets out the accounting requirements for investments in associates, unless an entity is preparing separate financial statements under IAS 27 *Consolidated and Separate Financial Statements*. It defines an **associate** as an entity over which an investor has significant influence, but which is not a subsidiary or an interest in a joint venture. The entity may be an unincorporated organization such as a partnership.

Investments in associates held by venture capital organizations or mutual funds, unit trusts, and similar organizations are **excluded** from complying with this IFRS. These investments are accounted for at fair value through profit or loss under IAS 39 *Financial Instruments: Recognition and Measurement*.

Significant Influence and the Equity Method

Significant Influence

Investors with significant influence over the entities they have invested in are required to use the **equity method of accounting** for their associates as set out in this standard. *Significant influence* is the **power to take part**

in the financial and operating policy decisions of the investee, but not to the extent of having control or joint control.[1] ***Control*** is a higher level of power in which an investor can **govern** the financial and operating policies of the investee and through this **obtain benefits** from its activities.

It is presumed that an investor that holds, either directly or indirectly, between 20% and 50% of the voting power of another entity is **able to exercise significant influence**. If this presumption is not correct, or if significant influence exists with an interest below 20%, the entity has to clearly demonstrate why significant influence does not exist in the first instance or how it is exercised in the latter instance.

The ability to significantly influence the strategic decisions of another entity without control may be illustrated by

(a) having representation on its board or governing body;
(b) participating in policy-making processes, including decisions about distributions such as dividends;
(c) entering into significant transactions with the investee;
(d) exchanging managerial personnel; or
(e) providing necessary technical information.[2]

Having potential voting rights such as those that are related to share warrants, call options, and convertible securities is a factor in determining significant influence **if the rights are currently exercisable**. They are not considered if they rely on management's intentions or on the entity's financial ability to exercise or convert them.

Significant influence is lost when an entity no longer has the power to participate in the financial and operating decisions of the investee. Significant influence may be lost or obtained by factors other than a change in share ownership.

Equity Method

The ***equity method*** is a method of accounting for investments in which the investment, originally recognized at cost, is adjusted after acquisition for the investor's share of the post-acquisition changes in the investee's book value or net assets. The investor's share of the investee's profit or loss is recognized in the profit or loss of the investor.[3] Consistent with this approach, distributions from the investee reduce the carrying amount of the investment, and the investor's share of the transactions that directly affect the other comprehensive income and retained earnings of the investee are recognized in the same accounts of the investor.

The equity method provides much better information in the statement of comprehensive income about the investor's (and associate's) performance than recognizing the dividend received. Under the equity method, if the investor exercises influence that is beneficial to the investee, it recognizes the positive effect on the investee's profit in its own profit and loss. The receipt of dividends from an investee, however, says little about the investor or investee's performance in a period.

APPLICATION OF THE EQUITY METHOD

There are very few exceptions to applying the equity method for investments in associates. The three exceptions are the following:

1. if the investment is classified as held for sale and accounted for under IFRS 5 *Non-current Assets Held for Sale and Discontinued Operations*;
2. if the investor's parent company is exempt from preparing consolidated financial statements under paragraph 10 of IAS 27 *Consolidated and Separate Financial Statements* (see Chapter 32); or

---

[1] IASCF, IAS 28.2.
[2] IASCF, IAS 28.7.
[3] IASCF, IAS 28.2. The investor's share of the investee's profit or loss does not take into account any potential voting rights, only those that currently exist.

3.   if the investor itself meets **all** the same criteria in 2 above that exempt a parent from preparing consolidated statements. These conditions require that the entity does not have or is not in the process of issuing any publicly traded securities, that the investor either is a wholly owned subsidiary or a partially owned subsidiary whose other owners do not object to the non-use of the equity method, and that at least one parent of the investor prepares and issues GAAP financial statements that comply with IFRSs.

The equity method is often called **one-line consolidation**. This refers to the fact that the procedures used in the equity method are similar to the procedures used to account for the acquisition of a subsidiary and for the subsequent consolidation procedures in IAS 27 *Consolidated and Separate Financial Statements*. Both methods are concerned with accounting for the investments as part of the reporting entity rather than as passive holdings.

How does the equity method work?

At Acquisition

The equity method begins when an associate is acquired. The investor prepares an analysis of the purchase cost similar to the one carried out in a business combination. From this, the investor identifies any difference between the investor's cost and its share of the fair value of the associate's identifiable net assets at acquisition as **goodwill**. The goodwill is not recognized separately from the investment itself, but **it represents a portion of the investment's carrying amount**. It is not amortized. If the goodwill calculated is negative, it is recognized in the investor's profit or loss in the year of acquisition, as part of the investor's share of the associate's profit or loss for the period.

The analysis of the investment at acquisition also identifies situations in which the fair values of the investee's identifiable net assets differ from their carrying amounts in the investee's accounts. The difference between the fair values and the carrying amounts on the investee's books **explains another portion of the purchase cost of the investment**, at least to the extent of the investor's interest. The investor's share of this fair value difference has to be amortized as the underlying assets are realized and liabilities are settled by the associate. Illustration 30-1 provides an explanation of how these amounts are related to the investment account.

Illustration 30-1 Investment Account—Equity Method	Investment in Associate Dr.	Investment in Associate Cr.		Represented by the total of the investor's % of		
				Associate's net book value	Associate's fair value differences	Goodwill
	1. Acquisition cost			1. dr.	1. dr.*	1 dr.
	2. Associate earns profit			2. dr.		
		3. Investor amortizes fair value differences			3. cr.	
		4. Associate pays a dividend		4. cr.		
	Balance of investment account, equity method			= % of associate's net book value	= Unrecognized fair value differences	= Goodwill

*This assumes fair values of the identifiable net assets exceed the carrying amounts.

After Acquisition

Illustration 30-1 also indicates how the equity method works after acquisition. As the associate **earns a profit** and its net assets increase, the investor recognizes its share of the profit and increases the carrying amount of the investment for its share of the increase in the associate's net assets:

Investment in Associate	$	
Investment Income		$

The **fair value differences** are not recognized in the associate's records and are not amortized in the profit or loss it reports. However, they need to be amortized by the investor because they are included in the investment account balance. This usually has the effect of reducing the investment income reported:

Investment Income	$	
Investment in Associate		$

As the associate distributes assets as **dividends**, its net assets decrease, and the investor recognizes this effect as its share of the dividend is received:

Cash	$	
Investment in Associate		$

This last entry reflects the realization or the conversion of the investment into cash by the investor. Another adjustment needed each period is the **elimination of profits and losses on intercompany transactions** between the investor and the associate. For both upstream (associate to investor) and downstream (investor to associate) transactions, the investor's share of any unrealized profits and losses are eliminated with adjustments to the investment and the investment income accounts.

To the extent that the associate recognizes changes in its net assets through other comprehensive income (OCI) or other equity accounts, the investor also adjusts the investment account and its OCI or other equity account for its share.

If an associate incurs losses and the investor's share of the losses is more than the carrying amount of the investment, the investor continues to recognize them and the resulting liability only to the extent it has legal or constructive obligations to make payments on behalf of the associate.[4]

Other specific guidance in IAS 28 includes the following:

- The **associate's accounting policies** for similar transactions and events are required to be the same as those of the investor; otherwise, the associate's policies are conformed to the investor's policies before its financial statements are used in applying the equity method.
- If the associate has a different reporting period than the investor, the associate's financial statements used must be dated no more than three months from the investor's reporting date, and adjusted for significant transactions and events that occurred in the intervening period.

---

[4] If the carrying amount of the investment includes additional financing extended to the associate (such as long-term loans, preferred share holdings, etc.) and these may not be recovered, losses may be recognized that are larger than the investor's common share interest. In this case, the excess losses are applied to the other components of the investment in reverse order of seniority.

Impairment Losses

When an associate experiences financial difficulties, the investment account is reduced by the investor's share of losses reported by the associate. The investor also applies the requirements of IAS 39 *Financial Instruments: Recognition and Measurement* to determine whether it needs to recognize an impairment loss.

The carrying amount of the investment as a whole is compared with its recoverable amount (the higher of value in use and fair value less selling costs) to determine whether the investment is impaired. Any resulting impairment loss is not allocated to specific assets underlying the investment. Although goodwill forms part of the carrying amount of the investment, the investment is tested for impairment as a single asset, as set out in IAS 36 *Impairment of Assets*. An impairment loss may be reversed in the future.

The value in use is determined by estimates of either the net cash flows expected from the associate's operations and the proceeds on the ultimate disposal of the investment, or the cash flows expected from dividends to be received and the proceeds from the investment's ultimate disposal.

Loss of Significant Influence

An investor stops using the equity method for an investment on the date it ceases to have significant influence over an associate. Unless the associate becomes a subsidiary or joint venture, the investment is accounted for under IAS 39 *Financial Instruments: Recognition and Measurement*. Any investment that remains is remeasured at its fair value and the proceeds on disposal are recognized. The difference between the total of these two amounts and the carrying value of the investment when significant influence is lost is recognized in profit or loss.

Amounts remaining in the entity's other comprehensive income that are attributable to the associate are accounted for at this time as if the associate had directly disposed of the assets or liabilities. Amounts are reclassified to profit and loss if that is what the associate would have done on disposal.

DISCLOSURE

Investments in associates accounted for by the equity method are reported as non-current assets with the following amounts disclosed:

(a) the carrying amount of the investments;
(b) the investor's share of the profit or loss for the period;
(c) the investor's share of any discontinued operations of associates, reported separately in discontinued operations;
(d) the investor's share of changes recognized in other comprehensive income by the associate, reported in other comprehensive income; and
(e) information about any related contingent liabilities.

In addition, other information is required that provides the reader of the financial statements with a better understanding of the circumstances and financial position of the associates. Examples include the following:

- summarized financial information about the assets, liabilities, revenues, and profit or loss of associates, and the fair value of any associates with published price quotations;
- reasons supporting the use of the equity method with holdings of less than 20% and for not using the equity method with holdings of between 20% and 50%;
- reasons why the financial statements used for the associate do not cover the same period as those of the investor, if applicable; and
- reasons why any associates are not accounted for using the equity method along with summarized financial information about them.

LOOKING AHEAD

Accounting for investments in associates is not a specific topic on the IASB's agenda, so basic application of the equity method as required by IAS 28 is not likely to change in the foreseeable future. However, there are a number of other projects in process that may have an effect on some aspects of significant influence investments. These include:

- The impairment provisions in the financial instruments (IAS 39 replacement) project. The IASB plans on issuing an Exposure Draft on this topic in late 2009 and revised accounting standards a year later.
- The Exposure Draft on *Derecognition: Proposed Amendments to IAS 39 and IFRS 7* (ED/2009/3). A final amendment to the derecognition guidance in IAS 39 is expected in 2010.
- An Exposure Draft *Consolidated Financial Statements* was issued late in 2008 to revise the definition of control in light of problems with special purpose (structured) entities. The amendments to the standard are expected in late 2009. Although there are no direct effects of this document on IAS 28 *Investments in Associates*, a change to the concept of control may have implications going forward.
- The IASB's fair value measurement project, expected to result in the convergence of international and U.S. GAAP, may affect some of the measurement guidance in this standard. An Exposure Draft (ED/2009/5) was issued in May 2009 with the publication of final guidance expected in 2010.

All of the projects identified are being worked on either closely or jointly with the FASB, with the goal of reducing or eliminating significant differences in standards.

END-OF-CHAPTER PRACTICE

30-1 Dundeed Ltd. (DL) has three investments.

DL owns 16% of Company A's common shares. This ownership interest was recently acquired when DL provided significant financing to Company A, a family-owned and controlled company that supplies DL with materials needed for its major product line. The financing helped the company through cash flow problems associated with a recent expansion. Company A's owner–manager is very appreciate of DL's assistance and has appointed two of DL's top management to its board of directors.

DL also owns 40% of Company B. The remainder of Company B's shares is owned by a major corporation that is Company B's largest customer.

Company C is 22% owned by DL. Most of the remainder of Company C's shares is widely held, although one other investor has a 25% interest through his wholly owned investment company. The investor has reached retirement age and no longer attends board meetings on a regular basis.

Instructions

Determine whether DL should account for each of the investments described above by using the equity method. In each case, explain why the equity method should be used or why the investment does not qualify for this treatment.

30-2 Leara Corp. (LC) acquired 25% of Gnome Ltd.'s common shares early in 2008 for $100 and classified Gnome as an associate. The carrying amount of Gnome's net assets at this time was $300, although the land on its books had a fair value of $12 more than its carrying amount, and an unrecorded patent with a remaining useful life of five years had a fair value of $60. The excess payment related to Gnome's unrecognized goodwill.

During 2008, Gnome reported a profit of $40 and an unrealized holding gain of $8 on an available-for-sale investment that was reported in other comprehensive income. The company also declared and paid out a $16 dividend.

Instructions
  (a) Construct a T account of LC's Investment in Gnome Ltd. Post all the entries that were made to this account during LC's year ended December 31, 2008.
  (b) Determine the investment income LC reports in profit or loss for 2008.
  (c) Briefly explain the relationship between the Investment in Gnome Ltd. at December 31, 2008 and the carrying amount of Gnome's net assets at the same date.

30-3 In this chapter, flag icons identify areas where there are GAAP differences between IFRS requirements and national standards.

Instructions
Access the website(s) identified on the inside back cover of this book, and prepare a concise summary of the differences that are flagged throughout the chapter material.

Chapter 31

Business Combinations: IFRS 3

U.S. GAAP Reference
FAS 141(R) Business Combinations

Related IFRSs
IAS 27 Consolidated and Separate Financial Statements
Framework for the Preparation and Presentation of Financial Statements

OBJECTIVE AND SCOPE

Business combinations, commonly referred to as mergers and acquisitions, are an important activity in the world's capital markets.[1] IFRS 3 *Business Combinations* sets out principles and other requirements for entities to follow in reporting the effects of their acquisitions. The standard covers three major areas:

1. how to recognize and measure the identifiable assets acquired, liabilities assumed, and non-controlling interest, if applicable;
2. how to recognize and measure any goodwill acquired, or a gain in a bargain purchase; and
3. the disclosures that are necessary to help users evaluate the nature and financial effects of the business combination.

A ***business combination,*** according to Appendix A of IFRS 3, is "a transaction or other event in which an acquirer obtains control of one or more businesses," including transactions sometimes referred to as mergers of equals.

The formation of a joint venture, the acquisition of an asset or group of assets that does not meet the definition of a business (see next page), and the combination of entities or businesses under common control **are not included in** the scope of IFRS 3.

---

[1] *Business Combinations Phase II: Project Summary, Feedback and Analysis,* January 2008, IASB (2008), p. 4 reports that there were more than 13,000 mergers and acquisition transactions worldwide with a combined value of more than €2 trillion in 2006.

IDENTIFYING A BUSINESS COMBINATION

A key element in determining whether a business combination has taken place is identifying whether the assets acquired constitute a business. If a transaction is only the acquisition of a group of assets and not a business, the total cost of the group is allocated to individual assets based on their relative fair values. A *business* is defined as "an integrated set of activities and assets that is capable of being conducted and managed for the purpose of providing a return in the form of dividends, lower costs or other economic benefits directly to investors or other owners, members or participants."[2]

Appendix B of IFRS 3 provides additional application guidance to help preparers distinguish between a group of assets and a business. For example, it discusses a business in terms of having two essential elements: it has **inputs** and **processes applied** to the inputs that together can be used to create outputs. It also acknowledges that having liabilities is common but not essential to being a business; that activities and assets in a development stage have to look to other factors; and while the existence of goodwill is strongly indicative of a business, it is not a required element.

THE ACQUISITION METHOD

When a business has been acquired, it must be accounted for by using the **acquisition method**, and most of IFRS 3 is dedicated to explaining how this method should be applied.

The first two issues that need to be resolved in applying this method are to determine **who the acquirer is** and **what the date of the acquisition is**. After this, the identifiable assets acquired, the liabilities assumed, and any non-controlling interest are recognized and measured, and any positive or negative goodwill is accounted for.

Identifying the Acquirer

The definition of a business combination refers to "an acquirer" and the standard requires that one of the combining entities be identified as the acquirer. The *acquirer* is the entity who obtains control of the acquired business, the **acquiree**. Therefore, to apply IFRS 3, the starting point is to identify which party ends up with *control* of the assets—the power to govern the financial and operating policies of an entity and so obtain benefits from its activities.

IFRS 3 sends the reader to the discussion and guidance in IAS 27 *Consolidated and Separate Financial Statements* to determine what is meant by control. IAS 27 explains that control means having more than half of the voting power over an entity, but also recognizes that control can exist with less than 50% of the voting shares, and, in extreme situations, may not exist with more than 50%. Ownership of share warrants, call options, convertible securities, or other instruments that are **currently exercisable or convertible** are considered as well. An entity also looks to factors other than share ownership in determining control, such as agreements with other investors, rights given under statute, and the power to appoint or remove members of the board or other governing body.

Appendix B of IFRS 3 offers additional guidance if IAS 27 does not clearly indicate which of the combining companies in a particular situation is the acquirer. If an entity acquires another business by transferring cash or other assets or incurring liabilities, identifying the acquirer is straightforward. It is the entity that gives up the assets or incurs the liabilities. However, if shares are exchanged to effect a combination, it may be more difficult to determine which party to the combination acquires the other. The acquirer is usually the entity that issues its equity interests, but sometimes so many new shares are issued for the business acquired that control of the assets ends up with the owners of the acquired entity. This is known as a **reverse acquisition**.

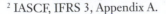

[2] IASCF, IFRS 3, Appendix A.

Circumstances to be considered in identifying the acquirer when equity interests are exchanged include the following:

(a) the relative voting rights of the owners, as a group, of the combining entities in the combined entity after the combination;

(b) the existence of a large minority voting interest in the combined entity if no other owner or group of owners has a significant voting interest;

(c) the composition of the governing body of the combined entity and which group of combining company owners can appoint and remove its members;

(d) the senior management team of the combined entity and which combining entity's management is dominant;

(e) the terms of the exchange and which combining entity pays a premium for its interests; and

(f) the relative size of the combining entities, and which entity initiated the combination.

There is a good accounting reason for having to identify an acquirer correctly. This is because the acquirer's net assets continue to be accounted for at their existing carrying amounts, whereas the net assets of the acquired company are remeasured to and reported at their fair values at the acquisition date.

Situation

Company A and Company B want to combine operations, and the combination can be carried out through a variety of legal avenues. The following summarized information sets out the financial position of each entity at the end of the most recent year.

	Company A	Company B
Assets	$ 30	$ 40
Liabilities	$ 20	$ 30
Equity	10	10
	$ 30	$ 40
Number of shares outstanding	10 shares	10 shares
Price per share	$1	$1.50

Alternative 1: Company A borrows $15 and purchases all of Company B's shares.

Alternative 2: Company A issues 15 new shares and exchanges them for all of Company B's outstanding shares.

Alternative 3: A new entity, Company AB, is incorporated. Company AB issues 20 AB shares to Company A's shareholders and 30 AB shares to Company B's shareholders in exchange for their shares of Company A and Company B, respectively. Which company is the acquirer in each of the transactions proposed?

Analysis

Under **Alternative 1**, Company A and its original shareholders as a group own all of Company B and its net assets. Company B's original shareholders have no equity interest in any of the assets. Therefore, Company A is the acquirer.

Under **Alternative 2**, Company A again owns all of Company B and its net assets. It, therefore, is the legal acquirer. However, who controls those net assets and is the acquirer **for accounting purposes** under IFRS 3? Company A now has 25 outstanding shares, 10 of which are owned by its original shareholders and 15 of which are held by Company B's original shareholders. Because Company B's original shareholders as a group can now elect the majority of the members of Company A's board of directors, Company B is identified as the acquirer. This is a reverse acquisition.

Under **Alternative 3**, the combined net assets of both Company A and Company B are owned by a new entity, Company AB. While AB is the legal acquirer, AB is not the acquirer under IFRS 3. Which combining company's shareholders as a group control the combined assets? The combined assets are owned by Company AB. AB has 50 shares outstanding, 20 (or 40%) of which are held by the original Company A shareholders and 30 (or 60%) of which are held by the original Company B shareholders. The original Company B shareholders as a group control the combined assets and therefore Company B is the acquirer for accounting purposes.

Determining the Acquisition Date

The *acquisition date* is the date on which the acquirer **obtains control** of the acquiree. This is usually the closing date for the transaction when the acquirer legally transfers the consideration and accepts ownership of the assets and assumes the liabilities. Written agreements may transfer control either before or after the closing date.

Recognition and Measurement of Identifiable Assets, Liabilities, and Non-controlling Interest

Three recognition and measurement principles are set out as a basis for applying the acquisition method. Although the principles are stated in few words, entities spend considerable time and resources to ensure that these are correctly applied.[3]

1. At the acquisition date, the acquirer recognizes the identifiable assets acquired, liabilities assumed, and any non-controlling interest in the acquiree, all separately from any goodwill. The identifiable assets and liabilities recognized must meet the definitions of assets and liabilities set out in the *Framework for the Preparation and Presentation of Financial Statements* and they are restricted to those that are part of the actual combination transaction. Assets or liabilities associated with any separate arrangements or side transactions are not included.

2. At the acquisition date, the acquirer classifies or designates the identifiable assets acquired and liabilities assumed so that they can be accounted for under the relevant IFRSs after acquisition. The classification and designation decisions are made based on the conditions, including contractual terms, operating and accounting policies, and economic and other relevant conditions that exist at the acquisition date, with two exceptions. Lease and insurance contracts are classified according to the terms and conditions at the inception of the contracts, not at the acquisition date.

3. The acquirer measures all of the **identifiable** assets acquired and liabilities assumed at their fair values on the acquisition date. A **choice is permitted for the measurement of any non-controlling interest** in the acquiree. It is measured at **either** its fair value including goodwill, **or** at its proportionate share of the fair value of the acquiree's identifiable net assets, i.e., excluding goodwill.

Exceptions to the Recognition and Measurement Principles

One exception to these principles relates to the recognition of contingent liabilities. Under IAS 37 *Provisions, Contingent Liabilities and Contingent Assets*, contingent liabilities are not recognized if a future outflow of resources is not probable. Under IFRS 3, they are recognized, even if the outflow is not probable. IFRS 3 is followed in this case.

Deferred tax assets and liabilities related to the assets acquired and liabilities assumed in the combination and any liability (or asset) under the acquiree's employee benefit arrangements are not fair valued. Instead they are recognized and measured under their respective IFRS (IAS 12 and IAS 19). Specific treatment is also provided for indemnification assets resulting from a seller's guarantee, reacquired rights, share-based payment awards, and assets held for sale.

Recognition and Measurement of Goodwill

In general, goodwill is the excess of the fair value of an entity over the fair value of its identifiable assets and liabilities. *Goodwill* is defined in Appendix A of IFRS 3 as "an asset representing the future economic benefits arising from other assets acquired in a business combination that are not individually identified and separately recognized." Illustration 31-1 indicates how goodwill is measured at the acquisition date of the combination.

---

[3] It is often particularly difficult to determine identifiable intangible assets separately from goodwill. IAS 38 *Intangible Assets* provides relevant guidance in this area.

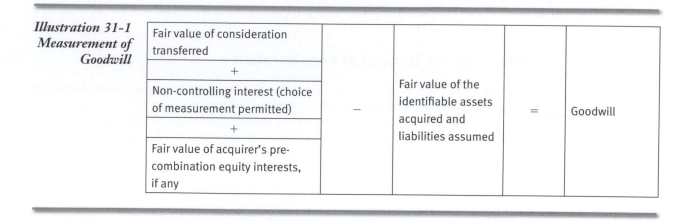

Illustration 31-1
Measurement of
Goodwill

Fair value of consideration transferred $+$ Non-controlling interest (choice of measurement permitted) $+$ Fair value of acquirer's pre-combination equity interests, if any	$-$	Fair value of the identifiable assets acquired and liabilities assumed	$=$	Goodwill

The "fair value" amounts indicated in Illustration 31-1 are acquisition-date values.

Consideration Transferred

The **consideration transferred** in a combination transaction can take a number of forms: assets, liabilities, or equity interests. For example, it could be any one or a combination of cash, other assets, a business or subsidiary of the acquirer, notes payable at a later date, ordinary or preferred shares, or share options and warrants.

Consideration also includes *contingent consideration*—additional assets or equity interests that are payable, or recoverable, if specified future events occur or conditions are met. The resulting liability or equity element (or asset if it relates to an amount that may be recoverable) is also measured at its fair value at the date of acquisition.

If only shares are exchanged and the fair value of the equity interests acquired can be measured more reliably than those given up by the acquirer, this value may be used instead. When an acquirer transfers assets as part of the consideration, any difference between their carrying amount and fair value is recognized by the acquirer in its profit or loss.[4]

Non-controlling Interest

The *non-controlling interest*, the equity in the acquired business that is not owned by the acquirer, may be measured at its fair value. If the shares **not held** by the acquirer-parent trade in an active market, their fair value is relatively easy to measure. Otherwise, other valuation methods have to be used. Their fair value cannot be automatically inferred from the fair value of the controlling interest's holdings because a premium is usually attached to ownership representing a controlling interest.

Alternatively, the non-controlling interest is measured at its proportionate share of the fair value of only the identifiable net assets.

Acquirer's Pre-combination Equity Interests

Often an investor acquires control of another entity in a step-acquisition, that is, by building up its holdings in stages until it reaches a control position. When control is reached, the investor becomes a **parent**, the investee becomes a **subsidiary**, and the transaction is accounted for as a business combination. How should the pre-combination investment be accounted for by the acquirer-parent?

In this situation, the acquirer brings its previous equity investment to its fair value at the date of the business combination and recognizes the resulting gain or loss in profit or loss. Any part of the investment balance

---

[4] If the assets transferred remain in the consolidated entity (see Chapter 32) and therefore under the control of the acquirer, the assets are transferred at their carrying amount, not at their fair value.

previously offset by amounts recognized in other comprehensive income is accounted for as if the investor had directly disposed of the investment.

Business Combination with No Transfer of Consideration

If a company buys back its own shares, it is possible for an investor in that company to attain a control position merely by holding a majority of the reduced number of voting shares. Alternatively, an agreement may expire that previously prevented an investor that holds the majority of voting shares from exercising control. In both these cases, a business combination results without any consideration being transferred by the acquirer. The acquisition method of accounting applies equally to such transactions.

Negative Goodwill—A Bargain Purchase

While not very common, there are situations when the goodwill calculated according to the formula in Illustration 31-1 results in a negative amount. The acquirer in such a case is required to carefully review and ensure it has correctly included all the assets acquired and liabilities assumed. After this, the amounts recognized for these assets and liabilities, for the non-controlling interest, for any previous holdings, and for the consideration transferred are reconsidered as of the acquisition date. If a negative balance still remains, the acquirer recognizes it in profit or loss as a gain.

Acquisition-related Costs

There are often significant costs incurred in bringing a combination to completion. These include finder's fees, a variety of professional and consulting costs, general administrative costs, and fees related to the registration of debt and equity securities. Except for the costs of issuing debt and equity securities that are accounted for according to IAS 32 *Financial Instruments: Presentation* and IAS 39 *Financial Instruments: Recognition and Measurement*, the acquirer recognizes all costs associated with the acquisition **as expenses in the period they are incurred**.

Before continuing, we will work through an example of how goodwill is calculated.

Situation

Acquirer Corp. enters into a business combination by purchasing 80% of the outstanding common shares of Acquiree Corp. from Acquiree Corp.'s shareholders in exchange for 100 newly issued Acquirer shares. On this date, Acquirer shares have a fair value of $8.80 each. The following information is available about Acquiree on the date of acquisition:

	Carrying Amount	Fair Value
Monetary assets	$ 100	$ 100
Property, plant, & equipment, net	900	1,150
Patent	—	200
	$1,000	$1,450
Liabilities	$ 550	$ 550
Equity (100 common shares)	450	
	$1,000	

- Acquirer incurs $50 of legal costs associated with the acquisition.
- The shares of Acquiree not purchased in the combination continue to trade in the market after the combination transaction, priced at $10 per share.
- Acquirer did not own any shares of Acquiree before this acquisition.

How much goodwill should be recognized as a result of this business combination?

Analysis

Step 1: Determine the fair value of the consideration transferred.

The fair value of the 100 shares given up by Acquirer is $8.80 × 100 = $880.

The transaction costs are expensed as incurred.

Step 2: Determine the non-controlling interest (NCI).

Under IFRS 3, a choice is permitted in measuring the non-controlling interest. It can be (A) the fair value of the interest of the non-controlling shareholders, or (B) the NCI's proportionate share of the fair value of Acquiree's identifiable net assets.

Under **option A**, the NCI is equal to the number of shares of Acquiree not held by Acquirer (20% × 100 shares = 20 shares) at their fair value of $10 each, for a total fair value of $200.

Under **option B**, the NCI is 20% of the fair value of the identifiable assets of $1,450 less 20% of the fair value of the liabilities of $550. This measure of the NCI, therefore, is 20% ($1,450 − $550) = $180.

Step 3: Determine the fair value of the acquirer's pre-combination equity interests, which in this case is $0.

Step 4: Determine the fair value of the identifiable assets acquired and liabilities assumed.

The fair value of the identifiable assets is $1,450 and of the liabilities is $550, for a net amount of $900.

Step 5: Calculate goodwill as follows: (Step 1 + Step 2 + Step 3) − Step 4

Under **option A**, goodwill is ($880 + $200 + $0) − $900 = $180.

Under **option B**, goodwill is ($880 + $180 + $0) − $900 = $160.

Under **option B**, the goodwill is the amount associated with Acquirer's interest only:

Fair value of the consideration exchanged	$880
80% of the fair value of the identifiable net assets: 80% × $900	720
Goodwill, controlling interest	$160

Under **option A**, the goodwill amount also includes the goodwill attributed to the NCI—implied by the difference between the NCI's fair value and its share of the fair value of the identifiable net assets:

Fair value of the NCI: 20 shares × $10 per share	$200
20% of the fair value of the identifiable net assets: 20% × $900	180
Goodwill, non-controlling interest	20
Goodwill, controlling interest	160
Option A goodwill	$180

Measurement Period

Because the information required to account for a business combination is extensive, IFRS 3 provides some flexibility in finalizing the amounts to be recognized and reported by identifying a measurement period. The **measurement period** is the period of time after the acquisition date, to a maximum of one year, during which an acquirer is permitted to adjust the provisional amounts initially recognized for a business combination.

If the initial accounting is not complete at the end of the reporting period when the combination takes place, the entity may report provisional amounts. These are changed retrospectively if new information that is obtained about facts and circumstances **that existed at the acquisition date** would have meant different measures originally. Changes in the provisional amounts are accounted for as adjustments to the goodwill recognized.

SUBSEQUENT MEASUREMENT AND ACCOUNTING

One of the recognition principles discussed earlier required that the identifiable assets acquired, liabilities assumed or incurred, and equity instruments issued be classified and designated in such a way that the IFRS that applies to each can be followed in the periods after the combination transaction. Therefore, IFRS 3 does not include requirements for their subsequent measurement and accounting. The standard does include specific guidance for reacquired rights, indemnification assets, contingent liabilities, and contingent consideration.

Contingent Liabilities

After initial recognition and until it no longer exists, a contingent liability recognized in a business combination is measured at the amount that would be recognized under IAS 37 *Provisions, Contingent Liabilities and Contingent Assets*, or the amount initially recognized reduced by any amortization under IAS 18 *Revenue*, whichever is higher.

Contingent Consideration

Changes that occur in the measurement of contingent consideration may be related to measurement period provisions, or they may be a result of meeting an earnings target, share price, or other event on which the contingency is based. If the fair value of the contingent consideration changes and the change is not a measurement period adjustment, the following applies:

(a) If the contingent consideration is classified as equity, no adjustment is made and only equity is affected when settled.
(b) If the contingent consideration is classified as an asset or liability and is a financial instrument to which IAS 39 *Financial Instruments: Recognition and Measurement* applies, it is measured at fair value with the gain or loss recognized in profit or loss or other comprehensive income, whichever is appropriate.
(c) If the contingent consideration is classified as an asset or liability and is not covered by IAS 39, changes in its fair value and its ultimate settlement are accounted for under its respective IFRS.

DISCLOSURES

The body of IFRS 3 sets out the disclosure objectives, leaving the detailed requirements in Appendix B, Application Guidance, which is an integral part of the IFRS.

> **Disclosure Objectives:** Disclose information to help users of the financial statements evaluate the nature and financial effect of
> * a business combination that occurs during the current period or after the end of the period but before the statements are released, and
> * adjustments recognized in the current period that relate to combinations that took place in the current or previous reporting periods.

Specific types of disclosure are required for each business combination:

(a) The name and description of the acquiree, the acquisition date, the percentage of voting equity interests acquired, reasons for the combination, and how control was obtained.
(b) A qualitative description of factors making up the goodwill recognized, the fair value of the consideration transferred in total and by major category, information about contingent consideration, indemnification assets, acquired receivables, and the amount of goodwill expected to be deductible for tax purposes.
(c) The amounts recognized for each major classification of assets acquired and liabilities assumed, and information about contingent liabilities.

(d) Information about transactions recognized separately from the acquisition transaction.

(e) An explanation of the reason for and amount of gain recognized in a bargain purchase.

(f) When less than 100% of the equity interests are held, and for a combination achieved in stages, detailed information about specific measures related to non-controlling interest and any gain or loss recognized.

(g) The actual revenue and profit or loss of the acquiree included in the acquirer's consolidated statement of comprehensive income, and what this would have been if held for an entire annual period.

If the combination takes place after the end of the reporting period, the information listed above is required to the extent possible.

If the initial accounting is incomplete at the balance sheet date, considerable additional information is required for each individually material combination or in total for combinations that are material collectively. These disclosures zero in on explaining why the accounting is incomplete, details about contingent consideration and contingent liabilities, and an explanation of changes in the carrying amount of goodwill.

Excerpts from the 2007 consolidated financial statements of the Nestlé Group that relate to business combinations are provided in Illustration 31-2 and Illustration 31-3.[5]

The Nestlé Group is based in Switzerland and reports amounts in millions of Swiss francs. Illustration 31-2 sets out information included in the Accounting Policies section of the statements. You may notice that some of the disclosures differ from those identified as required in this chapter. This is due to the fact that the chapter is based on the new standard that takes effect in 2009, whereas these excerpts are taken from the company's 2007 report. For example, Nestlé indicates that it applies the purchase method of accounting for newly acquired companies, while the new standard requires the acquisition method. The methods have many similarities, but also some fundamental differences in approach.

Illustration 31-2
The Nestlé Group
Accounting Policy
Notes

Consolidated companies

Companies, in which the Group has the power to exercise control, are fully consolidated. This applies irrespective of the percentage of interest in the share capital.

Control refers to the power to govern the financial and operating policies of a company so as to obtain the benefits from its activities. Minority interests are shown as a component of equity in the balance sheet and the share of the profit attributable to minority interests is shown as a component of profit for the period in the income statement.

Newly acquired companies are consolidated from the effective date of control, using the purchase method.

Business combinations and related goodwill

As from 1 January 1995, the excess of the cost of an acquisition over the fair value of the net identifiable assets, liabilities and contingent liabilities acquired is capitalized. Previously these amounts had been written off through equity.

Goodwill is not amortised but tested for impairment at least annually and upon the occurrence of an indication of impairment. The impairment testing process is described in the appropriate section of these policies.

Goodwill is recorded in the functional currencies of the acquired operations.

All assets, liabilities and contingent liabilities acquired in a business combination are recognized at the acquisition date and measured at their fair value.

---

[5] http://www.nestle.com/Resource.axd?Id=24E5A5E2-93F8-43A3-956E-0F259448CB90.

Illustration 31-3 reports detailed information about the company's acquisition activities in the year. Again, remember that this reflects accounting standards in 2007 and not 2009, as discussed in the chapter.

Illustration 31-3
The Nestlé Group
Business
Acquisitions
Note

23. Acquisition of businesses

In millions of CHF	Gerber	Novartis Medical Nutrition	Other acquisitions	2007	2006
Fair value of net assets acquired					
Property, plant and equipment	327	98	108	533	407
Intangible assets	1 886	1 518	206	3 610	749
Other assets	2 282	579	204	3 065	287
Minority interests	–	–	(2)	(2)	(20)
Purchase of minority interests in existing participations	–	–	130	130	19
Financial liabilities	(13)	(51)	(14)	(78)	(275)
Employee benefits, deferred taxes and provisions	(1 050)	(49)	(26)	(1 125)	(299)
Other liabilities	(1 266)	(198)	(122)	(1 586)	(179)
	2 166	1 897	484	4 547	689
Goodwill	4 515	1 186	1 202 [a]	6 903	2 581
Total acquisition cost	6 681	3 083	1 686	11 450	3 270
Cash and cash equivalents acquired	(75)	(24)	(33)	(132)	(18)
Consideration payable	(80)	(50)	(2)	(132)	(151)
Payment of consideration payable on prior years acquisition	–	–	46	46	3 368
Cash outflow on acquisitions	6 526	3 009	1 697	11 232	6 469

[a] Of which CHF 1006 million (2006: CHF 1099 million) resulting from Alcon's acquisition of own shares to satisfy obligations under the stock option plan of Alcon employees and for shares buy-back programme.

Since the valuation of the assets and liabilities of businesses recently acquired is still in process, the above values are determined provisionally. The carrying amounts of assets and liabilities determined in accordance with IFRSs immediately before the combination do not differ significantly from those disclosed above except for internally generated intangible assets and goodwill which were not recognized. The goodwill represents elements that cannot be recognized as intangible assets such as synergies, complementary market share and competitive position.

The profit for the period of Gerber and Novartis Medical Nutrition included in the Consolidated Financial Statements amount to CHF 0.09 billion and CHF 0.05 billion. The Group's sales and profit for the period would have amounted to CHF 109.8 billion and CHF 10.9 billion if the acquisitions had been effective 1 January 2007.

LOOKING AHEAD

The IFRS 3 requirements identified in Chapter 31 are applicable for business combinations with acquisition dates on or after the beginning of an entity's first annual reporting period that begins on or after July 1, 2009.[6] This standard, along with related amendments to IAS 27 *Consolidated and Separate Financial Statements*, is the output of the second phase of a major project conducted jointly with the FASB. FASB released FAS 141 (Revised 2007) *Business Combinations* and FAS 160 *Noncontrolling Interests in Consolidated Financial Statements* concurrently. While the IASB and FASB met their objective of substantially unifying merger and acquisition accounting across the world's major capital markets, some differences still exist, caused mainly by differences in other IFRSs and U.S. GAAP. While this major project has been completed, the related IAS 27 is still part of the IASB's active agenda.

As indicated in the chapter, the combination of entities or businesses under common control are excluded from the scope of IFRS 3. Because of this, accounting for such combinations diverges in practice. A recently added IASB project on common control transactions and demergers has been put on hold.

Two IASB projects nearing completion may have implications for IFRS 3. The first one is on consolidations, in which the IASB is providing more guidance on what constitutes control. The "Looking Ahead" feature in Chapter 32 explains the tentative decisions made in this area to date. The final standard is expected in late 2009.

The other project is the *Reporting Entity* portion of the larger and joint Conceptual Framework project with the FASB. In 2008, the IASB issued a Discussion Paper entitled *Preliminary Views on an Improved Conceptual Framework for Financial Reporting – The Reporting Entity* that looks at control-related issues from new perspectives. An Exposure Draft is planned for late 2009, with the finalized chapter expected in 2010.

END-OF-CHAPTER PRACTICE

31-1 The condensed statements of financial position of Hype Ltd. and Tense Ltd. at July 31, 2008 are as follows:

	Hype Ltd.	Tense Ltd.
Current assets	$ 600	$ 400
Plant and equipment	3,400	2,600
	$4,000	$3,000
Current liabilities	$ 200	$ 300
Common shares, no par value		
40 shares	1,200	
40 shares		2,000
Retained earnings	2,600	700
	$4,000	$3,000

Both companies are publicly traded, with Hype Ltd. shares averaging about $250 per share and Tense Ltd.'s averaging $125 per share in recent weeks. The fair value of the current assets and liabilities of both companies approximate their book value, and the fair values of the plant and equipment assets are $4,000 for Hype and $3,400 for Tense.

Two transactions that could be used to effect a business combination are described below.

Option 1: Hype Ltd. issues 1 new share in exchange for every 2 outstanding shares of Tense Ltd.

Option 2: A new company, HT Corp. is formed to acquire the net assets of Hype and Tense. HT Corp. issues 30 shares of its no par value shares to Hype Ltd. and 15 shares to Tense Ltd.

---

[6] IASCF, Introduction to IFRS 3, para. IN3.

The management of the two companies is trying to determine what the effect will be of carrying out the combination under each of the options described.

Instructions

    (a) Identify which company is the acquirer as described in IFRS 3 under each of the options presented. Explain briefly.

    (b) Explain why an acquirer must be identified in order to account for each business combination.

    (c) Identify the amount of goodwill, if any, that would be recognized as a result of the combination under each of the options.

31-2 Refer to the situation and Option 1 described in 31-1 above. Assume that Hype Ltd. acquires only 60% of the shares of Tense Ltd. by issuing one new Hype share for every two of the Tense shares acquired. Further assume that the Tense shares not acquired by Hype continue to have a fair value of $125 after the combination.

Instructions

Determine the goodwill that will be recognized in the business combination in Option 1 under each of the choices provided by IFRS 3.

31-3 Provide a short, but clear explanation of the following terms:

    (a) Reverse acquisition

    (b) Goodwill

    (c) Control

    (d) Identifiable net assets

31-4 In this chapter, flag icons identify areas where there are GAAP differences between IFRS requirements and national standards.

Instructions

Access the website(s) identified on the inside back cover of this book, and prepare a concise summary of the differences that are flagged throughout the chapter material.

Chapter 32

Consolidated and Separate Financial Statements: IAS 27

U.S. GAAP References
FAS 160 Noncontrolling Interests in Consolidated Financial Statements
FAS 94 Consolidation of all Majority-Owned Subsidiaries
ARB 51 Consolidated Financial Statements
FIN 46 (Revised) Consolidation of Variable Interest Entities

Related IFRSs
IFRS 3 Business Combinations
IAS 28 Investments in Associates
IAS 31 Interests in Joint Ventures
SIC 12 Consolidation—Special Purpose Entities

OBJECTIVE AND SCOPE

IAS 27 sets out the accounting and reporting requirements for

(a) entities with investments in subsidiaries; and

(b) entities with investments in subsidiaries, joint ventures, and associates that elect or that are required by local regulations to present separate financial statements.

The primary objective of this IFRS is to ensure useful information is provided to users about the economic entity under the control of a parent company and its management. One of its main features is an explanation of how to determine if control exists. The control criteria are currently under review by the IASB and are the subject of an Exposure Draft to be issued by the Board toward the end of 2008.

Standards set out in IFRS 3 *Business Combinations* affect consolidation by specifying how the identifiable assets and liabilities, goodwill acquired, and non-controlling interest are identified and measured. In turn, the criteria for control in IAS 27 affect what qualifies as a business combination and some aspects of how it is accounted for.

WHO PRESENTS CONSOLIDATED FINANCIAL STATEMENTS?

A number of key terms are used throughout this standard. *Consolidated financial statements* are defined as the financial statements of a parent company and all of its subsidiaries presented as one economic entity. They are the financial statements of the **group**. To be a *parent*, an entity must *control* another entity. This means having the power to govern the entity's financial and operating policies and, through this, being able to obtain benefits from its activities. A *subsidiary* is an entity controlled by a parent. A subsidiary may be an unincorporated entity such as a partnership.[1]

Except for a short list of specific exceptions, **all parent entities are required to consolidate** the financial statements of their subsidiaries and present consolidated financial statements.

A parent is excluded from this requirement only if all of the following apply:

(a) it is a wholly-owned subsidiary or a partially-owned subsidiary of another entity whose other owners have been informed and do not object to the non-consolidation;

(b) it does not have and is not in the process of having any debt or equity instruments that are publicly traded; and

(c) its ultimate or an intermediate parent prepares consolidated financial statements for public use that comply with IFRSs.

A parent that qualifies for exclusion is required to follow the IAS 27 requirements for presenting separate financial statements and for disclosure.

CONTROL

Another principle stated in IAS 27 is that the consolidated financial statements must include **all the subsidiaries** of the parent.[2] Previous provisions to exempt a variety of subsidiaries from consolidation, for reasons such as an inability to transfer funds to the parent or the type of activity carried out by the parent or subsidiary, no longer apply.

Because a subsidiary is defined in terms of control, establishing whether control exists is a fundamental aspect of this standard. The primary indication of control is **voting power**, the ability to elect members to the body that sets the operating and financial policies of the other entity. Unless it can be clearly demonstrated in an exceptional circumstance that such ownership does not provide control, the ownership of more than 50% of the voting power of one entity by another is presumed to qualify as control. A parent can hold the voting power **directly or indirectly** such as through a subsidiary. Illustration 32-1 provides an example of direct and indirect ownership giving control.

Control can also exist when the investor owns 50% or less of another entity, provided it has additional powers such as one of the following:

• An agreement with other shareholders results in the investor having more than half the voting rights.

• A statute or agreement gives the investor the right to govern the investee's financial and operating policies.

• The investee's governing body controls the investee and the investor has the power to appoint or remove the majority of its members.

• The investee's governing body controls the investee and the investor has the power to cast the majority of the votes at meetings of that body.

---

[1] IASCF, IAS 27.4.
[2] If a subsidiary meets the IFRS 5 criteria to be classified as held for sale when it is acquired, the parent applies IFRS 5 *Non-current Assets Held for Sale and Discontinued Operations* instead.

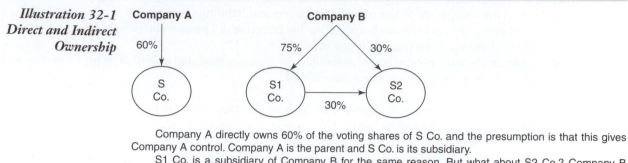

Illustration 32-1
Direct and Indirect
Ownership

Company A directly owns 60% of the voting shares of S Co. and the presumption is that this gives Company A control. Company A is the parent and S Co. is its subsidiary.

S1 Co. is a subsidiary of Company B for the same reason. But what about S2 Co.? Company B owns only 30% of S2 directly but, through its control of S1, Company B is also able to vote the entire 30% ownership interest of S2 held by S1. Therefore Company B has 60% of the voting power of S2, making S2 Co. an indirect subsidiary of Company B.

An entity also assesses whether **potential voting rights** contribute to control. Potential voting rights exist when an investor owns share warrants, call options, debt or equity securities convertible into voting shares, or other similar instruments that, if exercised, would give it the necessary voting power or reduce someone else's voting power over the financial and operating policies of the investee. Only potential rights that can be exercised or converted currently may contribute to control. Management's intentions and financial ability to exercise or convert these instruments are not considered in the assessment.

Basing the control definition primarily on voting power has presented problems with a variety of special purpose entities and whether and under what conditions they should be consolidated.[3] The objective of a current IASB project is to develop control criteria that can be used in all situations.

CONSOLIDATION PROCEDURES

Using uniform accounting policies for reporting like transactions, events, and circumstances, the parent presents its financial statements and those of all its subsidiaries together as if the group were a single economic entity. This means that all intercompany transactions and balances are eliminated, and then the items on each entity's statement of financial position and statement of comprehensive income are added together on a line-by-line basis to present group consolidated statements.

Beginning with the trial balance of the parent and the trial balances of each of the subsidiaries at the same date, the following calculations and adjustments are required to prepare the consolidated amounts:[4]

1. All intragroup transactions, income, and expenses and balances are eliminated.
2. Unrealized gains and losses remaining within the group of companies are eliminated.
3. The carrying amount of the parent's investment in each of its subsidiaries is eliminated, as is the parent's portion of the equity accounts of each subsidiary. The parent's share of any remaining fair value differences, deferred tax amounts, and goodwill indicated at acquisition are recognized.
4. The interest of the non-controlling shareholders in each consolidated subsidiary's net assets is determined. This amount is based on the fair value of the non-controlling interest established when each subsidiary was acquired, adjusted for its share of the changes in equity since acquisition. The non-controlling

---

[3] See SIC 12 *Consolidation—Special Purpose Entities*.
[4] IASCF, IAS 27.22 and 27.23. If the financial statements of the subsidiary are not at the same date as those of the parent, adjustments are made to the subsidiary's financial statements for the effects of significant transactions or events since the date of its statements. In no case can the statement dates be more than three months apart.

interest's portion of any remaining fair value differences, deferred income taxes, and goodwill indicated at acquisition are recognized in the consolidated assets and liabilities.

5. Adjustments are made to income and expense for any fair value differences and deferred taxes recognized at acquisition that have been realized in the year.

6. The interest of the non-controlling shareholders in each consolidated subsidiary's profit or loss and other items of comprehensive income is determined.

Illustration 32-2 summarizes what is represented by and the measurement bases of the assets that are reported on P Company's consolidated or group balance sheet, assuming it has a 75%-owned subsidiary, S Company. All classes of assets, such as the parent's inventory and the subsidiary's inventory, are added together on a line-by-line basis. Assume all intercompany balances and unrealized gains and losses have been eliminated. To simplify, income tax issues are ignored.

Illustration 32-2
Consolidated Assets

Consolidated (Group) Assets
P Company (P) and Subsidiary S Company (S)

	100% of P's assets at their carrying amount, excluding Investment in S
+	100% of S's assets
	• Acquisition-date assets at their unrealized acquisition-date fair values
	• Post-acquisition assets at their carrying amount
+	Goodwill at its acquisition-date fair value (see IFRS 3)
=	Consolidated assets

Illustration 32-3 indicates what is represented by the liabilities in the same consolidated statement of financial position for the same parent and 75%-owned subsidiary. The parent and subsidiary's individual line items are added together here as well, and the illustration assumes that all intercompany balances and unrealized gains and losses have already been eliminated.

Illustration 32-3
Consolidated Liabilities

Consolidated (Group) Liabilities
P Company (P) and Subsidiary S Company (S)

	100% of P's liabilities at their carrying amount
+	100% of S's liabilities
	• Acquisition-date liabilities at their unrealized acquisition-date fair values
	• Post-acquisition liabilities at their carrying amount
=	Consolidated liabilities

Illustration 32-4 shows the components of P Company's group equity and indicates what makes up each part. The same assumptions indicated for Illustrations 32-2 and 32-3 apply here as well.

Illustration 32-4
Consolidated Equity

Consolidated (Group) Equity
P Company (P) and Subsidiary S Company (S)

Equity attributable to owners of P Company

Share capital	= 100% of P's share capital
Retained earnings	= 100% of P's retained earnings + 75% of S's post-acquisition retained earnings +/− 75% of the acquisition-date fair value differences realized
Other equity	= 100% of P's other equity +/− 75% of S's post-acquisition other equity components
	P Company group equity attributable to P Company's owners

+ Non-controlling interests

    Fair value of non-controlling interest at acquisition (IFRS 3 calculation)

+	25% of changes in S's equity since acquisition
+/−	25% of acquisition-date fair value differences realized
=	P Company group equity attributable to non-controlling interests

=   Total consolidated (group) equity

The statement of financial position clearly illustrates that an **entity view** is taken of the consolidated group—it reports all of the resources under the control of the parent company management and how the total resources are financed. The non-controlling interest is reported as part of the group equity because the interest of the non-controlling shareholders **is** an equity interest. This total entity presentation and measurement basis is also carried over to the consolidated statement of comprehensive income.

Illustration 32-5 provides information on the basic components of profit or loss and other comprehensive income, again assuming that intercompany transactions, revenues and expenses, and unrealized gains and losses have been eliminated. These, too, are reported from a total entity perspective with all of the individual revenues, expenses, and other comprehensive income items added together on a line-by-line basis. Bottom line profit or loss and comprehensive income represent the interests of both the parent company shareholders and the non-controlling interest in the subsidiary.

Illustration 32-5
Consolidated
Comprehensive
Income

Consolidated (Group) Comprehensive Income
P Company (P) and S Company (S)

Revenue:

    100% of P's revenues, excluding investment income from S

+	100% of S's revenues
=	Consolidated revenues

Less expenses:

    100% of P's expenses

+	100% of S's expenses
+/−	100% of any acquisition-date fair value differences realized in the period
=	Consolidated expenses

=	Profit or loss	
+/−	Other comprehensive income (OCI):	
		100% of P's OCI
+		100% of S's OCI
=		Other comprehensive income
=	Total comprehensive income for the period	

Profit attributable to

Owners of the parent:	100% of P's profit excluding investment income from S + 75% of S's profit +/− 75% of any acquisition-date fair value differences realized in the period
Non-controlling interests:	25% of S's profit +/− 25% of any acquisition-date fair value differences realized in the period
=	Profit or loss for the period

Total comprehensive income attributable to

Owners of the parent:	Profit attributable to owners of the parent + 100% of P's OCI + 75% of S's OCI
Non-controlling interests:	+ Profit attributable to non-controlling interests + 25% of S's OCI
=	Total comprehensive income for the period

If a subsidiary has **cumulative preferred shares** outstanding that are classified as equity and that are not held by the parent company, the parent's share of the subsidiary's profit or loss is calculated only after adjusting for the preferred dividend, whether it has been declared or not.

Let us work through an example of a parent and subsidiary company and prepare the group financial statements.

Situation

The balance sheet and income statement accounts of Pot and its 60%-owned subsidiary Shot for their years ended December 31, 2008 are provided below. All intercompany transactions, balances, and unrealized profits and losses have already been eliminated from the account balances on this working paper, except for the dividend paid by Shot during the year. Pot accounts for Shot at cost and has recognized the dividend in investment income in its accounts.

	Pot $	Shot $
Cash	125	75
Other current assets	500	260
Plant and equipment	1,025	150
Intangibles	-0-	40
Investment in Shot, at cost	172	-0-
	1,822	525
Liabilities	250	250
Common shares	500	50
Retained earnings	1,020	220
Other equity	52	5
	1,822	525

Sales	490	200
Investment income	20	-0-
	510	200
Cost of sales	240	85
Depreciation and other expenses	160	65
	400	150
Profit	110	50
Other comprehensive income	-0-	-0-
Comprehensive income	110	50
Dividends paid in 2008	60	25

Pot acquired its 60% interest in Shot in a business combination on January 2, 2006, primarily to gain access to patents that Shot had developed. On this date, Shot's common shares were $50, retained earnings were $120, accumulated other comprehensive income was $0, and the fair value of the identifiable assets acquired and liabilities assumed was $260. The analyses carried out at that time to determine the goodwill acquired and fair value differences were as follows:

	Pot 60% $	Non-controlling interest – 40% $	Total $
Calculation of goodwill:			
Fair value of consideration paid	172		172
Fair value of non-controlling interest	—	108	108
	172	108	280
Fair value of identifiable net assets	156	104	260
Goodwill to be recognized	16	4	20
Identification of fair value differences of identifiable net assets:			
Carrying amount, January 2, 2006	102	68	170
Patents: fair value > carrying amount	48	32	80
Inventory: fair value > carrying amount	6	4	10
Fair value of identifiable net assets	156	104	260

The inventory at January 2, 2006 was sold within the year; and the patents had a remaining useful life of eight years. The excess of the fair value over the carrying amount therefore has to be amortized at $80 ÷ 8 years = $10 each year. Goodwill has not been impaired.

Prepare the consolidated (group) financial statements for Pot and its subsidiary for the year ended December 31, 2008. Ignore income taxes.

Analysis

Group Consolidated Statement of Financial Position
December 31, 2008

	$	$
Cash 125 + 75		200
Other current assets 500 + 260 + 10 − 10		760
Plant and equipment 1,025 + 150		1,175
Intangibles 0 + 40 + 80 − 3(10)		90
Goodwill 0 + 0 + 20		20
		2,245
Liabilities 250 + 250		500

Equity
    Attributable to Pot:
    Common shares   500
    Retained earnings $1{,}020 + .6(220 - 120)$
                     $- .6[10 + 3(10)]$ 1,056
        Other equity $52 + .6(5 - 0)$ 55
                                             1,611

    Non-controlling interest:
    At acquisition   108
    Change since acquisition:
           In retained earnings $.4(220 - 120)$ 40
           In other equity $.4(5 - 0)$ 2
    Fair value differences realized:
           $.4[10 + 3(10)]$ -16
                                       134   1,745
                                                 2,245

The assets and liabilities are, for the most part, based on the carrying amounts on Pot and Shot's books. The inventory's fair value at acquisition was $10 more than its carrying amount, so the fair value should be reported in the consolidated statement. However, the inventory has all been sold and the fair value difference realized, so the $10 amount realized is deducted from the fair value measure that had been added. Because the patents acquired had a fair value $80 higher than the carrying amount on Shot's books, the $80 fair value difference is added to the carrying amount of the patents on the consolidation working paper. Shot has been amortizing the carrying amount of the patents at acquisition, but not the fair value difference. The consolidated statements are adjusted to reflect this. The goodwill acquired is added to the consolidated assets, and the Investment in Shot account is removed from the assets.

Both the parent company's and the non-controlling shareholders' interests are reported as equity. Pot's interest in the consolidated net assets is based on its own common shares, retained earnings, and other equity items. In addition, Pot has a 60% interest in Shot's earnings since acquisition, reduced by its 60% share of the fair value differences amortized or realized, plus 60% of any other of Shot's equity changes since acquisition.

The non-controlling interest is the amount at acquisition plus its share of post-acquisition earnings (i.e., the change in retained earnings) and changes in other equity items. The earnings portion is adjusted for the 40% of the fair value differences realized over the three years since acquisition.

Group Consolidated Statement of Comprehensive Income
Year ended December 31, 2008

	$	$
Revenue $490 + 200$		690
Investment income $20 + 0 - .6(25)$		5
		695
Cost of sales $240 + 85$		325
Depreciation and other expenses $160 + 65 + 10$		235
		560
Group profit		135
OCI		-0-
Comprehensive income		135
Profit and comprehensive income attributable to:		
Owners of Pot $110 - .6(25) + .6(50) - .6(10)$	119	
Non-controlling interest $.4(50) - .4(10)$	16	135

The consolidated profit and loss is made up, for the most part, of the revenues and expenses reported by both companies. Because Shot paid a dividend of $25 during the current year and Pot reported it in investment income, it has to be eliminated from the consolidated statement. Amortization expense is increased by $10, the annual amortization of the fair value difference assigned to the patents. As the patents are used, this amount of the fair value difference is considered realized by the consolidated group.

> Pot's share of the $135 profit (and comprehensive income) is made up of its own profit reduced by the intercompany dividend, plus 60% of Shot's profit. In addition, Pot's share of the additional patent amortization on the fair value difference is recognized. The non-controlling shareholders of Shot are entitled to 40% of Shot's profit, and this is adjusted for 40% of the patent's fair value difference realized in the year.

CHANGES IN A PARENT'S OWNERSHIP INTERESTS

Changes without a Change in Control

When there is a change in the parent's shareholdings in a subsidiary but the parent continues to have a controlling interest, the transaction is treated as a **capital transaction**, i.e., a transaction with owners in their capacity as owners.

To account for this, the up-to-date interests of the controlling and non-controlling shareholders are adjusted for the change in relative interests. The difference between the adjustment to the non-controlling interest and the fair value of the amount paid or received by the parent is recognized directly in the parent's equity.

Loss of Control

A parent loses control of a subsidiary when it loses the power to govern its financial and operating policies. This may result from the sale of enough shares to tip the balance of voting power or from the subsidiary issuing new shares to others, diluting the parent's ownership. Alternatively, there may not even be a transaction. The loss of control may be a result of the expiration of a contract that previously gave the investor an ability to exercise control.

The loss of control is a significant event that brings the parent-subsidiary relationship to a close and, if there is any continuing interest, begins a new and different investor-investee relationship. For this reason, the parent takes the following steps:

1. It derecognizes all of the former subsidiary's individual assets and liabilities and all of the non-controlling interest at their carrying amounts when it lost control.
2. It recognizes any retained investment in the former subsidiary **at its fair value** on the date that it lost control.
3. It recognizes the fair value of any consideration received.
4. It removes amounts previously recognized in other comprehensive income related to the previous subsidiary, and deals with them as if the parent had directly disposed of the underlying related asset or liability. That is, they are reclassified to profit or loss or taken directly to retained earnings.
5. It recognizes any resulting difference as a gain or loss in the investor's profit or loss.

If the loss of control is related to a spin-off of the shares of the subsidiary to the parent's shareholders, the parent recognizes this distribution as well. The measurement basis for this type of distribution is not addressed by the standard.

After recognizing any remaining investment in the previous subsidiary at fair value when control is lost, the investor applies IAS 39 *Financial Instruments: Recognition and Measurement* to account for the investment.

If control is lost as a result of two or more transactions, a parent has to consider all the terms and conditions of the multiple transactions to determine whether they should be accounted for as one. This issue stems from the possibility that entities might engineer a disposal to get a predetermined financial result. For example, an entity could dispose of all but 51% of an investment with the resulting gain or loss reported directly in equity because it does not result in a loss of control. Any further disposal requires a gain or loss to be taken to profit or loss. Alternatively, if the transactions were considered together, all of the resulting gain or loss on disposal would be taken to profit or loss.

SEPARATE FINANCIAL STATEMENTS

As indicated earlier, a parent company that is exempt from preparing consolidated financial statements may prepare separate financial statements as its only financial statements. Other parent entities prepare separate financial statements in addition to consolidated ones. Regardless, all are required to apply the IAS 27 standards that set out how to account for investments in subsidiaries, jointly controlled entities, and associates in separate financial statements.

An entity that presents separate financial statements for its investments in subsidiaries, jointly controlled entities, and associates recognizes dividends from them in profit or loss when its rights to the dividend are established. It accounts for these investments in its separate statements either

- at cost, or
- according to IAS 39 *Financial Instruments: Recognition and Measurement.*

An entity chooses the same accounting for all investments in each category of investment. Those accounted for at cost apply IFRS 5 *Non-current Assets Held for Sale and Discontinued Operations* if they are classified later as held for sale, while those choosing IAS 39 continue to apply the provisions of IAS 39 for those later held for sale.

IAS 27 now also speaks to how the cost of an investment is determined for the separate financial statements in the very restricted situation when a parent reorganizes the structure of its group in such a way that establishes a new entity as its parent. The circumstances are limited to a situation in which there is no substantive change in ownership. Therefore the new cost is based on existing carrying amounts.

DISCLOSURE

The disclosures required under IAS 27 differ depending on whether they are related to consolidated financial statements, whether they are for separate financial statements presented when a parent elects not to prepare consolidated statements, or whether they are for separate financial statements when the investor also issues full GAAP reports.

Disclosures for Consolidated Financial Statements

The following disclosures are required when a parent presents consolidated statements:

(a) Explanations of why an entity is a subsidiary when the investor does not own more than half the voting power, and why an investee is not a subsidiary in situations when the investor holds more than half the voting power.

(b) Information about, and explanations of why, the date of a subsidiary's financial statements are different from the date of the parent company's statements.

(c) Information about any significant restrictions on the ability of the subsidiary to pay cash dividends and to transfer funds to the parent to repay loans or advances.

(d) The effects of changes in the parent's ownership interest in a subsidiary that do not result in a loss of control.

(e) The gain or loss recognized on the loss of control of a subsidiary, separately reporting the amount due to recognizing the investment retained at its fair value and the line item where the gain or loss is reported.

Disclosures for Separate Financial Statements with No Consolidated Statements

A parent that is exempt from providing consolidated statements and prepares only separate financial statements identifies the statements as separate, indicates that it has used the exemption permitted, and provides information about the related entity that has produced consolidated statements using IFRS so it can be located and the group statements obtained.

The parent also lists the names of its major investments in subsidiaries, jointly owned entities, and associates, providing for each its country of incorporation or where it resides; the proportionate ownership interest; the proportion of voting power, if different; and the method used to account for each.

Disclosures for Separate Financial Statements in Addition to Consolidated Statements

Parents other than those referred to in the preceding section, venturers with interests in jointly controlled entities, or investors in associates may prepare separate financial statements in addition to those provided using GAAP methods for these three types of investments. In addition to the information about the specific investments indicated in the preceding section for separate statements, the investor also identifies the financial statements that were prepared under the requirements of IAS 27, IAS 28 *Investments in Associates*, and IAS 31 *Interests in Joint Ventures*.

Illustrations 32-6 and 32-7 provide excerpts from the consolidated financial statements of Marks and Spencer Group plc for the 52 weeks ended March 29, 2008. These are examples of some of the consolidation-related reporting by this international retail organization. Marks and Spencer is based in the United Kingdom and reports its financial statements in millions of pounds sterling (£).[5]

In Illustration 32-6, Marks and Spencer indicates the interest of the Company (parent company) shareholders as well as the non-controlling (minority) interest in the Group's Equity and in the profit reported by the consolidated Group for the year.

Illustration 32-6 Marks and Spencer Group plc Financial Statement Excerpts

Consolidated Balance Sheet

	As at 29 March 2008 £m	As at 31 March 2007 £m
Total shareholders' equity	1,956.7	1,646.8
Minority interests in equity	7.3	1.4
Total equity	1,964.0	1,648.2

Consolidated Income Statement

	52 weeks ended 29 March 2008 £m	52 weeks ended 31 March 2007 £m
Profit for the year	821.0	659.9
Attributable to:		
Equity shareholders of the Company	821.7	659.9
Minority interests	(0.7)	–
	821.0	659.9

---

[5] http://annualreport.marksandspencer.com/financials/auditors_report.html.

Illustration 32-7 presents the Group's consolidation policy note. Many of the issues identified in this chapter are referred to in this note.

Illustration 32-7
Marks and Spencer
Group plc
Consolidation
Policy Note

1 Accounting policies
Basis of consolidation

The Group financial statements incorporate the financial statements of Marks and Spencer Group plc and all its subsidiaries made up to the year-end date. Where necessary, adjustments are made to the financial statements of subsidiaries to bring the accounting policies used in line with those used by the Group.

Subsidiary undertakings are all entities over which the Group has the power to govern the financial and operating policies generally accompanying a shareholding of more than one half of the voting rights. Subsidiary undertakings acquired during the year are recorded using the acquisition method of accounting and their results included from the date of acquisition.

The separable net assets, both tangible and intangible of the newly acquired subsidiary undertakings are incorporated into the financial statements on the basis of the fair value as at the effective date of control.

Results of subsidiary undertakings disposed of during the financial year are included in the financial statements up to the effective date of disposal. Where a business component representing a separate major line of business is disposed of, or classified as held-for-sale, it is classified as a discontinued operation. The post-tax profit or loss of the discontinued operation is shown as a single amount on the face of the income statement, separate from the other results of the Group.

Intercompany transactions, balances and unrealized gains on transactions between Group companies are eliminated.

Illustration 32-8 is the accounting policy note found in Marks and Spencer Company plc separate financial statements. The Company presents financial statements on a non-consolidated basis as well as on a Group basis. There is no non-controlling or minority interest reported in the unconsolidated statements of the parent company.

Illustration 32-8
Marks and Spencer
Company plc
Separate Financial
Statements Note

C1 Accounting policies

The Company's accounting policies are the same as those set out in <u>note 1</u> of the Group financial statements, except as noted below.

Investments in subsidiaries are stated at cost less, where appropriate, provisions for impairment.

LOOKING AHEAD

Amendments were made to IAS 27 in early 2008 and these have been incorporated in this chapter. The changes resulted primarily from the second phase of the business combinations project that the IASB has undertaken jointly with the FASB.

A project on consolidation has been on the IASB's agenda since mid-2003 with the goal of publishing a single IFRS to replace IAS 27 and SIC 12 *Consolidation—Special Purpose Entities*. The FASB is also working on a similar project and the hope is to develop convergent standards in this area. The IASB is developing a new working definition of control and a disclosure framework and issued an Exposure Draft in late 2008 that seeks to improve the definition of control so the same control criteria can be applied to all entities, including structured entities. A revised IAS 27 is expected to be published in late 2009.

Some of the tentative decisions made to date are summarized below. Caution has to be exercised, however, as nothing is considered final until the IFRS itself is released.

The definition of control. The Exposure Draft sets out a single definition of control that would apply to all entities:

"A reporting entity controls another entity when the reporting entity has the power to direct the activities of that other entity to generate returns for the reporting entity." The power to direct the activities of another entity means that the reporting entity can determine the other entity's strategic operating and financing policies. This power can be achieved in a number of ways. Examples include through voting rights or contractual arrangements, by having options or convertible instruments, or an agent that has the ability to direct the activities for the benefit of the controlling entity.

Power to direct activities without a majority of the voting rights. Control is possible without owning more than half the voting power and without any formal arrangements giving an entity a majority of the voting rights. An example is "de facto control," such as when a reporting entity with less than half of the voting rights has more voting rights than any other party, and these rights enable the reporting entity to determine the entity's strategic operating and financing policies. Other application guidance is also provided in an appendix to the Exposure Draft.

Structured entities. The Exposure Draft uses the term "structured entities" to refer to entities with characteristics similar to the special purpose entities referred to in SIC 12 and contains guidance on how to assess control of such entities. The ability to control is a function of the specific circumstances of how the returns from the entity's activities are shared and how decisions are made that cause those returns to vary. The facts and circumstances that need to be considered include the purpose and design of the structured entity, the extent to which the reporting entity is exposed to the variability of returns from its involvement, and the extent to which the reporting entity directs the activities that affect those returns.[6]

Changes to IAS 27 as a result of the 2008 Exposure Draft are not expected to change the basic accounting requirements for how financial statements are consolidated. Note also that an Exposure Draft on the derecognition of financial instruments is expected to be published in 2010. Because structured entities are sometimes used for this purpose, these projects are related.

Another project to watch is Phase D: Reporting Entity of the joint IASB/FASB's Conceptual Framework Project. Phase D's objective, as its name suggests, is to determine what constitutes a reporting entity for financial reporting purposes. The Boards have confirmed that an entity perspective is the correct approach, but changes to parts of IAS 27 may come out of these joint deliberations in the longer term.

END-OF-CHAPTER PRACTICE

32-1 Able Company owns 30% of Bay Company and 45% of Delta Company. Bay Company owns 75% of Chase Company. Chase owns 10% of Delta Company.

Instructions
Identify which companies, if any, are parent companies and which are subsidiaries, if any. Explain briefly.

32-2 Push Ltd. owns 65% of Shove Ltd. and has acquired a portion of the company's outstanding debentures. Shove's head office is located in a building owned by Push, and Push's management is very active in Shove's operating and financing policy

---

[6] IASCF, *Exposure Draft ED10 Consolidated Financial Statements* (December 2008).

decisions. Shove purchases raw materials from Push and manufactures a product for sale to non-associated third parties. Shove is very profitable and distributes a significant portion of its profits to its shareholders each year.

Instructions

Identify the eliminations and adjustments that are likely to be required when Push prepares its consolidated financial statements.

32-3 Prompt Co. reports a $100 profit for its most recent year at the same time that its 80%-owned subsidiary, Slow Corp., reports a profit of $50 and other comprehensive income of $5. Slow paid an annual dividend of $10 to its shareholders during the year.

When Prompt acquired Slow five years ago, Slow reported land in its accounts with a carrying amount $30 less than its fair value and a building with a carrying amount $40 less than its fair value. The building had a 20-year remaining life at that time.

Instructions

Determine the amount of the profit or loss and the amount of comprehensive income reported on Prompt Co.'s current consolidated statement of comprehensive income. Indicate how much of each is attributable to Prompt Co. and to the non-controlling shareholders of Slow Corp.

32-4 In this chapter, flag icons identify areas where there are GAAP differences between IFRS requirements and national standards.

Instructions

Access the website(s) identified on the inside back cover of this book, and prepare a concise summary of the differences that are flagged throughout the chapter material.

Chapter 33

Interests in Joint Ventures:
IAS 31

U.S. GAAP Reference
APB 18 The Equity Method of Accounting for Investments in Common Stock

Related IFRSs
SIC 13 Jointly Controlled Entities—Non-monetary Contributions by Venturers
IAS 27 Consolidated and Separate Financial Statements
IAS 28 Investments in Associates

OBJECTIVE AND SCOPE

IAS 31 sets out the accounting requirements for interests in joint ventures and how a joint venture's net assets and income statement items are reported in the financial statements of a venturer or investor. A *joint venture* differs from other types of investment in that it is a contractual arrangement where two or more parties share in an economic activity over which they have joint control. *Joint control* means that, regardless of actual ownership rights, the strategic financial and operating decisions, by contract, require unanimous consent of the venturers. Control in this IFRS has the same meaning as in other related IFRSs.[1]

Not all investors in a joint venture are venturers. A *venturer* is an entity that has joint control over a joint venture, whereas an *investor in a joint venture* is a party to the venture but does not have joint control.[2]

IAS 31 applies to all interests in joint ventures, regardless of how the venture is structured. The only **exceptions** are venturers' interests in jointly controlled entities held by venture capital organizations or mutual funds, unit trusts, and similar organizations that are accounted for at fair value through profit or loss under IAS 39 *Financial Instruments: Recognition and Measurement*. This could result from being designated as such when they

---

[1] IASCF, IAS 31.3.
[2] IASCF, IAS 31.3.

were first acquired or because they are classified as held for trading. In addition, under very limited conditions explained later in the chapter, some venturers are exempt from applying two of the major provisions of IAS 31.

JOINT VENTURES

Joint ventures may take a variety of forms. They may be **jointly controlled operations, assets,** or **entities**. Regardless of their form or structure, joint control by at least two parties must be contractually established. If one party has the power to determine the operating and financial policies of the venture, the investee is a subsidiary, not a joint venture.

The contractual arrangement may be set out in the articles of incorporation or bylaws of the joint venture or less formally through documentation of meetings between the venturers. The agreement, usually in writing, sets out the governance structure of the joint venture; the capital to be supplied by each venturer; how the output, income, and expenses will be shared; and the purpose and duration of the venture.

JOINTLY CONTROLLED OPERATIONS AND JOINTLY CONTROLLED ASSETS

Jointly Controlled Operations

Instead of setting up a separate entity to conduct joint activities, a venturer may enter into an agreement with one or more venturers to produce, market, and distribute a specific product, with each venturer providing its own particular area of operating expertise. This form of joint venture is used to take advantage of the resources and abilities of the individual venturers. In this case, they may agree to use their own assets, incur their own expenses and liabilities, and finance their own requirements. The joint venture agreement sets out how the revenue from the sale of the product worked on together is shared and how any shareable costs are allocated to the venturers.

Because the financial statement elements committed to the joint venture are already recognized on the venturer's financial statements, the venturer does not have to prepare any investment-related adjustments. Instead, for **jointly controlled operations, the venturer recognizes** the following in its financial statements:

(a)   the assets that it controls and the liabilities it incurs, and

(b)   the expenses that it incurs and its share of the income earned from the sale of goods or services by the joint venture.[3]

Jointly Controlled Assets

Consider a situation where individual oil and gas producers come together and set up the joint ownership and control of a pipeline that each producer uses to take its product to market. Rather than set up a separate legal entity to own and operate the pipeline, only the asset itself is owned jointly. Each party to the agreement takes a share of the output from the asset and pays an agreed share of the costs incurred to operate it. This form of joint venture, where each venturer has control over its share of future economic benefits through its share of the asset, is known as a **jointly controlled asset**. No legal or other entity is formed separately from the venturers themselves.

The accounting for this form of joint venture is consistent with its economic substance and usually the legal form of the joint venture. Similar to jointly controlled operations, the assets and liabilities are reported separately on the statement of financial position according to their nature, not as an investment; and the income from the asset and expenses incurred are reported on the operating statement. For jointly controlled assets, a venturer recognizes the following on its financial statements:

[3] IASCF, IAS 31.15.

(a) its share of the specific jointly controlled assets classified by their nature, and of any liabilities incurred jointly with the other venturers;

(b) any liabilities it has incurred on its own;

(c) any income from the sale or use of its share of the output of the venture along with its share of any expenses incurred by the venture; and

(d) any expenses it has incurred relative to its interest in the venture.

JOINTLY CONTROLLED ENTITIES

Illustration 33-1 represents a **jointly controlled entity**. The entity may be a corporation, a partnership, or other form of organization.

***Illustration 33-1
Jointly
Controlled Entity***

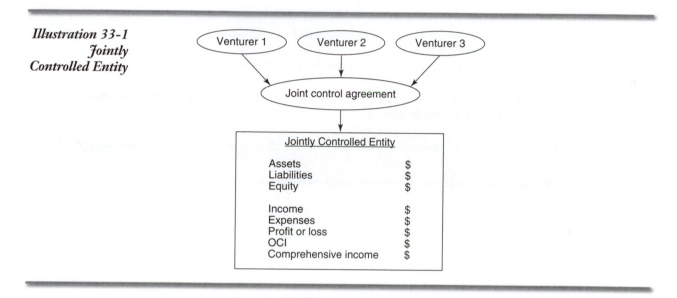

Unlike a joint venture that is a jointly controlled operation or asset, a separate entity controls the assets of the joint venture, incurs the liabilities and expenses, and earns income. For example, many developing countries require foreign investors to set up joint ventures in which the developing country government or local investors share in the control of the operating and financial policies of the entity. Each venturer usually has an ownership interest in the venture and is entitled to a share of its profits or output.

When the jointly controlled entity is organized, the individual venturers contribute cash or other assets in return for an ownership interest. These contributions are recognized in each venturer's accounting records as an investment in the joint venture. The jointly controlled entity records the receipt of the assets contributed in its own accounting records and later prepares and presents financial statements on the results of its operations and financial position.

Financial Statements of a Venturer

IAS 31 provides venturers with a choice of methods to account for their investment in a jointly controlled entity, but states a preference for one over the other.[4] A joint venturer is required to **apply proportionate**

---

[4] The IASB's Exposure Draft ED 9 *Joint Arrangements* proposes to eliminate the proportionate consolidation method, leaving the equity method as the required approach.

consolidation, the preferred approach, or the **equity method** of accounting for its investment in a jointly controlled entity **unless it is exempt** from having to use these methods.

Similar to entities excluded from accounting for associates by the equity method and from preparing consolidated financial statements for its subsidiaries, entities that meet **one of the following three conditions** are **excluded** from applying one of the two methods identified above for investments in jointly controlled entities:

1. The interest in the jointly controlled entity is classified as held for sale under IFRS 5 *Non-current Assets Held for Sale and Discontinued Operations.*

2. The venturer meets the exception in IAS 27.10 (*Consolidated and Separate Financial Statements*) that qualifies a parent with an interest in a jointly controlled entity not to present consolidated financial statements.

3. **All of the following** apply:

    (a) the venturer is a wholly owned subsidiary or a partially owned subsidiary of another entity whose other owners have been informed and do not object to the venturer not applying the proportionate consolidation or equity method;

    (b) the venturer does not have and is not in process of having any debt or equity instruments that are publicly traded; and

    (c) the venturer's ultimate or an intermediate parent produces consolidated financial statements for public use that comply with IFRSs.

Illustration 33-2 sets out the two methods permitted and provides an overview of how each is applied.

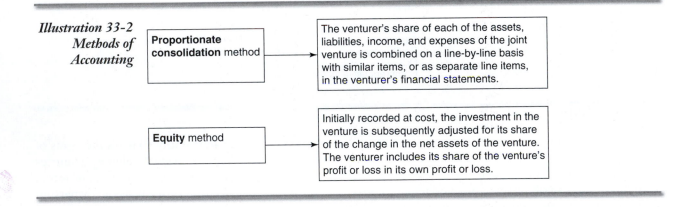

Illustration 33-2
Methods of
Accounting

Proportionate consolidation method → The venturer's share of each of the assets, liabilities, income, and expenses of the joint venture is combined on a line-by-line basis with similar items, or as separate line items, in the venturer's financial statements.

Equity method → Initially recorded at cost, the investment in the venture is subsequently adjusted for its share of the change in the net assets of the venture. The venturer includes its share of the venture's profit or loss in its own profit or loss.

Proportionate Consolidation

As Illustration 33-2 indicates, the term "proportionate consolidation" is descriptive of the method which uses many of the same procedures that are applied in full consolidation. This means that inter-entity transactions, balances, unrealized profits, and losses all need to be eliminated in proportion to the venturer's interests.

IAS 31 indicates that this is the preferred method because it reflects the "substance and economic reality of a venturer's interest in a jointly controlled entity . . . and control over the venturer's share of the future economic benefits."[5] Proportionate consolidation reports the type of assets and liabilities and the extent of the risks the venturer has taken on in its ownership of the jointly controlled entity, thereby providing useful information to financial statement readers. The netting of assets and liabilities or income and expenses is not permitted under

---

[5] IASCF, IAS 31.40.

this method unless a legal right of offset exists and the asset and liability are expected to be realized and settled, respectively, in this way.

There is a choice of reporting formats within this method.

Option 1: The venturer's share of each line item on the venture's financial statements is added to the venturer's line item on its financial statements, e.g., inventory to inventory, land to land, and rent expense to rent expense.

Option 2: The venturer's share of each major classification of assets, liabilities, income, and expenses are identified as separate line items within the same classification on the venturer's financial statements, e.g., within the current liability section on the venturer's statement of financial position, the venturer includes an item that reports "current liabilities of jointly controlled entity."

The totals of the major classifications of all financial statement elements are identical under both options.

Equity Method

The equity method, summarized in Illustration 33-2 and explained in Chapter 30 and IAS 28 *Investments in Associates*, is an allowed alternative to proportionate consolidation. However, if the proposals in the IASB Exposure Draft ED 9 *Joint Arrangements* issued in 2007 are retained in the final standard expected in 2009, the equity method will be the only method permitted. Many believe that having joint control is more similar to having **significant influence** than having **control**, and this supports the use of the equity method. Advocates for the equity method do not support adding together jointly controlled assets and liabilities with elements that are under the direct control of the venturer's management.

In a survey of companies reporting in accordance with IFRSs in 2005, the 144 companies reporting investments in jointly controlled entities were equally split in their use of proportionate consolidation and the equity method. There were significant country-specific differences in the use of each method, however, strongly influenced by the methods required by national reporting standards prior to the adoption of IFRSs.[6]

When Joint Control Is Lost

As indicated earlier, an interest in a jointly controlled entity that is classified as held for sale is accounted for according to IFRS 5 *Non-current Assets Held for Sale and Discontinued Operations*. If it no longer meets the criteria to be classified under IFRS 5, the venturer applies either proportionate consolidation or the equity method, **retroactive to the date of its classification as held for sale.**

When the venturer no longer has joint control over a previously jointly controlled entity and the investment has not become a subsidiary or associate, the investor accounts for its remaining investment under IAS 39 *Financial Instruments: Recognition and Measurement* from the date joint control was lost. If the investment **becomes a subsidiary,** the investor accounts for this as a business combination under IFRS 3 and then prepares consolidated financial statements according to IAS 27. If the investment becomes an investment in an associate, the investor applies IAS 28.

When joint control is lost, **any remaining investment is measured at its fair value** and a gain or loss on disposal is recorded. The gain or loss is the difference between the carrying amount of the investment when joint control is lost and the total of the fair value of the retained investment and the proceeds of disposal on the portion disposed of.

If the venturer has an interest in amounts reported in the other comprehensive income of a previously jointly controlled entity, the investor accounts for its interest as if it had directly disposed of the assets or liabilities to which the accumulated other comprehensive income amounts relate on the date that joint control was lost.

---

[6] Prof. Dr. Isabel von Keitz and KPMG IFRG Limited, *The Application of IFRS: Choices in Practice* (December 2006), pp. 27 and 28.

Separate Financial Statements

When a venturer prepares **separate financial statements**, it looks to IAS 27 *Consolidated and Separate Financial Statements* to determine the accounting for its interest in a jointly controlled entity. In effect, the investment is accounted for at cost or in accordance with IAS 39 *Financial Instruments: Recognition and Measurement*. **Separate financial statements** are those where subsidiaries and investments in associates and jointly controlled entities are accounted for on the basis of the direct equity interest rather than on a basis related to the investor's interest in the investee's net assets and reported results.

Transactions between a Venturer and a Joint Venture

Transactions between a venturer and its jointly controlled entity are accounted for as if the venturer conducts the transactions in part with the other non-related venturers and in part internally. To the extent the transaction is assumed to take place on an arm's-length basis, the venturer recognizes that portion of the transaction and any associated gain or loss; to the extent the venturer is dealing with its own ownership interest, that portion of the transaction and gains or losses is eliminated.

Therefore, IAS 31 requires that when a venturer contributes or sells assets to a joint venture that assumes the significant risks and rewards of ownership of the assets, and the joint venture continues to hold the assets, the venturer recognizes only the portion of any gain or loss that is associated with the other venturers' interests.[7] As the joint venture realizes the gain in its dealings with outside parties, the venturer then recognizes its portion of any gain or loss as realized. If a loss is evidence of a decline in the asset's net realizable value or an impairment, then the full loss is recognized immediately.

When a joint venture sells assets to a venturer and reports a gain on the sale, the venturer does not recognize its share of the gain until it has sold the asset in turn to a third party. Again, the venturer recognizes its share of any gain only when it is realized. The same principle applies to the recognition of any losses unless the loss is a true economic loss.[8]

Situation

Venturers A, B, and C sign an agreement on January 1, 2009 for the joint ownership and control of JV-ABC, each contributing assets of $54 for a one-third interest. Venturer A contributes equipment with a fair value of $54 and a carrying amount of $36 in exchange for its equity interest. The equipment has a remaining useful life of six years with no expected residual value. During 2009, JV-ABC reports a profit of $15 and pays a total dividend of $3 to its venturers.

Assuming Venturer A accounts for its interest in JV-ABC using the equity method, determine the 2009 income it will report from its investment and what the carrying amount of the investment will be on Venturer A's statement of financial position at December 31, 2009.

Analysis

Venturer A makes the following entries.

Jan. 1	Investment in JV-ABC	54	
	Equipment (net)		36
	Gain on disposal [(54 − 36) × 2/3]		12
	Investment in JV-ABC [(54 − 36) × 1/3]		6

[7] IASCF, SIC-13 *Jointly Controlled Entities—Non-monetary Contributions by Venturers* indicates that when assets are contributed by a venturer to a venture in exchange for an equity interest in the venture, this principle is applied unless the gain or loss on the non-monetary contribution cannot be measured reliably or the contribution transaction lacks commercial substance.
[8] IAS 31.50 indicates that in deciding whether an asset transferred inter-entity is impaired, the venturer determines its recoverable amount by applying IAS 36. The value in use is determined by the estimated future cash flows from the continued use of the asset and its ultimate disposal.

This entry records the disposal of the equipment at its carrying amount of $36 and the gain on disposal attributed to Venturers B and C of $12 (2/3 × $18). You might expect the investment in JV-ABC to be reported at the $54 fair value of the assets transferred; however, because SIC-13 indicates that A's share of the gain cannot be reported as a deferred gain, it is deducted instead from the carrying amount of the investment account.[9] As JV-ABC uses the equipment and recognizes depreciation on the full $54 cost to it, Venturer A will take its share of the gain into income. We adjust for this at year end.

| Dec. 31 | Investment in JV-ABC | 5 | |
| | Investment income | | 5 |

This entry is the equity method recognition of Venturer A's interest in JV-ABC's reported profit for the year ($15 × 1/3).

| Dec. 31 | Investment in JV-ABC | 1 | |
| | Investment income | | 1 |

This entry recognizes Venturer A's share of the gain on disposal realized in the year by the joint venture. When JV-ABC takes depreciation on the full $54 cost recognized for the asset on its books, this includes depreciation on the full $18 gain incorporated in the cost. The $18 is being depreciated over six years at a rate of $3 per year. Venturer A's share of the $3 is 1/3 × $3 = $1. This is recognized by Venturer A now because it has been realized by JV-ABC.

An alternative explanation is that the asset transferred by Venturer A is transferred at $54 − $6 or $48. The depreciation on $48 over six years is $8 each year. However, JV-ABC recognizes depreciation on the full $54 or $9 each year. The $1 difference relates to Venturer A's unrealized gain when the asset was transferred and that is realized as the asset is used.

| Dec. 31 | Cash | 1 | |
| | Investment in JV-ABC | | 1 |

This entry recognizes the dividend received from JV-ABC.

How much income has Venturer A reported on its investment in 2009? It is $5 + $1 = $6. This is its share of JV-ABC's reported profits plus the amount of A's gain on the transfer of the equipment that has been realized in the year.

What balance is reported in the investment account at December 31, 2009? From the entries above, we can see that the balance is $54 − $6 + $5 + $1 − $1 = $53. We should be able to reconcile this to prove it is the correct amount. It should be Venturer A's share of JV-ABC's net assets at December 31, 2009 reduced by Venturer A's share of any unrealized gains from the equipment transfer.

JV-ABC's net assets at December 31, 2009:		
January 1 capital contributions	$54 × 3 =	$162
Increase in net assets from profit		15
Decrease in net assets from dividend paid		− 3
		$174
Venturer A's share of net assets: 1/3 × $174	=	$ 58
Less Venturer A's share of unrealized gains in assets:		
Original unrealized gain in the		
cost of the equipment ($18 × 1/3)	$ 6	
Realized in year ($6 ÷ 6 years)	1	− 5
Balance in Investment in JV-ABC account		$ 53

---

[9] SIC-13 *Jointly Controlled Entities—Non-monetary Contributions by Venturers* indicates that "such unrealized gains or losses shall not be presented as deferred gains or losses in the venturer's consolidated statement of financial position." These deferrals do not meet the definitions of liabilities and assets in the *Framework*.

If JV-ABC sells assets to a venturer at a profit, the adjustments required are similar to those presented in the previous Applications box . For example, assume that JV-ABC sells inventory to Venturer A for $100 that cost $70. If the inventory remains in Venturer A's assets at $100, it contains a $30 profit that is reported in JV-ABC's profit or loss. When Venturer A recognizes its share of the venture's profit, Venturer A has to reduce its investment income and the investment in JV-ABC account by 1/3 of $30 or $10. Once the inventory is sold by Venturer A to an independent party, Venturer A recognizes its share of the profit. Remember that **all the adjustments** are made to the investment account and the investment income account when the equity method is used.

Operators of Joint Ventures

When a venturer acts as an operator or manager of a joint venture, it is usually paid a fee for these services. The joint venture recognizes the fee paid as an expense and the venturer refers to IAS 18 *Revenue* to determine how to account for the fee received.

Investments without Joint Control

If an investor has an equity interest in a joint venture but it is not a party to the joint control agreement, the investor applies IAS 28 *Investments in Associates* assuming it has significant influence in the joint venture. Otherwise, it applies IAS 39 *Financial Instruments: Recognition and Measurement*.

DISCLOSURE

A venturer is required to report basic information about the joint ventures in which it has an interest. This includes a description of the interest, the proportion of ownership interest it holds, and the method it uses to recognize this interest. In addition, if line-by-line proportionate consolidation or the equity method is used to account for the joint ventures, the venturer reports the total amount of current assets, long-term assets, current liabilities, long-term liabilities, income, and expenses that are related to its joint venture interests.

Other disclosures are required to provide readers with information about the venturer's potential obligations associated with contingent liabilities and commitments of the joint ventures separately from those of the venturer itself.

The following excerpts from the consolidated financial statements of BP plc (formerly British Petroleum) for its year ended December 31, 2007 are provided to illustrate some of the disclosures it made about its joint ventures.[10] BP is one of the world's largest energy companies, operating in over 100 countries worldwide. Illustration 33-3 shows how the income from BP's jointly controlled entities (and associates) is reported. The company's group financial statements are reported in millions of U.S. dollars.

Illustration 33-3
BP plc
Income
Statement
Excerpt

Group income statement

For the year ended 31 December		$ million
	Note	**2007**
Sales and other operating revenues	5	**284,365**
Earnings from jointly controlled entities–after interest and tax		**3,135**
Earnings from associates–after interest and tax		**697**
Interest and other revenues	6	**754**
Total revenues		**288,951**

[10] http://www.bp.com/liveassets/bp_internet/globalbp/globalbp_uk_english/set_branch/STAGING/common_assets/downloads/pdf/ara_2007_annual_report_and_accounts.pdf.

Illustration 33-4 provides part of the company's accounting policy note on how it accounts for its joint ventures, indicating that it uses the equity method.

<table>
<tr><td>

Illustration 33-4
BP plc
Accounting Policy
Note Excerpt

</td><td>

1. Significant accounting policies

Interests in joint ventures

A joint venture is a contractual arrangement whereby two or more parties (venturers) undertake an economic activity that is subject to joint control. Joint control exists only when the strategic financial and operating decisions relating to the activity require the unanimous consent of the venture. A jointly controlled entity is a joint venture that involves the establishment of a company, partnership or other entity to engage in economic activity that the group jointly controls with its fellow venturers.

The results, assets and liabilities of a jointly controlled entity are incorporated in these financial statements using the equity method of accounting. Under the equity method, the investment in a jointly controlled entity is carried in the balance sheet at cost, plus post acquisition changes in the group's share of net assets of the jointly controlled entity, less distributions received and less any impairment in value of the investment. Loans advanced to jointly controlled entities are also included in the investment on the group balance sheet. The group income statement reflects the group's share of the results after tax of the jointly controlled entity. The group statement of recognized income and expense reflects the group's share of any income and expense recognized by the jointly controlled entity outside profit and loss.

The group ceases to use the equity method of accounting on the date from which it no longer has joint control over, or significant influence in the joint venture, or when the interest becomes held for sale.

</td></tr>
</table>

Illustration 33-5 provides some of the specific disclosures BP makes about the entities making up its investment in jointly controlled entities, and the extent to which they are included in various subtotals reported in the consolidated financial statements.

<table>
<tr><td>

Illustration 33-5
BP plc
Joint Venture
Details

</td><td>

26 Investments in jointly controlled entities

The significant jointly controlled entities of the BP Group at 31 December 2007 are shown in Note 46. The principal joint venture is the TNK-BP joint venture. Summarized financial information for the group's share of jointly controlled entities is shown below.

			2007
	TNK-BP	Other	Total
Sales and other operating revenues	19,463	7,245	26,708
Profit before interest and taxation	3,743	1,299	5,042
Finance costs and other finance expense	264	176	440

</td></tr>
</table>

Profit before taxation	3,479	1,123	4,602
Taxation	993	259	1,252
Minority interest	215	–	215
Profit for the year from continuing operations	2,271	864	3,135
Non-current assets	12,433	9,841	22,274
Current assets	6,073	2,642	8,715
Total assets	18,506	12,483	30,989
Current liabilities	3,547	1,552	5,099
Non-current liabilities	5,562	3,620	9,182
Total liabilities	9,109	5,172	14,281
Minority interest	580	–	580
	8,817	7,311	16,128
Group investment in jointly controlled entities			
Group share of net assets (as above)	8,817	7,311	16,128
Loans made by group companies to jointly controlled entities	–	1,985	1,985
	8,817	9,296	18,113

46 Subsidiaries, jointly controlled entities and associates

Jointly controlled entities	%	Country of incorporation or registration	Principal activities
Atlantic 4 Holdings	38	US	LNG manufacture
Atlantic LNG 2/3 Company of Trinidad and Tobago	43	Trinidad and Tobago	LNG manufacture
Elvary Neftegaz Holdings BV	49	Netherlands	Exploration and appraisal
LukArco	46	Netherlands	Exploration and production, pipelines
Pan American Energy[a]	60	US	Exploration and production
Ruhr Oel	50	Germany	Refining and marketing and petrochemicals
Shanghai SECCO Petrochemical Co.	50	China	Petrochemicals
TNK-BP	50	British Virgin Islands	Integrated oil operations

[a] Pan American Energy is not controlled by BP as certain key business decisions require joint approval of both BP and the minority partner. It is therefore classified as a jointly controlled entity rather than as a subsidiary.

LOOKING AHEAD

Accounting for investments in joint ventures was originally a part of the IASB's short-term convergence project with the FASB, but the IASB is now conducting the joint ventures project alone. The objective of the project is limited to eliminating the choice now allowed in IAS 31 and clarifying the definitions of joint assets and joint operations.[11]

As this book goes to print, the IASB is reviewing the feedback and responses on its 2007 Exposure Draft, ED 9 *Joint Arrangements*, and it expects to issue a final IFRS entitled *Joint Arrangements* in late 2009. The following tentative decisions were exposed in ED 9.

- The types of interests parties could have in a joint arrangement are either direct interests, where parties have contractual rights to individual assets or contractual responsibility for individual liabilities (an interest in a joint operation), and indirect interests, where parties have rights to a share of the net common outcome expected to be generated from a group of assets and liabilities jointly controlled by all the venturers (interest in a joint venture).
- A party to a joint arrangement should recognize its contractual rights and obligations (and the related income and expenses) according to applicable IFRSs.
- A party should recognize its interest in a joint venture using the equity method; that is, proportionate consolidation is not an acceptable method of accounting for interests in a share of the outcome expected to be generated from a group of net assets subject to joint control.
- Disclosures should be aligned with those required for investments in associates; information about the nature of operations conducted through joint arrangements should be reported, as should summarized financial statement information for each individually material joint venture and in total for all other joint ventures.[12]

Except for the elimination of the use of proportionate consolidation, these changes are not expected to result in significant differences in the profit or loss and financial position of parties to these joint arrangements.

END-OF-CHAPTER PRACTICE

33-1 Arguments have been made on both sides about the advantages of using proportionate consolidation and of using the equity method of accounting for a venturer's interests in a jointly controlled entity.

Instructions
(a) Prepare a list of the strengths and weaknesses associated with each of the two methods.
(b) Will the changes to the accounting for interests in joint ventures proposed in Exposure Draft ED 9 *Joint Arrangements* correct any of the weaknesses you identified for proportionate consolidation in part (a)? Explain briefly.

33-2 Explain briefly how an investor differentiates between an investment in a jointly owned operation, an investment in jointly controlled assets, and an interest in a jointly controlled entity.

33-3 Able, Bain, and Cohn are the three parties to a joint control arrangement over the net assets of ABC Joint Venture, each having contributed $20 for each one percent of equity interest on Day 1, Year 1. Able's equity interest in the joint venture is 25%, Bain's is 15%, and Cohn's is 60%. Toward the end of Year 1, ABC Joint Venture sells inventory to Able, Bain, and Cohn in the amount of $100, $90, and $180, respectively. ABC's gross profit rate is 40%. ABC reports a profit of $200 for Year 1 and pays a total dividend of $50.

Instructions
(a) How much of ABC Joint Venture does Able, Bain, and Cohn each own? How much of ABC Joint Venture does each control? Comment.
(b) Determine how much of ABC's Year 1 profit will be recognized by Able, Bain, and Cohn respectively, assuming the inventory purchased from ABC Joint Venture remains in each of the venturer's inventory at the end of Year 1

---

[11] IASCF, IASB *Joint Ventures Project Update*, June 2008.
[12] IASCF, IASB *Joint Ventures Project Update*, June 2008, and ED 9 *Joint Arrangements*, September 2007.

and each of the venturers uses the equity method. Would your answer be different if each uses the proportionate consolidation method? Explain briefly.

(c)   Prepare the equity basis T account of Cohn's investment in ABC Joint Venture for all transactions and events in Year 1.

33-4 In this chapter, flag icons identify areas where there are GAAP differences between IFRS requirements and national standards.

Instructions

Access the website(s) identified on the inside back cover of this book, and prepare a concise summary of the differences that are flagged throughout the chapter material.

Chapter 34

Operating Segments: IFRS 8

U.S. GAAP Reference
FAS 131 Disclosures about Segments of an Enterprise and Related Information

Related IFRS
NA

OBJECTIVE AND SCOPE

The purpose of this standard is to provide external users with a glimpse of how management views its operations in terms of resource allocation and performance measurements. The standard therefore seeks to present information about the various business and geographical segments of the entity so users can better assess the risks and returns of each segment.

IFRS 8 identifies the core principle as ensuring that sufficient information is disclosed to allow users to evaluate the nature and financial effects of the business and the economic environment within which the entity operates.[1]

It applies to separate as well as consolidated statements of entities that have debt or equity instruments traded in a public market or that file or are in the process of filing financial information with a securities regulator (if both reports are presented in the same document, then only the consolidated statements need report this information).

In essence, public companies or those planning to go public must follow the standard, although private companies may voluntarily adopt it. If the entity voluntarily adopts but does not completely adhere to the standard, it may not describe the information as segment information.

---

[1] IASCF, IFRS 8.1.

OPERATING SEGMENTS

An *operating segment* is defined as follows:[2]

> An operating segment is a component of an entity:
>
> (a) that engages in business activities from which it may earn revenues and incur expenses (including revenues and expenses relating to transactions with other components of the same entity),
> (b) whose operating results are regularly reviewed by the entity's chief operating decision maker (CODM) to make decisions about resources to be allocated to the segment and assess its performance, and
> (c) for which discrete financial information is available.

An operating segment may engage in business activities for which it has yet to earn revenues, for example, start-up operations may be operating segments before earning revenues.

To summarize—operating segments have three defining characteristics:

1. They must engage in a business activity.
   - The head office function would likely not qualify as it does not earn revenues from a specific business itself. Rather, it supports the rest of the business.
2. The operating results must be reviewed by senior management for resource allocation and performance evaluation.
   - This is often the chief executive officer or chief operating officer but it may be a group of senior executives.
   - The operating segment usually has a segment manager who manages the segment and reports to the chief operating decision-maker.
3. Separate information must be available.
   - If separate information is not available, it is unlikely that the segment will meet the first two criteria. If it were a separate segment from a business perspective, the entity should be managing it, including capturing and assessing financial information.

Sometimes the entity may have overlapping segments, for example, by product lines versus by geographic areas. This is referred to as a matrix organization. The entity must choose which set of segments constitutes the operating segments for the purposes of this section by referring to the standard's core principles noted earlier in the chapter.

REPORTABLE SEGMENTS

Aggregation Criteria

Where two or more operating segments have similar economic characteristics, they may be combined for reporting purposes. According to IFRS 8.12, the entity reviews the following aspects when making this assessment:

- the nature of products/services,
- the nature of the production processes,
- the type of customer,
- distribution methods, and
- the nature of the regulatory environment.

---

[2] IASCF, IFRS 8.5.

Quantitative Thresholds

The entity reports only those operating segments that exceed a size test. Otherwise the segmented disclosures might be overwhelming in terms of volume and this in turn might obscure the information content. The following quantitative thresholds are identified in IFRS 8.13:

1. Reported revenue (including intersegment sales) is equal to or greater than 10% of the combined revenues of all operating segments.
2. Absolute amount of profit or loss is equal to or greater than the higher of combined profits (for those operating segments reporting profits) and combined losses (for those operating segments reporting losses).
3. Assets are equal to or greater than 10% of the combined assets of all operating segments.

If an operating segment meets any one of the above criteria, it is reportable. In addition, management may identify other operating segments as reportable, if they think that the information presented would be useful to users.

Once management have identified the reporting segments, they assess whether additional segments shall be reported. For this test, if the total external revenues for the reportable segments are less than 75% of the entity's revenues, the entity identifies additional reportable segments. The minimum that is reported is 75%. Once the entity has identified sufficient reportable segments to meet the 75% threshold, the rest of the non-reportable segments are added together under "other operating segments" and disclosed. The entity presents comparatives, which include all reportable segments. If a segment was reportable in the prior period but does not meet the size test in the current period, it is still presented in the current period.[3]

DISCLOSURE

The entity should present the following categories of information:

- general information;
- information about the reported segment's profit or loss, assets and liabilities, and bases of measurement; and
- reconciliations of segment revenues to reported revenues.

Each of these will be discussed in more detail below.

General Information

The following general disclosures are required under IFRS 8.22:

- Factors used to identify the reportable segments—how did management choose to organize the entity in order to make key resource allocation decisions and to assess performance?
- Types of products/services.

Information about Profit or Loss, and Assets and Liabilities

The entity must present the amount of profit or loss and total assets for each reportable segment under IFRS 8.23 and 8.24. In addition to this basic information, supplementary information is disclosed where it is regularly presented to the CODM (either as part of profit or loss, assets, or otherwise) as follows:

- liabilities;
- revenues (external);
- revenues (intersegment);

---

[3] IASCF, IFRS 8.17–8.19.

- interest revenue/expense (revenue and expense may have to be disclosed separately);
- depreciation and amortization;
- material items of income and expense;
- interest in the profit or loss of associates and joint ventures accounted for by the equity method;
- income tax expense income;
- material non-cash items other than depreciation and amortization;
- investment in associates/joint ventures accounted for by the equity method; and
- additions to non-current assets (other than financial instruments, deferred tax assets, employment benefits, and rights under insurance contracts).

This adheres to the general principle that if the CODM thinks the information is important for decision-making, it should be presented to the external users.

MEASUREMENT

As noted above, the numbers should be measured the way they are measured for presentation to CODM. To understand how these numbers are put together, the following is relevant and should therefore be disclosed:[4]

- the basis of accounting for intersegment transactions;
- the nature of any differences between the segment profit or loss and the entity profit or loss;
- the nature of any differences between the segment assets/liabilities and the entity assets/liabilities;
- the nature of any changes from prior periods; and
- the nature and effect of asymmetrical allocations to reportable segments (e.g., depreciation may be allocated to one but not all of the segments).

Reconciliations

Most users focus on the consolidated numbers and would therefore find it useful to be able to reconcile back to these numbers from the reportable segment numbers. The following reconciliations between reportable segments and financial statement numbers are therefore required:

- revenues,
- profit and loss,
- assets,
- liabilities (if liabilities are presented for the segments), and
- any other material segments amounts presented (to the corresponding amount on the entity financial statements).

The entity should identify and describe material reconciling items.

Restatement of Previously Reported Information

Where the entity restructures or reorganizes the information presented to its CODM, it presents the new information and restates the comparative information unless the costs to produce it are excessive or the information is not available.

---

[4] IASCF, IFRS 8.27.

ENTITY-WIDE DISCLOSURES

The following are required to be disclosed by all entities including those that have only a single segment. The information is developed unless the costs to produce it are excessive or the information is not available. It would be based on information used to produce the entity's financial statements.

Information about products and services

- External revenues by product/service (or group thereof)

Information about geographical areas

- External revenues attributed to the entity's

  o   domestic operations (entity's country of domicile, e.g., United States for a U.S. operation)

  o   foreign operations in other countries (if revenues from external customers attributed to a specific country are material, this should be disclosed also)

- Non-current assets (other than financial instruments, deferred tax assets, post-employment benefit assets, and rights under insurance contracts)

  o   domestic (located in country of domicile)

  o   foreign (located in foreign countries). If non-current assets in certain countries are material, this should be disclosed also.

Information about major customers

If revenues to a customer amount to 10% or more, this fact should be disclosed along with the amount.[5]

Illustration 34-1 is an excerpt from the 2007 financial statements of Siemens.[6] Siemens is a Germany-based multinational corporation with activities predominantly in the area of electronics and electrical engineering. The company reports its consolidated financial statements under IFRSs in euros. The excerpt below is only a part of the segmented disclosures, which are quite voluminous given the nature of the consolidated entity. Note how the company has identified its reportable segments in terms of differing types of businesses.

Illustration 34-1
Excerpt from
the Segmented
Information
Note for Siemens

Description of business segments

The **Operations** Groups are comprised of the following businesses:

Siemens IT Solutions and Services (SIS) – SIS provides information and communications services to customers primarily in the manufacturing industry, telecommunications and media, the public sector, service industries, the healthcare sector, the transportation and airports sector and utilities. SIS designs, builds and operates both discrete and large-scale information and communications-systems.

Automation and Drives (A&D) – A&D produces and installs manufacturing automation systems, motion control and drive systems, low voltage controllers and installation systems, process automation systems and instrument products, and electronic assembly systems and provides related solutions and services.

Industrial Solutions and Services (I&S) – I&S is a solution provider for Infrastructure and Industry with own standard products worldwide. I&S aims to optimize the production and operational processes of customers in the sectors water, metals, traffic control, airport logistics, postal automation, marine solutions, oil and gas, paper, cement and opencast mining.

Siemens Building Technologies (SBT) – SBT provides products, systems and services for monitoring and regulating the temperature and ventilation, fire safety, security and energy efficiency of commercial and industrial property, as well as special applications for airports, tunnels, harbors or stadiums.

Power Generation (PG) – PG provides customers worldwide with a full range of equipment necessary for the efficient conversion of energy into electricity and heat. PG's offerings include engineering and

---

[5] IASCF, IFRS 8.34.

[6] http://w1.siemens.com/en/investor_relations/financial_publications/annual_reports.htm.

manufacturing of key components, equipment, and systems, individualized planning, engineering and construction of coal and gas fired power plants as well as comprehensive servicing, retrofitting and modernizing of existing facilities. PG also engineers and manufactures wind energy plants and customizes smaller gas turbines, steam turbines and compressors for industrial applications. It also supplies control technology for all plant types.

Power Transmission and Distribution (PTD) – PTD supplies energy utilities and large industrial power users with equipment, systems and services used to process and transmit electrical power from the source, typically a power plant, to various points along the power transmission network and to distribute power via a distribution network to the end-user.

Transportation Systems (TS) – TS provides products and services for the rail industry, including signaling and control systems, railway electrification systems, complete heavy rail systems including rapid transit systems, locomotives, light rail systems and other rail vehicles.

Medical Solutions (Med) – Med develops, manufactures and markets diagnostic and therapeutic systems, devices and consumables, as well as information technology systems for clinical and administrative purposes. Med provides technical maintenance, professional and consulting services and works with Siemens Financial Services to provide financing and related services to the customers.

Osram – Osram designs, manufactures and sells a full spectrum of lighting products for a variety of applications such as general lighting and automotive, photo-optic and opto-semiconductor lighting.

The **Financing and Real Estate** Groups are comprised of the following two businesses:

Siemens Financial Services (SFS) – SFS, the Company's international financial services segment, provides a variety of customized financial solutions both to third parties and to other Siemens business Groups and their customers.

Siemens Real Estate (SRE) – SRE owns and manages a substantial part of Siemens' real estate portfolio and offers a range of services encompassing real estate development, real estate disposal and asset management, as well as lease and services management.

LOOKING AHEAD

The IASB issued IFRS 8 in November 2006. The standard eliminated all material differences in the accounting treatment of operating segments between IFRSs and U.S. GAAP. No further work is planned on the standard at this time. IFRS 8 is effective for fiscal years beginning on or after January 1, 2009 and earlier application was encouraged.

END-OF-CHAPTER PRACTICE

34-1 Segmented information may be presented using a different basis than that of the rest of the annual financial statements. Is this a good thing or bad?

Instructions
Discuss.

34-2 Krause Inc. is a multinational company with two subsidiaries as follows:

Subsidiary A – revenues $100
Subsidiary B – assets $200

There are no intersegment sales. Combined revenues are $900 and combined assets are $1,900. Subsidiary A manufactures car parts and Subsidiary B provides engineering consulting.

Instructions
Discuss whether these are operating segments under IFRS 8.

34-3 Refer to the excerpt from the Siemens' financial statements presented in the chapter.

Instructions

Explain why each of the separately disclosed segments meets the definition of an operating segment. Is there another test that has to be passed before these segments are reported separately in the financial statements?

34-4 Litton Inc. is in the research and development business. It operates in the U.S. only, and the research and development division accounts for about 60% of its combined revenues. There are a number of small divisions, each of which has very few assets and contributes between 1% and 5% of combined revenues. The following is a list of what each division does:

Division 1 – produces generic drugs
Division 2 – does website development
Division 3 – manufactures medical equipment
Division 4 – runs a small medical center

Instructions

Discuss whether these divisions should be presented as operating segments.

34-5 In this chapter, flag icons identify areas where there are GAAP differences between IFRS requirements and national standards.

Instructions

Access the website(s) identified on the inside back cover of this book, and prepare a concise summary of the differences that are flagged throughout the chapter.

Chapter 35

The Effects of Changes in Foreign Exchange Rates: IAS 21

U.S. GAAP Reference
FAS 52 Foreign Currency Translation

Related IFRS
NA

OBJECTIVE AND SCOPE

An entity's financial statements are sensitive to changes in foreign exchange rates. This is due to several factors, which stem from the entity's underlying business model and business environment. The standard identifies three of these as follows:

1. foreign transactions (e.g., buying or selling in other countries)
2. foreign operations (e.g., operating a business in other countries)
3. presentation currency (e.g., presenting financial statements in another currency)

Transactions—Many entities, especially multinational ones, enter into transactions denominated in other currencies as part of their normal day-to-day business activities. For instance, a manufacturing entity may source its raw materials in another country because the quality and price is optimal. The contract would likely be denominated in the foreign currency and the entity would have to pay the invoice using foreign currency. The entity must weigh the cash flow risk associated with payment in a foreign currency against the need to obtain the best raw materials. Any contract that is entered into (written or otherwise), which is denominated in another currency and/or requires settlement in another currency, will be affected by changes in exchange rates. Other examples are foreign purchases and borrowing/lending in another currency.

Operations—Entities may also own businesses that are located in different countries. It may be more advantageous to locate in another country due to tax incentives, access to raw materials, access to customers, and myriad other reasons. IAS 21.8 defines a foreign operation as follows:

Foreign operation is an entity that is a subsidiary, associate, joint venture, or branch of a reporting entity, the activities of which are based or conducted in a country or currency other than those of the reporting entity.

Presentation of financial statements—Finally, an entity may choose to present its financial statements in a foreign currency. For instance, some Canadian companies report in U.S. dollars. An entity may do this because it accesses capital markets in another country so needs to make the statements more comparable and understandable to the local users. A number of Canadian companies access capital on the New York Stock Exchange or NASDAQ.

Given the above, IAS 21.8 categorizes and defines various currencies as follows:

Foreign currency is a currency other than the functional currency of the entity.

Functional currency is the currency of the primary economic environment in which the entity operates.

Presentation currency is the currency in which the financial statements are presented.

The standard looks at each of these factors and provides guidance on measurement, recognition, presentation, and disclosures. Like many IFRSs, the standard is accompanied by a Basis for Conclusion document, which is not meant to be a part of the actual standard but rather provide some background and insight.

Derivatives, hedges, and balances covered by IAS 39 are not covered by this standard except when the entity translates these items from its functional currency into its presentation currency.

SUMMARY OF THE APPROACH REQUIRED BY THIS STANDARD

An entity must first identify its functional currency—the currency of the primary economic environment in which it operations, as defined above and in the standard. The other currencies are then relative to the functional currency. A Canadian company, for instance, would generally have the Canadian dollar as its functional currency if it was located in Canada and most of its transactions were done in Canadian dollars (i.e., it has Canadian customers and suppliers). A foreign currency would therefore be any other currency, such as euros.

As previously noted, the entity could choose to present the statements in its functional currency or another currency, which would be referred to as the presentation currency. Identification of the functional currency is a very important starting point. An entity determines its own functional currency and, in addition, the functional currency of its foreign operations. It uses the functional currency to measure the transactions.

The process has multiple steps.

Step 1: Determine functional currency for both the parent and any foreign operations. This will be used for measurement in step 2.
Step 2: Translate items into the functional currency.
Step 3: Identify and translate items into the presentation currency.

Illustration 35-1 shows the process.

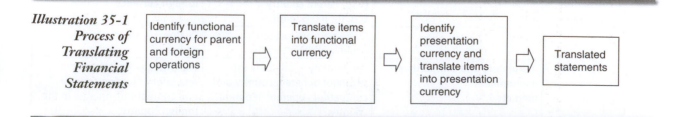

Illustration 35-1 Process of Translating Financial Statements

Identify functional currency for parent and foreign operations ⇨ Translate items into functional currency ⇨ Identify presentation currency and translate items into presentation currency ⇨ Translated statements

Factors to consider in making the step 1 fundamental decision regarding functional currency include the following:[1]

- *Sales*—What is the currency in which sales prices are denominated and settled? Which currency do customers pay in?
- *Regulatory and competitive environment*—What is the currency of the regulatory and competitive environment? In the United States, this would be the U.S. dollar for most U.S. companies since the Securities Exchange Commission is American and many competitors would operate in a U.S.-dollar environment.
- *Labor and raw materials*—What is the currency that influences labor and raw material prices? Which currency are employees and suppliers paid in?
- *Financing currency*—Which capital markets does the entity use to obtain funding? What currencies does it finance in?
- *Operating currency*—What currency does the entity maintain cash from operations in? What is the currency of the operating bank accounts?

In addition, for foreign subsidiaries, the following are also taken into account:

- *Independence*—Are the activities of a foreign operation carried out as an extension of the parent or independently? Does the foreign operation make its own decisions, buy and sell in local markets, and manage its own cash flows? If the foreign operation is relatively independent, then the local foreign currency would likely be the functional currency for the foreign operation.
- *Relative volume/size of transactions with parent*—Do the transactions with the parent company represent a large percentage of the foreign operation's transactions? If they do not, then the local foreign currency would likely be the functional currency for the foreign operation.
- *Cash management*—Are the cash flows of the foreign operation available for remittance to the parent? Are cash flows managed centrally? If not, then the local foreign currency would likely be the functional currency for the foreign operation.
- *Self-sufficiency*—Are cash flows from the foreign operation sufficient to run its day-to-day operations? If so, then the local foreign currency would likely be the functional currency for the foreign operation.

Sometimes it is not so clear-cut and management must use their judgment. In this case, management would give priority to the following factors from above in the analysis:

- sales markets,
- the regulatory and competitive environment, and
- labor and raw materials markets.[2]

Illustration 35-2 summarizes the factors affecting the functional currency.

Illustration 35-2 Factors Affecting Functional Currency	Functional currency = parent country currency (e.g., Parent country = U.S. for a U.S. entity)	Functional currency = foreign currency
Sales	Customers are located in country of parent entity.	Customers are in a foreign country.
Regulatory and competitive environment markets	The primary regulator is the regulator of parent country and competitors operate in parent country.	The primary regulator is the regulator of foreign country and competitors operate in the foreign country.

[1] IASCF, IAS 21.9-14.
[2] IASCF, IAS 21.12.

Labor and raw materials	Suppliers and employees are located in the country of parent entity.	Suppliers and employees are located in the foreign country.
Financing currency	Financing is denominated in the currency of parent country.	Financing is denominated in the foreign currency.
Operating currency	Main bank accounts are in the currency of parent country.	Main bank accounts are in the foreign currency.
Foreign operations—Independence	Activities are interdependent with the parent; the parent makes decisions.	Independent/activities are carried out with significant autonomy.
Foreign operations—Volume/size of transactions with parent	There are many transactions or ones with large dollar values between the parent and foreign operation.	There are few transactions or ones with small dollar values.
Foreign operations—Cash management	Cash is managed centrally by the parent. It is remitted by the foreign operation to the parent or is available to remit.	Cash is managed independently by foreign operation. It is retained by the operation or is not available to remit to the parent.
Foreign operations—Self-sufficiency	The foreign operation relies on the parent for cash flow shortfalls.	The foreign operation's cash flow is sufficient to cover its own cash outflows.

Once the functional currency is identified, it is not changed unless the underlying business or economic environment changes.

The entity then translates the transactions and operations in accordance with the standard and presents the financial statements (steps 2 and 3). The rest of the chapter will focus on aspects of the translation.

REPORTING FOREIGN CURRENCY TRANSACTIONS IN THE FUNCTIONAL CURRENCY

Initial Recognition

Foreign currency transactions are initially recognized in the functional currency. The current exchange rate (known as the spot rate) is used in translating the foreign currency amount. The standard allows the use of an average weekly or monthly rate where there are numerous transactions and the exchange rate does not fluctuate significantly.[3]

Situation

Multi Inc. is headquartered in the United States. Most of its customers and suppliers are located there and the entity raises capital through the New York Stock Exchange (and is therefore regulated by the SEC). During the year, it purchased raw material abroad. The materials cost 100 FCU (foreign currency units) and the entity paid cash from its FCU bank account. Note that the entity's main bank account is in U.S. dollars.

At the date of the transaction, 1 FCU = $1.50. There were many such transactions (all fairly small transactions) during the month and the average exchange rate was 1 FCU = $1.30. How should Multi Inc. recognize the transaction in its financial statements?

---

[3] IASCF, IAS 21.22.

Analysis

First, the functional currency of Multi Inc. must be identified. Multi is headquartered in the United States and most of its customers and suppliers are also located there. It raises funds locally; keeps its main bank account in dollars; and is regulated by the SEC, which is American. Therefore, in the absence of any other information, the functional currency is the U.S. dollar. Judgment is required in making this determination.

The transaction would then be converted to the functional currency, which is dollars. Which rate should be used? Technically, the rate on the date the transaction occurred would be used (1 FCU = $1.50); however, the standard allows for practicality purposes the use of an average rate where there are numerous transactions and the rate is fairly stable. This is the case here and so $1.30 could be used to value this and all similar transactions that took place during the month.

The entry to record the transaction would be as follows:

Dr. Inventory $130
    Cr. Cash   130

Reporting at the Ends of Subsequent Reporting Periods

In many cases, transactions result in balances that remain at the financial statement date. For instance, if the entity still owes money to a foreign supplier at year end and the payable is denominated in a foreign currency, it must be translated.

Before looking at the guidance provided in the standard, it may be useful to inspect the different types of balances that may need translating. For this purpose, balances are divided into two categories—monetary and non-monetary. IAS 21.8 provides the following definition of monetary items:

> *Monetary items* are units of currency held and assets and liabilities to be received or paid in a fixed or determinable number of units of currency.

Examples of monetary items would be receivables, payables, and cash balances. Monetary items may be in any currency. The defining attribute is that they are fixed in terms of the amount of currency units that they represent. A receivable for $100— whether it is to be collected in Canadian or U.S. dollars—is a monetary item. The amount of the currency is fixed, although the measurement value may be different depending on what the functional currency is determined to be.

Non-monetary items are everything else.

The standard provides the following guidance for translating balances at the ends of subsequent periods:

- Monetary items—at the year-end spot rate. A payable or receivable outstanding at year end, which is denominated in a foreign currency, would be translated at the year-end spot exchange rate.
- Non-monetary items that are measured in terms of historical cost in a foreign currency—at the historical exchange rate. A building held by a foreign subsidiary (that was measured at amortized historical cost in the financial statements) would be translated at the exchange rate in effect when the asset was originally purchased.
- Non-monetary items that are measured at fair value in a foreign currency—at the rate in effect when the fair value was determined. An investment in equity shares might be valued at fair value as available for sale. It would be revalued at the reporting date and this would also be the date that the exchange rate is determined for translation.

Illustration 35-3 summarizes the standard as it relates to translation of monetary and non-monetary items.

Illustration 35-3 *Translation of Monetary and Non-monetary Assets and Liabilities where Foreign Operations Have Same Functional Currency as Parent*		**Monetary/non-monetary**	**Foreign exchange rate**
	Balances related to foreign currency transactions	Monetary	Closing rate
	Foreign operations	Monetary	Closing rate
		Non-monetary, where the item is measured in terms of historical cost in a foreign currency	Exchange rate at the original date of the transaction
		Non-monetary, where the item is measured at fair value in a foreign currency	Exchange rate at the date the fair value is determined (generally at the reporting date)

The carrying values are determined by other IFRSs. For instance, the entity has a choice to carry its buildings at amortized costs or at fair value under the revaluation method.

There is a complication here where impairments and writedowns occur. For example, consider inventories that are carried at the lower of cost and net realizable value as per IAS 2. According to IAS 21, if the inventory is at cost, it would be translated at the historical rate. If, on the other hand, it was written down to net realizable value, it would be translated at the rate in effect when the net realizable value was determined. In terms of carrying value, in the final statements, the lower of cost and net realizable value prevails. Therefore, the test has to be done based on the translated values. To determine whether a writedown is needed in the translated statements, the inventory cost would be translated at the historic rate and the net realizable value at the current exchange rate. The two balances would then be compared and the lower one reported in the statements. This might have the unusual outcome of triggering a loss (or not) in the translated statements.[4]

Where the foreign operation is reporting in a different functional currency than the parent, this first translation is not required. The balances are already in the functional currency (even though it is a different functional currency than the parent). These operations are translated separately when the statements are translated into the presentation currency (step 3).

Recognition of Exchange Differences

Any gains/losses produced on translation are recognized in profit or loss in the period they arise.[5] Following are three exceptions:

- Hedges, which are not covered by IAS 21.
- Non-monetary items, where IFRSs require all related gains/losses to be booked, for instance, to other comprehensive income. Related foreign exchange gains/losses should also be booked to other comprehensive income (for instance, unrealized gains/losses on available for sale securities are booked to other comprehensive income).
- A monetary item (such as a long-term receivable from a foreign operation), which is treated as part of the investment in the foreign operation, is booked to other comprehensive income (and subsequently reclassified to profit or loss on disposal).[6]

---

[4] IASCF, IAS 21.25.
[5] IASCF, IAS 21.28.
[6] IASCF, IAS 21.32 and 21.33.

Change in Functional Currency

Where an entity changes its functional currency, the change is applied prospectively.[7]

USE OF A PRESENTATION CURRENCY OTHER THAN THE FUNCTIONAL CURRENCY

Translation to the Presentation Currency

Step 3 of the process results in an additional translation, where the entity chooses to present its statements in a currency other than the functional currency. The following guidance is provided in IAS 21.39:

- Assets and liabilities are recorded at the closing exchange rate.
- Income and expenses are recorded at the rate in effect when the transactions occurred.
- Resulting translations gains/losses are booked through other comprehensive income. For practical purposes, an average rate may be used as long as exchange rates do not fluctuate significantly over the period in question.

The translation gains and losses are not recognized in profit or loss initially because they have little or no effect on present or future cash flows from operations.[8] They will be recognized through profit or loss on disposal of the foreign operation.

Where a hyperinflationary economy exists, all amounts are translated at the closing rates except for comparatives, which shall remain at the prior year's translation rates. When the entity's functional currency is that of a hyperinflationary economy, additional guidance is provided.

Translation of a Foreign Operation

Intercompany payables expose either the parent or foreign operation to an exchange risk and therefore related gains/losses are booked through profit or loss, unless they are part of the net investment, in which case they are booked to other comprehensive income.

It is acceptable for the foreign operation to have a different year end than the reporting entity as long as the year end is within three months and any significant changes or transactions in the intervening period are adjusted for. The statements of the foreign operation would be translated at the rates in effect at the date they are produced. Adjustments would be made for significant changes in exchange rates.

Goodwill and fair value increments arising from business combinations are treated as assets of the foreign operation.

Disposal or Partial Disposal of a Foreign Operation

Upon disposal of the foreign operation, any foreign exchange gains/losses previously booked through other comprehensive income will be booked through profit or loss. Disposals include loss of control, loss of significant influence, and/or loss of joint control. The portion of exchange gains/losses attributable to the non-controlling interest is derecognized but not through profit or loss.[9]

Partial disposals include payment of dividends when the dividend payment is itself a return of investment or includes a return of investment.

---

[7] IASCF, IAS 21.35.
[8] IASCF, IAS 21.41.
[9] IASCF, IAS 21.48.

DISCLOSURE

The following should be disclosed as per IAS 21:

- exchange gains and losses booked through profit and loss and comprehensive income;
- the fact that the presentation currency is different from the functional currency, if this is the case; and
- where there has been a change in functional currency.

Additional disclosures are required in certain situations.

LOOKING AHEAD

Since the IASB and FASB have largely converged the standards, this topic is not part of the short-term convergence project and there are no plans to study issues relating specifically to foreign currency translation, as covered by IAS 21.

END-OF-CHAPTER PRACTICE

35-1 Foreign Company Limited has its headquarters in Canada but does a substantial amount of business in the United States. Because most of its customers are American, the entity has financed its business using U.S. debt with a Canadian bank. The manufacturing plant for the company is in Mexico. The company has issued shares on the Toronto Stock Exchange and the New York Stock Exchange.

Instructions
Foreign Company Limited is unsure about whether its functional currency should be U.S. dollars, Canadian dollars, or Mexican pesos. Discuss the pros and cons of each.

35-2 IAS 21 identifies various currency labels (functional currency, etc.).

Instructions
What is the difference between a functional currency and a presentation currency? Does the company have any choice in selecting these? Discuss.

35-3 Lactose Inc. entered into the following transactions this year. The functional currency is U.S. dollars, which is also the presentation currency.

- Issued a long-term receivable to a foreign subsidiary. Lactose does not intend to collect this money within the foreseeable future. The receivable is denominated in the functional currency of the foreign subsidiary.
- Sold inventory for 100 FCUs in a foreign country when the exchange rate was $1FCU = $1.1. As a result of this, the receivables are still due at year end when the rate is $1FCU = $1.5.
- Established a foreign subsidiary with a functional currency of FCUs.
- Established a foreign subsidiary with a functional currency of U.S. dollars.
- Took out a loan in FCUs with a U.S. bank due in 10 years.

Instructions
Discuss how each of these would be accounted for.

35-4 Grunge Inc. has a foreign subsidiary whose functional currency is U.S. dollars (the same as Grunge). Grunge is currently preparing its annual financial statements and is in the process of translating the foreign subsidiary statements for consolidation purposes. Grunge would like to know how to handle the following:

- Goodwill that arose when the subsidiary was first acquired.
- Fair value increment (arising from the same acquisition) allocated to buildings. The buildings are accounted for under the revaluation method.

- Inventory that is carried at the lower of cost and net realizable value (cost is 100 FCUs and net realizable value is 90 FCUs). The inventory was acquired when the exchange rate was 1 FCU = $ .90.

The year-end exchange rate is 1 FCU = $1.1.

Instructions
Discuss how each item should be accounted for in Grunge Inc.'s year-end statements.

35-5 In this chapter, flag icons identify areas where there are GAAP differences between IFRS requirements and national standards.

Instructions
Access the website(s) identified on the inside back cover of this book, and prepare a concise summary of the differences that are flagged throughout the chapter.

Chapter 36

Specialized Industries and Hyperinflation: IFRS 4, IAS 26, and IAS 29

This chapter covers specialized areas dealing with insurance contracts, accounting and reporting by retirement benefit plans, and financial reporting in hyperinflationary economies. Because these topics do not have general applicability to most entities, the coverage is at a summary level only.

PART 1—INSURANCE CONTRACTS: IFRS 4

U.S. GAAP References
FAS 163 Accounting for Financial Guarantee Insurance Contracts
FAS 120 Accounting and Reporting by Mutual Life Insurance Enterprises and by Insurance Enterprises for Certain Long-Duration Participating Contracts
FAS 113 Accounting and Reporting for Reinsurance of Short-Duration and Long-Duration Contracts
FAS 97 Accounting and Reporting by Insurance Enterprises for Certain Long-Duration Contracts and for Realized Gains and Losses from the Sale of Investments
FAS 60 Accounting and Reporting by Insurance Enterprises

Related IFRSs
Framework for the Preparation and Presentation of Financial Statements
IAS 37 Provisions, Contingent Liabilities and Contingent Assets
IAS 39 Financial Instruments: Recognition and Measurement

Objective and Scope

IFRS 4 is the result of Phase 1 of a longer-term IASB project on accounting for insurance contracts by both insurers and policyholders. The IFRS applies only to the financial reporting for insurance contracts **by the issuer** of such contracts pending completion of the project's second phase. It makes limited improvements to existing diverse accounting practices and requires issuers of insurance contracts to disclose basic relevant information about those contracts to users of financial statements.

This standard is limited to

(a) insurance contracts, including reinsurance contracts that an entity issues and reinsurance contracts that it holds; and
(b) financial instruments that an entity issues with a discretionary participation feature.

An *insurance contract* is a contract where one party (the **insurer**) accepts significant insurance risk from another party (the **policyholder**). The insurer agrees to compensate the policyholder if an uncertain future event adversely affects the policyholder. The term insurance contract also covers a reinsurance contract. A *reinsurance contract* is one issued by an insurer (the **reinsurer**) to compensate another insurer (the **cedant**) if an insured event occurs.[1]

IFRS 4 clarifies that an insurer does not need to apply the requirements of IAS 39 *Financial Instruments: Recognition and Measurement* to separately account for an embedded derivative at fair value if the embedded derivative meets the definition of an insurance contract. It requires an insurer to unbundle the deposit components of some insurance contracts to ensure that the full assets and liabilities are reported on the insurer's financial statements. When they are unbundled, the insurer applies IAS 39 to the asset portion and IFRS 4 to the insurance component.

Recognition and Measurement

Temporary Exemption from Other IFRSs

This IFRS temporarily exempts insurers from the provisions of IAS 8 *Accounting Policies, Changes in Accounting Estimates and Errors* that specify how accounting policies are chosen. In effect, an insurer is not required to apply the *Framework for the Preparation and Presentation of Financial Statements* in determining how to account for insurance contracts it issues or reinsurance contracts it holds. Still, specific accounting policies are prohibited and others are required:

(a) Liabilities cannot be recognized for possible future claims under contracts that do not exist at the financial statement date.
(b) Liabilities must be tested at the end of each reporting period to ensure the amounts recognized are adequate.
(c) Reinsurance assets (a cedant's net contractual rights) must be tested for impairment.
(d) Insurance liabilities are removed from the statement of financial position only when the related obligation is discharged, cancelled, or it expires.
(e) Reinsurance assets cannot be offset against related insurance liabilities, and the income or expense from reinsurance contracts also cannot be offset against the income or expense from the related insurance contracts.

Changes in Accounting Policies

To improve the financial accounting related to insurance contracts by contract issuers, IFRS 4 sets out requirements related to accounting changes that move the insurers closer to the criteria in IAS 8 *Accounting Policies, Changes in Accounting Estimates and Errors*. It allows insurers to change their accounting policies only if

---

[1] IASCF, IFRS 4, Appendix A—Defined Terms.

(i) the resulting financial statement information is more relevant and not less reliable, or (ii) it is more reliable and not less relevant. They may continue to use, but are not permitted to change to, the following specific policies:

(a) measuring insurance liabilities on an undiscounted basis;
(b) measuring contractual rights to future management fees at more than their fair value, as implied by the current fee levels charged by others for similar services; and
(c) applying non-uniform accounting policies for subsidiaries' insurance liabilities.

Alternatively, the standard allows an insurer to remeasure designated insurance liabilities using current market interest rates, taking the resulting changes to profit or loss, as well as to introduce other policies that use current estimates and assumptions for the same designated liabilities. This election permits an insurer to move to these preferred measurements on a piecemeal basis rather than having to apply the new policy to all similar liabilities.

An insurer that uses excessively conservative or prudent accounting policies may, but is not required to, change to policies that are less conservative. However, the standard does not allow an entity with appropriate policies to change to excessively prudent ones.

IFRS 4 also specifies that introducing an accounting policy that incorporates future investment margins in the measurement of insurance contracts is not acceptable on the basis that this makes the financial statements less relevant and reliable. This presumption is rebuttable. For example, if this policy is used with other new policies that increase the relevance and reliability of the financial statements, the result may be a net improvement.

Lastly, the standard permits, but does not require, an entity to change to a practice known as "shadow accounting," which is ensuring the accounting effects of recognized but unrealized gains or losses on an insurer's assets are the same as for recognized but realized gains or losses.

Contracts Acquired in a Business Combination or Portfolio Transfer

An insurer is also permitted, but not required, to use an expanded form of presentation to split up the fair value of insurance contracts acquired in a business combination or in the acquisition of a portfolio of such contracts. The expanded presentation results in the recognition of intangible assets that are excluded from IAS 38 *Intangible Assets* and from IAS 36 *Impairment of Assets*.

Discretionary Participation Features

IFRS 4 addresses limited recognition and measurement issues related to **discretionary participation features** contained in some insurance contracts. This feature refers to the contractual right of a policyholder to receive significant benefits supplementary to those guaranteed by the contract. The benefits are contractually based on the performance of a specified group of assets, and the amount or timing is at the discretion of the issuer.[2]

Disclosure

The disclosure requirements of IFRS 4 have two main objectives:

1. to identify and explain the amounts in an insurer's financial statements that arise from insurance contracts, and
2. to provide information useful to users of financial statements in their assessment of the nature and extent of risks associated with these contracts.

---

[2] IASCF, IFRS 4, Appendix A—Defined Terms.

Examples of required disclosures meant to satisfy the first objective include

- the accounting policies for the contracts and all related assets, liabilities, income, and expenses, as well as the amounts recognized for each;
- the process used to determine the underlying assumptions on which key measurements are based, and the effect of any changes in those assumptions; and
- reconciliations of changes in insurance liabilities, reinsurance assets, and related deferred acquisition costs, if any.

Examples of disclosures designed to meet the second objective include

- policies and methods used to manage risks related to insurance contracts;
- information about insurance risk, i.e., risks other than financial risks that are transferred from the policyholder to the insurer;
- IFRS 7 *Financial Instruments: Disclosures* requirements for information about credit risk, liquidity risk, and market risk; and
- sensitivity analyses relating changes in risk variables and their effect on profit or loss.

LOOKING AHEAD

The IASB developed a project on insurance contracts because these contracts are excluded from other relevant IFRSs such as provisions, financial instruments, and intangible assets, because of the diversity of accounting policies being applied by entities with such contracts, and the divergence of these policies and practices from those used in other sectors. IFRS 4 *Insurance Contracts* is the result of the first phase of the project. The second phase, expected to address accounting by both insurers and policyholders, will eventually replace this existing interim standard.[3]

In 2007, the IASB released a Discussion Paper, *Preliminary Views on Insurance Contracts*, which focuses on the measurement of insurance liabilities. This project is not part of the IASB's Memorandum of Understanding with the FASB. However, the FASB included the IASB's discussion document in its 2007 Invitation to Comment, *An FASB Agenda Proposal: Accounting for Insurance Contracts by Insurers and Policyholders*. The FASB decided in October 2008 to add this topic to its agenda, and it is now a joint IASB-FASB project.

The IASB expects to issue an Exposure Draft in late 2009 and a final standard in 2011.

PART 2—ACCOUNTING AND REPORTING BY RETIREMENT BENEFIT PLANS: IAS 26

U.S. GAAP Reference
FAS 35 Accounting and Reporting by Defined Benefit Pension Plans

Related IFRS
IAS 19 Employee Benefits

---

[3] IASCF, IASB *Insurance Contracts Project Update*, May 2008.

Objective and Scope

IAS 26 sets out the accounting and reporting standards for retirement benefit plans as a basis for the plans' reporting to all participants as a group.

A ***retirement benefit plan*** is an arrangement in which an entity provides annual income or lump sum benefits to employees at or after the termination of their service. The standard applies to both defined benefit and defined contribution plans. Most retirement benefit plans are based on formal agreements and require separate funds to be established to receive contributions and pay the benefits. Such funds are usually administered by an independent party, often called a **trustee**.

Defined Contribution Plans

Under a **defined contribution plan**, the benefits paid to plan participants are a function of the amounts the participant and employer contribute into the plan, the return earned on the plan assets, and the operating efficiency of the plan's management. The objective of financial reporting to the participants, therefore, is to provide financial statements that include the following:

(a) a description of the significant activities for the period, and the effect of changes relating to the plan, its membership, terms, and conditions;

(b) a report on the period's transactions and investment performance, and the plan's financial position at the end of the period; and

(c) a description of the investment policies.[4]

IAS 26 requires a defined contribution plan's financial statements to present, at a minimum, a **statement of net assets available for benefits** and a description of the **funding policy**.

Defined Benefit Plans

As explained more fully in Chapter 25 on IAS 19 *Employee Benefits*, a **defined benefit plan** is one in which the benefits paid are determined by a formula, usually based on an employees' earnings and/or length of service. Under this type of plan, the ultimate payment of the promised benefits is dependent on the financial position of the plan, the ability of contributors—especially the employer-sponsor—to make future contributions, and the investment performance and operating efficiency of the plan itself.

The objectives of reporting for this type of plan then are similar to the three objectives identified above for a defined contribution plan, with the important addition of another. Participants in this type of plan need to have actuarial information on the plan's obligations and the extent to which these have been provided for.

IAS 26 provides options for what a defined benefit plan's actual financial statements should contain, but both options require that the following information be provided:

- the **net assets available for benefits;**
- the **actuarial present value of the obligation** for vested retirement benefits and for non-vested benefits, and the basis used to measure the obligation; and
- an explanation of the resulting excess or deficiency of assets available, and its relationship to the funding policy.

The actuarial present value of the obligation is based either on **current** or **projected** salary levels, with disclosure required for the measure not used in the statement. Any significant effects resulting from changes in actuarial assumptions are required to be reported, along with the date of the most recent actuarial valuation.

The actual format of the statements provided is controversial, particularly around the issue of whether the actuarial present value of the promised benefits is a liability of the entity that is the benefit plan. For this reason

---

[4]IASCF, IAS 26.16.

a variety of formats are allowed as long as the information is set out either in the statements or in the statements and an attached actuary's report to which the statements refer.

All Plans: Valuation of Plan Assets

Retirement benefit plan investments are carried at fair value, which in the case of marketable securities is market value. When it is not possible to determine an investment's fair value, the reason must be provided. Other assets used in the operations of the plan are accounted for under applicable IFRSs.

Disclosure

In addition to the required financial statement information identified above, the following are required for both defined contribution and defined benefit plans:

1. a statement of changes in net assets available for benefits,
2. a summary of significant accounting policies, and
3. a description of the plan and the effect of any changes to it during the period.[5]

The **statement of net assets available for benefits** contains the assets at the statement date and the basis of their valuation, details of any single investment or type of security making up more than 5% of the net assets available or any investment in the employer entity, and the liabilities other than the actuarial present value of the benefit obligation.

The **statement of changes in net assets available for benefits** is similar to an income statement and reports

- contributions into the plan, both from the employer and the employee;
- investment income such as interest and dividends, and other income;
- benefits paid or payable, classified by type;
- administrative expenses, and other expenses;
- income taxes;
- profits and losses on disposals of investments and changes in the value of the investments; and
- transfers to and from other plans.

In addition, the plan provides information about its **benefit obligation** identified earlier and describes its **funding policy** and the **significant actuarial assumptions** made.

A detailed description of the plan is also provided, either in the financial statements or in the report containing the statements. This should identify the employer-sponsor and employee groups covered, the type of plan and the retirement benefits promised to participants, the terms of any plan termination, and changes in any features during the period.

LOOKING AHEAD

Accounting for retirement benefit plans is not on the IASB's current agenda, so changes are not likely in the near future. Looking further into the future, there may be consequential changes as the FASB and IASB work on their long-term convergence project on the employer's accounting for employee benefits, to the extent any decisions from this project affect measurements within the plans.

---

[5] IASCF, IAS 26.34.

PART 3—FINANCIAL REPORTING IN HYPERINFLATIONARY ECONOMIES: IAS 29

U.S. GAAP Reference
FAS 52 Foreign Currency Translation

Related IFRS
IAS 21 The Effects of Changes in Foreign Exchange Rates

Objective and Scope

IAS 29 sets out how an entity whose functional currency is the currency of a hyperinflationary economy should restate its financial statements, including consolidated financial statements, to account for the currency's significant decline in purchasing power.

Two terms need to be explained. ***Functional currency*** is relatively straightforward and is defined as the currency of the primary economic environment in which an entity operates.[6] ***Hyperinflation***, on the other hand, is a matter of degree. How high does inflation have to be to be considered hyperinflation? Instead of pinpointing a specific rate, the standard indicates that this is a matter of judgment and identifies conditions that are characteristic of a hyperinflationary environment:

- The country's wealth is kept in non-monetary assets or in a stable currency, and local currency is invested to maintain purchasing power.
- Prices may be quoted in another more stable currency.
- Business transactions take place with credit terms that compensate for the expected loss of purchasing power during the credit period.
- Key economic variables such as interest rates, wages, and prices are linked to a price index.
- Cumulative inflation over three years is high, at close to 100% or more.[7]

Restatement of Financial Statements

IAS 29 requires an entity whose functional currency is the currency of a hyperinflationary economy to restate its current period financial statements in terms of the measuring unit at the end of the reporting period, and to restate the comparative figures for the previous periods reported in the same way. This requirement applies whether the entity uses a historical cost approach or a current cost approach on its primary statements.

The standard emphasizes that the precise accuracy of the resulting amounts in the restated financial statements is less important than the consistent application of procedures and judgment.

An entity applies IAS 21 *The Effects of Changes in Foreign Exchange Rates* if these statements are to be presented in a different presentation currency. This is likely if a parent company reports its financial statements in its own local currency.

Historical Cost Financial Statements

Even financial statements that are based primarily on historic cost include some recognition of changing prices. Investments carried at fair value, investment properties carried on a revaluation basis, and agricultural products

---

[6] IASCF, IASB *International Financial Reporting Standards 2008*, Glossary, page 2639.
[7] IASCF, IAS 29.3.

measured at selling price less costs to sell are all examples of a move toward more current values. However, this is not the same thing as statements that are prepared on a current or replacement cost basis. Current cost financial statements are those that have been adjusted to reflect the effects of changes in the specific prices of assets held.

Illustration 36-1 sets out how historical cost-based financial statements are restated to the measuring unit current at the end of the period. The general price index referred to is the relationship between the end-of-period price level and that of an earlier date.

Illustration 36-1
Price Level
Adjustments:
Historic
Cost-Based
Statements

Financial Statement Item	Restatement
Monetary assets and monetary liabilities	No restatement. These are already in end-of-period currency units.
Non-monetary assets and liabilities carried at cost or amortized cost	Restate using the change in price level from the acquisition date to the end of the current period.
Non-monetary assets carried at net realizable value or fair value	No restatement. These are already at amounts current at the end of the period.
Assets and liabilities linked by agreement to changes in prices	Adjust to end-of-the-period amounts according to the agreement.
Non-monetary assets and liabilities carried at revaluation amounts	Adjust using the change in price level from the date of the revaluation of the element's carrying amount.
Statement of comprehensive income items	Restate all items to end-of-period measuring units using the change in price level from the date the items were first recorded in the financial statements.
Components of owners' equity	Restate by applying the general price level from the beginning of the period or date of contribution, if later.
An entity holding net monetary liabilities in a period of inflation gains purchasing power; an entity holding net monetary assets loses purchasing power. The net gain or loss can be independently derived or estimated by applying the change in the general price index to the weighted average difference between monetary assets and liabilities for the period.[8]	

The restated items cannot be reported at amounts greater than their recoverable amount, so each non-monetary item is reduced to its recoverable amount if it is less than its restated value. Restated inventory is reduced to a lower net realizable value, if applicable.

The gain or loss on the entity's net monetary position is included in profit or loss and is reported as a separate line item.

---

[8] IASCF, IASB 29.27 indicates that the net purchasing power gain or loss is derived "as the difference resulting from the restatement of non-monetary assets, owners' equity and items in the statement of comprehensive income and the adjustment of index linked assets and liabilities."

Current Cost Financial Statements

If an entity in a hyperinflationary economy prepares current cost financial statements, the adjustment process is somewhat different. This is because an item's current cost or replacement cost at the balance sheet date is already expressed in a measuring unit that is current at the end of the period. Illustration 36-2 summarizes the restatement procedures when current cost financial statements are restated.

Illustration 36-2 Price Level Adjustments: Current Cost-Based Statements

Financial Statement Item	Restatement
Current cost items on the statement of financial position	No restatement. They are already in period-end measuring units.
Other items on the statement of financial position	Use the same method to restate as for historic cost-based statement items.
Statement of comprehensive income items	All expenses on a current cost statement, including cost of goods sold and depreciation amounts, are reported at their current cost when consumed in the current period. Therefore they are already in current period currency units. Use a general price index to restate them to end-of-period units.
A gain or loss on the holding of net monetary balances is determined when current cost financial statements are restated as well.	

As indicated above, the gain or loss on the net monetary position during the year is included in profit or loss and is reported as a separate line item.

Other Issues

A variety of other items are addressed by this standard:

- The general price index used is one that reflects the changes in general purchasing power.
- Differences between restated amounts and their carrying values in the statement of financial position may give rise to deferred taxes. These are accounted for under IAS 12 *Income Taxes*.
- All items in the statement of cash flows are expressed in terms of the measuring unit current at the end of the reporting period.
- Corresponding figures on comparative financial statements are restated and presented in terms of the current period-end measuring unit.
- Guidance is provided for parent companies that report in the currency of a hyperinflationary economy.
- When an entity no longer presents financial statements under this standard because an economy ceases to be hyperinflationary, it uses the amounts expressed in the measuring unit current at the end of the last reporting period as the beginning carrying amounts in its subsequent statements.

Disclosures

Disclosures are needed in restated financial statements so that the basis for dealing with the effects of inflation is clear and the results are understandable.

An entity that applies this IFRS reports that its current and comparative financial statements have been restated for changes in the general purchasing power of the functional currency and that they are restated into the measuring unit current at the balance sheet date. The entity identifies whether the statements restated were based on historic cost or current cost, and provides information about the general price levels and changes in them during the current and previous periods.

LOOKING AHEAD

The IASB has not included reporting in hyperinflationary economies on its current project list, so it is unlikely there will be significant changes in this IFRS in the near to medium term. As standard-setting processes continue to move toward an expanded use of fair values, however, conventional financial statements will report more and more assets at amounts closer to measures based on current period-end measuring units. This is only one small step in reflecting the effects of general price-level changes on an entity's financial statements.

END-OF-CHAPTER PRACTICE

36-1 A retirement benefit plan is required to present a statement of changes in net assets.

Instructions
   (a)   What financial statement prepared by a business is most similar to a statement of changes in net assets?
   (b)   In what way are the statement of changes in net assets and the statement you identified in (a) similar? In what way are they different?

36-2 A variety of presentations are permitted for a retirement benefit plan's statement of net assets available for benefits.

Instructions
Read IAS 26 *Accounting and Reporting by Retirement Benefit Plans* and briefly explain why different presentations are allowed. What are the issues?

36-3 Assume a company in Inflationland acquires equipment on January 1, Year 1 at a cost of 100 FCUs (functional currency units). The equipment has a useful life of 10 years and no residual value. Between the beginning of Year 1 and the end of Year 3 general prices in Inflationland tripled.

Instructions
   (a)   Explain briefly why financial statements in countries with hyperinflation need to be restated into current currency units.
   (b)   Briefly explain, by giving an example, why holding monetary assets during a period of inflation results in a purchasing power loss and why holding monetary liabilities has the opposite effect.
   (c)   Explain how the equipment referred to above is reported on the company's unadjusted cost-based financial statements at the end of Year 3 and how it would be reported on its price level-adjusted financial statements.

36-4 In this chapter, flag icons identify areas where there are GAAP differences between IFRS requirements and national standards.

Instructions
Access the website(s) identified on the inside back cover of this book, and prepare a concise summary of the differences that are flagged throughout the chapter material.

Chapter 37

First-Time Adoption of International Financial Reporting Standards: IFRS 1

U.S. GAAP Reference
NA

Related IFRS
NA

OBJECTIVE AND SCOPE

No corresponding standards in North American GAAP relate specifically to the transition to IFRSs. This standard, despite its complexity, is meant to provide relief from the onerous task of conversion.

The standard provides guidance on how to transition over to IFRSs. Specifically, an entity would apply this the first time it issues statements with an explicit and unreserved statement that it is in compliance with IFRSs (including the interim period covered by the first IFRS financial statements). In essence, an entity must comb through its statements to see where there are differences between the existing accounting and IFRSs. This analysis requires a thorough knowledge of IFRSs and so this chapter has been left until the end of this book.

In general, the standard requires retrospective application since this will allow users to have greater comparability. However, there are two caveats:

1. Cost benefit—in many cases it will be very difficult and time consuming to go back and collect the information needed to apply IFRSs. The information may never have been captured by the entity's accounting information systems. Therefore, the standard allows some relief and has articulated several exceptions to the retrospective application principle.

2. No hindsight—because hindsight is 20/20, bias might be introduced when applying the standards retrospectively. The standard is quite explicit in that only information that was available at the time may be used for estimates. However, this is difficult to apply in practice. Therefore, certain several specific prohibitions have been articulated in the standards.

The overall objective of the IFRS is to ensure the following:[1]

- transparency,
- a suitable starting point, and
- costs do not exceed the benefits.

It may not be clear which statements are the entity's first IFRS statements. There are two components to this:

1. full adoption of IFRS, and
2. an explicit and unreserved statement of compliance with IFRSs.

Many multinational companies may have already prepared some form of IFRS financial statements. Do these statements qualify as the first IFRS statements? The standard provides the following guidance. An entity's financial statements are the first IFRS statements if[2]

- the most recent financial statements were presented
  - under national GAAP,
  - in conformity with IFRSs but with no explicit statement to that effect,
  - under national GAAP with partial application of IFRSs, or
  - under national GAAP with a reconciliation of some amounts to IFRSs;
- the entity has prepared IFRS statements for internal use only;
- the entity has prepared an IFRS reporting package for consolidation purposes only; or
- the entity did not prepare financial statement at all previously.

The standard is accompanied by a comprehensive Basis for Conclusion document and lengthy guidance, which are not part of the standard. The dates in the standard are geared toward the European changeover in 2005.

RECOGNITION AND MEASUREMENT

Opening IFRS Statement of Financial Position

IFRS 1 requires that an entity prepare and present an opening statement as the starting point. This is the beginning of the first period for which comparative statements are presented and is known as the *date of transition*.

Accounting Policies

The financial statements should reflect IFRSs as at the end of the *first reporting period*. The first reporting period is defined as the period in which the entity first presents its IFRS statements. In the United States, this would be 2011 (with the balance sheet date December 31, 2011 for entities with a calendar year end). The full set of statements, including comparatives and the opening balance sheet, is prepared on the basis of December 31, 2011 IFRSs.

The opening statement of financial position will

- recognize all and only assets/liabilities required/allowed under IFRSs,
- present all assets/liabilities in accordance with IFRSs, and
- measure all assets/liabilities in accordance with IFRSs.

---

[1] IASCF, IFRS 1.1.
[2] IASCF, IFRS 1.3.

Any adjustments should be recognized through retained earnings at the date of transition (or other category of equity if appropriate). An entity should look to how the item would have been accounted for had IFRSs always applied.[3] The rest of the chapter will examine the exemptions from other IFRSs (exceptions based on cost-benefit) and the exemptions from the general principle of retrospective application (prohibitions to prevent the undue use of hindsight).

Following are the exemptions from other IFRSs:[4]

1. business combinations
2. fair value or revaluation as deemed cost
3. employee benefits
4. cumulative translation differences
5. compound financial instruments
6. assets and liabilities of subsidiaries, associates, and joint ventures
7. designation of previously recognized financial instruments
8. share-based payment transactions
9. insurance contracts
10. decommissioning liabilities included in the cost of property, plant, and equipment
11. leases
12. fair value measurement of financial assets or financial liabilities at initial recognition
13. a financial asset or an intangible asset accounted for in accordance with IFRIC 12 *Service Concession Arrangements*
14. borrowing costs

Following are the exemptions from the retrospective application:[5]

1. derecognition of financial assets and financial liabilities
2. hedge accounting
3. estimates
4. assets classified as held for sale and discontinued operations
5. some aspects of accounting for non-controlling interests

Exemptions from Other IFRSs

As previously mentioned, these exemptions are meant to provide some relief from the fairly onerous task of transitioning to IFRSs. The entity may also use this opportunity for a fresh start, i.e., if it has made some decisions in the past that are proving to be unwieldy from a cost-benefit perspective (for instance, designation of an investment in debt securities as available for sale securities).

The following pages will go through each of the exemptions one by one giving a brief overview.

Business Combinations[6]

Because it is very difficult to go back and gather information about past business combinations and because the entity's accounting information systems may not have originally captured information required to implement IFRS 3 on business combinations, IAS 21 (on foreign currency translation as it relates to business combinations), and IAS 27 (on consolidations), the standard allows some relief.

---

[3] IASCF, IFRS 1.11.
[4] IASCF, IFRS 1.13.
[5] IASCF, IFRS 1.26.
[6] IASCF, IFRS 1.15 and Appendix B.

The entity need not apply these standards retrospectively or may choose to go back only to a certain point in time to apply the standards. For example, an entity might elect to apply the standard only to business combinations that happened after December 31, 2001.

As a caution, even if this exemption is taken, the entity would still have to ensure that financial statement elements of subsidiaries that are being consolidated comply with other IFRSs. That is, all assets/liabilities being consolidated must meet the present definition of assets/liabilities and be measured and presented in accordance with IFRSs in general (other than IFRS 3, IAS 21, and IAS 27, as noted above). Therefore, although this exemption allows some relief, there is still a considerable amount of work to be done in terms of identifying differences between prior GAAP and IFRSs where numerous business combinations have taken place. As a general rule, the adjustment would be booked through retained earnings (or another category of equity if appropriate) unless it deals with intangible assets, which are then adjusted through goodwill.[7]

To illustrate, if the subsidiary has deferred costs that do not qualify as assets under IFRSs, they are not picked up on consolidation. The amount of deferred costs would be debited to goodwill so that the statements balanced (i.e., deferred costs would be decreased and goodwill correspondingly increased).

Adjustments resulting from changes in measurement required under other current IFRSs (such as valuation of inventory) would be booked through retained earnings.

An additional caution—this and other exemptions are sometime layered; that is, there may be exemptions within exemptions. For instance, some financial assets or liabilities from past business combinations already derecognized under previous GAAP are not required to be picked up even though they may be required to be recognized under present IFRSs. This is another exemption that will be discussed further below.

The entity should ensure that all assets and liabilities that are required to be recognized under present IFRSs (if there are no other exemptions under IFRS 1) are recognized. For instance, if a lease was treated as an operating lease under prior GAAP and yet qualifies for treatment as a finance lease under present IFRS, the related assets and liabilities will be recognized on consolidation.

Goodwill should be tested for impairment.

Where an entity had not previously consolidated an entity that meets the definition of a subsidiary under present IFRSs, the entity would consolidate that entity using values that IFRSs would require in the subsidiary's financial statements.

The entity goes through the same process with the balance sheets of its subsidiaries (looking for GAAP differences) as it does for its own assets and liabilities.

Fair Value or Revaluation as Deemed Cost[8]

According to IFRS 1.16, an entity has the option to measure an item of property, plant, and equipment (or intangible asset or investment property) at fair value at the date of transition. This fair value may then be deemed to be the asset cost at the date of transition. The option allows an entity to come up with a suitable starting value without having to go back in time to recreate a value based on historical cost. Just because it makes this election does not mean that the entity has to continue to use fair value as a measurement base. After determining the starting point, the entity would then decide how the asset will be valued going forward under IFRSs. This is an accounting policy choice. If the entity chooses the revaluation model under IAS 16, the cumulative revaluation surplus is booked to a separate component of equity.

If the entity has already revalued the asset prior to transition, the value established by the valuation (referred to as the revaluation amount) may also be used as a starting point as long as the value is broadly comparable to either fair value or cost/depreciated cost under IFRSs.[9]

---

[7] IASCF, IFRS 1.B2.
[8] IASCF, IFRS 1.16–1.19.
[9] IASCF, IFRS 1.17.

If the exemption is used for an intangible asset, there must be an active market for the asset, thus reducing measurement uncertainty.

The entity may apply this exemption selectively to different assets.

Employee Benefits[10]

IAS 19 allows an entity to use a "corridor" approach for unrecognized actuarial gains and losses. If the entity were to apply this retrospectively, it would have to identify actuarial gains and losses that were recognized versus not recognized. This could be time consuming and costly.

The exemption allows the entity to recognize all actuarial gains and losses at the date of transition (through retained earnings). On a going forward basis, the entity has an accounting policy choice whether to use the corridor approach.

Cumulative Translation Differences[11]

The entity may elect to deem any cumulative translation adjustments booked through other comprehensive income as zero. This reduces complexity regarding the accounting upon disposition of the foreign operation.

Compound Financial Instruments[12]

Under IAS 39, compound instruments are split between their debt and equity components. If the debt components are already settled at transition, the standard would still require the instrument to be split with part of the amount being booked as retained earnings (related to the debt portion, which is no longer outstanding).

Under the exemption, the entity need not split the compound instrument if the debt portion is no longer outstanding.

Assets and Liabilities of Subsidiaries, Associates, and Joint Ventures[13]

If a subsidiary becomes a first-time adopter after its parent, the subsidiary has some options on how to measure its assets and liabilities in its own statements. The subsidiary may value the assets/liabilities

1. at the carrying amounts that would be included in the parent's consolidated statements; or
2. at the carrying amounts required by the rest of IFRS 1, based on the subsidiary's transition date.

If the entity becomes a first-time adopter after the subsidiary, the entity measures the assets or liabilities at the same amounts as the subsidiary after adjusting for consolidation adjustments.

Designation of Previously Recognized Financial Instruments[14]

IAS 39 allows an entity to designate financial assets as available for sale (AFS) or as fair value through profit or loss (FVTPL) only upon initial recognition.

Under IFRS 1, the entity may make these designations at transition as long as the relevant criteria for AFS and FVTPL are met. This allows the entity another opportunity to ensure the information is presented in the most useful manner.

---

[10] IASCF, IFRS 1.20 and 1.20A.
[11] IASCF, IFRS 1.21 and 1.22.
[12] IASCF, IFRS 1.23.
[13] IASCF, IFRS 1.24 and 1.25.
[14] IASCF, IFRS 1.25A.

Share-based Payment Transactions[15]

Under IFRS 1, the entity may choose to adopt IFRS 2 for equity instruments granted on or before November 7, 2002 and for those granted after that date that have vested. It may only do so if it has disclosed fair values. Conversely, the entity need not adopt IFRS 2 and is not allowed to if it did not previously disclose the fair values. For items that have already vested, there would be no impact on current compensation expense either way since the items have vested.

In addition, the entity **may** apply IFRS 2 to liabilities arising from share-based payment transactions that were settled before the date of transition to IFRSs. Conversely, the entity need not apply IFRS 2 to these transactions.

Insurance Contracts[16]

The entity has the option to apply the transitional provisions in IFRS 4.

Changes in Existing Decommissioning, Restoration, and Similar Liabilities Included in the Cost of Property, Plant, and Equipment[17]

Normally an entity would calculate costs related to the above and add to the cost of the related asset for depreciation purposes. The costs of applying this retrospectively may be onerous and so the standard allows the entity to measure the liability at transition and estimate what would have been included in the asset by discounting the liability backwards. Accumulated depreciation would then be calculated based on this estimated amount.

Leases[18]

The entity may determine whether an arrangement contains a lease as at the transition date (based on facts and circumstances at that date). This saves the entity from having to go back in time and determine this information.

Fair Value Measurement of Financial Assets or Financial Liabilities[19]

Under this exemption, the entity may apply the guidance regarding valuation techniques in IAS 39 on a prospective basis to transactions entered into after January 1, 2004 or after October 25, 2002. Therefore, the practice of only restrictively recognizing "day 1 profits" may be applied prospectively. Day 1 profits would arise upon subsequent revaluation to fair value of a financial instrument; for instance, the day after the transaction.

Service Concession Arrangements[20]

The standard allows the entity to apply the transitional provisions in IFRIC 12.

Borrowing Costs[21]

The standard allows the entity to apply the transitional provisions in IAS 23.

---

[15] IASCF, IFRS 1.25B and 1.25C.
[16] IASCF, IFRS 1.25D.
[17] IASCF, IFRS 1.25E.
[18] IASCF, IFRS 1.25F.
[19] IASCF, IFRS 1.25G.
[20] IASCF, IFRS 1.25H.
[21] IASCF, IFRS 1.25I.

Exceptions to Retrospective Application of Other IFRSs

Derecognition of Financial Assets and Financial Liabilities[22]

The derecognition provisions in IAS 39 must be applied prospectively for transactions occurring on or after January 1, 2004. Financial instruments that have already been derecognized prior to that would not be re-recognized. The entity is allowed to apply the derecognition provisions from IAS 39 retrospectively only if sufficient information is and was available at the time of initially accounting for the transaction.

Hedge Accounting[23]

Hedging relationships (under a previous GAAP) that do not qualify as such under IFRS should not be recognized on transition. The entity may not retrospectively designate hedges.

Estimates[24]

The entity may not use hindsight for estimates. Any subsequent information regarding estimates would be dealt with under IAS 10 *Events after the Reporting Period*.

Assets Classified as Held for Sale and Discontinued Operations[25]

IFRS 5 is to be applied retrospectively. The exemption incorporated in IFRS 1 is not available to entities with transition dates after January 1, 2005.

Non-controlling Interests[26]

The entity applies certain requirements from IAS 27 prospectively from the date of transition unless the entity elects to apply IFRS 3 and IAS 21 retrospectively, in which case it must also apply IAS 27 retrospectively.

PRESENTATION AND DISCLOSURE

Comparative Information

Non-IFRS Comparative Information and Historical Summaries

Entities often present summary information of selected data. These are not required under IFRSs. In addition, where the entity provides additional comparatives under previous GAAP, the entity must clearly label this information as non-IFRS and provide additional disclosures.[27]

Explanation of Transition to IFRSs

As a general rule, the entity should explain how the transition affects its financial statements.

---

[22] IASCF, IFRS 1.27 and 1.27A.
[23] IASCF, IFRS 1.28–1.30.
[24] IASCF, IFRS 1.31–1.34.
[25] IASCF, IFRS 1.34A and 1.34B.
[26] IASCF, IFRS 1.34C.
[27] IASCF, IFRS 1.37.

Reconciliations

In order to achieve the above, the entity must present various reconciliations, including

- equity under previous GAAP to equity under IFRSs, and
- total comprehensive income under previous GAAP to comprehensive income under IFRSs.

The entity must also include additional information about impairment booked on transition.

Designation of Financial Assets or Financial Liabilities

Where an entity chooses to designate a financial instrument as FVTPL, additional information is required regarding fair values of those specific instruments.

Use of Fair Value as Deemed Cost

Where an entity uses fair value as deemed cost, it must disclose additional information, including the amount of the adjustment.

Interim Financial Reports

The entity must present interim information for the period covered by its first IFRS statements. The standard provides detail about the additional requirements relating to interim information.[28]

The table in Illustration 37-1 summarizes the exemptions under IFRS 1.

	Relevant standards	Exemption	Cautions
Business combinations	IFRS 3—Business Combinations IAS 21—The Effects of Changes in Foreign Exchange Rates IAS 27—Consolidated and Separate Financial Statements	Need not apply relevant standards (as defined in the prior column) to business combinations occurring prior to transition. May select a date prior to transition and apply standards from that date.	Even if the entity does not apply the relevant standards retrospectively, it must still ensure that any assets or liabilities that are consolidated comply with other IFRSs as at transition. This may result in new assets or liabilities being recognized/derecognized or remeasured. Watch for layered exemptions (exemptions within exemptions).
Fair value or revaluation as deemed cost	IAS 16—Property, Plant & Equipment IAS 38—Intangible Assets	May elect to value the asset at fair value or the revaluation amount (previous revaluation). This becomes the deemed cost.	An active market must exist for intangible assets for this exemption to apply. Additional disclosures are required where fair value is deemed as cost.

---

[28] IASCF, IFRS 1.45 and 1.46.

	Relevant standards	Exemption	Cautions
Employee benefits	IAS 19—Employee Benefits	May recognize cumulative actuarial gains and losses (through retained earnings).	
Cumulative translation differences	IAS 21—Effects of Changes in Foreign Exchange Rates	May set the cumulative translation account at zero at transition.	
Compound financial instruments	IAS 32—Financial Instruments: Presentation	Need not bifurcate compound financial instruments of the issuer if the debt portion is no longer outstanding.	
Assets and liabilities of subsidiaries, associates, and joint ventures		If the subsidiary becomes a first-time adopter after the parent, it has a choice of how to value assets and liabilities in its own statements.	
Designation of previously recognized financial instruments	IAS 39—Financial Instruments: Recognition and Measurement	May designate financial assets at AFS or FVTPL at transition.	Criteria for AFS and FVTPL must be met. Additional disclosures are required.
Share-based payment transfers	IFRS 2—Share-based Payment	Need not apply IFRS 2 to equity instruments granted before November 7, 2002 or those granted after that have already vested. Need not apply to liabilities that were settled prior to the transition date.	
Insurance contracts	IFRS 4—Insurance Contracts	May adopt transition provisions in IFRS 4.	
Changes in existing decommissioning, and other costs	IFRIC 1—Changes in Existing Decommissioning, Restoration and Similar Liabilities	May estimate decommissioning and other costs by calculating at the transition date and discounting back in time to estimate accumulated depreciation.	
Leases	IFRIC 4—Determining Whether an Arrangement Contains a Lease	May determine if arrangement contains a lease as at transition date and assume facts and circumstances at that date.	
Fair value measurement of financial assets or financial liabilities	IAS 39—Financial Instruments: Recognition and Measurement	May apply more restrictive guidance in IAS 39 relating to "day 1" profit recognition on a prospective basis.	
Service concession arrangements	IFRIC 12—Service Concession Arrangements	May apply transitional provisions in IFRIC 1.	
Borrowing costs	IAS 23—Borrowing Costs	May apply transitional provisions in IAS 23.	
Derecognition of financial assets and financial liabilities	IAS 39—Financial Instruments: Recognition and Measurement	May not apply derecognition criteria to transactions prior to 2004 unless the information needed to apply IAS 39 was obtained at the time of those transactions.	

Hedge accounting	IAS 39—Financial Instruments: Recognition and Measurement	May not retrospectively designate hedges.	
Estimates		May not use hindsight.	
Assets classified as held for sale and discontinued operations	IFRS 5—Non-current Assets Classified as Held for Sale and Discontinued Operations	Exemption not available to entities with a transition date after January 1, 2005.	
Non-controlling interests	IAS 27—Consolidated and Separate Financial Statements	Must apply IAS 27 retrospectively where the entity chooses to apply IFRS 3 and IAS 21.	

Illustration 37–1 Exemptions under IFRS 1

LOOKING AHEAD

On September 25, 2008, the IASB issued an Exposure Draft with some additional exemptions for first-time adopters. The comment period ended January 23, 2009.

The Exposure Draft proposes to allow an exemption from retrospective application for oil and gas companies using the full cost method and for rate-regulated entities. In addition, entities with existing lease contracts accounted for under IFRIC 4 (*Determining whether an arrangement contains a lease*) need not reassess these contracts for embedded leases.

On November 24, 2008, a restructured version of IFRS 1 was issued. The content remains substantially the same as the existing standard; however, the standard has been reorganized to allow for greater understanding and to accommodate future changes.

END-OF-CHAPTER PRACTICE

37-1 IFRS 1 is a very important standard for entities transitioning to IFRSs.

Instructions
Explain the basic philosophy of the standard and discuss why the exemptions are necessary.

37-2 Yodel Limited has various classes of fixed assets.

Instructions
What exemptions relate to fixed assets? Identify the exemptions and note how the entity would account for the fixed assets upon transition to IFRSs without the exemption and with the exemption.

37-3 IFRS 1 generally requires retrospective application of all IFRSs that exist at the year end balance sheet date in the first IFRS financial statements.

Instructions
Discuss any situations where the entity is not allowed to use retrospective application or may opt to apply IFRSs prospectively. Why are these deviations allowed? Discuss.

37-4 Hene Limited is a U.S. public company following U.S. GAAP. As a subsidiary of Hene Inc., Hene Limited prepares annual financial statements that are in accordance with IFRSs. The statements are used only for consolidation purposes. It is now 2011 and Hene Limited must prepare IFRS financial statements as a U.S. public company.

Instructions
Discuss whether 2011 is the first IFRS reporting period for Hene Limited.

Index